EDMUND'S

1992 used car prices

Volume U2604
Library of Congress Catalog Card Number: 71-80099
Standard Book Number: 87759-403-1 • ISSN Number: 0424-5059

CONTENTS

How To Use This Book 2
Mileage Deduction Table 2
Optional Equipment Tables 3-14
How To Determine Model Year 15
DISCOUNT CAR BUYING (new cars for as little as $50 above cost) 202, 204

AMERICAN

American Motors 17
Buick 18
Cadillac 25
Chevrolet 28
Chrysler 36
Dodge 40
Eagle 45
Ford 47
Lincoln 55
Mercury 57
Oldsmobile 62
Plymouth 68
Pontiac 67
Saturn 78

IMPORT

Acura 78
Alfa Romeo 80
Audi 82
BMW 85
Challenger 87
Colt 87
Conquest 88
Daihatsu 89
Dodge D-50 90
Geo 90
Honda 91
Hyundai 94
Infiniti 96
Isuzu 96
Jaguar 100
Lexus 102
Mazda 102
Mercedes-Benz 108
Mitsubishi 112
Nissan 118
Peugeot 124
Porsche 126
Range Rover 129
Renault 129
Saab 130
Sapporo 132
Sterling 132
Subaru 133
Suzuki 137
Toyota 138
Vista 147
Volkswagen 148
Volvo 152
Yugo 156

TRUCKS

Chevrolet 156
Dodge 166
Ford 173
GMC 181
Jeep 191
Oldsmobile 195
Plymouth 195
Pontiac 196

EDMUND PUBLICATIONS CORPORATION

JOHN BARTLETT
Publisher

WILLIAM BADNOW
Editor-In-Chief

JOHN IAFOLLA
Editor

KELLY HULITZKY
Director, Operations & Production

KATHY McMANUS
Production Manager

MIKE GERARDO
Circulation Director

200 Baker Avenue, Concord, MA 01742, publishes the Edmund's Car Price Guides ten times a year as follows: Used Car editions four times a year in January, April, July and October; New Car editions three times a year in February, June and December; Import Car editions three times a year in March, July and October. SUBSCRIPTION RATES: U.S. and its possessions—$54.95.

Edmund books are available at special quantity discounts when purchased in bulk by corporations, credit unions, organizations, and other special interest groups. Custom covers and/or customized copy on certain pages is also available. For further information write to: Edmund Publications Corp., 200 Baker Avenue, Concord, MA 01742. Business Office: (508) 371-9788; Editorial Office: (516) 292-0044.

how to use this book

ORIGINAL LIST PRICE: This term applies to the original suggested retail price. **American Car Valuations:** include automatic transmission, stereo, power steering and air conditioning. **Foreign Car Valuations (1983-1988):** include standard transmission and stereo. **Foreign Car Valuations (1989-1992):** include standard transmission, stereo, air conditioning and power steering. Original List Prices do not include state and local taxes or original transportation charges.

AVERAGE RETAIL: The current average price the buyer may expect to pay.

CURRENT WHOLESALE: This term applies to the approximate average current sum a seller may expect to receive from a dealer for a "clean" car in fine mechanical condition. For cars needing repairs or reconditioning, the cost of said work should be deducted.

CONDITION: Within the industry, the generally accepted classification of used cars is as follows: "Extra Clean or Cream Puff"—this refers to a car in exceptionally fine condition that warrants a premium price. "Clean"—this is the classification for the valuations in Edmund's *Used Car Prices*; as mentioned, it is a car in fine mechanical and physical condition. "Average"—is a car that shows obvious wear and tear, but is still passable. "Rough"—is a below average car, still usable, but with body wear and needing mechanical repair.

excessive mileage deduction table

EXCESSIVE MILEAGE: The following table represents generally accepted deductions for clean cars in good mechanical condition with excessive mileage. It is most important to keep in mind that the *condition* of the car is more important than the mileage. Late model cars with excessive mileage should be given special consideration. At the same time, older cars with low mileage have an additional worth. At no point is the deduction to be over 50% of the wholesale valuation. Using the table, deduct the lower figure for sub-compacts, compacts and intermediate cars. Deduct the higher figure for standard and luxury cars.

	1991	1990	1989	1988	1987	1986	1985
TO 15,000 Miles	—	—	—	—	—	—	—
15,000 to 20,000	$300 - $400	—	—	—	—	—	—
20,000 to 25,000	450 - 600	—	—	—	—	—	—
25,000 to 30,000	575 - 750	$275 - $325	—	—	—	—	—
30,000 to 35,000	725 - 950	375 - 500	—	—	—	—	—
35,000 to 40,000	900 - 1150	550 - 700	$200 - $275	—	—	—	—
40,000 to 45,000	1050 - 1300	725 - 900	350 - 500	—	—	—	—
45,000 to 50,000	1200 - 1500	850 - 1100	525 - 650	$200 - $250	—	—	—
50,000 to 55,000	1350 - 1700	1025 - 1300	675 - 850	350 - 425	—	—	—
55,000 to 60,000	1525 - 1900	1175 - 1500	850 - 1050	500 - 650	$175 - $200	—	—
60,000 to 65,000	1800 - 2100	1325 - 1700	1000 - 1250	650 - 825	300 - 400	—	—
65,000 to 70,000	1825 - 2300	1500 - 1900	1150 - 1450	800 - 1025	450 - 600	$125 - $150	$100 - $125
GENERALLY ACCEPTED MILEAGE	10,000 to 15,000	15,000 to 30,000	30,000 to 40,000	40,000 to 45,000	45,000 to 50,000	50,000 to 55,000	55,000 to 60,000

IMPORTANT!

Optional Equipment Tables

AMERICAN CARS: Automatic transmission, power steering, stereo and air conditioning included in all domestic passenger car valuations. **For diesel engine models:** Deduct 30% of wholesale and retail for cars manufactured from 1983 through 1985.

FOREIGN CARS, ALL TRUCKS AND VANS: Valuations for 1983 through 1988 models include standard transmission and stereo unless specifically noted. Valuations for 1989 through 1992 models include standard transmission, stereo, air conditioning and power steering unless specifically noted.

First turn to the Option Schedule Locaters on pages 4 through 8 to determine which schedule applies to your vehicle. Then use the Optional Equipment Schedules on pages 9 through 14 to determine values for factory installed accessories. Each model indicates the equipment schedule you should use. The reader is cautioned to note additional option valuations that frequently appear at the end of each model year in the main text.

If "No Schedule" is indicated for your vehicle, the model is only sold fully equipped with all options included.

IMPORTANT: *The value adjustments in these tables apply only to vehicles that did not have this equipment as standard, or that do not have specific values for this equipment assigned to them in the main text.*

Observe closely the NOTES section at the end of each model year. It contains information regarding standard equipment levels for each model.

ABBREVIATIONS: Auto - automatic transmission, A/C - air conditioning, PS - power steering, PW - power windows, PSeat - power seat, PDL - power door locks, Tilt - tilt steering wheel, Cruise - cruise control, Sun-M - manual sunroof, Sun-P - power sunroof, Stereo - AM/FM stereo, 4WD - four wheel drive, SRW - sliding rear window.

NOTICE

The symbol "—" frequently appears in the body of this publication. In the pricing section, it indicates that the price was unavailable at the time of publication. In the 'Note' section, it indicates that no additional amount is to be added.

Option Schedule Locater

Use this table to determine which schedule applies to your vehicle.

DOMESTIC

Make	A	B	E	F
AMERICAN MOTORS	Alliance Eagle Encore GTA			
BUICK	Skyhawk Skylark	Century Electra Estate Wagon LeSabre Park Avenue Reatta Regal Riviera		
CADILLAC		All Models		
CHEVROLET	Beretta Cavalier Chevette Citation Corsica Nova Spectrum Sprint	Camaro Caprice Celebrity Corvette Lumina Monte Carlo	Blazer El Camino Lumina APV Safari Std-Size Pickups Std-Size Vans Suburban	S-10 Pickups
CHRYSLER		All Cars	Town & Country Van	
DODGE	Aries Charger Omni Shadow	600 Daytona Dynasty Diplomat Lancer Monaco Spirit Stealth	Caravan Dakota Raider Std-Size Pickup Std-Size Van	Ram 50
EAGLE	Summit	Medallion Premier Talon		

Use this table to determine which schedule applies to your vehicle.

Make	A	B	E	F
FORD	Escort EXP Festiva Tempo	Crown Victoria LTD Mustang Probe Taurus Thunderbird	Aerostar Bronco Bronco II Explorer Std-Size Pickup Std-Size Van	Ranger
GMC			Caballero Jimmy Safari Std-Size Pickup Std-Size Van Suburban	Sonoma
JEEP			Cherokee Comanche Grand Wagoneer J-10 J-20 Wrangler	CJ
LINCOLN		All Models		
MERCURY	Capri (FWD) Lynx Topaz Tracer	Capri (RWD) Cougar Gran Marquis Marquis Merkur Sable		
OLDSMOBILE	Cutlass Calais Firenza	Custom Cruiser Cutlass Ciera Cutlass Supreme Eighty-Eight Ninety-Eight Toronado	Bravada Silhouette	
PLYMOUTH	Horizon Reliant Sundance Turismo	Acclaim Caravelle Gran Fury Laser	Voyager	

Use this table to determine which schedule applies to your vehicle.

Make	A	B	E	F
PONTIAC	1000 Fiero Grand Am LeMans Sunbird	6000 Bonneville Firebird Grand Prix Parisienne Safari	Trans Sport	
SATURN	All Models			

IMPORT

Make	C	D	E	F	No Schedule
ACURA	Integra	Legend			
ALFA ROMEO	Spider	164 Milano			
AUDI		All Models			
BMW		318 325			525 535 635 735 750
COLT	All Models				
CONQUEST		All Models			
DAIHATSU	Charade	Rocky			
GEO	Metro Prizm Spectrum Storm	Tracker			
HONDA	Civic CRX	Accord Prelude			
HYUNDAI	Excel Scoupe	Sonata			

Use this table to determine which schedule applies to your vehicle.

Make	C	D	E	F	No Schedule
ISUZU	I-Mark Stylus	Impulse	Trooper	Amigo Pickups Rodeo	
JAGUAR		XJ6 Base			Sovereign Vanden Plas
LEXUS		All Models			
MAZDA	323 GLC Miata Protege	626 929 MX-6 RX-7		Pickups	
MERCEDES		190 300 350 380 420			560
MITSUBISHI	Mirage Precis Tredia	300 GT Cordia Eclipse Galant Sigma Starion	Montero Van	Trucks	
INFINITI		G-20 M30			Q45
NISSAN	200 SX NX Pulsar Sentra	240 SX 300 ZX Maxima Stanza	Axxess Pathfinder	Pickups Vans	
PEUGEOT		All Models			
PORSCHE		924S			911 944
RANGE ROVER			All Models		
RENAULT	Fuego	Sportwagon			

Use this table to determine which schedule applies to your vehicle.

Make	C	D	E	F	No Schedule
SAAB		All Models			
STERLING		All Models			
SUBARU	Brat DL GL Justy Loyale RX Standard XT-6	Legacy			
SUZUKI	Swift	Samurai Sidekick			
TOYOTA	Corolla MR2 Tercel	Camry Celica Cressida Supra	Land Cruiser Previa Van	Trucks	
VISTA	All Models				
VW	Fox Golf Jetta	Corrado Passat Quantum		Vanagon	
VOLVO		All Models			
YUGO	All Models				

Optional Equipment Schedule A

ADD FOR:

	1992	1991	1990	1989	1988	1987	1986	1985
	wh/ret	**wh/ret**	**wh/ret**	**wh/ret**	**wh/ret**	**wh/ret**	**wh/ret**	**wh/ret**
PW	—/—	150/175	125/150	100/125	75/100	50/75	50/50	50/50
PSeat	—/—	125/150	100/125	50/75	50/75	25/25	25/25	25/25
PDL	—/—	100/125	100/125	50/75	50/75	50/50	25/25	25/25
Tilt	—/—	125/150	100/125	50/75	50/75	50/75	50/50	25/25
Cruise	—/—	125/150	125/150	75/100	50/75	50/75	50/50	25/25
Sun-M	—/—	150/200	150/175	125/150	100/125	75/100	50/75	50/75
Sun-P	—/—	375/425	350/400	300/350	250/300	200/250	175/200	150/175

DEDUCT IF NO:

	1992	1991	1990	1989	1988	1987	1986	1985
	wh/ret	**wh/ret**	**wh/ret**	**wh/ret**	**wh/ret**	**wh/ret**	**wh/ret**	**wh/ret**
Auto	—/—	475/525	450/500	450/500	350/400	325/375	250/300	225/275
A/C	—/—	525/575	500/550	450/500	375/425	325/375	275/325	200/250
PS	—/—	125/150	125/150	100/125	100/125	75/100	75/100	50/75
Stereo	—/—	100/150	75/100	75/100	75/100	50/75	50/75	50/75

IMPORTANT: *The value adjustments in these tables apply only to vehicles that did not have this equipment as standard, or that do not have specific values for this equipment assigned to them in the main text.*

Optional Equipment Schedule B

ADD FOR:

	1992	1991	1990	1989	1988	1987	1986	1985
	wh/ret	**wh/ret**	**wh/ret**	**wh/ret**	**wh/ret**	**wh/ret**	**wh/ret**	**wh/ret**
PW	—/—	175/200	150/175	125/150	100/125	75/100	75/100	50/50
PSeat	—/—	150/175	100/125	75/100	75/100	50/75	50/50	25/25
PDL	—/—	150/175	125/150	100/125	75/100	50/75	50/50	50/50
Tilt	—/—	150/175	125/150	100/125	75/100	50/75	50/75	50/50
Cruise	—/—	150/175	150/175	125/150	100/125	75/100	50/75	50/50
Sun-M	—/—	150/200	150/175	125/150	100/125	75/100	50/75	50/75
Sun-P	—/—	550/625	375/450	350/425	325/400	250/300	200/250	175/200

DEDUCT IF NO:

	1992	1991	1990	1989	1988	1987	1986	1985
	wh/ret	**wh/ret**	**wh/ret**	**wh/ret**	**wh/ret**	**wh/ret**	**wh/ret**	**wh/ret**
Auto	—/—	575/675	500/575	475/550	450/500	425/475	375/425	300/325
A/C	—/—	650/725	575/650	500/575	450/500	400/450	375/425	275/300
PS	—/—	225/250	225/250	200/225	175/200	175/200	125/150	100/125
Stereo	—/—	100/150	100/150	75/100	75/100	50/75	50/75	50/75

IMPORTANT: *The value adjustments in these tables apply only to vehicles that did not have this equipment as standard, or that do not have specific values for this equipment assigned to them in the main text.*

Optional Equipment Schedule C

ADD FOR:

	1992	1991	1990	1989	1988	1987	1986	1985
	wh/ret	wh/ret	wh/ret	wh/ret	wh/ret	wh/ret	wh/ret	wh/ret
Auto	—/—	450/500	450/500	425/475	325/375	325/375	225/275	200/225
A/C	—/—	—/—	—/—	—/—	375/425	350/400	275/325	200/250
PS	—/—	—/—	—/—	—/—	75/100	75/100	50/75	50/75
PW	—/—	150/175	125/150	100/125	75/100	50/75	50/50	50/50
PSeat	—/—	125/150	100/125	50/75	50/75	25/25	25/25	25/25
PDL	—/—	100/125	100/125	50/75	50/75	50/50	25/25	25/25
Tilt	—/—	125/150	100/125	50/75	50/75	50/75	50/50	25/25
Cruise	—/—	125/150	125/150	75/100	50/75	50/75	50/50	25/25
Sun-M	—/—	150/200	150/175	125/150	100/125	75/100	50/75	50/75
Sun-P	—/—	375/425	350/400	300/350	250/300	200/250	175/200	150/175

DEDUCT IF NO:

	1992	1991	1990	1989	1988	1987	1986	1985
	wh/ret	wh/ret	wh/ret	wh/ret	wh/ret	wh/ret	wh/ret	wh/ret
A/C	—/—	525/575	500/550	475/500	—/—	—/—	—/—	—/—
PS	—/—	125/150	125/150	100/125	—/—	—/—	—/—	—/—
Stereo	—/—	100/150	75/100	75/100	75/100	50/75	50/75	50/75

IMPORTANT: *The value adjustments in these tables apply only to vehicles that did not have this equipment as standard, or that do not have specific values for this equipment assigned to them in the main text.*

Optional Equipment Schedule D

ADD FOR:

	1992	1991	1990	1989	1988	1987	1986	1985
	wh/ret	wh/ret	wh/ret	wh/ret	wh/ret	wh/ret	wh/ret	wh/ret
Auto	—/—	575/650	500/575	450/525	450/500	400/450	375/425	275/300
A/C	—/—	—/—	—/—	—/—	450/500	400/450	350/400	250/275
PS	—/—	—/—	—/—	—/—	150/175	125/150	100/125	50/75
PW	—/—	175/200	150/175	125/150	100/125	75/100	75/100	50/50
PSeat	—/—	150/175	100/125	75/100	75/100	50/75	50/50	25/25
PDL	—/—	150/175	125/150	100/125	75/100	50/75	50/50	50/50
Tilt	—/—	150/175	125/150	100/125	75/100	50/75	50/75	50/50
Cruise	—/—	150/175	150/175	125/150	100/125	75/100	50/75	50/50
Sun-M	—/—	150/175	150/175	125/150	100/125	75/100	50/75	50/75
Sun-P	—/—	575/650	400/475	350/425	325/400	250/300	200/250	175/200

DEDUCT IF NO:

	1992	1991	1990	1989	1988	1987	1986	1985
	wh/ret	wh/ret	wh/ret	wh/ret	wh/ret	wh/ret	wh/ret	wh/ret
A/C	—/—	650/725	575/650	500/575	—/—	—/—	—/—	—/—
PS	—/—	225/250	225/250	200/225	—/—	—/—	—/—	—/—
Stereo	—/—	100/150	100/150	100/125	100/125	75/100	50/75	50/75

IMPORTANT: *The value adjustments in these tables apply only to vehicles that did not have this equipment as standard, or that do not have specific values for this equipment assigned to them in the main text. However, it is likely that luxury models are fully equipped with the above optional equipment.*

Optional Equipment Schedule E

ADD FOR:

	1992	1991	1990	1989	1988	1987	1986	1985
	wh/ret	wh/ret	wh/ret	wh/ret	wh/ret	wh/ret	wh/ret	wh/ret
Auto	—/—	475/550	450/525	425/475	400/450	350/400	300/350	250/300
A/C	—/—	—/—	—/—	—/—	450/500	400/450	325/375	275/325
PS	—/—	—/—	—/—	—/—	175/200	175/200	150/175	100/125
PW	—/—	175/200	150/175	125/150	125/150	100/125	75/100	50/75
PSeat	—/—	150/175	100/125	100/125	75/100	50/75	50/50	25/25
PDL	—/—	100/125	100/125	75/100	75/100	50/75	50/75	25/25
Tilt	—/—	125/150	125/150	100/125	75/100	50/75	50/50	50/50
Cruise	—/—	150/175	125/150	100/125	75/100	50/75	50/75	50/50
4WD	—/—	1500/1700	1400/1600	1250/1400	1150/1300	1000/1100	900/1050	800/925
SRW	—/—	75/100	75/100	50/75	50/75	50/50	50/50	25/25
Sun-M	—/—	175/200	150/175	125/150	100/125	75/100	50/75	50/75
Sun-P	—/—	475/550	375/450	325/375	300/350	250/300	200/250	150/200

DEDUCT IF NO:

	1992	1991	1990	1989	1988	1987	1986	1985
	wh/ret	wh/ret	wh/ret	wh/ret	wh/ret	wh/ret	wh/ret	wh/ret
A/C	—/—	550/625	525/600	525/600	—/—	—/—	—/—	—/—
PS	—/—	275/300	275/300	250/275	—/—	—/—	—/—	—/—
Stereo	—/—	100/150	100/150	75/100	75/100	50/75	50/75	50/75

IMPORTANT: *The value adjustments in these tables apply only to vehicles that did not have this equipment as standard, or that do not have specific values for this equipment assigned to them in the main text.*

Optional Equipment Schedule F

ADD FOR:

	1992	1991	1990	1989	1988	1987	1986	1985
	wh/ret	**wh/ret**	**wh/ret**	**wh/ret**	**wh/ret**	**wh/ret**	**wh/ret**	**wh/ret**
Auto	—/—	400/475	350/425	325/375	325/375	300/350	250/300	200/250
A/C	—/—	—/—	—/—	—/—	375/425	300/350	250/300	200/225
PS	—/—	—/—	—/—	—/—	125/150	125/150	100/125	75/100
PW	—/—	150/175	125/150	100/125	75/100	50/75	25/50	25/25
PSeat	—/—	100/125	75/100	75/100	50/75	25/25	25/25	—/—
PDL	—/—	75/100	75/100	50/75	50/75	25/25	25/25	25/25
Tilt	—/—	100/125	100/125	75/100	75/100	50/75	50/50	25/25
Cruise	—/—	125/150	100/100	75/100	50/75	50/75	50/50	25/25
4WD	—/—	1400/1600	1300/1500	1150/1300	1100/1300	900/1050	800/900	750/850
SRW	—/—	75/100	75/100	50/75	50/75	50/50	50/50	25/25
Sun-M	—/—	150/200	150/175	125/150	100/125	75/100	50/75	50/75
Sun-P	—/—	450/525	350/400	300/350	275/325	225/275	175/200	150/175

DEDUCT IF NO:

	1992	1991	1990	1989	1988	1987	1986	1985
	wh/ret	**wh/ret**	**wh/ret**	**wh/ret**	**wh/ret**	**wh/ret**	**wh/ret**	**wh/ret**
A/C	—/—	500/575	500/575	425/475	—/—	—/—	—/—	—/—
PS	—/—	175/200	175/200	150/175	—/—	—/—	—/—	—/—
Stereo	—/—	100/150	100/150	75/100	75/100	50/75	50/75	50/75

IMPORTANT: *The value adjustments in these tables apply only to vehicles that did not have this equipment as standard, or that do not have specific values for this equipment assigned to them in the main text.*

How To Determine Model Year

To be sure you are paying the correct price for the car you want to buy you must be sure that the model year is correct. Fortunately, checking out the model year is not difficult.

Just find the VIN (Vehicle Identification Number) usually located on the dash near the front window. The letter in the tenth position in the VIN identifies the model year.

The following chart shows the letter and the corresponding years.

VIN LETTER	YEAR
B	1981
C	1982
D	1983
E	1984
F	1985
G	1986
H	1987
J	1988
K	1989
L	1990
M	1991
N	1992
P	1993

For example, here is a VIN for a 1987 Chevrolet Cavalier:

1G1JE1119<u>H</u>J162212

The tenth position is "H" — this confirms that the car is a 1987 model.

FREE RECALL INFORMATION

An important part of buying a used car is to know the model's recall history; it will tell you what problems the manufacturer recalled the auto for.

A lot of recalls could mean that the model had problems. You should try to get the auto's service records to see if all recalls were complied with by the owner.

To get recall data, call the National Highway Traffic Safety Administration at the following toll-free number:

1-800-424-9393

They will send you the auto's up-to-date recall history. There is no charge for this service.

Also, you can report any safety problems you have had with an auto to the same number.

AMERICAN MOTORS

Year-Model-Body Type	Original List	Current Whlse	Average Retail
1987			
ALLIANCE 4			
2 Dr Base Sdn	**7917**	675	1275
4 Dr Base Sdn	**8117**	775	1500
3 Dr Htchbk	**7917**	725	1375
2 Dr DL Sdn	**8944**	1000	1725
4 Dr DL Sdn	**9219**	1100	1825
2 Dr DL Conv	**13418**	2625	3525
3 Dr DL Htchbk	**8994**	1050	1775
5 Dr DL Htchbk	**9269**	1150	1875
2 Dr L Sdn	**8443**	850	1550
4 Dr L Sdn	**8718**	900	1625
2 Dr L Conv	**12418**	2475	3350
3 Dr L Htchbk	**8397**	875	1600
5 Dr L Htchbk	**8672**	950	1675
3 Dr GS Htchbk	**9818**	1325	2050
GTA 4			
2 Dr Sdn	**9704**	1450	2225
2 Dr Conv	**13604**	3025	3925
EAGLE 6			
4 Dr Sdn	**12927**	2775	3675
4 Dr Wgn	**13743**	3050	3950
EAGLE LIMITED 6			
4 Dr Wgn	**14475**	3050	3950
ADD FOR:			
Eagle Sport Pkg (Eagle)	**456**	100	125

NOTE: Power brakes standard on all models.

Year-Model-Body Type	Original List	Current Whlse	Average Retail
1986			
ALLIANCE 4			
2 Dr Base Sdn	**7473**	475	875
4 Dr Base Sdn	**7673**	575	1075
2 Dr DL Sdn	**8391**	775	1500
4 Dr DL Sdn	**8414**	875	1600
2 Dr DL Conv	**12966**	2150	3000
2 Dr L Sdn	**7891**	625	1175
4 Dr L Sdn	**8141**	725	1375
2 Dr L Conv	**12611**	2000	1850
EAGLE 6			
4 Dr Sdn	**12196**	800	1500
4 Dr Wgn	**12966**	2125	2975
EAGLE LIMITED 6			
4 Dr Wgn	**13656**	2475	3350
ENCORE 4			
3 Dr S Lftbk	**7931**	625	1175
5 Dr S Lftbk	**8181**	725	1375
3 Dr LS Lftbk	**8591**	775	1500
5 Dr LS Lftbk	**8841**	875	1600
3 Dr GS Lftbk	**9089**	1050	1775
3 Dr Electronic Lftbk	**8619**	775	1500
ADD FOR:			
Eagle Sport Pkg (Eagle)	**431**	75	90

NOTE: Vinyl top standard on Eagle Sedan. Power brakes standard on all models.

Year-Model-Body Type	Original List	Current Whlse	Average Retail
1985			
ALLIANCE 4			
2 Dr Base Sdn	**7200**	325	600
2 Dr DL Sdn	**8114**	550	1025
4 Dr DL Sdn	**8364**	650	1225
2 Dr DL Conv	**12316**	1750	2600
2 Dr L Sdn	**7514**	450	825
4 Dr L Sdn	**7764**	550	1025
2 Dr L Conv	**11637**	1675	2525
4 Dr Limited Sdn	**8764**	875	1600
EAGLE 6			
4 Dr Sdn	**11698**	1275	2000
4 Dr Wgn	**12459**	1475	2300
EAGLE LIMITED 6			
4 Dr Wgn	**13135**	1800	2650
ENCORE 4			
3 Dr Base Lftbk (4 spd)	**5986**	325	600
3 Dr S Lftbk	**7702**	475	875
5 Dr S Lftbk	**7952**	575	1075
3 Dr LS Lftbk	**8402**	575	1075
5 Dr LS Lftbk	**8652**	675	1275
3 Dr GS Lftbk	**8902**	825	1525

NOTE: 5 speed transmission standard on Encore LS and GS. Power brakes standard on all models.

Year-Model-Body Type	Original List	Current Whlse	Average Retail
1984			
ALLIANCE 4			
2 Dr Base Sdn	**7346**	110	300
2 Dr L Sdn	**7734**	110	300
4 Dr L Sdn	**7984**	175	375
2 Dr DL Sdn	**8334**	150	350
4 Dr DL Sdn	**8634**	225	475
4 Dr Limited Sdn	**9296**	325	600
2 Dr Diamond Edit. Sdn	**8984**	225	475
4 Dr Diamond Edit. Sdn	**9284**	300	575
EAGLE 4*			
4 Dr Sdn	**10331**	675	1275
4 Dr Wgn	**11061**	850	1550
EAGLE LIMITED 4*			
4 Dr Wgn	**11531**	1150	1875

* For 6 cylinder models add $200 wholesale and $200 retail.

Refer To Optional Equipment Schedules

Year-Model-Body Type	Original List	Current Whlse	Average Retail
ENCORE 4			
3 Dr Base Sdn	**7142**	110	300
3 Dr S Lftbk	**7668**	110	300
5 Dr S Lftbk	**7618**	150	350
3 Dr LS Lftbk	**8298**	125	325
5 Dr LS Lftbk	**8498**	200	400
3 Dr GS Lftbk	**8850**	225	475
3 Dr Diamond Edit. Lftbk	**8873**	300	575
5 Dr Diamond Edit. Lftbk	**9073**	375	675
1983 — ALL BODY STYLES			
ALLIANCE 4	—	110	300
BASE CONCORD	—	225	475
CONCORD DL	—	375	675
CONCORD LIMITED	—	475	875
EAGLE	—	650	1225
EAGLE LIMITED	—	875	1600
EAGLE SX/4	—	375	675
EAGLE SX/4 DL	—	475	775
SPIRIT DL	—	200	400
SPIRIT GT	—	250	500

BUICK

1992

Year-Model-Body Type	Original List	Current Whlse	Average Retail
CENTURY CUSTOM 4*			
4 Dr Sdn	**14755**	—	—
2 Dr Cpe	**14550**	—	—
4 Dr Wgn	**15660**	—	—
CENTURY LIMITED 4*			
4 Dr Sdn	**15695**	—	—
4 Dr Wgn	**16395**	—	—
CENTURY SPECIAL 4*			
4 Dr Sdn	**13795**	—	—
* For 6 cylinder models add $— wholesale and $— retail.			
ADD FOR:			
Leather Seat Trim	**500**	—	—
Aluminum Wheels	**295**	—	—
LE SABRE CUSTOM 6			
4 Dr Sdn	**18695**	—	—
LE SABRE LIMITED 6			
4 Dr Sdn	**20775**	—	—
ADD FOR:			
Leather Seat Trim	**500**	—	—
Aluminum Wheels	**325**	—	—
PARK AVENUE 6			
4 Dr Base Sdn	**25285**	—	—
4 Dr Ultra Sdn	**28780**	—	—
ADD FOR:			
Leather Seat Trim (Base Sdn)	**500**	—	—
REGAL CUSTOM 6			
4 Dr Sdn	**16865**	—	—
2 Dr Cpe	**16610**	—	—
REGAL GRAN SPORT 6			
4 Dr Sdn	**19300**	—	—
2 Dr Cpe	**18600**	—	—
REGAL LIMITED 6			
4 Dr Sdn	**18110**	—	—
2 Dr Cpe	**17790**	—	—
ADD FOR:			
3.8 Liter 6 Cyl Eng (Custom, Limited)	**395**	—	—
Anti-Lock Brakes (Custom)	**450**	—	—
Leather Seat Trim	**500**	—	—
Aluminum Wheels (Custom, Limited)	**295**	—	—
Wire Wheels (Custom, Limited)	**240**	—	—
RIVIERA 6			
2 Dr Cpe	**25415**	—	—
ADD FOR:			
Vinyl Roof	**695**	—	—
Leather Seat Trim	**600**	—	—
ROADMASTER 8			
4 Dr Base Sdn	**21865**	—	—
4 Dr Limited Sdn	**24195**	—	—
4 Dr Estate Wgn	**23040**	—	—
ADD FOR:			
Vinyl Roof	**695**	—	—
Leather Seat Trim	**700**	—	—
Wire Wheel Covers (Base, Limited)	**240**	—	—
Aluminum Wheels (Base, Limited)	**325**	—	—
SKYLARK 4*			
4 Dr Sdn	**14705**	—	—
2 Dr Cpe	**14705**	—	—
* For 6 cylinder models add $— wholesale and $— retail.			
SKYLARK GRAN SPORT 6			
4 Dr Sdn	**16700**	—	—
2 Dr Cpe	**16700**	—	—
ADD FOR:			
Automatic Leveling System (Base)	**380**	—	—

NOTE: Power windows standard on LeSabre, Park Avenue, Riviera and Roadmaster. Power door locks standard on Century, Park Avenue, Regal, Riviera, Roadmaster and Skylark. Power

Year-Model-Body Type	Original List	Current Whlse	Average Retail

seat standard on Century, Park Avenue Ultra and Roadmaster Limited. Tilt steering wheel standard on Park Avenue, Regal, Riviera and Roadmaster. Cruise control standard on Park Avenue, Riviera and Roadmaster Base.

1991

Year-Model-Body Type	Original List	Current Whlse	Average Retail
CENTURY CUSTOM 4*			
4 Dr Sdn	**13685**	8400	9700
2 Dr Cpe	**13785**	8300	9575
4 Dr Wgn	**15310**	8800	10175
CENTURY LIMITED 4*			
4 Dr Sdn	**14795**	9025	10400
4 Dr Wgn	**16230**	9425	10850
CENTURY SPECIAL 4*			
4 Dr Sdn	**13240**	8000	9300

* For 6 cylinder models add $425 wholesale and $425 retail.

Year-Model-Body Type	Original List	Current Whlse	Average Retail
LE SABRE 6			
2 Dr Cpe	**17180**	10825	12500
LE SABRE CUSTOM 6			
4 Dr Sdn	**17180**	10975	12675
LE SABRE LIMITED 6			
4 Dr Sdn	**18430**	11950	13800
2 Dr Cpe	**18330**	11825	13650
PARK AVENUE 6			
4 Dr Sdn	**24385**	15025	17675
4 Dr Ultra Sdn	**27420**	18025	20675
REATTA 6			
2 Dr Cpe	**29300**	17500	20150
2 Dr Conv	**35965**	—	—
REGAL CUSTOM 6			
4 Dr Sdn	**15910**	9200	10600
2 Dr Cpe	**15690**	9200	10600
REGAL LIMITED 6			
4 Dr Sdn	**16735**	9750	11225
2 Dr Cpe	**16455**	9750	11225
RIVIERA 6			
2 Dr Cpe	**24560**	15875	18525
ROADMASTER 8			
4 Dr Base Sdn	**20890**	16550	19200
4 Dr Limited Sdn	**23245**	17800	20450
4 Dr Estate Wgn	**21445**	16350	19000
SKYLARK 4*			
2 Dr Cpe	**11570**	4975	5900
4 Dr Sdn	**11470**	4975	5900
SKYLARK CUSTOM 4*			
4 Dr Sdn	**12765**	5500	6425
2 Dr Cpe	**12765**	5500	6425
SKYLARK GRAN SPORT 4*			
2 Dr Cpe	**14410**	5950	6875
SKYLARK LUXURY EDITION 4*			
4 Dr Sdn	**14610**	6125	7125

* For 6 cylinder or quad 4 engine models add $400 wholesale and $400 retail.

ADD FOR:

	Original List	Current Whlse	Average Retail
Anti-lock Brakes (Le Sabre, Regal, Skylark Gran Sport)	**925**	450	525
Vinyl Landau Roof (Roadmaster)	**695**	260	320
Leather Seats (Le Sabre Limited, Park Ave. Base, Regal)	**500**	250	300
(Reatta)	**680**	300	350
(Roadmaster Sdn)	**760**	300	350
(Roadmaster Estate Wgn)	**540**	250	300
CD Player (Reatta)	**396**	150	180
(Regal)	**414**	150	180

NOTE: Power windows, power door locks and power seat standard on Park Avenue, Reatta, Riviera and Roadmaster. Anti-lock brakes and driver side air bag standard on Park Avenue, Reatta and Roadmaster. Power brakes standard on all models.

1990

Year-Model-Body Type	Original List	Current Whlse	Average Retail
CENTURY CUSTOM 4*			
4 Dr Sdn	**13150**	5950	6875
2 Dr Cpe	**13250**	5850	6775
4 Dr Wgn	**14570**	6300	7325
CENTURY LIMITED 4*			
4 Dr Sdn	**14075**	6500	7575
4 Dr Wgn	**15455**	6850	7975

* For 6 cylinder models add $400 wholesale and $400 retail.

Year-Model-Body Type	Original List	Current Whlse	Average Retail
ELECTRA LIMITED 6			
4 Dr Sdn	**20225**	10275	11850
ELECTRA PARK AVENUE 6			
4 Dr Sdn	**21750**	11200	12925
ELECTRA PARK AVENUE ULTRA 6			
4 Dr Sdn	**27825**	13825	16200
ELECTRA T TYPE 6			
4 Dr Sdn	**23025**	10750	12400
ESTATE WAGON 8			
4 Dr Wgn	**17940**	9425	11100
LE SABRE 6			
2 Dr Cpe	**16145**	7975	9250
LE SABRE CUSTOM 6			
4 Dr Sdn	**16050**	8125	9375
LE SABRE LIMITED 6			
2 Dr Cpe	**17300**	8875	10250
4 Dr Sdn	**17400**	9025	10400

Refer To Optional Equipment Schedules

Year-Model-Body Type	Original List	Current Whlse	Average Retail
REATTA 6			
2 Dr Cpe	**28335**	13125	15450
2 Dr Conv	**34995**	17025	19675
REGAL CUSTOM 6			
2 Dr Cpe	**15200**	5850	6775
REGAL LIMITED 6			
2 Dr Cpe	**15860**	6300	7325
RIVIERA 6			
2 Dr Cpe	**23040**	11725	13550
SKYLARK 4			
2 Dr Cpe	**11285**	4975	5900
4 Dr Sdn	**11185**	4975	5900
SKYLARK CUSTOM 4*			
2 Dr Cpe	**12180**	5500	6425
4 Dr Sdn	**12180**	5525	6450
SKYLARK GRAN SPORT 4*			
2 Dr Cpe	**13655**	5950	6875
SKYLARK LUXURY EDITION 4*			
4 Dr Sdn	**13865**	6125	7125

* For 6 cylinder or quad 4 engine models add $350 wholesale and $350 retail.

ADD FOR:			
Anti-lock Brakes (Electra Limited & Park Ave., Le Sabre, Regal, Riviera)	**925**	425	500
3.8 Liter V6 Eng (Regal)	**395**	200	240
Leather Bucket Seats (Reatta)	**680**	275	340
4-Seater Pkg (Regal)	**409**	200	250
Delco/Bose Music System (Riviera)	**1399**	395	480

NOTE: Power windows standard on Electra Series, Reatta and Riviera. Power door locks standard on Electra Park Avenue, Electra Ultra, Reatta and Riviera. Power driver's seat standard on Electra Series, Reatta and Riviera. Full vinyl roof standard on Skylark Luxury Edition. Power brakes standard on all models.

1989

Year-Model-Body Type	Original List	Current Whlse	Average Retail
CENTURY CUSTOM 4*			
4 Dr Sdn	**13554**	4400	5325
2 Dr Cpe	**13324**	4300	5225
4 Dr Wgn	**14396**	4675	5600
CENTURY ESTATE WAGON 4*			
4 Dr Wgn	**15196**	5350	6275
CENTURY LIMITED 4*			
4 Dr Sdn	**14481**	4900	5825

* For 6 cylinder models add $375 wholesale and $375 retail.

Year-Model-Body Type	Original List	Current Whlse	Average Retail
ELECTRA LIMITED 6			
4 Dr Sdn	**18525**	7725	8975
ELECTRA ESTATE WAGON 8			
4 Dr Wgn	**19860**	8575	9900
ELECTRA PARK AVENUE 6			
4 Dr Sdn	**20460**	8525	9850
ELECTRA PARK AVENUE ULTRA 6			
4 Dr Sdn	**26218**	10875	12550
ELECTRA T TYPE 6			
4 Dr Sdn	**21325**	8200	9500
LE SABRE 6			
2 Dr Cpe	**15425**	6525	7600
LE SABRE CUSTOM 6			
4 Dr Sdn	**15330**	6650	7750
LE SABRE ESTATE WAGON 8			
4 Dr Wgn	**16770**	7000	8150
LE SABRE LIMITED 6			
2 Dr Cpe	**16630**	7325	8500
4 Dr Sdn	**16730**	7475	8675
REATTA 6			
2 Dr Cpe	**26700**	9975	11500
REGAL CUSTOM 6			
2 Dr Cpe	**14614**	5850	6775
REGAL LIMITED 6			
2 Dr Cpe	**15139**	6300	7325
RIVIERA 6			
2 Dr Cpe	**22540**	8875	10250
SKYHAWK 4			
2 Dr Cpe	**10420**	4050	4950
4 Dr Sdn	**10420**	4150	5075
4 Dr Wgn	**11365**	4350	5275
SKYLARK CUSTOM 4*			
2 Dr Cpe	**11691**	4650	5575
4 Dr Sdn	**11691**	4650	5575
SKYLARK LIMITED 4*			
2 Dr Cpe	**12921**	4950	5875
4 Dr Sdn	**12921**	4950	5975

* For 6 cylinder models add $325 wholesale and $325 retail. For quad 4 engine add $275 wholesale and $275 retail.

ADD FOR:			
S/E Pkg (Skyhawk Cpe)	**1095**	400	500
(Skylark Custom)	**1134**	450	550
4-Seater Pkg (Regal)	**409**	175	210
Gran Sport Pkg (Regal Custom)	**1212**	500	600
T-Type Pkg (Le Sabre)	**1005**	400	500
16-way Adj. Driver's Seat (Riviera)	**1230**	250	300
(Reatta)	**895**	200	250
Anti-Lock Brakes (Regal, Le Sabre, Electra Limited, Electra Park Ave.,			

Year-Model-Body Type	Original List	Current Whlse	Average Retail
Riviera)	**925**	350	425
Leather Seats (Regal Limited, Le Sabre)	**450**	175	200

NOTE: Power brakes standard on all models. Power windows standard on Electra Series, Riviera and Reatta. Power locks standard on Electra Park Ave., Riviera and Reatta. Power seat standard on Electra Park Ave., Ultra Riviera and Reatta. Vinyl roof standard on Le Sabre Coupe and Electra Park Avenue Ultra. Anti-Lock brakes standard on Electra T Type, Electra Park Avenue and Reatta.

1988

Year-Model-Body Type	Original List	Current Whlse	Average Retail
CENTURY CUSTOM 4*			
4 Dr Sdn	**12679**	3500	4400
2 Dr Cpe	**12529**	3400	4300
4 Dr Wgn	**13346**	3750	4650
CENTURY ESTATE WAGON 4*			
4 Dr Wgn	**14553**	4225	5150
CENTURY LIMITED 4*			
4 Dr Sdn	**13729**	3975	4875
2 Dr Cpe	**13526**	3875	4775

* For 6 cylinder models add $350 wholesale and $350 retail.

Year-Model-Body Type	Original List	Current Whlse	Average Retail
ELECTRA LIMITED 6			
4 Dr Sdn	**17479**	6075	6975
ELECTRA ESTATE WAGON 8			
4 Dr Wgn	**18954**	6800	7925
ELECTRA PARK AVENUE 6			
4 Dr Sdn	**19464**	6775	7875
ELECTRA T TYPE 6			
4 Dr Sdn	**20229**	6475	7525
LE SABRE 6			
2 Dr Cpe	**14560**	5050	5975
LE SABRE CUSTOM 6			
4 Dr Sdn	**14405**	5200	6125
LE SABRE LIMITED 6			
4 Dr Sdn	**15475**	5925	6850
2 Dr Cpe	**16350**	5775	6700
LE SABRE ESTATE WAGON 8			
4 Dr Wgn	**16040**	5350	6275
REATTA 6			
2 Dr Cpe	**25000**	8600	9925
REGAL CUSTOM 6			
2 Dr Cpe	**13452**	4650	5575
REGAL LIMITED 6			
2 Dr Cpe	**14015**	4950	5875
RIVIERA 6			
2 Dr Cpe	**21615**	6575	7650
SKYHAWK 4			
4 Dr Sdn	**9974**	3325	4225
2 Dr Cpe	**9974**	3325	4225
4 Dr Wgn	**10887**	3600	4500
SKYLARK CUSTOM 4*			
4 Dr Sdn	**11074**	3625	4525
2 Dr Cpe	**11359**	3625	4525
SKYLARK LIMITED 4*			
4 Dr Sdn	**12396**	3925	4825
2 Dr Cpe	**12466**	3925	4825

* For quad 4 or 6 cylinder models add $275 wholesale and $275 retail.

ADD FOR:

Year-Model-Body Type	Original List	Current Whlse	Average Retail
T-Type Pkg (Le Sabre Custom Cpe)	**1958**	700	800
(Riviera)	**1844**	650	750
Turbo Pkg (Skyhawk Limited)	**1547**	500	600
Anti-Lock Brakes (Electra Limited Park Ave., Le Sabre, Riviera)	**925**	275	350
Cellular Telephone (Riviera)	**2850**	200	250
231 CID V6 Eng (Century)	**745**	200	240

NOTE: Power brakes standard on all models. Power windows standard on Electra Series, Riviera and Reatta. Power door locks standard on Electra Park Avenue, Electra Estate Wagon, Riviera and Reatta. Power seat standard on Electra Series, Riviera and Reatta.

1987

Year-Model-Body Type	Original List	Current Whlse	Average Retail
CENTURY CUSTOM 4*			
4 Dr Sdn	**11764**	2675	3575
2 Dr Cpe	**11619**	2600	3475
4 Dr Wgn	**12253**	2900	3800
CENTURY ESTATE WAGON 4*			
4 Dr Wgn	**12773**	3275	4175
CENTURY LIMITED 4*			
4 Dr Sdn	**12368**	3075	3975
2 Dr Cpe	**12172**	3000	3900

* For 6 cylinder models add $300 wholesale and $300 retail.

Year-Model-Body Type	Original List	Current Whlse	Average Retail
ELECTRA LIMITED 6			
4 Dr Sdn	**16902**	4200	5125
ELECTRA ESTATE WAGON 8			
4 Dr Wgn	**17697**	5000	5925
ELECTRA PARK AVENUE 6			
4 Dr Sdn	**18769**	4825	5750
2 Dr Cpe	**18577**	4700	5625
ELECTRA T TYPE 6			
4 Dr Sdn	**18224**	4600	5525

Refer To Optional Equipment Schedules

Year-Model-Body Type	Original List	Current Whlse	Average Retail
LE SABRE 6			
4 Dr Sdn	**13438**	3700	4600
LE SABRE CUSTOM 6			
4 Dr Sdn	**13616**	4000	4900
2 Dr Cpe	**13616**	3850	4750
LE SABRE LIMITED 6			
4 Dr Sdn	**14918**	4575	5500
2 Dr Cpe	**14918**	4425	5350
LE SABRE ESTATE WAGON 8			
4 Dr Wgn	**14724**	4050	4950
REGAL 6*			
2 Dr Cpe	**12337**	3250	4150
REGAL LIMITED 6*			
2 Dr Cpe	**13078**	3650	4550

* For 8 cylinder models add $350 wholesale and $350 retail.

Year-Model-Body Type	Original List	Current Whlse	Average Retail
RIVIERA 6			
2 Dr Cpe	**20337**	4800	5725
SKYHAWK CUSTOM 4			
4 Dr Sdn	**9949**	2225	3075
2 Dr Cpe	**9912**	2150	3000
4 Dr Wgn	**10639**	2350	3225
SKYHAWK LIMITED 4			
4 Dr Sdn	**10893**	2550	3425
2 Dr Cpe	**10835**	2475	3350
4 Dr Wgn	**11231**	2675	3575
SKYHAWK SPORT 4			
2 Dr Htchbk	**10355**	2225	3075
SKYLARK CUSTOM 4*			
4 Dr Sdn	**11080**	2600	3475
SKYLARK LIMITED 4*			
4 Dr Sdn	**12168**	2850	3750
SOMERSET CUSTOM 4*			
2 Dr Cpe	**11122**	2600	3475
SOMERSET LIMITED 4*			
2 Dr Cpe	**12168**	2850	3750

* For 6 cylinder models add $300 wholesale and $300 retail.

Year-Model-Body Type	Original List	Current Whlse	Average Retail
ADD FOR:			
Grand National Package (Regal)	**3574**	1000	1200
T-Type Pkg (Le Sabre Custom Cpe)	**1975**	500	600
(Riviera)	**1844**	450	525
T Pkg (Skyhawk, Skylark, Somerset)	**592**	170	200
(Le Sabre, Electra, Regal)	**508**	140	170
(Riviera)	**581**	160	200
(Electra Park Ave)	**407**	150	200
Turbo Pkg (Skyhawk)	**1607**	350	400
(Regal)	**1422**	400	450
231 CID V6 Eng (Century)	**745**	150	175
307 CID V8 Eng (Regal)	**590**	175	200
Hatch Roof (Regal)	**895**	250	300

NOTE: Power brakes standard on all models. Power windows standard on Riviera and Electra Series. Power locks standard on Riviera and Electra Park Avenue.

1986

Year-Model-Body Type	Original List	Current Whlse	Average Retail
CENTURY CUSTOM 4*			
4 Dr Sdn	**11259**	1850	2700
2 Dr Cpe	**11078**	1775	2625
4 Dr Wgn	**11689**	2050	2900
CENTURY ESTATE WAGON 4*			
4 Dr Wgn	**12162**	2350	3225
CENTURY LIMITED 4*			
4 Dr Sdn	**11772**	2175	3025
2 Dr Cpe	**11582**	2100	2950
CENTURY T TYPE 6			
4 Dr Sdn	**13304**	2525	3400

* For 6 cylinder models add $300 wholesale and $300 retail.

Year-Model-Body Type	Original List	Current Whlse	Average Retail
ELECTRA 6			
4 Dr Sdn	**16071**	3300	4200
2 Dr Cpe	**15873**	3175	4075
ELECTRA ESTATE WAGON 8			
4 Dr Wgn	**16911**	3575	4475
ELECTRA PARK AVENUE 6			
4 Dr Sdn	**17875**	3850	4750
2 Dr Cpe	**17690**	3700	4600
ELECTRA T TYPE 6			
4 Dr Sdn	**17348**	3650	4550
LE SABRE CUSTOM 6			
4 Dr Sdn	**12699**	3150	4050
2 Dr Cpe	**12699**	3000	3900
LE SABRE LIMITED 6			
4 Dr Sdn	**13838**	3600	4500
2 Dr Cpe	**13838**	3450	4350
LE SABRE ESTATE WAGON 8			
4 Dr Wgn	**14044**	2800	3700
REGAL 6*			
2 Dr Cpe	**11770**	2325	3200
REGAL LIMITED 6*			
2 Dr Cpe	**12485**	2625	3525
REGAL T TYPE 6			
2 Dr Cpe	**14153**	3825	4725

* For 8 cylinder models add $325 wholesale and $325 retail.

Year-Model-Body Type	Original List	Current Whlse	Average Retail
RIVIERA 6			
2 Dr Cpe	**20267**	3875	4775
RIVIERA T TYPE 6			
2 Dr Cpe	**22052**	4250	5175
SKYHAWK CUSTOM 4			
4 Dr Sdn	**9682**	1775	2625

Year-Model-Body Type	Original List	Current Whlse	Average Retail
2 Dr Cpe	**9444**	1775	2625
4 Dr Wgn	**10044**	1875	2725
SKYHAWK LIMITED 4			
4 Dr Sdn	**10220**	2075	2925
2 Dr Cpe	**10024**	1975	2825
4 Dr Wgn	**10541**	2150	3000
SKYHAWK T TYPE 4			
2 Dr Cpe	**10528**	2250	3100
2 Dr Htchbk	**10983**	2350	3225
SKYLARK CUSTOM 4*			
4 Dr Sdn	**10997**	1950	2800
SKYLARK LIMITED 4*			
4 Dr Sdn	**11681**	2175	3025
SOMERSET CUSTOM 4*			
2 Dr Cpe	**10797**	1950	2800
SOMERSET LIMITED 4*			
2 Dr Cpe	**11482**	2175	3025
SOMERSET T TYPE 6			
2 Dr Cpe	**11241**	2600	3475

* For 6 cylinder models add $275 wholesale and $275 retail.

ADD FOR:

110 CID Turbo Eng (Skyhawk T Type)	**800**	150	180
173 CID V6 Eng (Century except T Type)	**485**	90	110
181 CID V6 Eng (Skylark, Somerset except T Type)	**660**	120	140
231 CID V6 Eng (Century except T Type)	**745**	100	135
307 CID V8 Eng (Regal except T Type)	**590**	110	130
Hatch Roof (Regal)	**895**	160	200

NOTE: Power windows and power seat standard on Electra and Riviera.

1985

Year-Model-Body Type	Original List	Current Whlse	Average Retail
CENTURY CUSTOM 4*			
4 Dr Sdn	**10485**	1250	1975
2 Dr Cpe	**10315**	1275	2000
4 Dr Wgn	**10890**	1425	2175
CENTURY LIMITED 4*			
4 Dr Sdn	**10965**	1525	2375
2 Dr Cpe	**10790**	1425	2175
4 Dr Wgn	**11335**	1675	2525
CENTURY T TYPE 6			
4 Dr Sdn	**12395**	1625	2475
2 Dr Cpe	**12225**	1625	2475

* For 6 cylinder models add $300 wholesale and $300 retail.

Year-Model-Body Type	Original List	Current Whlse	Average Retail
ELECTRA 6			
4 Dr Sdn	**14883**	2475	3350
2 Dr Cpe	**14697**	2350	3225
ELECTRA ESTATE WAGON 8			
4 Dr Wgn	**15629**	2825	3725
ELECTRA PARK AVENUE 6			
4 Dr Sdn	**16566**	2900	3800
2 Dr Cpe	**16398**	2300	3175
ELECTRA T TYPE 6			
4 Dr Sdn	**15879**	2725	3625
2 Dr Cpe	**15694**	2600	3475
LE SABRE CUSTOM 6*			
4 Dr Sdn	**11565**	2000	2850
2 Dr Cpe	**11412**	1875	2725
LE SABRE ESTATE WAGON 8			
4 Dr Wgn	**12958**	2275	3150
LE SABRE LTD COLLECTORS EDIT 6*			
4 Dr Sdn	**12904**	2200	3050
2 Dr Cpe	**12736**	2075	2925

* For 8 cylinder models add $400 wholesale and $400 retail.

Year-Model-Body Type	Original List	Current Whlse	Average Retail
REGAL 6			
2 Dr Cpe	**10879**	1700	2550
REGAL LIMITED 6			
2 Dr Cpe	**11543**	1950	2800
REGAL T TYPE 6			
2 Dr Cpe	**12890**	2900	3800
RIVIERA 8			
2 Dr Cpe	**17044**	2725	3625
RIVIERA CONVERTIBLE 8			
2 Dr Conv	**27335**	5650	6575
RIVIERA T TYPE 6			
2 Dr Cpe	**17995**	2275	3150
SKYHAWK CUSTOM 4			
4 Dr Sdn	**9019**	1325	2050
2 Dr Cpe	**8798**	1250	1975
4 Dr Wgn	**9362**	1375	2125
SKYHAWK LIMITED 4			
4 Dr Sdn	**9529**	1550	2400
2 Dr Cpe	**9325**	1450	2225
4 Dr Wgn	**9832**	1625	2475
SKYHAWK T TYPE 4			
2 Dr Cpe	**9851**	1700	2550
SKYLARK CUSTOM 4*			
4 Dr Sdn	**9061**	1075	1800
SKYLARK LIMITED 4*			
4 Dr Sdn	**9649**	1275	2000
SOMERSET REGAL 4*			
2 Dr Cpe	**10104**	1450	2225
SOMERSET REGAL LIMITED 4*			
2 Dr Cpe	**10725**	1625	2475

* For 6 cylinder models add $200 wholesale and $200 retail.

Year-Model-Body Type	Original List	Current Whlse	Average Retail
ADD FOR:			
110 CID Turbo Eng (Skyhawk T Type)	**800**	100	120
173 CID MFI V6 Eng (Skylark)	**510**	60	80
181 CID MFI V6 Eng (Somerset Regal)	**560**	70	80
231 CID MFI V6 Eng (Century Custom & Limited)	**595**	70	90
231 CID V6 Turbo Eng (Riviera)	**735**	90	115

NOTE: Power windows standard on Electra and Riviera. Power door locks standard on Electra. Power brakes standard on all models. Power seat standard on Electra, Le Sabre Ltd Collector's Edit and Riviera.

1984

Year-Model-Body Type	Original List	Current Whlse	Average Retail
CENTURY CUSTOM 4*			
4 Dr Sdn	**10004**	1050	1775
2 Dr Cpe	**9840**	950	1675
4 Dr Wgn	**10390**	1175	1900
CENTURY LIMITED 4*			
4 Dr Sdn	**10459**	1225	1950
2 Dr Cpe	**10292**	1150	1875
4 Dr Wgn	**10817**	1325	2050

* For 6 cylinder models add $200 wholesale and $200 retail.

Year-Model-Body Type	Original List	Current Whlse	Average Retail
CENTURY T TYPE 6			
4 Dr Sdn	**11404**	1275	2000
2 Dr Cpe	**11240**	1275	2000
ELECTRA LIMITED 6*			
4 Dr Sdn	**13530**	1775	2625
2 Dr Cpe	**13353**	1675	2525
ELECTRA PARK AVENUE 6*			
4 Dr Sdn	**15044**	2175	3025
2 Dr Cpe	**14888**	2050	2900

* For 8 cylinder models add $300 wholesale and $300 retail.

Year-Model-Body Type	Original List	Current Whlse	Average Retail
ESTATE WAGON 8			
4 Dr Wgn	**14681**	1725	2575
LE SABRE CUSTOM 6*			
4 Dr Sdn	**10971**	1300	2025
2 Dr Cpe	**10826**	1200	1925
LE SABRE LIMITED 6*			
4 Dr Sdn	**11782**	1550	2400
2 Dr Cpe	**11622**	1425	2175

* For 8 cylinder models add $300 wholesale and $300 retail.

Year-Model-Body Type	Original List	Current Whlse	Average Retail
REGAL 6			
4 Dr Sdn	**10513**	1075	1800
2 Dr Cpe	**10329**	1250	1975
REGAL LIMITED 6			
4 Dr Sdn	**11105**	1300	2025
2 Dr Cpe	**10967**	1450	2225
REGAL T TYPE 6			
2 Dr Cpe	**12230**	2150	3000
RIVIERA 6*			
2 Dr Cpe	**15967**	2075	2925
RIVIERA CONVERTIBLE 6*			
2 Dr Conv	**25832**	4850	5775

* For 8 cylinder models add $300 wholesale and $300 retail.

Year-Model-Body Type	Original List	Current Whlse	Average Retail
RIVIERA T TYPE 6			
2 Dr Cpe	**17050**	1775	2625
SKYHAWK CUSTOM 4			
4 Dr Sdn	**8574**	800	1500
2 Dr Cpe	**8362**	725	1375
4 Dr Wgn	**8906**	850	1550
SKYHAWK LIMITED 4			
4 Dr Sdn	**9066**	925	1650
2 Dr Cpe	**8870**	875	1600
4 Dr Wgn	**9356**	975	1700
SKYHAWK T TYPE 4			
2 Dr Cpe	**9306**	1000	1725
SKYLARK CUSTOM 4*			
4 Dr Sdn	**8862**	625	1175
2 Dr Cpe	**8700**	575	1075
SKYLARK LIMITED 4*			
4 Dr Sdn	**9438**	800	1500
2 Dr Cpe	**9274**	725	1375

* For 6 cylinder models add $150 wholesale and $150 retail.

Year-Model-Body Type	Original List	Current Whlse	Average Retail
SKYLARK T TYPE 6			
2 Dr Cpe	**10712**	900	1625

1983 — ALL BODY STYLES

Year-Model-Body Type	Original List	Current Whlse	Average Retail
CENTURY CUSTOM	—	875	1600
CENTURY LIMITED	—	975	1700
CENTURY T TYPE	—	1050	1775
ELECTRA LIMITED	—	1250	1975
ELECTRA PARK AVENUE	—	1525	2375
ESTATE WAGON	—	1300	2025
LE SABRE CUSTOM	—	975	1700
LE SABRE ESTATE WAGON	—	1125	1850
LE SABRE LIMITED	—	1200	1925
REGAL	—	1000	1725
REGAL ESTATE WAGON	—	900	1625
REGAL LIMITED	—	1200	1925
REGAL T TYPE	—	1000	1725
RIVIERA	—	1625	2475
RIVIERA CONV	—	4375	5300
SKYHAWK CUSTOM	—	550	1025
SKYHAWK LIMITED	—	675	1275
SKYHAWK T TYPE	—	700	1325

Year-Model-Body Type	Original List	Current Whlse	Average Retail
SKYLARK CUSTOM	—	425	775
SKYLARK LIMITED	—	550	1025
SKYLARK T TYPE	—	650	1225

CADILLAC

Year-Model-Body Type	Original List	Current Whlse	Average Retail
1992			
ALLANTE 8			
Cpe/Conv	**62790**	—	—
Conv	**57170**	—	—
ADD FOR:			
Digital Instrument Cluster (Conv)	**495**	—	—
Pearl White Paint	**700**	—	—
BROUGHAM 8			
Sdn	**31740**	—	—
ADD FOR:			
5.7 Liter 8 Cyl Eng	**250**	—	—
D'Elegance, Cloth	**1875**	—	—
D'Elegance, Leather	**2445**	—	—
Leather Seat Trim	**570**	—	—
Wire Wheels	**1000**	—	—
DE VILLE 8			
Cpe	**31740**	—	—
Sdn	**31740**	—	—
Touring Sdn	**35190**	—	—
ADD FOR:			
Cabriolet Roof	**1095**	—	—
Phaeton Roof	**1095**	—	—
Full Vinyl Roof	**925**	—	—
Leather Seat Trim (Base)	**570**	—	—
ELDORADO 8			
Cpe	**32470**	—	—
ADD FOR:			
Sports & Stripes Pkg	**1900**	—	—
Touring Pkg	**4000**	—	—
Leather Seat Trim	**650**	—	—
FLEETWOOD 8			
Cpe	**36360**	—	—
Sdn	**36360**	—	—
Sixty Special Sdn	**39860**	—	—
ADD FOR:			
Leather Seat Trim	**570**	—	—
SEVILLE 8			
Sdn	**34975**	—	—
Touring Sdn	**37975**	—	—
ADD FOR:			
Leather Seat Trim	**650**	—	—

NOTE: Power windows, power door locks, power seat, cruise control and tilt steering wheel standard on all models.

Year-Model-Body Type	Original List	Current Whlse	Average Retail
1991			
ALLANTE 8			
Cpe/Conv	**62810**	32925	36625
Conv	**57260**	30525	33950
BROUGHAM 8			
Sdn	**30455**	18400	21400
DE VILLE 8			
Cpe	**30455**	17575	20225
Sdn	**30455**	17775	20425
ELDORADO 8			
Cpe	**31495**	19275	22325
FLEETWOOD 8			
Cpe	**35195**	19775	22825
Sdn	**35195**	19975	23025
Sixty Special Sdn	**38695**	21025	24325
SEVILLE 8			
Sdn	**34195**	17175	19825
Touring Sdn	**37395**	19650	22700
TOURING SEDAN 8			
Sdn	**33455**	19675	22725
ADD FOR:			
D'Elegance, Cloth (Brougham)	**1875**	1000	1300
D'Elegance, Leather (Brougham)	**2445**	1250	1550
Touring Coupe Pkg (Eldorado)	**2050**	1200	1475
Spring Edit Pkg (Coupe De Ville)	**1481**	800	900
Leather Seats (Brougham, De Ville, Fleetwood ex. 60 Special)	**570**	325	400
(Eldorado)	**555**	325	400
(Seville Base)	**460**	300	375
Formal Cabriolet Roof (Coupe De Ville)	**925**	345	420
Full Cabriolet Roof (Coupe De Ville, Eldorado)	**1095**	360	440
Full Padded Vinyl Roof (Sedan De Ville)	**925**	345	420
(Eldorado)	**1095**	360	440
Phaeton Roof (Sedan De Ville)	**1095**	360	440
(Seville Base)	**1195**	445	540

NOTE: Power windows, power door locks, power seat, and power anti-lock brakes standard on all models. Vinyl roof standard on Brougham and Fleetwood. Air bag standard on Allante, De Ville, Eldorado, Fleetwood and Seville.

Refer To Optional Equipment Schedules

CADILLAC

Year-Model-Body Type	Original List	Current Whlse	Average Retail
1990			
ALLANTE 8			
Cpe/Conv	**58638**	27550	30900
Conv	**53050**	25475	28800
BROUGHAM 8			
Sdn (307 CID V8)	**27400**	13175	15500
Sdn (350 CID V8)	**28250**	13525	15900
DE VILLE 8			
Cpe	**26960**	13975	16350
Sdn	**27540**	14175	16650
ELDORADO 8			
Cpe	**28855**	15025	17675
FLEETWOOD 8			
Cpe	**32400**	15425	18075
Sdn	**32980**	15625	18275
Sixty Special Sdn	**36980**	16950	19600
SEVILLE 8			
Sdn	**31830**	14475	17000
Touring Sdn	**36320**	16525	19175
ADD FOR:			
Anti-Lock Brakes (De Ville, Eldorado, Seville Base)	**925**	450	550
Cellular Telephone (Allante)	**1195**	195	240
D'Elegance, Cloth (Brougham)	**2171**	850	1000
D'Elegance, Leather (Brougham)	**2731**	950	1150
Formal Cabriolet Roof (Coupe De Ville)	**825**	235	285
Full Cabriolet Roof (Coupe De Ville, Eldorado)	**1095**	310	375
Full Padded Vinyl Roof (Eldorado)	**1095**	310	375

NOTE: Power windows, power door locks, power seat and power brakes standard on all models. Air bag standard on all models except Brougham. Anti-lock brakes standard on Allante, Brougham, Fleetwood Series and Seville Touring Sedan. Full vinyl roof standard on Brougham and Fleetwood Series. Formal cabriolet roof standard on Fleetwood Coupe.

Year-Model-Body Type	Original List	Current Whlse	Average Retail
1989			
ALLANTE 8			
Cpe/Conv	**57183**	20650	23700
BROUGHAM 8			
Sdn	**25699**	9800	11300
DE VILLE 8			
Cpe	**25285**	10925	12600
Sdn	**25760**	11100	12825
ELDORADO 8			
Cpe	**26915**	11700	13525
FLEETWOOD 8			
Cpe	**30365**	11925	13775
Sdn	**30840**	12100	13975
Sixty Special Sdn	**34840**	13100	15425
SEVILLE 8			
Sdn	**29935**	11725	13550
ADD FOR:			
Biarritz, Cloth (Eldorado)	**2875**	780	975
Biarritz, Leather (Eldorado)	**3325**	950	1200
Full Vinyl Roof (Eldorado)	**1095**	260	315
D'Elegance, Cloth (Brougham)	**2286**	800	1050
D'Elegance, Leather (Brougham)	**2846**	950	1250
STS Pkg (Seville)	**5754**	2400	2800
Anti-Lock Brakes (De Ville, Eldorado, Seville)	**925**	350	450

NOTE: Power windows, power door locks, and power brakes standard on all models.

Year-Model-Body Type	Original List	Current Whlse	Average Retail
1988			
ALLANTE 8			
Cpe/Conv	**56533**	18075	20750
BROUGHAM 8			
Sdn	**23486**	8250	9525
CIMARRON 6			
Sdn	**16486**	5050	5975
DE VILLE 8			
Cpe	**23049**	7925	9200
Sdn	**23404**	8125	9375
ELDORADO 8			
Cpe	**24891**	8475	9800
FLEETWOOD 8			
d'Elegance	**28025**	9025	10400
Sixty Special	**34750**	9700	11175
SEVILLE 8			
Sdn	**27627**	8625	9950
ADD FOR:			
Biarritz, Cloth (Eldorado)	**2845**	590	680
Biarritz, Leather (Eldorado)	**3255**	650	745
D'Elegance, Cloth (Brougham)	**2335**	520	600
D'Elegance, Leather			

Year-Model-Body Type	Original List	Current Whlse	Average Retail
(Brougham)	**2895**	600	700
Elegante, Cloth (Seville)	**3345**	660	760
Elegante, Leather (Seville)	**3755**	715	830
Touring Car Opt. (De Ville)	**2880**	900	1075
Anti-Lock Brakes (De Ville, Eldorado, Seville, Fleetwood d'Elegance)	**925**	300	400
Full Vinyl Roof (Eldorado)	**995**	300	165
Formal Cabriolet Roof (De Ville Cpe)	**713**	200	270
Phaeton Roof (Seville)	**1095**	350	425
Premier Formal Vinyl Roof (Brougham)	**1095**	350	425

NOTE: Power windows, power door locks, and power brakes standard on all models. Sunroof standard on Allante.

1987

Year-Model-Body Type	Original List	Current Whlse	Average Retail
ALLANTE 8			
Cpe/Conv	**54700**	14150	16600
CIMARRON 4*			
Sdn	**15032**	3150	4050

* For 6 cylinder models add $425 wholesale and $425 retail.

Year-Model-Body Type	Original List	Current Whlse	Average Retail
DE VILLE 8			
Cpe	**21316**	6075	6975
Sdn	**21659**	6275	7300
ELDORADO 8			
Cpe	**23740**	6625	7700
FLEETWOOD 8			
Limousine	**36510**	7025	8150
Formal Limousine	**38580**	8550	9875
Brougham	**22637**	5800	6725
d'Elegance	**26104**	6900	8025
Sixty Special	**34850**	7600	8825
SEVILLE 8			
Sdn	**26326**	6775	7875
ADD FOR:			
Biarritz, Cloth (Eldorado)	**3095**	455	515
Biarritz, Leather (Eldorado)	**3505**	500	655
D'Elegance, Cloth (Brougham)	**1950**	360	400
D'Elegance, Leather (Brougham)	**2510**	410	475
Elegante, Cloth (Seville)	**3595**	600	750
Elegante, Leather (Seville)	**4005**	700	875
Touring Car Opt (De Ville)	**2880**	750	900
Formal Cabriolet Roof (De Ville)	**713**	150	200

NOTE: Power windows, power brakes, and power seat standard on all models.

1986

Year-Model-Body Type	Original List	Current Whlse	Average Retail
CIMARRON 4*			
Sdn	**13974**	2450	3325

* For 6 cylinder models add $400 wholesale and $400 retail.

Year-Model-Body Type	Original List	Current Whlse	Average Retail
DE VILLE 8			
Cpe (FWD)	**20254**	4175	5100
Sdn (FWD)	**20585**	4375	5300
ELDORADO 8			
Cpe	**25032**	5200	6125
FLEETWOOD 8			
Limousine	**34934**	5200	6125
Formal Limousine	**36934**	6475	7525
Brougham Sdn	**21633**	4825	5750
SEVILLE 8			
Sdn	**27618**	5775	6700
ADD FOR:			
Biarritz, Cloth (Eldorado)	**3095**	300	345
Biarritz, Leather (Eldorado)	**3505**	350	425
D'Oro (Cimarron)	**975**	140	200
Elegante, Cloth (Seville)	**3595**	350	440
Elegante, Leather (Seville)	**4005**	400	500
Fleetwood Cloth Opt (De Ville)	**3150**	325	450
Fleetwood Leather Opt (De Ville)	**3700**	375	500
Touring Car Opt (De Ville)	**2880**	400	550
Formal Cabriolet Roof (De Ville)	**713**	125	150

NOTE: Power windows and power brakes standard on all models. Power seat standard on Formal Limousine and Fleetwood Brougham Sedan. Vinyl top standard on Limousines and Fleetwood Brougham Sedan.

Refer To Optional Equipment Schedules

Year-Model-Body Type	Original List	Current Whlse	Average Retail
1985			
DE VILLE 8			
Cpe (FWD)	**18355**	3125	4025
Sdn (FWD)	**18947**	3300	4200
FLEETWOOD 8			
Cpe (FWD)	**21495**	3500	4400
Sdn (FWD)	**21466**	3700	4600
Limousine (FWD)	**32640**	3950	4850
Brougham Cpe (RWD)	**21219**	3225	4125
Brougham Sdn (RWD)	**21835**	3425	4325
Eldorado Cpe	**21355**	4050	4950
Eldorado Biarritz Conv.	**32105**	8350	9650
Seville Sdn	**23729**	4050	4950
Cimarron Sdn (4 cyl)	**13312**	1475	2300
ADD FOR:			
Brougham d'Elegance, Cloth	**1295**	150	200
Brougham d'Elegance, Leather	**1845**	200	250
Fleetwood d'Elegance, Leather	**1845**	200	250
Formal Cabriolet (De Ville Cpe, Fleetwood Sdn)	**698**	90	100
Full Cabriolet (Eldorado Cpe, Seville)	**995**	120	150
D'Oro (Cimarron)	**975**	120	150

NOTE: Power brakes standard on all models. Power windows, power door locks and power seat standard on all models except Cimarron.

Year-Model-Body Type	Original List	Current Whlse	Average Retail
1984			
CIMARRON 4			
Sdn	**12605**	1250	1975
DE VILLE 8			
Cpe (RWD)	**17128**	2050	2900
Sdn (RWD)	**17613**	2175	3025
Cpe (FWD)	**17472**	—	—
Sdn (FWD)	**17957**	—	—
FLEETWOOD 8			
Eldorado Cpe	**20330**	2900	3800
Eldorado Biarritz Conv.	**31274**	6575	7650
Brougham Cpe	**19930**	2450	3325
Brougham Sdn	**20439**	2550	3425
Limousine	**30439**	3125	4025
Formal Limousine	**31497**	3650	4550
Seville Sdn	**22456**	2950	3850

NOTE: Power windows (except Cimarron), tinted glass, and power disc brakes standard on all models. Cabriolet roof standard on Brougham Coupe. Full vinyl roof standard on Brougham Sedan, Limousine and Formal Limousine.

Year-Model-Body Type	Original List	Current Whlse	Average Retail
1983 — ALL BODY STYLES			
CIMARRON	—	1000	1725
DE VILLE	—	1775	2625
FLEETWOOD ELDORADO	—	2325	3200
FLEETWOOD BROUGHAM	—	2150	3000
FLEETWOOD LIMOUSINE	—	2925	3825
FLEETWOOD FORMAL LIMOUSINE	—	3250	4150
SEVILLE	—	2600	3475

CHEVROLET

Year-Model-Body Type	Original List	Current Whlse	Average Retail
1992			
BERETTA 4*			
2 Dr Base Cpe	**12359**	—	—
* For 6 cylinder models add $— wholesale and $— retail.			
BERETTA GTZ 4			
2 Dr Cpe	**16755**	—	—
BERETTA GT 4*			
2 Dr Cpe	**13935**	—	—
* For 6 cylinder models add $— wholesale and $— retail.			
DEDUCT FOR:			
6 Cyl Engine (GTZ)	—	—	—
CAMARO 6*			
2 Dr RS Cpe	**13435**	—	—
2 Dr RS Conv	**19415**	—	—
* For 8 cylinder models add $— wholesale and $— retail.			
CAMARO 8			
2 Dr Z28 Cpe	**17415**	—	—
2 Dr Z28 Conv	**22860**	—	—
ADD FOR:			
5.7 Liter 8 Cyl Eng (Z28 Cpe)	**300**	—	—
Custom Cloth Seats	**327**	—	—
Leather Seats	**850**	—	—
Aluminum Wheels (RS)	**225**	—	—
Removable Roof Panels	**895**	—	—
CAPRICE 8			
4 Dr Sdn	**17300**	—	—
4 Dr Wgn	**18700**	—	—
CAPRICE CLASSIC 8			
4 Dr Sdn	**19300**	—	—
ADD FOR:			
5.7 Liter Engine	**250**	—	—
Leather Seat Trim	**645**	—	—
Wire Wheel Covers (Base)	**215**	—	—

Year-Model-Body Type	Original List	Current Whlse	Average Retail
CAVALIER 4*			
2 Dr VL Cpe	**10471**	—	—
4 Dr VL Sdn	**10571**	—	—
4 Dr VL Wgn	**11176**	—	—
2 Dr RS Cpe	**11239**	—	—
2 Dr RS Conv	**17175**	—	—
4 Dr RS Sdn	**11439**	—	—
4 Dr RS Wgn	**11944**	—	—
* For 6 cylinder models add $— wholesale and $— retail.			
CAVALIER 6			
2 Dr Z24 Sport Cpe	**14235**	—	—
2 Dr Z24 Conv	**19545**	—	—
CORSICA LT 4*			
4 Dr Ntchbk Sdn	**12359**	—	—
* For 6 cylinder models add $— wholesale and $— retail.			
ADD FOR:			
Sport Handling Pkg	**395**	—	—
CORVETTE 8			
Htchbk Cpe	**33635**	—	—
Conv	**40145**	—	—
ADD FOR:			
ZR1 Spec Perf Pkg	**31378**	—	—
Handling Pkg	**2045**	—	—
Removable Hardtop Roof	**1995**	—	—
Removable Roof Panels	**650**	—	—
Dual Removable Roof Panels	**950**	—	—
Leather Seat Trim	**475**	—	—
Sport Leather Seat Trim	**1100**	—	—
Selective Ride & Handling Suspension	**1695**	—	—
LUMINA 4*			
2 Dr Cpe	**14030**	—	—
4 Dr Sdn	**14230**	—	—
* For 6 cylinder models add $— wholesale and $— retail.			
LUMINA 6			
2 Dr Euro Cpe	**15600**	—	—
4 Dr Euro Sdn	**15800**	—	—
2 Dr Z34 Cpe	**18600**	—	—
ADD FOR:			
Euro 3.4 Pkg (Euro Sdn)	**1885**	—	—
Anti-Lock Brakes (Base)	**450**	—	—
Custom Cloth Bench Seats	**234**	—	—
Custom Cloth Bucket Seats	**284**	—	—

NOTE: Power windows standard on Cavalier Convertible & Z24 and Corvette. Power door locks standard on Caprice Classic and Corvette. Tilt steering wheel standard on Camaro, Caprice, Corvette and Lumina Z34. Cruise control standard on Corvette and Lumina Z34.

1991

Year-Model-Body Type	Original List	Current Whlse	Average Retail
BERETTA 4*			
2 Dr Base Cpe	**11725**	7250	8425
2 Dr GTZ Cpe	**15005**	9275	10675
* For Base Cpe with 6 cylinder engine add $375 wholesale and $375 retail.			
BERETTA GT			
2 Dr GT Cpe	**13705**	8900	10275
CAMARO RS 6*			
2 Dr Cpe	**13010**	7775	9025
2 Dr Conv	**18790**	—	—
* For 8 cylinder models add $450 wholesale and $450 retail.			
CAMARO Z28 8			
2 Dr Cpe	**16805**	11650	13450
2 Dr Conv	**22175**	—	—
CAPRICE 8			
4 Dr Sdn	**16515**	9675	11150
4 Dr Wgn	**17872**	12450	14600
CAPRICE CLASSIC 8			
4 Dr Sdn	**18470**	11250	13000
CAVALIER 4*			
2 Dr VL Cpe	**9567**	5700	6625
4 Dr VL Sdn	**9842**	5800	6725
4 Dr VL Wgn	**10302**	6100	7000
2 Dr RS Cpe	**10305**	6350	7400
4 Dr RS Sdn	**10505**	6450	7500
4 Dr RS Wgn	**11015**	6750	7850
* For 6 cylinder models add $375 wholesale and $375 retail.			
CAVALIER 6			
2 Dr RS Conv	**16454**	9900	11400
4 Dr Z24 Sport Cpe	**13290**	9125	10500
CORSICA LT 4*			
4 Dr Ntchbk Sdn	**11430**	6775	7875
5 Dr Htchbk Sdn	**12105**	6975	8125
* For 6 cylinder models add $375 wholesale and $375 retail.			
CORVETTE 8			
Cpe	**32455**	22225	25525
Conv	**38770**	26975	30300
LUMINA 4*			
2 Dr Base Cpe	**13500**	8400	9700
4 Dr Base Sdn	**13700**	8400	9700
* For 6 cylinder models add $475 wholesale and $475 retail.			
LUMINA 6			
2 Dr Euro Cpe	**14795**	9700	11175

Refer To Optional Equipment Schedules

Year-Model-Body Type	Original List	Current Whlse	Average Retail
4 Dr Euro Sdn	**14995**	9700	11175
2 Dr Z34 Cpe (NA w/Auto Trans)	**17275**	—	—
ADD FOR:			
Special Perf Pkg (ZR-1) (Corvette)	**31683**	18500	21400
Leather Seats			
(Camaro)	**850**	420	490
(Caprice Classic)	**645**	335	390
(Corvette)	**1100**	510	600
Removable Roof Panels			
(Camaro Cpe)	**895**	435	525
(Corvette Cpe)	**650**	345	425
Dual Removable Roof Panels (Corvette Cpe)	**950**	475	625

NOTE: Power brakes standard on all models. Power door locks and power windows standard on Caprice Classic, Corvette and Cavalier RS Convertible & Z24. Anti-lock brakes standard on Caprice and Corvette. Air bag standard on Beretta, Camaro, Caprice and Corvette.

1990

Year-Model-Body Type	Original List	Current Whlse	Average Retail
BERETTA 4*			
2 Dr Cpe	**11640**	5800	6725
* For 6 cylinder models add $350 wholesale and $350 retail.			
BERETTA GTZ 4			
2 Dr Cpe (NA w/auto trans)	**13750**	7350	8525
BERETTA GT 6			
2 Dr Cpe	**13040**	7350	8475
CAMARO 6*			
2 Dr RS Cpe	**12315**	5775	6700
* For 8 cylinder models add $400 wholesale and $400 retail.			
CAMARO 8			
2 Dr RS Conv	**18200**	—	—
2 Dr IROC-Z Cpe	**15875**	9225	10625
2 Dr IROC-Z Conv	**21515**	—	—
CAPRICE 8			
4 Dr Sdn	**14525**	6650	7750
CAPRICE CLASSIC 8			
4 Dr Sdn	**15125**	7925	9200
4 Dr Wgn	**15725**	8275	9550
CAPRICE CLASSIC BROUGHAM 8			
4 Dr Sdn	**16325**	8675	10025
4 Dr LS Sdn	**17525**	9450	10875
CAVALIER 4*			
2 Dr VL Cpe	**9369**	3850	4750
4 Dr VL Sdn	**8962**	3950	4900
4 Dr VL Wgn	**9350**	4200	5125
2 Dr Cpe	**9805**	4450	5375
4 Dr Sdn	**10005**	4550	5475
4 Dr Wgn	**10380**	4750	5675
* For 6 cylinder models add $300 wholesale and $300 retail.			
CAVALIER 6			
2 Dr Z24 Cpe	**12690**	6950	8100
CELEBRITY 4*			
4 Dr 2 Seat Wgn	**13200**	6600	7675
4 Dr 3 Seat Wgn	**13450**	6725	7825
* For 6 cylinder models add $400 wholesale and $400 retail.			
CORSICA 4*			
4 Dr LT Ntchbk Sdn	**10815**	5275	6200
4 Dr LT Htchbk Sdn	**11215**	5500	6425
* For 6 cylinder models add $350 wholesale and $350 retail.			
CORSICA 6			
4 Dr LTZ Ntchbk Sdn	**13335**	7050	8175
CORVETTE 8			
Htchbk Cpe	**31979**	18575	21625
Conv	**37264**	22875	26175
LUMINA 4*			
2 Dr Cpe	**12945**	5650	6575
4 Dr Sdn	**13145**	5650	6575
* For 6 cylinder models add $475 wholesale and $475 retail.			
LUMINA EURO 6			
2 Dr Euro Cpe	**14040**	6750	7850
4 Dr Euro Sdn	**14240**	6750	7850
ADD FOR:			
5.7 Liter Engine	**300**	160	190
Estate Equipment (Caprice Classic Wgn)	**307**	160	190
Eurosport Pkg (Celebrity)	**2011**	950	1100
Performance Handling Pkg (Corvette Htchbk)	**460**	240	290
Selective Ride Handling Pkg (Corvette Htchbk)	**1695**	800	1000
Leather Bucket Seats			
(Camaro)	**800**	350	425
(Corvette)	**425**	220	295
Leather Sport Bucket Seats (Corvette Htchbk)	**1050**	400	525
Removable Roof Panels			
(Camaro Cpe)	**866**	400	500
(Corvette Htchbk)	**615**	300	375
Dual Removable Roof Panels (Corvette Htchbk)	**915**	450	550

NOTE: Power windows and power door locks standard on Beretta Convertible and Corvette.

Year-Model-Body Type	Original List	Current Whlse	Average Retail
Power brakes standard on all models.			
1989			
BERETTA 4*			
2 Dr Cpe	**11860**	4425	5350
* For 6 cylinder models add $300 wholesale and $300 retail.			
BERETTA GT 6			
2 Dr Cpe	**13200**	4825	5750
CAMARO 6*			
2 Dr RS Cpe	**12805**	4775	5700
* For 8 cylinder models add $350 wholesale and $350 retail.			
CAMARO 8			
2 Dr RS Conv	**18305**	9100	10475
2 Dr IROC Spt Cpe	**15455**	7925	9200
2 Dr IROC Conv	**20255**	11850	13675
CAPRICE 8			
4 Dr Sdn	**13865**	5125	6050
CAPRICE CLASSIC 8			
4 Dr Sdn	**14445**	6325	7350
4 Dr Wgn	**15025**	6625	7700
CAPRICE CLASSIC BROUGHAM 8			
4 Dr Sdn	**15615**	6975	8125
4 Dr LS Sdn	**16835**	7650	8875
CAVALIER 4*			
2 Dr VL Cpe	**8919**	3125	4025
2 Dr Cpe	**9530**	3650	4550
4 Dr Sdn	**9730**	3750	4650
4 Dr Wgn	**10110**	3950	4850
* For 6 cylinder models add $300 wholesale and $300 retail.			
CAVALIER 6			
2 Dr Z24 Sport Cpe	**12435**	5900	6825
2 Dr Z24 Conv	**17725**	8500	9825
CELEBRITY 4*			
4 Dr Sdn	**12290**	4025	4925
4 Dr 2 Seat Wgn	**12720**	4325	5250
4 Dr 3 Seat Wgn	**12970**	4425	5350
* For 6 cylinder models add $350 wholesale and $350 retail.			
CORSICA 4*			
4 Dr Ntchbk Sdn	**11270**	3925	4825
5 Dr Htchbk Sdn	**11660**	4125	5050
* For 6 cylinder models add $300 wholesale and $300 retail.			
CORSICA 6			
4 Dr LTZ Ntchbk Sdn	**13340**	5425	6350
CORVETTE 8			
Htchbk Cpe	**31545**	15525	18175
Conv	**36785**	19350	22400
ADD FOR:			
Eurosport Pkg (Celebrity)	**230**	100	120
Estate Equipment (Caprice Wgn)	**307**	140	160
Removable Roof Panels (Camaro Cpe)	**866**	350	425
(Corvette)	**615**	250	300
Dual Removable Roof Panels (Corvette)	**915**	350	425
Removable Hardtop (Corvette Conv)	**1995**	750	950
Leather Sport Bucket Seats (Corvette Cpe)	**1050**	375	450
Selective Ride & Handling Suspension (Corvette Cpe)	**1695**	600	775
NOTE: Power brakes standard on all models. Power windows and power door locks standard on Cavalier Z24 Convertible and Corvette.			
1988			
BERETTA 4*			
2 Dr Cpe	**11375**	3775	4675
* For 6 cylinder models add $300 wholesale and $300 retail.			
CAMARO 6*			
Sport Cpe	**12260**	3925	4825
* For 8 cylinder models add $325 wholesale and $325 retail.			
CAMARO 8			
Sport Cpe Conv	**17520**	7800	9050
IROC-Z Sport Cpe	**14755**	6725	7825
IROC-Z Sport Cpe Conv	**19280**	10250	11825
CAPRICE 6*			
4 Dr Sdn	**12805**	3500	4400
CAPRICE CLASSIC 6*			
4 Dr Sdn	**12575**	4775	5700
CAPRICE CLASSIC BROUGHAM 6*			
4 Dr Sdn	**13645**	5300	6225
4 Dr LS Sdn	**14820**	5950	6875
* For 8 cylinder models add $475 wholesale and $475 retail.			
CAPRICE CLASSIC 8			
4 Dr Wgn	**14340**	5475	6400
CAVALIER 4*			
2 Dr VL Cpe	**8310**	2400	3275
2 Dr Cpe	**9435**	2850	3750
4 Dr Sdn	**9510**	2950	3850
4 Dr Wgn	**9805**	3100	4000
2 Dr RS Cpe	**10265**	3325	4225

Refer To Optional Equipment Schedules

CHEVROLET

Year-Model-Body Type	Original List	Current Whlse	Average Retail
4 Dr RS Sdn	**10475**	3425	4325
* For 6 cylinder models add $250 wholesale and $250 retail.			
CAVALIER 6			
2 Dr Z24 Sport Cpe	**11815**	4725	5650
2 Dr Z24 Conv	**17080**	7100	8250
CELEBRITY 4*			
2 Dr Cpe	**11360**	2925	3825
4 Dr Sdn	**11800**	3000	3900
4 Dr 2 Seat Wgn	**12125**	3225	4125
4 Dr 3 Seat Wgn	**12365**	3325	4225
* For 6 cylinder models add $325 wholesale and $325 retail.			
CORSICA 4*			
4 Dr Sdn	**10795**	3275	4175
* For 6 cylinder models add $300 wholesale and $300 retail.			
CORVETTE 8			
Htchbk Cpe	**29480**	13675	16050
Conv	**34820**	17025	19675
MONTE CARLO 6*			
2 Dr LS Cpe	**13105**	4275	5200
* For 8 cylinder models add $375 wholesale and $375 retail.			
MONTE CARLO 8			
2 Dr SS Sport Cpe	**15095**	6550	7625
NOVA 4			
4 Dr Ntchbk Sdn	**10310**	2875	3775
4 Dr Twin Cam Ntchbk Sdn	**12860**	3525	4425
5 Dr Htchbk Sdn	**10565**	2975	3875
SPECTRUM			
4 Dr Ntchbk Sdn	**9587**	2050	2900
4 Dr Turbo Ntchbk Sdn (NA w/auto trans, power steering or radio)	**8900**	2650	3550
2 Dr Htchbk Cpe	**9800**	1950	2800
2 Dr Express Htchbk Cpe (NA w/auto trans, power steering or radio)	**7155**	1175	1900
SPRINT 3			
2 Dr Metro Htchbk Cpe (NA w/power steering)	**6996**	1100	1825
2 Dr Htchbk Cpe (NA w/power steering)	**7881**	1400	2150
2 Dr Turbo Htchbk Cpe (NA w/auto trans or power steering)	**9017**	1875	2725
4 Dr Htchbk Sdn (NA w/power steering)	**8086**	1500	2350
ADD FOR:			
Sport Handling Pkg (Corvette)	**970**	300	400
Perf Handling Pkg (Corvette)	**1295**	375	475
Dual Removable Roof Panels (Corvette)	**915**	300	375
Removable Roof Panels			
(Camaro Cpe)	**866**	275	350
(Corvette)	**615**	200	250
(Monte Carlo)	**895**	275	350
5.0 Liter V8 TPI Eng (Camaro IROC-Z)	**745**	250	300
5.7 Liter V8 TPI Eng (Camaro IROC-Z Cpe)	**1045**	375	450

NOTE: Power brakes standard on all models. Power windows and power door locks standard on Cavalier Z24 Convertible and Corvette.

1987

Year-Model-Body Type	Original List	Current Whlse	Average Retail
CAMARO 6*			
Sport Cpe	**11260**	2825	3725
Convertible	**15689**	—	—
* For 8 cylinder models add $300 wholesale and $300 retail.			
CAMARO 8			
Z28 Sport Cpe	**14084**	4825	5750
Z28 Convertible	**18483**	—	—
CAPRICE 6*			
4 Dr Sdn	**11770**	2375	3250
CAPRICE CLASSIC 6*			
2 Dr Sport Cpe	**12167**	3275	4175
4 Dr LS Sdn	**12335**	3425	4325
CAPRICE CLASSIC BROUGHAM 6*			
4 Dr Sdn	**13324**	3850	4750
4 Dr LS Sdn	**14580**	4225	5150
* For 8 cylinder models add $450 wholesale and $450 retail.			
CAPRICE 8			
4 Dr Wgn	**12770**	2900	3800
CAPRICE CLASSIC 8			
4 Dr Wgn	**13361**	4000	4900
CAVALIER 4*			
2 Dr Cpe	**8737**	2200	3050
4 Dr Sdn	**8961**	2275	3150
4 Dr Wgn	**9127**	2400	3275
2 Dr CS Htchbk Cpe	**9368**	2400	3275
4 Dr CS Sdn	**9343**	2400	3275
4 Dr CS Wgn	**9530**	2500	3375
2 Dr RS Conv	**14611**	4875	5800
2 Dr RS Cpe	**9483**	2525	3400
2 Dr RS Htchbk Cpe	**9685**	2600	3475
4 Dr RS Sdn	**9664**	2600	3475
4 Dr RS Wgn	**9842**	2725	3625
* For 6 cylinder models add $200 wholesale and $200 retail.			

Year-Model-Body Type	Original List	Current Whlse	Average Retail
CAVALIER 6			
2 Dr Z24 Sport Cpe	**11078**	3800	4700
2 Dr Z24 Htchbk	**11280**	3900	4800
CELEBRITY 4*			
2 Dr Cpe	**10770**	2100	2950
4 Dr Sdn	**11040**	2175	3025
4 Dr 2 Seat Wgn	**11200**	2375	3250
4 Dr 3 Seat Wgn	**11447**	2475	3350
* For 6 cylinder models add $300 wholesale and $300 retail.			
CHEVETTE 4			
2 Dr CS Htchbk Cpe	**6345**	1075	1800
4 Dr CS Htchbk Sdn	**6845**	1175	1900
CORVETTE 8			
Htchbk Cpe	**27999**	10800	12475
Conv	**33172**	13925	16300
MONTE CARLO 6*			
2 Dr LS Cpe	**12081**	3225	4125
* For 8 cylinder models add $350 wholesale and $350 retail.			
MONTE CARLO 8			
2 Dr SS Sport Cpe	**14238**	5300	6225
2 Dr SS Aero Cpe	**15613**	—	—
NOVA 4			
4 Dr Ntchbk Sdn	**9200**	2200	3050
5 Dr Htchbk Sdn	**9630**	2275	3150
SPECTRUM 4			
4 Dr Ntchbk Sdn	**9200**	1600	2450
2 Dr Htchbk Cpe	**8903**	1500	2350
SPRINT 3			
2 Dr Htchbk Cpe	**7486**	1050	1775
2 Dr ER Htchbk Cpe	**7601**	1100	1825
2 Dr Turbo Htchbk Cpe	**9181**	1425	2175
4 Dr Htchbk Sdn	**7686**	1150	1875
ADD FOR:			
LT Opt Pkg 1 (Camaro Base Sport Cpe)	**1522**	400	500
LT Opt Pkg 2 (Camaro Base Sport Cpe)	**1938**	500	600
LT Opt Pkg 3 (Camaro Base Sport Cpe)	**2387**	625	750
LT Opt Pkg 4 (Camaro Base Sport Cpe)	**2858**	750	900
Nova CL Opt Pkg 1	**2405**	600	750
Nova CL Opt Pkg 2	**2625**	650	800
Nova CL Opt Pkg 3	**3200**	750	900
5.7 Liter TPI V8 Eng (Camaro)	**1045**	300	360
Removable Glass Roof Panels (Camaro, Monte Carlo)	**895**	250	300
(Corvette)	**615**	170	210
Dual Removable Glass Roof Panels (Corvette)	**915**	250	310

NOTE: Power windows standard on Cavalier Convertible and Corvette. Power brakes standard on all models except Chevette.

1986

Year-Model-Body Type	Original List	Current Whlse	Average Retail
CAMARO 4			
Sport Cpe	**10414**	1925	2775
CAMARO 6*			
Berlinetta Cpe	**12963**	3025	3925
* For 8 cylinder models add $300 wholesale and $300 retail.			
CAMARO 8			
Z28 Sport Cpe	**12963**	4125	5050
CAPRICE 6*			
4 Dr Sdn	**11264**	1875	2725
CAPRICE CLASSIC 6*			
2 Dr Sport Cpe	**11665**	2650	3550
4 Dr Sdn	**11829**	2800	3700
4 Dr Brougham Sdn	**12478**	3175	4075
4 Dr Wgn (8 cyl)	**12562**	3275	4175
* For 8 cylinder models add $400 wholesale and $400 retail.			
CAVALIER 4*			
2 Dr Cpe	**8258**	1425	2175
4 Dr Sdn	**8443**	1525	2375
4 Dr Wgn	**8606**	1625	2475
2 Dr CS Htchbk Cpe	**8940**	1625	2475
4 Dr CS Sdn	**8916**	1625	2475
4 Dr CS Wgn	**9097**	1700	2550
2 Dr RS Conv	**13996**	3550	4450
2 Dr RS Cpe	**8988**	1700	2550
2 Dr RS Htchbk Cpe	**9183**	1775	2625
4 Dr RS Sdn	**9163**	1775	2625
4 Dr RS Wgn	**9335**	1875	2725
* For 6 cylinder models add $200 wholesale and $200 retail.			
CAVALIER 6			
2 Dr Z24 Sport Cpe	**10256**	2625	3525
2 Z24 Htchbk Sport Cpe	**10451**	2725	3625
CELEBRITY 4*			
2 Dr Cpe	**10243**	1525	2375
4 Dr Sdn	**10444**	1625	2475
4 Dr 2 Seat Wgn	**10598**	1775	2625
4 Dr 3 Seat Wgn	**10836**	1825	2675
* For 6 cylinder models add $300 wholesale and $300 retail.			
CHEVETTE 4			
CS Htchbk Cpe	**7125**	875	1600
CS Htchbk Sdn	**7309**	925	1650
CS Diesel Htchbk Cpe	**6507**	400	725
CS Diesel Htchbk Sdn	**6712**	500	925
(Diesel models not available w/automatic transmission)			

Refer To Optional Equipment Schedules

Year-Model-Body Type	Original List	Current Whlse	Average Retail
CORVETTE 8			
Htchbk Cpe	**27405**	9325	10750
Conv	**32480**	12200	14100
MONTE CARLO 6*			
2 Dr Sport Cpe	**10344**	2175	3025
2 Dr LS Cpe	**13640**	2250	3100

* For 8 cylinder models add $325 wholesale and $325 retail.

Year-Model-Body Type	Original List	Current Whlse	Average Retail
MONTE CARLO 8			
2 Dr SS Sport Cpe	**13640**	4075	5000
NOVA 4			
4 Dr Ntchbk Sdn	**9176**	1500	2350
4 Dr Htchbk Sdn	**9417**	1600	2450
SPECTRUM 4			
4 Dr Ntchbk Sdn	**8728**	1275	2000
2 Dr Ntchbk Cpe	**8444**	1175	1900
SPRINT 3			
2 Dr Htchbk Cpe	**6891**	850	1550
2 Dr ER Htchbk Cpe	**6996**	875	1600
4 Dr Plus Htchbk Sdn	**7101**	900	1625
(Power steering not available)			

ADD FOR:

	Original List	Current Whlse	Average Retail
Performance Handling Pkg (Corvette)	**470**	80	100
Nova CL Pkg 1	**1780**	300	350
Nova CL Pkg 2	**2190**	375	450
Nova CL Pkg 3	**2590**	420	500
Nova CL Pkg 4	**2700**	450	550
I.R.O.C. Sport Equipment Pkg (Camaro)	**669**	120	150
2.8 Liter MFI V6 Eng (Celebrity)	**610**	110	150
(Cavalier except Z24)	**660**	110	150
5.0 Liter TPI V8 Eng (Camaro)	**745**	140	160
5.0 Liter HO V8 Eng (Camaro)	**745**	140	160
Removable Glass Roof Panels (Camaro, Monte Carlo)	**866**	160	190
(Corvette)	**615**	110	140
Dual Removable Glass Roof Panels (Corvette)	**915**	170	200

NOTE: Power brakes standard on all models except Chevette. Power windows standard on Corvette.

1985

Year-Model-Body Type	Original List	Current Whlse	Average Retail
CAMARO 4*			
Sport Cpe	**9705**	1400	2150

* For models with 6 cylinder engine add $350 wholesale and $350 retail. For models with 5.0 liter T.P.I. V8 engine add $450 wholesale and $450 retail. For models with 5.0 liter H.O. V8 engine add $600 wholesale and $600 retail. For models with 5.0 liter V8 4 bbl. engine add $600 wholesale and $600 retail.

Year-Model-Body Type	Original List	Current Whlse	Average Retail
CAMARO 6*			
Berlinetta Cpe	**12456**	2225	3075

* For models with 5.0 liter T.P.I. V8 engine add $300 wholesale and $300 retail. For models with 5.0 liter H.O. V8 engine add $300 wholesale and $300 retail. For models with 5.0 liter V8 4 bbl. engine add $300 wholesale and $300 retail.

Year-Model-Body Type	Original List	Current Whlse	Average Retail
CAMARO 8			
Z28 Sport Cpe	**12456**	3050	3950
CAPRICE CLASSIC 6*			
2 Dr Sport Cpe	**10917**	1650	2500
4 Dr Sdn	**11071**	1775	2625

* For 8 cylinder models add $350 wholesale and $350 retail.

Year-Model-Body Type	Original List	Current Whlse	Average Retail
CAPRICE CLASSIC WAGON 8			
4 Dr 3 Seat Wgn	**11760**	2200	3050
CAVALIER 4*			
4 Dr Sdn	**8003**	1125	1850
4 Dr Wgn	**8164**	1200	1925
2 Dr Conv	**12997**	2525	3400
2 Dr Cpe Type 10	**8157**	1225	1950
2 Dr Htchbk Cpe Type 10	**8342**	1300	2025
4 Dr CS Sdn	**8323**	1250	1975
4 Dr CS Wgn	**8492**	1300	2025

* For 6 cylinder models add $150 wholesale and $150 retail.

Year-Model-Body Type	Original List	Current Whlse	Average Retail
CELEBRITY 4*			
2 Dr Cpe	**9464**	1075	1800
4 Dr Sdn	**9654**	1175	1900
4 Dr 2 Seat Wgn	**9849**	1325	2050
4 Dr 3 Seat Wgn	**10073**	1350	2100

* For 6 cylinder models add $250 wholesale and $250 retail. For 6 cylinder M.F.I. engines add $250 wholesale and $250 retail.

Year-Model-Body Type	Original List	Current Whlse	Average Retail
CHEVETTE 4			
CS Htchbk Cpe	**6755**	625	1175
CS Htchbk Sdn	**7075**	725	1375
CS Diesel Htchbk Cpe	**7265**	225	475
CS Diesel Htchbk Sdn	**7600**	225	475
CITATION 4*			
2 Dr Htchbk	**8494**	650	1225
4 Dr Htchbk	**8647**	750	1475

* For 6 cylinder models add $175 wholesale and $175 retail. For V6 M.F.I. engine models add $175 wholesale and $175 retail.

Year-Model-Body Type	Original List	Current Whlse	Average Retail
CORVETTE 8			
Htchbk Cpe	**24891**	7575	8800
IMPALA 6*			
4 Dr Sdn	**10541**	925	1650

Year-Model-Body Type	Original List	Current Whlse	Average Retail
MONTE CARLO 6*			
2 Dr Sport Cpe	**10481**	1675	2525
* For 8 cylinder models add $300 wholesale and $300 retail.			
MONTE CARLO SS 8			
2 Dr SS Sport Cpe	**12358**	3250	4150
NOVA 4			
4 Dr Ntchbk	**8410**	1325	2050
SPECTRUM 4			
2 Dr Htchbk Cpe	**7689**	875	1600
4 Dr Ntchbk Sdn	**7969**	925	1650
SPRINT 3			
2 Dr Htchbk Cpe	**5941**	625	1175
ADD FOR:			
X-11 Sport Equipment Pkg (Citation II)	**1016**	130	150
I.R.O.C. Sport Equipment Pkg (Camaro)	**659**	80	100
Removable Glass Roof Panels (Camaro, Monte Carlo)	**850**	110	130

NOTE: Power windows standard on Corvette. Power brakes standard on Camaro, Impala, Caprice Classic, Cavalier, Celebrity, Chevette Diesel, Corvette, Monte Carlo, Sprint and Spectrum.

1984

Year-Model-Body Type	Original List	Current Whlse	Average Retail
CAMARO 4*			
Sport Cpe	**9352**	1325	2050
* For models with 6 cylinder engine add $200 wholesale and $200 retail. For models with 5.0 liter C.F.I. V8 engine add $350 wholesale and $350 retail. For models with 5.0 liter 4 bbl. V8 engine add $350 wholesale and $350 retail.			
CAMARO 6*			
Berlinetta Cpe	**12022**	1775	2625
* For models with 5.0 liter C.F.I. V8 engine add $200 wholesale and $200 retail. For models with 5.0 liter 4 bbl. V8 engine add $200 wholesale and $200 retail.			
CAMARO 8			
Z28 Sport Cpe	**11745**	2450	3325
CAPRICE CLASSIC 6*			
2 Dr Sport Cpe	**10084**	1025	1750
4 Dr Sdn	**10230**	1150	1875
* For 8 cylinder models add $300 wholesale and $300 retail.			
CAPRICE CLASSIC WAGON 8			
4 Dr Wgn	**11040**	1175	1900
CAVALIER 4			
4 Dr Sdn	**7555**	525	975
4 Dr Wgn	**7708**	575	1075
2 Dr Conv	**12428**	1700	2550
2 Dr Cpe Type 10	**7698**	600	1125
2 Dr Htchbk Cpe Type 10	**7875**	675	1275
4 Dr CS Sdn	**7887**	625	1175
4 Dr CS Wgn	**8042**	675	1275
CELEBRITY 4*			
2 Dr Cpe	**8857**	825	1525
4 Dr Sdn	**9036**	900	1625
4 Dr 2 Seat Wgn	**9360**	1000	1725
4 Dr 3 Seat Wgn	**9575**	1025	1750
* For 6 cylinder models add $200 wholesale and $200 retail.			
CHEVETTE 4			
CS Htchbk Cpe	**6711**	200	400
CS Htchbk Sdn	**6858**	300	575
Htchbk Cpe	**6301**	110	300
Htchbk Sdn	**6555**	150	350
CS Diesel Htchbk Cpe	**7221**	95	300
CS Diesel Htchbk Sdn	**7383**	125	325
CITATION 4*			
2 Dr Cpe	**7801**	300	575
2 Dr Htchbk Cpe	**8256**	375	675
4 Dr Htchbk Sdn	**8402**	425	775
* For 6 cylinder models add $150 wholesale and $150 retail.			
CORVETTE 8			
Htchbk Cpe	**23346**	6900	8025
IMPALA 6*			
4 Dr Sdn	**9726**	475	875
MONTE CARLO 6*			
2 Dr Sport Cpe	**9768**	1275	2000
* For 8 cylinder models add $200 wholesale and $200 retail.			
MONTE CARLO SS 8			
2 Dr SS Sport Cpe	**11530**	2650	3550

NOTE: Power brakes standard on all models except Chevette gasoline models. Power windows standard on Corvette.

1983 — ALL BODY STYLES

Year-Model-Body Type	Original List	Current Whlse	Average Retail
CAMARO SPORT CPE	—	925	1650
CAMARO BERLINETTA	—	1175	1900
CAMARO Z28	—	2150	3000
CAPRICE CLASSIC	—	900	1625
CAPRICE WAGON	—	900	1625
CAVALIER	—	375	675
CELEBRITY	—	675	1275
CHEVETTE	—	110	300
CITATION	—	250	500
IMPALA	—	275	550
MALIBU	—	700	1325
MONTE CARLO	—	1050	1775
MONTE CARLO SS	—	2075	2925

Refer To Optional Equipment Schedules

CHRYSLER

Year-Model-Body Type	Original List	Current Whlse	Average Retail
1992			
IMPERIAL 6			
4 Dr Sdn	**28453**	—	—
ADD FOR:			
Electronics Feature Group	**1011**	—	—
Electronic Air Suspension	**650**	—	—
LE BARON 4*			
2 Dr Cpe	**13988**	—	—
2 Dr Conv	**17565**	—	—
4 Dr Sdn	**13998**	—	—
4 Dr Landau Sdn	**15710**	—	—
* For 6 cylinder models add $— wholesale and $— retail.			
LE BARON 6			
2 Dr LX Cpe	**16094**	—	—
2 Dr LX Conv	**20130**	—	—
2 Dr GTC Cpe	**16844**	—	—
2 Dr GTC Conv	**19665**	—	—
4 Dr LX Sdn	**16079**	—	—
ADD FOR:			
4 Cyl Turbo Engine	**694**	—	—
Anti-Lock Brakes	**899**	—	—
Leather Seat Trim (LX Cpe & GTC Cpe)	**1016**	—	—
(GTC Conv)	**1233**	—	—
(Landau Sdn)	**668**	—	—
Cast Aluminum Wheels (Base)	**328**	—	—
(LX)	**532**	—	—
(GTC)	**188**	—	—
NEW YORKER 6			
4 Dr Fifth Ave Sdn	**21874**	—	—
4 Dr Salon Sdn	**18849**	—	—
ADD FOR:			
3.8 Liter 6 Cyl Eng (Fifth Ave)	**262**	—	—
Anti-Lock Brakes	**899**	—	—
Vinyl Landau Roof (Salon)	**325**	—	—
Leather Seat Trim (Salon)	**590**	—	—
Wire Wheels	**240**	—	—
Cast Aluminum Wheels (Fifth Ave)	**278**	—	—
TOWN & COUNTRY 6			
2 Dr FWD Wgn	**24716**	—	—
2 Dr AWD Wgn	**26611**	—	—

NOTE: Power windows standard on Imperial, LeBaron Coupe & Convertible and New Yorker. Power door locks standard on Imperial and New Yorker Fifth Avenue. Power seat standard on Imperial, LeBaron LX Convertible and New Yorker Fifth Avenue. Tilt steering wheel and cruise control standard on Imperial, LeBaron Sedan and New Yorker Fifth Avenue.

Year-Model-Body Type	Original List	Current Whlse	Average Retail
1991			
IMPERIAL 6			
4 Dr Sdn	**26978**	15125	17775
LE BARON 4*			
2 Dr Highline Cpe	**13816**	7325	8500
2 Dr Highline Conv	**16797**	10775	12425
2 Dr Premium LX Cpe (6 cyl)	**15520**	8825	10200
2 Dr Premium LX Conv (6 cyl)	**19226**	12250	14200
2 Dr GTC Cpe (6 cyl)	**15977**	9500	10950
2 Dr GTC Conv (6 cyl)	**18533**	12875	15200
4 Dr Sdn (6 cyl)	**16501**	9850	11350
* For 6 cylinder or 4 cylinder turbo engine models add $— wholesale and $— retail.			
NEW YORKER 6			
4 Dr Fifth Avenue Sdn	**20875**	12650	14975
4 Dr Salon Sdn	**17971**	10650	12300
TC MASERATI 6			
2 Dr Conv (auto)	**37000**	—	—
TOWN & COUNTRY 6			
4 Dr Wgn	**23956**	16400	19050
ADD FOR:			
Anti-lock Brakes (New Yorker)	**899**	475	575
Electronic Features Pkg (Imperial, New Yorker Fifth Avenue)	**1689**	830	970
Mark Cross Pkg (Imperial)	**649**	450	550
(New Yorker Fifth Avenue)	**2089**	980	1150
Leather Premium Seats (Le Baron Cpe)	**1006**	375	455
(Le Baron GTC Conv)	**1223**	415	510
Leather Sport Seats (Le Baron GTC Cpe)	**639**	285	340
Leather Ultrahyde Seats (Le Baron Sdn)	**668**	300	355

NOTE: Power brakes standard on all models. Air bag standard on Imperial, Le Baron, New Yorker & TC by Maserati. Anti-lock brakes standard on Imperial, TC by Maserati and Town & Country. Power windows standard on Imperial, Le Baron,

Year-Model-Body Type	Original List	Current Whlse	Average Retail

New Yorker, TC by Maserati and Town & Country. Power door locks standard on Imperial, Le Baron Permium LX, Le Baron GTC, Le Baron Sedan, New Yorker Fifth Avenue, TC by Maserati and Town & Country. Power seat standard on Imperial, New Yorker Fifth Ave., TC by Maserati and Town & Country. Vinyl roof standard on Imperial, Le Baron Sedan and New Yorker Fifth Ave.

1990

Year-Model-Body Type	Original List	Current Whlse	Average Retail
IMPERIAL 6			
4 Dr Sdn	**25495**	12375	14450
LE BARON 4*			
2 Dr Highline Cpe	**13300**	6350	7400
2 Dr Highline Conv	**15800**	9475	10925
2 Dr Premium Cpe (6 cyl)	**16415**	7700	8900
2 Dr Premium Conv (6 cyl)	**19595**	10775	12450
2 Dr GT Cpe (6 cyl)	**16214**	7875	9150
2 Dr GT Conv (6 cyl)	**18293**	10925	12600
2 Dr GTC Cpe	**17811**	8175	9450
2 Dr GTC Conv	**20052**	11200	12925
4 Dr Sdn (6 cyl)	**15995**	7550	8775

* For 6 cylinder models add $400 wholesale and $400 retail.

Year-Model-Body Type	Original List	Current Whlse	Average Retail
NEW YORKER 6			
4 Dr Fifth Avenue Sdn	**20860**	10500	12125
4 Dr Landau Sdn	**19080**	9150	10550
4 Dr Salon Sdn	**17147**	8075	9325
TC MASERATI 4			
2 Dr Conv (5 spd)	**35000**	—	—
TC MASERATI 6			
2 Dr Conv (auto)	**35000**	—	—
TOWN & COUNTRY 6			
4 Dr Wgn	**23500**	12475	14450
ADD FOR:			
Anti-Lock Brakes (New Yorker)	**926**	400	500
Electronics Feature Pkg (Imperial)	**1572**	560	660
(New Yorker ex. Salon)	**1216**	460	535
2.5 Liter Turbo Eng (Le Baron Highline)	**680**	340	400
Mark Cross Pkg (New Yorker Fifth Avenue)	**2129**	900	1100
(New Yorker Landau)	**2324**	1000	1200

NOTE: Power brakes standard on all models. Anti-lock brakes standard on Imperial. Power seat standard on Imperial, Le Baron GTC Convertible, New Yorker Fifth Avenue and Maserati. Vinyl roof standard on New Yorker Landau. Power windows standard on Le Baron Series except Sedan, New Yorker Landau, New Yorker Fifth Avenue, Maserati and Town & Country. Power door locks standard on Imperial, Le Baron Premium Coupe, Le Baron GT Coupe, Le Baron GTC Coupe, Le Baron Premium Convertible, Le Baron GT Convertible, Le Baron GTC Convertible, New Yorker Fifth Avenue, Maserati and Town & Country.

1989

Year-Model-Body Type	Original List	Current Whlse	Average Retail
FIFTH AVENUE 8			
4 Dr Sdn	**18345**	6700	7800
LE BARON 4			
2 Dr Highline Cpe	**12806**	4700	5650
2 Dr Highline Conv	**15306**	7175	8475
5 Dr Highline Spt Sdn	**12806**	4100	5075
2 Dr Premium Cpe	**14695**	5500	6425
2 Dr Premium Conv	**18195**	7975	9250
5 Dr Premium Spt Sdn	**14031**	4875	5800
LE BARON GT 4			
2 Dr Cpe	**15331**	5900	6825
2 Dr Conv	**17731**	8375	9675
LE BARON GTC 4			
2 Dr Cpe	**17435**	6550	7625
2 Dr Conv	**19666**	9000	10400
LE BARON GTS 4			
5 Dr Sport Sdn	**17095**	6125	7125
NEW YORKER 6			
4 Dr Sdn	**17416**	6775	7875
NEW YORKER LANDAU 6			
4 Dr Sdn	**19509**	7750	9000
TC 4			
2 Dr Conv	**33000**	—	—
ADD FOR:			
Power Leather Seats (Le Baron GTC)	**627**	250	300
Leather Seats (Le Baron Premium Cpe)	**627**	225	300
(Le Baron Premium Conv)	**1080**	230	300
(Le Baron GT Cpe)	**867**	230	300
(Le Baron GT Conv)	**1080**	230	300
(Le Baron Premium Sdn)	**625**	200	275
(Le Baron GTS Sdn)	**566**	200	275
Mark Cross Edit. (New Yorker Base)	**2069**	800	950
(New Yorker Landau)	**2467**	900	1050
Anti-Lock Brakes (New Yorker)	**670**	300	375

Refer To Optional Equipment Schedules

Year-Model-Body Type	Original List	Current Whlse	Average Retail
2.5 Liter Turbo Engine			
(Le Baron Highline Sdn)	**536**	225	275
(Le Baron Premium Sdn)	**678**	225	275
(Le Baron Highline & Premium Conv)	**678**	250	300

NOTE: Power brakes standard on all models. Power windows standard on Le Baron GTC, Le Baron GTS Sport Sedan, New Yorker Series, Town & Country and Fifth Avenue. Power door locks standard on Le Baron Premium, Le Baron GTC, Le Baron Premium Sport Sedan, New Yorker Landau and Town & Country.

1988

Year-Model-Body Type	Original List	Current Whlse	Average Retail
FIFTH AVENUE 8			
4 Dr Sdn	**17243**	5000	5925
LE BARON 4			
2 Dr Highline Cpe	**12306**	3675	4575
2 Dr High Conv	**14806**	5900	6825
2 Dr Premium Cpe	**13995**	4375	5300
2 Dr Premium Conv	**17495**	6575	7650
4 Dr Sdn	**12061**	3200	4100
LE BARON GTS 4			
5 Dr High Sport Sdn	**12109**	3150	4050
5 Dr Premium Sport Sdn	**13507**	3675	4575
NEW YORKER 6			
4 Dr Sdn	**17416**	5800	6725
NEW YORKER LANDAU 6			
4 Dr Sdn	**19509**	6675	7775
NEW YORKER TURBO 4			
4 Dr Sdn	**17373**	5050	5975
TOWN & COUNTRY 4			
4 Dr Wgn	**13664**	3975	4875
ADD FOR:			
Electronic Feature Pkg			
(Le Baron GTS Premium)	**272**	100	120
(Le Baron Premium Cpe & Conv)	**477**	175	200
Mark Cross Pkg (Le Baron Town & Country)	**1019**	350	400
(New Yorker Std)	**2374**	700	850
(New Yorker Landau)	**2066**	650	800
Turbo Coupe Pkg (Le Baron Highline Cpe)	**4000**	1000	1200
(Le Baron Highline Conv)	**3848**	1000	1200
2.2 Liter Turbo Engine			
(Le Baron, Le Baron GTS Premium)	**678**	200	250
(Le Baron GTS Highline)	**399**	200	250
Leather Seating Pkg			
(Le Baron Highline Cpe, Le Baron Premium Cpe)	**627**	170	225
(Le Baron Premium Conv)	**1080**	275	350
(Le Baron GTS Premium)	**625**	170	225

NOTE: Power brakes standard on all models. Power door locks standard on Le Baron GTS Premium, New Yorker Landau and New Yorker Turbo. Power seat standard on New Yorker Landau. Power windows standard on Fifth Avenue, Le Baron GTC Convertible, Le Baron Highline Convertible, Le Baron Premium, New Yorker Turbo and New Yorker Series.

1987

Year-Model-Body Type	Original List	Current Whlse	Average Retail
FIFTH AVENUE 8			
4 Dr Sdn	**15966**	3950	4850
LE BARON COUPE 4			
2 Dr Highline Cpe	**12606**	3150	4050
2 Dr Premium Cpe	**13742**	3650	4550
LE BARON 4			
4 Dr Sdn	**11489**	2350	3225
2 Dr Conv	**14899**	5175	6100
LE BARON GTS 4			
5 Dr High Sport Sdn	**11077**	2375	3250
5 Dr Premium Sport Sdn	**12692**	2750	3650
NEW YORKER 4			
4 Dr Sdn	**15321**	3625	4525
TOWN & COUNTRY 4			
4 Dr Wgn	**13037**	3050	3950
ADD FOR:			
Electronic Feature Pkg			
(Le Baron GTS Premium)	**382**	125	150
(Le Baron Premium Cpe)	**687**	150	200
Leather Seating Pkg			
(Le Baron GTS Premium)	**625**	175	200
(Le Baron Premium Cpe)	**807**	175	200
Mark Cross Pkg			
(Le Baron Sdn, Town & Country)	**1018**	200	250
Turbo Coupe Pkg			
(Le Baron Cpe)	**1434**	275	350
Turbo Engine Pkg			

Year-Model-Body Type	Original List	Current Whlse	Average Retail
(Le Baron GTS)	**678**	125	175
2.2 Liter Turbo Engine (Le Baron, New Yorker)	**678**	100	150

NOTE: Power windows standard on Fifth Avenue and New Yorker. Power brakes standard on all models.

1986

Year-Model-Body Type	Original List	Current Whlse	Average Retail
FIFTH AVENUE 8			
4 Dr Sdn	**14910**	3150	4050
LASER 4			
2 Dr Htchbk	**10625**	1650	2500
LASER XE 4			
2 Dr Htchbk	**12762**	2175	3025
LASER XT TURBO 4			
2 Dr Htchbk	**13115**	2375	3250
LE BARON GTS 4			
5 Dr High Sport Sdn	**11015**	1925	2775
5 Dr Premium Sport Sdn	**11941**	2275	3150
LE BARON 4			
2 Dr Cpe	**10734**	1600	2450
4 Dr Sdn	**10884**	1675	2525
2 Dr Conv	**13452**	2875	3775
LE BARON MARK CROSS CONV. 4			
2 Dr Conv	**16595**	3400	4300
2 Dr Town & Country Convertible	**17595**	4050	4950
NEW YORKER 4			
4 Dr Sdn	**14309**	2500	3375
TOWN & COUNTRY 4			
4 Dr Wgn	**12127**	2300	3175
ADD FOR:			
Electronic Feature Pkg (Le Baron GTS)	**382**	70	80
Mark Cross Pkg (Le Baron, Town & Country)	**1009**	150	200
2.2 Liter Turbo Eng			
(Base Laser)	**990**	175	200
(Laser XE)	**730**	175	200
(Le Baron, New Yorker)	**628**	100	150
2.5 Liter EFI Engine (Base Laser, Le Baron except Mark Cross Conv. and Town & Country Wgn)	**279**	75	100
T-Bar Roof (Laser)	**1316**	200	250

NOTE: Vinyl top and power windows standard on Fifth Avenue and New Yorker. Power brakes standard on all models.

1985

Year-Model-Body Type	Original List	Current Whlse	Average Retail
EXECUTIVE LIMOUSINE 4			
4 Dr Limousine	**26318**	—	—
FIFTH AVENUE 8			
4 Dr Sdn	**14428**	2325	3200
LASER 4			
2 Dr Htchbk	**10030**	975	1700
LASER XE 4			
2 Dr Htchbk	**11952**	1325	2050
LE BARON 4			
2 Dr Cpe	**10331**	1300	2025
4 Dr Sdn	**10176**	1375	2125
2 Dr Conv	**12809**	2400	3275
LE BARON GTS 4			
5 Dr High Sport Sdn	**10465**	1250	1975
5 Dr Premium Sport Sdn	**11379**	1625	2475
LE BARON MARK CROSS CONV. 4			
2 Dr Conv	**16951**	2825	3725
2 Dr Town & Country Convertible	**17951**	3350	4250
NEW YORKER 4			
4 Dr Sdn	**13678**	1975	2825
TOWN & COUNTRY 4			
4 Dr Wgn	**11252**	1950	2800
ADD FOR:			
Mark Cross Pkg			
(Le Baron Cpe)	**833**	110	120
(Le Baron Sdn, Town & Country Wgn)	**1009**	130	150
Turbo Sport Pkg			
(Le Baron GTS High)	**1098**	140	160
(Le Baron GTS Premium)	**1050**	140	160
2.2 Liter Turbo Eng			
(Base Laser)	**964**	120	140
(Laser XE)	**872**	120	140
(Le Baron, New Yorker)	**610**	100	120

NOTE: Power brakes standard on Executive Limousine, Fifth Avenue, Laser, Le Baron, Le Baron GTS and New Yorker. Vinyl top standard on Executive Limousine, Fifth Avenue, Le Baron Sedan, Le Baron Coupe and New Yorker. Power windows standard on Executive Limousine, Fifth Avenue and New Yorker. Power locks and power seat standard on Executive Limousine.

Refer To Optional Equipment Schedules

Year-Model-Body Type	Original List	Current Whlse	Average Retail
1984			
E CLASS 4			
4 Dr Sdn	**10294**	725	1375
EXECUTIVE 4			
4 Dr Sdn	**18967**	—	—
4 Dr Limousine	**21967**	—	—
LASER 4			
2 Dr Htchbk	**9814**	625	1175
LASER XE 4			
2 Dr Htchbk	**11712**	925	1650
LE BARON 4			
2 Dr Cpe	**9951**	875	1600
4 Dr Sdn	**9796**	925	1650
2 Dr Convertible	**12324**	1775	2625
LE BARON MARK CROSS CONV. 4			
2 Dr Conv	**16224**	1950	2800
2 Dr Town & Country Convertible	**17724**	2375	3250
NEW YORKER 4			
4 Dr Sdn	**13179**	1500	2350
NEW YORKER FIFTH AVE. 8			
4 Dr Sdn	**13978**	1800	2650
TOWN & COUNTRY 4			
4 Dr Wgn	**10856**	1325	2050

NOTE: Vinyl roof standard on New Yorker, Executive, Le Baron Coupe & Sedan, and New Yorker Fifth Avenue. Power windows standard on New Yorker, Executive and New Yorker Fifth Avenue.

1983 — ALL BODY STYLES			
CORDOBA	—	700	1325
E CLASS	—	550	1025
IMPERIAL	—	1625	2475
LE BARON	—	750	1475
LE BARON CONV.	—	1550	2400
LE BARON MARK CROSS CONV.	—	1725	2575
NEW YORKER	—	1275	2000
NEW YORKER FIFTH AVE	—	1500	2350
TOWN & COUNTRY	—	1050	1775

DODGE

Year-Model-Body Type	Original List	Current Whlse	Average Retail
1992			
DAYTONA 4*			
2 Dr Htchbk	**11857**	—	—
2 Dr ES Htchbk	**12898**	—	—
2 Dr IROC R/T Htchbk	**19222**	—	—

* For 6 cylinder models add $— wholesale and $— retail.

Year-Model-Body Type	Original List	Current Whlse	Average Retail
DAYTONA 6			
2 Dr IROC Htchbk (NA w/auto trans)	**13636**	—	—
ADD FOR:			
V6 Perf Pkg (ES)	**319**	—	—
Anti-Lock Brakes (ES, IROC)	**899**	—	—
Leather Enthusiast Seats	**1412**	—	—
Cloth Enthusiast Seats (ES, IROC, IROC R/T)	**761**	—	—
Cast Aluminum Wheels (Base)	**328**	—	—
DYNASTY 4*			
4 Dr Sdn	**15108**	—	—

* For 6 cylinder models add $— wholesale and $— retail.

Year-Model-Body Type	Original List	Current Whlse	Average Retail
DYNASTY LE 6			
4 Dr Sdn	**16598**	—	—
ADD FOR:			
Anti-Lock Brakes	**899**	—	—
Vinyl Landau Roof	**325**	—	—
Leather Seat Trim	**590**	—	—
Wire Wheel Covers	**240**	—	—
Cast Aluminum Wheels	**278**	—	—
MONACO 6			
4 Dr LE Sdn	**15241**	—	—
4 Dr ES Sdn	**17203**	—	—
ADD FOR:			
Anti-Lock Brakes	**799**	—	—
Leather Seat Trim	**891**	—	—
Cast Aluminum Wheels	**523**	—	—
SHADOW 4			
2 Dr America Htchbk	**9733**	—	—
4 Dr America Sdn Htchbk	**10133**	—	—
2 Dr Highline Htchbk	**10793**	—	—
4 Dr Highline Sdn Htchbk	**11193**	—	—
2 Dr ES Htchbk	**10762**	—	—
4 Dr ES Sdn Htchbk	**11162**	—	—
2 Dr Highline Conv	**14836**	—	—
2 Dr ES Conv	**15042**	—	—
ADD FOR:			
Cast Aluminum Wheels	**328**	—	—
2.5 Liter 4 Cyl Eng (America, Highline Htchbk & Sdn Htchbk)	**286**	—	—
2.5 Liter 4 Cyl Turbo Eng (Highline Conv & ES)	**760**	—	—
3.0 Liter 6 Cyl Eng			
(ES)	**694**	—	—
(Conv)	**905**	—	—

Year-Model-Body Type	Original List	Current Whlse	Average Retail
SPIRIT 4*			
4 Dr Sdn	**12858**	—	—
4 Dr LE Sdn	**14361**	—	—
4 Dr ES Sdn	**15829**	—	—
4 Dr R/T Sdn (NA w/auto trans)	**18674**	—	—

* For 6 cylinder models add $— wholesale and $— retail.

Year-Model-Body Type	Original List	Current Whlse	Average Retail
ADD FOR:			
2.5 Liter 4 Cyl Turbo Eng (LE)	**725**	—	—
Anti-Lock Brakes	**899**	—	—
Cast Aluminum Wheels	**328**	—	—
STEALTH 6			
2 Dr Base Cpe	**18167**	—	—
2 Dr ES Cpe	**20594**	—	—
2 Dr R/T Cpe	**25747**	—	—
2 Dr R/T Turbo Cpe (NA w/auto trans)	**31185**	—	—
ADD FOR:			
Anti-Lock Brakes	**1395**	—	—
Leather Seat Trim	**843**	—	—
VIPER 10			
2 Dr Sport Cpe (NA w/auto trans)	**50000**	—	—

NOTE: Power windows standard on Shadow Convertible, Stealth R/T & R/T Turbo. Power door locks and power seat standard on Stealth R/T & R/T Turbo. Tilt steering wheel standard on Spirit LE & ES, Stealth and Viper. Cruise control standard on Spirit LE, ES & R/T, Stealth R/T & R/T Turbo.

1991

Year-Model-Body Type	Original List	Current Whlse	Average Retail
DAYTONA 4*			
2 Dr Htchbk	**12080**	6550	7625
2 Dr ES Htchbk	**13325**	7150	8300
2 Dr Shelby Turbo Htchbk	**14596**	—	—

* For 6 cylinder models add $400 wholesale and $400 retail.

Year-Model-Body Type	Original List	Current Whlse	Average Retail
DAYTONA 6			
2 Dr IROC Htchbk	**14626**	—	—
DYNASTY 4*			
4 Dr Sdn	**14518**	8000	9300

* For 6 cylinder models add $400 wholesale and $400 retail.

Year-Model-Body Type	Original List	Current Whlse	Average Retail
DYNASTY LE 6			
4 Dr Sdn	**15958**	8500	9825
MONACO 6			
4 Dr LE Sdn	**14624**	6575	7650
4 Dr ES Sdn	**16492**	7500	8700
SHADOW 4			
2 Dr America Htchbk	**9321**	5375	6300
4 Dr America Htchbk	**9621**	5475	6400
2 Dr Highline Htchbk	**10286**	6175	7200
4 Dr Highline Htchbk	**10586**	6275	7300
2 Dr ES Htchbk	**11762**	7050	8175
4 Dr ES Htchbk	**12062**	7150	8300
2 Dr Highline Conv	**14333**	9300	10725
2 Dr ES Conv	**15406**	10175	11750
SPIRIT 4*			
4 Dr Sdn	**11523**	6800	7925
4 Dr LE Sdn	**13797**	7400	8600
4 Dr ES Sdn	**15128**	8225	9500
4 Dr R/T Sdn (NA w/auto trans)	**17871**	—	—

* For 6 cylinder models add $400 wholesale and $400 retail.

Year-Model-Body Type	Original List	Current Whlse	Average Retail
STEALTH 6			
2 Dr Base Cpe	**17952**	14250	16725
2 Dr ES Cpe	**19715**	15175	17825
2 Dr R/T Cpe	**24968**	18325	21250
2 Dr R/T Turbo Cpe (NA w/auto trans)	**29267**	20950	24050
ADD FOR:			
Anti-lock Brakes (Dynasty, Spirit)	**899**	500	600
(Monaco)	**799**	450	525
V6 Perf. Pkg (Daytona ES)	**1013**	575	700
Leather Seats (Stealth)	**843**	400	500
50/50 Leather Seats (Dynasty LE)	**590**	300	375
Power 8-Way Leather Seat (Daytona ex. Base)	**1402**	730	845
Opt Pkg 2 (Stealth Base)	**836**	475	550
(Stealth ES)	**766**	425	550
(Stealth RT)	**424**	200	275
Opt Pkg 3 (Stealth Base)	**969**	500	620
(Stealth ES)	**1186**	650	775
Opt Pkg 4 (Stealth Base)	**1445**	750	900
(Stealth ES)	**2436**	1220	1525
Opt Pkg 5 (Stealth Base)	**2219**	1140	1325
(Stealth ES)	**2860**	1485	1720
Opt Pkg 6 (Stealth Base)	**3119**	1685	1945
(Stealth ES)	**3221**	1700	2000

NOTE: Power brakes standard on all models. Air bag standard on Base Daytona, Dynasty, Shadow, Spirit and Stealth. Anti-lock brakes and power door locks standard on Stealth R/T. Power windows standard on Stealth R/T and Shadow Highline Convertible and ES.

Refer To Optional Equipment Schedules

Year-Model-Body Type	Original List	Current Whlse	Average Retail
1990			
DAYTONA 4*			
2 Dr Htchbk	**11335**	5075	6000
2 Dr ES Htchbk	**12535**	5650	6575
2 Dr ES Turbo Htchbk	**13431**	6500	7575
2 Dr Shelby Turbo Htchbk (NA w/auto trans)	**15403**	7050	8175
* For 6 cylinder models add $400 wholesale and $400 retail.			
DYNASTY 4*			
4 Dr Sdn	**13800**	5875	6800
* For 6 cylinder models add $375 wholesale and $375 retail.			
DYNASTY LE 6			
4 Dr Sdn	**15200**	6850	7975
OMNI 4			
5 Dr Htchbk	**7998**	3025	3925
MONACO 6			
4 Dr LE Sdn	**15855**	5925	6850
4 Dr ES Sdn	**17595**	6725	7825
SHADOW 4			
3 Dr Lftbk Cpe	**10096**	4800	5725
5 Dr Lftbk Sdn	**10296**	4875	5800
SPIRIT 4*			
4 Dr Sdn	**11031**	5275	6200
4 Dr LE Sdn	**13246**	5850	6775
4 Dr ES Sdn	**14546**	6525	7600
* For 6 cylinder models add $400 wholesale and $400 retail.			
ADD FOR:			
Anti-Lock Brakes (Dynasty)	**926**	450	520
Competition Pkg (Shadow Cpe)	**2558**	1100	1310
C/S Competition Pkg (Base Daytona)	**2702**	1300	1525
C/S Performance Discount Pkg (Base Daytona)	**1502**	750	875
Power 8-way Leather Seat (Daytona ex. Base)	**974**	380	450
3.0 Liter V6 Engine (Base Daytona)	**680**	350	410

NOTE: Power brakes standard on all models.

Year-Model-Body Type	Original List	Current Whlse	Average Retail
1989			
ARIES AMERICA 4			
2 Dr Sdn	**9298**	3000	3900
4 Dr Sdn	**9298**	3075	3975
DAYTONA 4			
2 Dr Htchbk	**10606**	4000	4900
2 Dr ES Htchbk	**11706**	4500	5425
2 Dr ES Turbo Htchbk	**12531**	5125	6050
2 Dr Shelby Turbo Htchbk (NA w/auto trans)	**13295**	5600	6525
DIPLOMAT 8			
4 Dr Salon Sdn	**12850**	4050	4950
4 Dr SE Sdn	**14795**	4825	5750
DYNASTY 4*			
4 Dr Sdn	**13070**	4525	5450
* For 6 cylinder models add $400 wholesale and $400 retail.			
DYNASTY LE 6			
4 Dr Sdn	**14370**	5100	6025
LANCER 4			
5 Dr Sport Sdn	**12506**	4400	5325
5 Dr ES Turbo Sport Sdn	**14231**	4900	5825
5 Dr Shelby Spt Sdn	**17220**	6125	7125
OMNI AMERICA 4			
5 Dr Htchbk	**8298**	2325	3200
SHADOW 4			
3 Dr Lftbk Cpe	**9706**	3625	4525
5 Dr Lftbk Sdn	**9906**	3725	4625
SPIRIT 4			
4 Dr Sdn	**10531**	4325	5250
4 Dr LE Sdn	**12506**	4800	5725
4 Dr ES Turbo Sdn	**13886**	5475	6400
ADD FOR:			
Competition Pkg (Shadow Cpe)	**1515**	650	750
ES Pkg (Shadow Cpe)	**1977**	800	925
(Shadow Sdn)	**2039**	800	925
C/S Competition Pkg (Base Daytona)	**2879**	1150	1345
C/S Performance Pkg (Base Daytona)	**1443**	600	700
T-Bar Roof Pkg (Base Daytona, Daytona ES)	**1513**	550	700
(Daytona ES Turbo, Daytona Shelby)	**1298**	550	700
Turbo Engine Pkg (Shadow)	**923**	400	475
(Base Lancer)	**536**	250	280

NOTE: Power windows standard on Lancer Shelby. Power locks standard on Lancer ES and Lancer Shelby.

Year-Model-Body Type	Original List	Current Whlse	Average Retail
1988			
600 4			
4 Dr Sdn	**11434**	2875	3775
4 Dr SE Sdn	**12403**	3225	4125
ARIES AMERICA 4			
2 Dr Sdn	**9064**	2425	3300
4 Dr Sdn	**9064**	2525	3400
4 Dr Wgn	**9458**	2900	3800
DAYTONA 4			
2 Dr Base Htchbk	**10299**	2825	3725
2 Dr Pacifica Htchbk	**15054**	4175	5100
2 Dr Shelby Z Htchbk	**14650**	4050	4950
DIPLOMAT 8			
4 Dr Base	**12127**	3350	4250
4 Dr Salon	**12237**	2950	3850
4 Dr SE	**14221**	3650	4550
DYNASTY 4*			
4 Dr Sdn	**12441**	3850	4750
4 Dr Premier Sdn	**13001**	4125	5050
* For 6 cylinder models add $375 wholesale and $375 retail.			
LANCER 4			
5 Dr Sport Sdn	**11793**	3025	3925
5 Dr ES Sport Sdn	**13251**	3475	4375
OMNI AMERICA 4			
5 Dr Htchbk	**7868**	1775	2625
SHADOW 4			
2 Dr Lftbk Cpe	**9225**	2700	3600
4 Dr Lftbk Sdn	**9475**	2800	3700
ADD FOR:			
Electronic Features Pkg (Lancer ES)	**571**	175	200
Lancer Shelby Pkg (Lancer ES)	**3830**	1200	1475
T-Bar Roof Pkg			
(Daytona)	**1468**	425	500
(Daytona Shelby Z)	**1258**	425	500
(Daytona Pacifica)	**955**	425	500
Turbo Engine Pkg (Shadow)	**780**	300	340
Turbo I Engine Pkg (Base Daytona)	**837**	320	370
Turbo Sport Discount Pkg (Lancer ES)	**1465**	500	600
2.2 Liter 4 Cyl Turbo Eng (Base 600, Base Lancer)	**399**	150	180
(600 SE, Lancer ES)	**678**	200	275
(Dynasty)	**660**	200	275

NOTE: Power brakes standard on all models. Power door locks standard on Lancer ES.

Year-Model-Body Type	Original List	Current Whlse	Average Retail
1987			
600 4			
4 Dr Sdn	**10792**	2150	3000
4 Dr SE Sdn	**11454**	2275	3150
* For 158 CID 4 cylinder engine add $— wholesale and $— retail.			
ARIES 4*			
2 Dr Sdn	**9430**	1625	2475
4 Dr Sdn	**9430**	1700	2550
2 Dr LE Sdn	**9915**	1950	2800
4 Dr LE Sdn	**9915**	2050	2900
4 Dr LE Wgn	**10359**	2350	3225
* For 158 CID 4 cylinder engine add $— wholesale and $— retail.			
CHARGER 4			
3 Dr Base Htchbk	**9199**	1775	2500
3 Dr Shelby Htchbk (NA w/auto trans)	**10541**	2400	3275
DAYTONA 4			
2 Dr Base Htchbk	**11110**	2225	3075
2 Dr Pacifica Htchbk	**14441**	3125	4025
2 Dr Shelby Z Htchbk (NA w/auto trans)	**12749**	3100	4000
DIPLOMAT 8			
4 Dr Salon	**11435**	2075	2925
2 Dr SE	**12515**	2600	3475
LANCER 4*			
5 Dr Sport Sdn	**11163**	2275	3150
5 Dr ES Sport Sdn	**12117**	2650	3550
* For 158 CID 4 cylinder models add $— wholesale and $— retail.			
OMNI 4			
5 Dr America Htchbk	**7799**	1325	2050
SHADOW 4			
2 Dr Lftbk Cpe	**8722**	2075	2925
4 Dr Lftbk Sdn	**8922**	2175	3025
ADD FOR:			
Electronic Features Pkg (Lancer ES)	**681**	150	200
Leather Seating Pkg			
(Daytona Shelby Z)	**939**	225	275
(Daytona Pacifica)	**488**	150	175
(Lancer ES)	**625**	175	200
Shadow ES Pkg	**1720**	150	185
T-Bar Roof Pkg			
(Daytona)	**1468**	375	435
(Daytona Shelby Z)	**1560**	375	435
(Daytona Pacifica)	**1165**	375	435
Turbo Engine Pkg (Shadow Sdn)	**806**	200	250
Turbo I Engine Pkg (Base Daytona)	**837**	225	275
2.2 Liter Turbo Eng (600, Lancer)	**678**	200	230

Refer To Optional Equipment Schedules

DODGE

Year-Model-Body Type	Original List	Current Whlse	Average Retail
NOTE: Sunroof standard on Shelby Charger. Power brakes standard on all models.			
1986			
600 4			
2 Dr Cpe	**10034**	1225	1950
2 Dr Convertible	**12682**	2425	3300
4 Dr Sdn	**10127**	1300	2025
600 ES TURBO CONVERTIBLE 4			
2 Dr Convertible (power steering NA)	**15613**	2550	3425
600 SE 4			
4 Dr Sdn	**10785**	1575	2425
ARIES 4*			
2 Dr	**8675**	1175	1900
4 Dr	**8792**	1275	2000
ARIES LE 4*			
2 Dr Sdn	**9578**	1475	2300
4 Dr Sdn	**9698**	1575	2425
4 Dr Wgn	**10197**	1850	2700
ARIES SE 4*			
2 Dr	**9130**	1325	2050
4 Dr	**9250**	1400	2150
4 Dr Wgn	**9677**	1700	2550
* For 158 CID 4 cylinder models add $50 wholesale and $50 retail.			
CHARGER 4*			
2 Dr Htchbk	**8297**	1300	2025
CHARGER 2.2 4*			
2 Dr Htchbk	**9129**	1700	2550
SHELBY CHARGER 4			
2 Dr Htchbk	**10528**	1900	2750
DAYTONA 4			
2 Dr Htchbk	**10274**	1650	2500
DAYTONA TURBO Z 4			
2 Dr Htchbk	**12562**	2475	3350
DIPLOMAT SALON 8			
4 Dr	**10898**	1475	2300
DIPLOMAT SE 8			
4 Dr	**11978**	1950	2800
LANCER 4			
5 Dr Sport Sdn	**10687**	1750	2600
LANCER 'ES' 4			
5 Dr Sport Sdn	**11583**	2125	2975
OMNI 4*			
4 Dr Htchbk	**7719**	900	1625
OMNI GLH 4			
4 Dr Htchbk (automatic transmission NA)	**8581**	1550	2400
OMNI SE 4*			
4 Dr Htchbk	**7955**	1225	1950
* For 135 CID 4 cylinder engine add $50 wholesale and $50 retail.			
ADD FOR:			
Electronics Features Pkg (Lancer)	**637**	120	150
(Daytona Turbo)	**583**	100	125
(Base Daytona)	**272**	50	75
T-Bar Roof Pkg (Dodge, Daytona, Turbo Z)	**1351**	250	300
Turbo Sport Pkg (Lancer ES)	**1415**	250	300
2.2 Liter Turbo Eng (600, Lancer)	**628**	120	140
(Base Daytona, Omni GLH)	**898**	170	200
NOTE: Power brakes standard on all models.			
1985			
600 4*			
2 Dr Cpe	**9931**	1025	1750
2 Dr Convertible	**12028**	2125	2975
600 ES TURBO CONVERTIBLE 4			
2 Dr Convertible	**15171**	2450	3325
600 SE 4*			
4 Dr Sdn	**9838**	1125	1850
ARIES 4			
2 Dr	**8432**	875	1600
4 Dr	**8547**	950	1675
ARIES LE 4			
2 Dr	**9054**	1150	1875
4 Dr	**9187**	1250	1975
4 Dr Wgn	**9554**	1450	2225
ARIES SE 4			
2 Dr	**8716**	1000	1725
4 Dr	**8834**	1100	1825
4 Dr Wgn	**9334**	1325	2050
CHARGER 4*			
2 Dr Htchbk	**7885**	1100	1700
CHARGER 2.2 4*			
2 Dr Htchbk	**8816**	1375	2125
SHELBY CHARGER 4			
2 Dr Htchbk	**10077**	1475	2300
DAYTONA 4			
2 Dr Htchbk	**9681**	975	1700
DAYTONA TURBO 4			
2 Dr Htchbk	**11462**	1325	2050
DAYTONA TURBO Z 4			
2 Dr Htchbk	**12796**	1750	2600
DIPLOMAT SALON 8			
4 Dr	**10470**	1050	1775
DIPLOMAT SE 8			
4 Dr	**11513**	1400	2150

Year-Model-Body Type	Original List	Current Whlse	Average Retail
LANCER 4			
5 Dr Sport Sdn	**10148**	1250	1975
LANCER 'ES' 4			
5 Dr Sport Sdn	**11093**	1625	2475
OMNI 4*			
4 Dr Htchbk	**7413**	725	1375
OMNI GLH 4			
4 Dr Htchbk	**9034**	1250	1975
OMNI SE 4			
4 Dr Htchbk	**7756**	975	1700
ADD FOR:			
Turbo Sport Pkg			
(Base Lancer)	**1098**	140	160
(Lancer ES)	**1397**	175	200
Turbo Engine			
(Lancer, 600)	**610**	80	90
(Base Daytona)	**964**	125	150
(Omni GLH)	**872**	125	150

NOTE: Power brakes standard on all models. Vinyl top standard on 600 Coupe.

1984

Year-Model-Body Type	Original List	Current Whlse	Average Retail
600			
2 Dr Cpe	**9544**	600	1125
2 Dr Convertible	**11543**	1425	2175
4 Dr Sdn	**9632**	700	1325
4 Dr 'ES' Sdn	**10254**	900	1625
ARIES			
2 Dr	**8337**	400	725
4 Dr	**8449**	475	875
ARIES CUSTOM			
4 Dr Wgn	**9123**	650	1225
ARIES SPECIAL EDITION			
2 Dr	**8840**	575	1075
4 Dr	**8976**	650	1225
4 Dr Wgn	**9363**	850	1550
CHARGER 4*			
2 Dr Htchbk	**7900**	525	975
CHARGER 2.2			
2 Dr Htchbk	**8581**	775	1500
DAYTONA			
2 Dr Htchbk	**9474**	625	1175
DAYTONA TURBO			
2 Dr Htchbk	**10954**	900	1625
DIPLOMAT SALON			
4 Dr	**9961**	800	1500
DIPLOMAT SE			
4 Dr	**10957**	975	1700
OMNI			
4 Dr Htchbk	**7236**	250	500
OMNI SE			
4 Dr Htchbk	**7441**	475	875
SHELBY CHARGER			
Shelby Charger	**9834**	950	1675

NOTE: Power brakes standard on all models.

1983 — ALL BODY STYLES

Year-Model-Body Type	Original List	Current Whlse	Average Retail
400	—	750	1475
400 CONV	—	1425	2175
600	—	575	1075
ARIES	—	250	500
ARIES CUSTOM	—	425	775
ARIES SPECIAL EDITION	—	400	725
CHARGER	—	250	500
CHARGER 2.2	—	450	825
DIPLOMAT MEDALLION	—	725	1375
DIPLOMAT SALON	—	600	1125
MIRADA	—	750	1475
OMNI	—	110	300
OMNI CUSTOM	—	175	375

EAGLE

1992

Year-Model-Body Type	Original List	Current Whlse	Average Retail
PREMIER 6			
4 Dr LX Sdn	**15716**	—	—
4 Dr ES Sdn	**18057**	—	—
4 Dr ES Limited Sdn	**20212**	—	—
ADD FOR:			
Anti-Lock Brakes (LX, ES)	**799**	—	—
Leather Seat Trim (ES)	**873**	—	—
Cast Aluminum Wheels			
(LX)	**523**	—	—
(ES)	**301**	—	—
SUMMIT 4			
3 Dr Htchbk	**9326**	—	—
4 Dr Sdn	**10710**	—	—
3 Dr ES Htchbk	**9739**	—	—
4 Dr ES Sdn	**11871**	—	—
4 Dr DL Wgn	**13173**	—	—
4 Dr LX Wgn	**13617**	—	—
4 Dr AWD Wgn	**15571**	—	—
ADD FOR:			
2.4 Liter 4 Cyl Eng			
(Wgns)	**181**	—	—
Anti-Lock Brakes (Wgn)	**913**	—	—
Cast Aluminum Wheels			
(ES Sdn)	**275**	—	—
TALON 4			
2 Dr Cpe	**15390**	—	—
2 Dr TSi Turbo Cpe	**17847**	—	—
2 Dr 4WD TSi Turbo			

Refer To Optional Equipment Schedules

Year-Model-Body Type	Original List	Current Whlse	Average Retail
Cpe	**19854**	—	—
ADD FOR:			
Anti-Lock Brakes	**943**	—	—
Leather Seat Trim (TSi)	**435**	—	—
Cast Aluminum Wheels (TSi 2WD)	**284**	—	—

NOTE: Power windows and power seat standard on Premier ES Limited. Power door locks and cruise control standard on Premier ES & ES Limited. Tilt steering wheel standard on Premier ES & ES Limited, Sundance ES Sdn, LX Wagon & AWD Wagon and Talon.

1991

Year-Model-Body Type	Original List	Current Whlse	Average Retail
PREMIER 6			
4 Dr LX Sdn	**15051**	7675	8900
4 Dr ES Sdn	**17238**	8600	9925
4 Dr ES Limited Sdn	**19478**	9875	11375
SUMMIT 4			
3 Dr Htchbk	**7132**	4800	5725
4 Dr Sdn	**10333**	5675	6600
3 Dr ES Htchbk	**9573**	5250	6175
4 Dr ES Sdn	**11079**	6125	7125
TALON 4			
2 Dr Cpe	**14489**	9250	10650
2 Dr TSi Turbo Cpe	**17026**	10450	12050
2 Dr 4WD TSi Turbo Cpe	**18930**	12875	15200
ADD FOR:			
Anti-lock Brakes (Premier LX & ES)	**799**	450	550
(Talon ex. TSi 4WD)	**925**	500	600
(Talon TSi 4WD)	**681**	450	550
Leather Seats (Talon)	**427**	225	275

NOTE: Power brakes standard on all models. Power windows, power seat and anti-lock brakes standard on Eagle Premier ES Limited. Power door locks standard on Eagle Premier ES & ES Limited.

1990

Year-Model-Body Type	Original List	Current Whlse	Average Retail
PREMIER 6			
4 Dr LX Sdn	**16210**	5675	6600
4 Dr ES Sdn	**17845**	6500	7575
4 Dr ES Limited Sdn	**20284**	7650	8875
SUMMIT 4			
4 Dr Sdn	**10582**	3600	4500
4 Dr DL Sdn	**11330**	3900	4800
4 Dr LX Sdn	**12014**	4400	5325
4 Dr ES Sdn	**13052**	4825	5750
TALON 4			
2 Dr Cpe	**14479**	7750	9000
2 Dr TSI Turbo Cpe (NA w/auto trans)	**15555**	8850	10225
2 Dr 4WD TSi Turbo Cpe (NA w/auto trans)	**17239**	10925	12600
ADD FOR:			
1.6 Liter DOHC Pkg (Summit LX)	**1319**	650	800
45/45 Leather/Vinyl Seats (Premier ES)	**566**	275	325
Leather Bucket Seats (Talon TSi)	**430**	200	250

NOTE: Power windows and power door locks standard on Eagle ES Limited. Power brakes standard on all models.

1989

Year-Model-Body Type	Original List	Current Whlse	Average Retail
MEDALLION 4			
4 Dr DL Sdn	**11204**	2100	2950
4 Dr DL Wgn	**12448**	2425	3300
4 Dr LX Sdn	**11737**	2250	3100
4 Dr LX Wgn	**13074**	2600	3475
PREMIER LX 4*			
4 Dr Sdn	**14406**	4025	4925

* For 6 cylinder models add $375 wholesale and $375 retail.

Year-Model-Body Type	Original List	Current Whlse	Average Retail
PREMIER ES 6			
4 Dr Sdn	**16689**	4925	5850
PREMIER ES LIMITED 6			
4 Dr Sdn	**19181**	6100	7000
SUMMIT 4			
4 Dr DL Sdn	**11281**	3025	3925
4 Dr LX Sdn	**11617**	3525	4425
ADD FOR:			
Enthusiast Group (Premier LX)	**640**	275	325
Driving Group (Medallion LX)	**404**	150	200

NOTE: Power brakes standard on all models.

1988

Year-Model-Body Type	Original List	Current Whlse	Average Retail
EAGLE 6			
4 Dr Wgn	**12995**	3400	4300
MEDALLION 4			
4 Dr DL Sdn	**11200**	1400	2150
4 Dr DL Wgn	**11928**	1775	2625
4 Dr LX Sdn	**11714**	1575	2425

Year-Model-Body Type	Original List	Current Whlse	Average Retail
PREMIER LX 4			
4 Dr Sdn	**13304**	3550	4450
PREMIER ES 6			
4 Dr Sdn	**14909**	4025	4925
ADD FOR:			
Driving Group (Medallion LX, DL Wgn)	**417**	125	175

NOTE: Power brakes standard on all models.

FORD

Year-Model-Body Type	Original List	Current Whlse	Average Retail
1992			
CROWN VICTORIA 8			
4 Dr Sdn	**19563**	—	—
4 Dr LX Sdn	**20887**	—	—
4 Dr Touring Sdn	**23832**	—	—
ADD FOR:			
Anti-Lock Brakes (Base, LX)	**695**	—	—
Leather Seat Trim (LX)	**555**	—	—
(Touring Sdn)	**339**	—	—
Spoke Wheel Covers	**311**	—	—
Cast Aluminum Wheels (Base)	**440**	—	—
ESCORT PONY 4			
2 Dr Htchbk (NA w/power steering)	**9399**	—	—
ESCORT GT 4			
2 Dr Htchbk	**13362**	—	—
ESCORT LX 4			
2 Dr Htchbk	**10807**	—	—
4 Dr Htchbk	**11235**	—	—
4 Dr Sdn	**11547**	—	—
4 Dr Wgn	**11819**	—	—
ESCORT LX-E 4			
4 Dr Sdn	**13424**	—	—
ADD FOR:			
Sport Appearance Grp (LX)	**757**	—	—
FESTIVA 4			
2 Dr L Htchbk (NA w/auto trans, or power steering)	**7253**	—	—
2 Dr GL Htchbk (NA w/power steering)	**9358**	—	—
ADD FOR:			
Sport Opt Pkg	**341**	—	—
MUSTANG 4			
2 Dr LX Sdn	**11627**	—	—
2 Dr LX Htchbk	**11538**	—	—
2 Dr LX Conv	**18311**	—	—
MUSTANG 8			
2 Dr LX 5.0L Sdn	**14834**	—	—
2 Dr LX 5.0L Htchbk	**15619**	—	—
2 Dr LX 5.0L Conv	**21056**	—	—
2 Dr GT Htchbk	**16655**	—	—
2 Dr GT Conv	**21611**	—	—
ADD FOR:			
Leather Seat Trim (LX 5.0L, GT)	**523**	—	—
Cast Aluminum Wheels	**401**	—	—
PROBE 4			
2 Dr GL Htchbk	**13806**	—	—
2 Dr GT Htchbk	**16406**	—	—
PROBE 6			
2 Dr LX Htchbk	**14806**	—	—
ADD FOR:			
Anti-Lock Brakes	**924**	—	—
Leather Seat Trim	**523**	—	—
Electronic Instrument Cluster (LX)	**463**	—	—
Cast Aluminum Wheels (GL)	**313**	—	—
TAURUS 6			
4 Dr L Sdn	**15821**	—	—
4 Dr L Wgn	**16854**	—	—
4 Dr GL Sdn	**16121**	—	—
4 Dr GL Wgn	**17131**	—	—
4 Dr LX Sdn	**17775**	—	—
4 Dr LX Wgn	**19464**	—	—
4 Dr SHO Sdn (NA w/auto trans)	**23839**	—	—
ADD FOR:			
3.8 Liter 6 Cyl Eng (GL, LX Sdn)	**555**	—	—
Anti-Lock Brakes (L, GL, LX)	**595**	—	—
Leather Seat Trim	**515**	—	—
Cast Aluminum Wheels	**389**	—	—
TEMPO 4*			
2 Dr GL Sdn	**11367**	—	—
4 Dr GL Sdn	**11517**	—	—
4 Dr LX Sdn	**12495**	—	—

* For 6 cylinder models add $— wholesale and $— retail.

Year-Model-Body Type	Original List	Current Whlse	Average Retail
TEMPO 6			
2 Dr GLS Sdn	**13215**	—	—
4 Dr GLS Sdn	**13363**	—	—
THUNDERBIRD 6			
2 Dr Cpe	**16345**	—	—
2 Dr LX Cpe	**18783**	—	—
2 Dr Super Cpe	**22641**	—	—
THUNDERBIRD 8			
2 Dr Sport Cpe	**18611**	—	—

Refer To Optional Equipment Schedules

Year-Model-Body Type	Original List	Current Whlse	Average Retail
ADD FOR:			
8 Cyl (Standard & LX)	**1080**	—	—
Anti-Lock Brakes (Base Sport, LX)	**1085**	—	—
Leather Seat Trim (LX, Sport)	**515**	—	—
(Super Cpe)	**648**	—	—

NOTE: Power windows standard on Crown Victoria, Mustang LX Convertible, LX 5.0L & GT, Taurus LX & SHO and Thunderbird. Power door locks standard on Mustang LX Convertible, LX 5.0L & GT and Taurus LX & SHO. Power seat standard on Crown Victoria LX & Touring Sedan, Taurus LX & SHO and Thunderbird LX. Tilt steering wheel standard on Crown Victoria, Taurus, Tempo LX, Thunderbird Sport & LX. Cruise control standard on Crown Victoria Touring Sedan and Taurus SHO.

1991

Year-Model-Body Type	Original List	Current Whlse	Average Retail
ESCORT PONY 4			
2 Dr Htchbk (NA w/power steering)	**8993**	5200	6125
ESCORT GT 4			
2 Dr Htchbk	**13000**	7300	8475
ESCORT LX 4			
2 Dr Htchbk	**10419**	5725	6650
4 Dr Htchbk	**10847**	5750	6675
4 Dr Wgn	**11432**	6025	6950
FESTIVA 4			
2 Dr L Htchbk (NA w/auto trans or power steering)	**6893**	4050	4950
2 Dr GL Htchbk	**9111**	4650	5575
LTD CROWN VICTORIA 8			
4 Dr Standard Sdn	**18227**	9675	11150
4 Dr LX Sdn	**18863**	11500	13275
4 Dr Standard Crown Victoria Wgn	**18083**	10775	12425
4 Dr Standard Country Squire Wgn	**18335**	11175	12900
4 Dr LX Wgn	**18833**	11625	13425
4 Dr Country Squire LX Wgn	**19085**	11800	13625
MUSTANG 4			
2 Dr LX Sdn	**11727**	6950	8100
2 Dr LX Htchbk	**12233**	7075	8225
2 Dr LX Conv	**17692**	10625	12250
MUSTANG 8			
2 Dr LX 5.0L Spt Sdn	**14740**	8375	9675
2 Dr LX 5.0L Spt Htchbk	**15525**	8525	9850
2 Dr LX 5.0L Spt Conv	**20712**	12050	13925
2 Dr GT Htchbk	**16504**	10200	11775
2 Dr GT Conv	**21334**	13750	16125
PROBE 4			
2 Dr GL Htchbk	**13412**	7625	8850
2 Dr GT Htchbk	**16748**	9950	11450
PROBE 6			
2 Dr LX Htchbk	**15013**	8575	9900
TAURUS 4*			
4 Dr L Sdn	**14751**	8075	9325
4 Dr GL Sdn	**14980**	8675	10025

* For 6 cylinder models add $500 wholesale and $500 retail.

Year-Model-Body Type	Original List	Current Whlse	Average Retail
TAURUS 6*			
4 Dr L Wgn	**15662**	9200	10600
4 Dr GL Wgn	**15868**	9900	11400
4 Dr LX Sdn	**17434**	10450	12050
4 Dr LX Wgn	**19024**	11200	12925
4 Dr SHO Sdn (NA w/auto trans)	**22132**	13675	16050
TEMPO 4			
2 Dr L Sdn	**9730**	5450	6375
4 Dr L Sdn	**9873**	5575	6500
2 Dr GL Sdn	**10967**	6075	6975
4 Dr GL Sdn	**11117**	6175	7200
2 Dr GLS Sdn	**11785**	6475	7525
4 Dr GLS Sdn	**11932**	6550	7625
4 Dr LX Sdn	**12089**	6850	7975
4 Dr All Wheel Drive Sdn	**12253**	7625	8850
THUNDERBIRD 6			
2 Dr Standard Cpe	**15385**	9125	10500
2 Dr LX Cpe	**17801**	10050	11600
2 Dr Super Cpe	**21661**	12975	15300
ADD FOR:			
Anti-Lock Brakes (Probe LX & GT)	**924**	510	635
(Taurus)	**985**	565	700
(Thunderbird ex. Super Cpe)	**1085**	575	710
Electronic Instrument Cluster (Probe LX)	**396**	210	260
Leather Bucket Seats (Taurus LX & SHO)	**489**	300	365
(Taurus GL)	**593**	365	450
Leather Seats (Thunderbird LX)	**489**	300	365
(Thunderbird Super Cpe)	**622**	385	470
5.0L V8 EFI HO Eng (Thunderbird ex. Super Cpe)	**1080**	625	760
Half Brougham Roof (LTD Crown Victoria)	**726**	375	455

Refer To Optional Equipment Schedules

Year-Model-Body Type	Original List	Current Whlse	Average Retail
NOTE: Power brakes standard on all models. Air bag standard on Crown Victoria, Mustang and Taurus. Anti-lock brakes standard on Thunderbird Super Coupe. Power windows standard on Crown Victoria, Mustang LX Standard Convertible, LX 5.0L Sport & GT, Taurus LX Sedan & LX Wagon, SHO and Thunderbird. Power seat standard on Taurus LX Sedan & LX Wagon, SHO and Thunderbird LX.			
1990			
ESCORT PONY 4			
2 Dr Htchbk (NA w/power steering)	**7995**	3350	4250
ESCORT GT 4			
2 Dr Htchbk (NA w/auto trans)	**10588**	5225	6150
ESCORT LX 4			
2 Dr Htchbk	**9324**	3800	4700
4 Dr Htchbk	**9654**	3900	4800
4 Dr Wgn	**10179**	4125	5050
FESTIVA 4			
2 Dr L Htchbk (NA w/auto trans or power steering)	**6564**	2550	3425
2 Dr L Plus Htchbk	**8710**	2850	3750
2 Dr LX Htchbk	**9244**	3125	4025
LTD CROWN VICTORIA 8			
4 Dr Standard Sdn	**17257**	7975	9250
4 Dr LX Sdn	**17894**	8700	10050
4 Dr Standard Crown Victoria Wgn	**17668**	7875	9150
4 Dr Country Squire Wgn	**17921**	8325	9625
4 Dr LX Wgn	**18418**	8800	10175
4 Dr Country Squire LX Wgn	**18671**	9250	10650
MUSTANG 4			
2 Dr LX Sdn	**11051**	5725	6625
2 Dr LX Htchbk	**11557**	5875	6775
2 Dr LX Conv	**16636**	8825	9950
MUSTANG 8			
2 Dr LX 5.0L Spt Sdn	**12842**	6600	7675
2 Dr LX 5.0L Spt Htchbk	**13685**	6725	7825
2 Dr LX 5.0L Spt Conv	**18861**	9800	11300
2 Dr GT Htchbk	**14664**	8350	9650
2 Dr GT Conv	**19483**	11575	13375
PROBE 4			
2 Dr GL Htchbk	**13139**	6250	7275
2 Dr GT Htchbk	**16275**	8350	9650
PROBE 6			
2 Dr LX Htchbk	**14557**	7100	8250
TAURUS 4*			
4 Dr L Sdn	**13457**	5350	6275
4 Dr GL Sdn	**13930**	6000	6925
* For 6 cylinder models add $450 wholesale and $450 retail.			
TAURUS 6			
4 Dr L Wgn	**15089**	6450	7500
4 Dr GL Wgn	**15539**	7075	8225
4 Dr SHO Sdn (NA w/auto trans)	**21633**	10400	12000
4 Dr LX Sdn	**16180**	7475	8675
4 Dr LX Wgn	**17771**	8125	9375
TEMPO 4			
2 Dr GL Sdn	**10863**	4625	5550
4 Dr GL Sdn	**11013**	4725	5650
2 Dr GLS Sdn	**11680**	4950	5875
4 Dr GLS Sdn	**11828**	5050	5975
4 Dr LX Sdn	**11985**	5300	6225
4 Dr All Wheel Drive Sdn	**12148**	6125	7125
THUNDERBIRD 6			
2 Dr Standard Cpe	**14980**	7500	8700
2 Dr LX Cpe	**17263**	8375	9675
2 Dr Super Cpe	**20985**	10950	12625
ADD FOR:			
Air Bag Restraint System (Tempo GL)	**815**	380	460
(Tempo LX)	**690**	270	330
Anti-Lock Brakes (Probe)	**924**	435	530
(Taurus GL Sdn & LX Sdn)	**985**	435	530
(Thunderbird)	**1085**	485	595
Leather Upholstery (Thunderbird LX)	**489**	215	265
(Thunderbird Super Cpe)	**622**	270	330
Brougham Roof (LTD Crown Victoria)	**665**	215	265
NOTE: Power brakes standard on all models. Power seat standard on Taurus LX & SHO and Thunderbird LX. Power door locks standard on Mustang LX Standard Convertible, Mustang LX 5.0L Sport & GT, Taurus SHO and Thunderbird LX. Power windows standard on Mustang LX Standard Convertible & GT, LTD Crown Victoria Series, Taurus LX & SHO, Thunderbird Series.			
1989			
CROWN VICTORIA 8			
4 Dr S Sdn	**15434**	5700	6625

Refer To Optional Equipment Schedules

Year-Model-Body Type	Original List	Current Whlse	Average Retail
4 Dr Sdn	**15851**	6700	7800
4 Dr Wgn	**16209**	6550	7625
4 Dr LX Sdn	**16727**	7350	8525
4 Dr LX Wgn	**17238**	7400	8600
4 Dr Country Squire Wgn	**16527**	7050	8200
4 Dr Country Squire LX Wgn	**17556**	7800	9050
ESCORT PONY 4			
2 Dr Htchbk (NA w/power steering)	**7508**	2400	3250
ESCORT GT 4			
2 Dr Htchbk (NA w/auto trans)	**10003**	3750	4650
ESCORT LX 4			
2 Dr Htchbk	**8877**	2775	3625
4 Dr Htchbk	**9207**	2850	3700
4 Dr Wgn	**9733**	3000	3875
FESTIVA 4			
2 Dr L Htchbk (NA w/auto trans or power steering)	**6124**	1675	2525
2 Dr L Plus Htchbk (NA w/power steering)	**7943**	1925	2775
2 Dr LX Htchbk (NA w/power steering)	**8567**	2175	3025
MUSTANG 4			
2 Dr LX Sdn	**10745**	3725	4625
2 Dr LX Htchbk	**11251**	3875	4775
2 Dr LX Conv	**15835**	6825	7950
MUSTANG 8			
2 Dr LX Spt Sdn	**13105**	4850	5775
2 Dr LX Spt Htchbk	**13960**	5000	5925
2 Dr LX Spt Conv	**18696**	7975	9250
2 Dr GT Htchbk	**14967**	6600	7675
2 Dr GT Conv	**19207**	9500	10950
PROBE 4			
2 Dr GL Htchbk	**12246**	4525	5450
2 Dr LX Htchbk	**13072**	5050	5975
2 Dr GT Htchbk (NA w/auto trans)	**14865**	6475	7525
TAURUS 4*			
4 Dr L Sdn	**12566**	4000	4900
4 Dr GL Sdn	**12990**	4600	5525

* For 6 cylinder models add $400 wholesale and $400 retail.

Year-Model-Body Type	Original List	Current Whlse	Average Retail
TAURUS 6			
4 Dr L Wgn	**13931**	4900	5825
4 Dr GL Wgn	**14332**	5550	6475
4 Dr SHO Sdn	**19739**	8300	9575
4 Dr LX Sdn	**15282**	5850	6775
4 Dr LX Wgn	**16524**	6450	7500
TEMPO 4			
2 Dr GL Sdn	**10360**	3450	4350
4 Dr GL Sdn	**10510**	3600	4500
2 Dr GLS Sdn	**11000**	3775	4675
4 Dr GLS Sdn	**11151**	3925	4825
4 Dr LX Sdn	**11459**	4050	4950
4 Dr All Wheel Drive Sdn	**11648**	4675	5600
THUNDERBIRD 6			
2 Dr Cpe	**14612**	6100	7000
2 Dr LX Cpe	**16817**	6850	7975
2 Dr Super Cpe	**19823**	8800	10175
ADD FOR:			
Sport App Group (Tempo GLS)	**1178**	460	560
Air Bag Restraint System (Tempo GL)	**815**	365	450
(Tempo LX)	**751**	365	450
3.8 Liter 6 Cyl Eng (Taurus GL Wgn & LX Sdn)	**400**	185	225
(Taurus GL Sdn)	**1072**	275	335
Anti-Lock Brakes (Thunderbird Base & LX)	**1085**	415	505

NOTE: Power brakes standard on all models. Power windows standard on Mustang Convertible and Thunderbird. Power door locks standard on Thunderbird LX.

1988½

Year-Model-Body Type	Original List	Current Whlse	Average Retail
ESCORT PONY 4			
2 Dr Htchbk (NA w/power steering)	**7291**	1800	2650
ESCORT LX 4			
2 Dr Htchbk	**8540**	2075	2925
4 Dr Htchbk	**8870**	2150	2925
4 Dr Wgn	**9396**	2150	3000
ESCORT EXP 4			
2 Dr Luxury Cpe	**9362**	2275	3150
ESCORT GT 4			
2 Dr Htchbk (NA w/auto trans)	**10196**	3150	4050

NOTE: Power brakes standard on all models.

1988

Year-Model-Body Type	Original List	Current Whlse	Average Retail
ESCORT PONY 4			
2 Dr Htchbk	**7115**	1700	2550
ESCORT GL 4			
2 Dr Htchbk	**8362**	1975	2825
4 Dr Htchbk	**8692**	2075	2925

Year-Model-Body Type	Original List	Current Whlse	Average Retail
4 Dr Wgn	**9205**	2200	3050
ESCORT GT 4			
2 Dr Htchbk (NA w/auto trans)	**9665**	3050	3950
ESCORT EXP 4			
2 Dr Luxury Cpe	**9364**	2175	3025
FESTIVA 4			
2 Dr L Htchbk (NA w/auto trans or power steering)	**5652**	1200	1925
2 Dr L Plus (NA w/auto trans or power steering)	**7002**	1375	2125
2 Dr LX Htchbk (NA w/auto trans or power steering)	**7489**	1650	2500
LTD CROWN VICTORIA 8			
4 Dr S Sdn	**14675**	3825	4725
4 Dr Std Sdn	**15241**	4725	5650
4 Dr LX Sdn	**16157**	5275	6200
4 Dr Crown Victoria Wgn	**15311**	4575	5500
4 Dr Country Squire Wgn	**15744**	4875	5800
4 Dr LX Crown Victoria Wgn	**16455**	5275	6200
4 Dr LX Country Squire Wgn	**16773**	5675	6600
MUSTANG 4			
2 Dr LX Sdn	**10138**	3000	3900
2 Dr LX Htchbk	**10644**	3125	4025
2 Dr LX Conv	**15005**	5825	6750
2 Dr GT Htchbk (8 cyl)	**14048**	5525	6450
2 Dr GT Conv (8 cyl)	**17193**	8100	9350
TAURUS 4*			
4 Dr L Sdn	**12351**	3250	4150
4 Dr GL Sdn	**12958**	3725	4625
4 Dr MT-5 Sdn (NA w/auto trans)	**13471**	3225	4125

* For 6 cylinder models add $400 wholesale and $400 retail.

Year-Model-Body Type	Original List	Current Whlse	Average Retail
TAURUS 6			
4 Dr L Wgn	**13655**	4125	5050
4 Dr GL Wgn	**14138**	4650	5575
4 Dr LX Sdn	**14966**	4900	5825
4 Dr LX Wgn	**15698**	5475	6400
TEMPO 4			
2 Dr GL Sdn	**9913**	2800	3700
4 Dr GL Sdn	**10063**	2900	3800
2 Dr GLS Sdn	**10504**	3075	3975
4 Dr GLS Sdn	**10655**	3150	4050
4 Dr LX Sdn	**10992**	3300	4200
4 Dr All Wheel Drive Sdn	**11186**	4000	4900
THUNDERBIRD 6			
2 Dr Std	**13495**	4450	5375
2 Dr LX	**15782**	5675	6600
2 Dr Turbo Cpe (4 cyl)	**17661**	5350	6275
2 Dr Sport (8 cyl)	**15927**	5675	6600
ADD FOR:			
Leather Seat Trim (Thunderbird)	**415**	150	185
Leather Articulated Sport Seats (Mustang LX Conv)	**780**	285	345
(Mustang GT Conv)	**415**	150	185
Electronic Instrument Cluster (Taurus L, GL & MT-5)	**351**	130	160
(Taurus LX)	**239**	95	115
Premium Lux Pkg (Thunderbird)	**832**	300	370
5.0 Liter 8 Cyl EFI Eng (Thunderbird Base & LX)	**721**	265	320
5.0 Liter HO 8 Cyl Eng (Mustang LX)	**2007**	715	875

NOTE: Power brakes standard on all models. Power seat standard on Taurus LX. Power locks standard on Tempo LX, Taurus LX and Thunderbird LX. Power windows standard on Taurus LX, Thunderbird LX and Turbo Coupe, Crown Victoria LX and Country Squire LX.

1987

Year-Model-Body Type	Original List	Current Whlse	Average Retail
ESCORT PONY 4			
2 Dr Htchbk	**6625**	1325	2050
(NA w/automatic transmission or power steering)			
ESCORT GL 4			
2 Dr Htchbk	**8362**	1475	2300
4 Dr Htchbk	**8576**	1575	2425
4 Dr Wgn	**8857**	1700	2550
ESCORT GT 4			
2 Dr Htchbk (NA w/auto trans)	**9548**	2450	3325
ESCORT EXP 4			
2 Dr Luxury Cpe	**9129**	1725	2575
2 Dr Sport Cpe (NA w/auto trans)	**9653**	2175	3025
LTD CROWN VICTORIA 8			
2 Dr Std Cpe	**14709**	3100	4000
4 Dr Std Sdn	**14349**	3225	4125
2 Dr LX Cpe	**15378**	3575	4475
4 Dr LX Sdn	**15410**	3725	4625
4 Dr Crown Victoria Wgn	**14315**	3050	3950

FORD

Year-Model-Body Type	Original List	Current Whlse	Average Retail
4 Dr Country Squire Wgn	**14567**	3325	4225
4 Dr LX Crown Victoria Wgn	**15489**	3600	4500
4 Dr LX Country Squire Wgn	**15741**	3900	4800
MUSTANG 4			
2 Dr LX Sdn	**9574**	2375	3250
2 Dr LX Htchbk	**9993**	2500	3375
2 Dr LX Conv	**14355**	4925	5850
2 Dr GT Htchbk (8 cyl)	**13409**	4625	5550
2 Dr GT Conv (8 cyl)	**17155**	6850	7975
TAURUS 4			
4 Dr L Sdn	**11438**	2375	3250
4 Dr GL Sdn	**12410**	2800	3700
4 Dr MT5 Sdn (NA w/auto trans)	**12117**	2325	3200
4 Dr MT5 Wgn (NA w/auto trans)	**12678**	2800	3700
TAURUS 6			
4 Dr L Wgn	**12658**	3075	3975
4 Dr GL Wgn	**13590**	3500	4400
4 Dr LX Sdn	**14633**	3700	4600
4 Dr LX Wgn	**15243**	4175	5100
TEMPO 4			
2 Dr GL Sdn	**9415**	1975	2825
4 Dr GL Sdn	**9565**	2075	2925
2 Dr Sport GL Sdn	**10191**	2175	3025
4 Dr Sport GL Sdn	**10341**	2250	3100
2 Dr LX Sdn	**10576**	2250	3100
4 Dr LX Sdn	**10775**	2350	3225
2 Dr All Wheel Drive Sdn	**10817**	2800	3700
4 Dr All Wheel Drive Sdn	**10967**	2900	3800
THUNDERBIRD 6			
2 Dr Std	**13028**	3000	3900
2 Dr LX	**15357**	4075	5000
2 Dr Turbo Cpe (4 cyl)	**16600**	3650	4550
2 Dr Sport (8 cyl)	**15065**	4100	5025
ADD FOR:			
Electronic Instrument Cluster (Taurus)	**351**	105	125
3.0 Liter 6 Cyl Eng w/overdrive trans (Taurus Sdn)	**672**	255	310
5.0 Liter 8 Cyl EFI Eng (Thunderbird Std & LX)	**639**	245	300
5.0 Liter HO 8 Cyl Eng (Mustang)	**1885**	710	865

NOTE: Power brakes standard on all models. Power windows standard on Taurus LX, 2 Door Crown Victoria, Thunderbird LX and Turbo Coupe.

Year-Model-Body Type	Original List	Current Whlse	Average Retail
1986			
ESCORT PONY 4			
2 Dr Htchbk (NA w/auto trans)	**6052**	825	1525
ESCORT L 4			
2 Dr Htchbk	**7676**	1025	1750
4 Dr Htchbk	**7890**	1125	1850
4 Dr Wgn	**8171**	1200	1925
ESCORT LX 4			
2 Dr Htchbk	**8281**	1275	2000
4 Dr Htchbk	**8495**	1325	2050
4 Dr Wgn	**8776**	1425	2175
ESCORT EXP 4			
2 Dr Luxury Cpe	**8415**	1350	2100
2 Dr Sport Cpe	**9238**	1725	2575
ESCORT GT 4			
2 Dr Htchbk	**9177**	1775	2625
LTD 6			
4 Dr Sdn	**10794**	1375	2100
4 Dr Brougham Sdn	**11182**	1700	2475
4 Dr Wgn	**10894**	1550	2350
LTD CROWN VICTORIA 8			
2 Dr Cpe	**13784**	2575	3450
2 Dr LX Cpe	**14514**	2975	3875
4 Dr Sdn	**13324**	2700	3600
4 Dr LX Sdn	**14546**	3100	4000
4 Dr S Sdn	**12950**	2100	2950
Country Squire Wagon	**13417**	2750	3650
Country Squire LX Wgn	**14579**	3150	4050
Crown Victoria Wgn	**13167**	2525	3400
Crown Victoria LX Wgn	**14329**	2950	3850
Crown Victoria S Wgn	**13230**	1900	2750
MUSTANG 4*			
2 Dr LX Sdn	**8461**	1600	2450
3 Dr LX Htchbk	**9016**	1725	2575
2 Dr LX Conv (6 cyl)	**13641**	4075	5000
3 Dr GT Htchbk (8 cyl)	**12162**	3500	4400
2 Dr GT Convertible (8 cyl)	**15994**	5300	6225
2 Dr SVO Htchbk (auto trans NA on SVO)	**15272**	4150	5075

* For 6 cylinder models add $300 wholesale and $300 retail.

Year-Model-Body Type	Original List	Current Whlse	Average Retail
TAURUS 4			
4 Dr L Sdn	**10407**	1575	2425
4 Dr L Wgn	**11586**	1975	2825
4 Dr MT5 Sdn	**11038**	1700	2550
4 Dr MT5 Wgn	**11503**	2100	2950
TAURUS 6			
4 Dr GL Sdn	**12145**	2300	3175
4 Dr GL Wgn	**12613**	2700	3600
4 Dr LX Sdn	**13412**	2700	3600
4 Dr LX Wgn	**13921**	3125	4025

Year-Model-Body Type	Original List	Current Whlse	Average Retail
TEMPO GL 4			
2 Dr Sdn	**8772**	1300	2025
4 Dr Sdn	**8922**	1400	2150
TEMPO LX 4			
2 Dr Sdn	**9769**	1550	2400
4 Dr Sdn	**9968**	1625	2475
THUNDERBIRD 6*			
2 Dr	**11782**	2175	3025
2 Dr Turbo (4 cyl)	**14905**	2550	3425
2 Dr Elan	**13316**	3000	3900

* For 8 cylinder models add $325 wholesale and $325 retail.

Year-Model-Body Type	Original List	Current Whlse	Average Retail
ADD FOR:			
Sport GL Pkg (Tempo GL)	**983**	190	235
"T" Roof (Mustang)	**1100**	235	285
Moonroof (Taurus, Thunderbird)	**701**	130	150
Interior Luxury Group (LTD Base Wgn)	**388**	75	90
3.0 Liter 6 Cyl Eng w/overdrive trans (Taurus L Sdn)	**672**	255	310
5.0 Liter 8 Cyl EFI Eng (Thunderbird)	**639**	245	300
5.0 Liter HO 8 Cyl Eng (Mustang LX Sdn & Htchbk)	**1211**	455	550
DEDUCT FOR:			
2.0 Liter 4 Cyl Diesel Eng (Escort)	**591**	400	400
(Tempo)	**509**	400	400

NOTE: Power windows standard on Mustang SVO and Thunderbird Elan. Power brakes standard on all models.

1985½

Year-Model-Body Type	Original List	Current Whlse	Average Retail
ESCORT 4			
2 Dr Htchbk	**6361**	725	1375
ESCORT GL 4			
2 Dr Htchbk	**7146**	1025	1750
4 Dr Htchbk	**7360**	1125	1850
4 Dr Wgn	**7641**	1175	1900
2 Dr Diesel Htchbk	**7710**	300	575
4 Dr Diesel Htchbk	**7924**	350	625
4 Dr Diesel Wgn	**8205**	425	775
ESCORT L 4			
2 Dr Htchbk	**6632**	875	1600
4 Dr Htchbk	**6846**	800	1500
4 Dr Wgn	**7127**	975	1700
2 Dr Diesel Htchbk	**7196**	250	500
4 Dr Diesel Htchbk	**7410**	325	600
4 Dr Diesel Wgn	**7691**	375	675

1985

Year-Model-Body Type	Original List	Current Whlse	Average Retail
ESCORT 4			
2 Dr Htchbk	**6956**	700	1325
4 Dr Htchbk	**7163**	800	1500
ESCORT GL 4			
2 Dr Htchbk	**7670**	1000	1725
4 Dr Htchbk	**7884**	1100	1825
4 Dr Wgn	**8061**	1150	1875
2 Dr Diesel Htchbk	**8228**	300	575
4 Dr Diesel Htchbk	**8442**	350	625
4 Dr Diesel Wgn	**8618**	375	675
ESCORT GT 4			
2 Dr Htchbk	**8806**	1275	2000
2 Dr Turbo Htchbk	**9686**	1275	2000
ESCORT L 4			
2 Dr Htchbk	**7212**	875	1600
4 Dr Htchbk	**7427**	900	1625
4 Dr Wgn	**7641**	975	1700
2 Dr Diesel Htchbk	**7770**	250	500
4 Dr Diesel Htchbk	**7984**	300	575
4 Dr Diesel Wgn	**8198**	350	625
ESCORT LX 4			
4 Dr Htchbk	**9136**	1025	1750
4 Dr Wgn	**9227**	1200	1925
EXP 4			
3 Dr Cpe	**7918**	800	1500
3 Dr Luxury Cpe	**8806**	1000	1725
3 Dr Turbo Cpe	**11003**	825	1525
LTD 4*			
4 Dr Sdn	**9828**	975	1700
4 Dr Brougham Sdn	**10216**	1225	1950

* For 6 cylinder models add $300 wholesale add $300 retail.

Year-Model-Body Type	Original List	Current Whlse	Average Retail
LTD 6			
4 Dr Wgn	**10417**	1250	1975
LTD 8			
4 Dr LX Sdn	**12457**	1775	2625
LTD CROWN VICTORIA 8			
2 Dr Sdn	**12674**	1750	2600
4 Dr Sdn	**12674**	1875	2725
Country Squire Wagon	**12862**	1900	2750
4 Dr S Sdn	**12322**	1350	2100
4 Dr Wgn	**12612**	1700	2550
4 Dr S Wgn	**12675**	1200	1925
MUSTANG 4*			
2 Dr LX Sdn	**8221**	1150	1875
3 Dr LX Sdn	**8741**	1250	1975
2 Dr LX Conv (6 cyl)	**12999**	3100	4000
3 Dr GT Sdn (8 cyl)	**11456**	2650	3550
2 Dr GT Conv (8 cyl)	**15162**	4350	5275
3 Dr SVO Sdn (NA w/auto trans)	**15568**	3600	4550

* For 6 cylinder models add $300 wholesale and $300 retail.

Refer To Optional Equipment Schedules

Year-Model-Body Type	Original List	Current Whlse	Average Retail
TEMPO GL 4			
2 Dr	**8489**	1000	1725
4 Dr	**8489**	1025	1750
2 Dr Diesel	**8968**	575	1075
4 Dr Diesel	**8968**	675	1275
TEMPO GLX 4			
2 Dr	**9359**	1200	1925
4 Dr	**9408**	1275	2000
2 Dr Diesel	**9838**	775	1500
4 Dr Diesel	**9887**	825	1525
TEMPO L 4			
2 Dr	**8381**	850	1550
4 Dr	**8381**	925	1650
2 Dr Diesel	**8860**	325	600
4 Dr Diesel	**8860**	425	775
THUNDERBIRD 6*			
2 Dr	**11205**	1600	2450
2 Dr Turbo Cpe (4 cyl)	**14340**	1900	2750
2 Dr Elan	**12886**	2300	3175
2 Dr Fila	**15956**	2525	3400

* For 8 cylinder models add $275 wholesale and $275 retail.

ADD FOR:			
Sport GL Pkg (Tempo GL)	**677**	90	105
"T" Roof (Mustang)	**1100**	200	275
302 V8 Engine (Mustang LX Sdn)	**1020**	450	550

NOTE: Power brakes standard on all models except Base Escort. Vinyl top standard on LTD Crown Victoria Sedan. Power door locks standard on Tempo GLX.

1984

Year-Model-Body Type	Original List	Current Whlse	Average Retail
ESCORT 4			
2 Dr Htchbk	**6956**	275	550
4 Dr Htchbk	**7163**	350	625
ESCORT GL 4			
2 Dr Htchbk	**7671**	500	925
4 Dr Htchbk	**7885**	575	1075
4 Dr Wgn	**8062**	650	1225
2 Dr Diesel Htchbk	**8229**	125	325
4 Dr Diesel Htchbk	**8443**	175	375
4 Dr Diesel Wgn	**8658**	225	475
ESCORT GT 4			
2 Dr Htchbk	**8806**	725	1375
2 Dr Turbo Htchbk	**9497**	725	1375
ESCORT L 4			
2 Dr Htchbk	**7212**	375	675
4 Dr Htchbk	**7427**	450	825
4 Dr Wgn	**7641**	525	975
2 Dr Diesel Htchbk	**7770**	50	225
4 Dr Diesel Htchbk	**7984**	150	350
4 Dr Diesel Wgn	**8198**	175	375
ESCORT LX 4			
4 Dr Wgn	**9152**	675	1275
4 Dr Htchbk	**9061**	600	1125
EXP 4			
3 Dr Cpe	**7866**	325	600
3 Dr Luxury Cpe	**8752**	500	925
3 Dr Turbo Cpe	**11110**	400	725
LTD 4*			
4 Dr Sdn	**9405**	775	1500
4 Dr Brougham Sdn	**9793**	900	1625
4 Dr Wgn (6 cyl)	**9902**	875	1600

* For 6 cylinder models add $200 wholesale and $200 retail.

Year-Model-Body Type	Original List	Current Whlse	Average Retail
LTD CROWN VICTORIA 8			
2 Dr Sdn	**11686**	1275	2000
4 Dr Sdn	**11686**	1375	2125
4 Dr S Sdn	**10558**	950	1675
LTD CROWN VICTORIA WAGONS 8			
Country Squire	**11842**	1375	2125
4 Dr Wgn	**11592**	1200	1925
4 Dr S Wgn	**10867**	800	1500
MUSTANG 4*			
2 Dr L Sdn	**8473**	825	1525
3 Dr L Sdn	**8644**	875	1600
2 Dr LX Sdn	**8665**	900	1625
3 Dr LX Sdn	**8871**	1000	1725
2 Dr LX Convertible (6 cyl)	**12785**	2225	3075
3 Dr GT Sdn	**10956**	1800	2650
3 Dr GT Turbo Sdn	**11140**	1325	2025
2 Dr GT Conv (8 cyl)	**14429**	3075	3975
2 Dr GT Turbo Convertible	**14623**	2600	3475
3 Dr SVO Sdn	**16530**	2700	3600

* For 6 cylinder models add $200 wholesale and $200 retail.

Year-Model-Body Type	Original List	Current Whlse	Average Retail
TEMPO GL 4			
2 Dr	**8556**	425	775
4 Dr	**8556**	525	975
2 Dr Diesel	**9114**	70	250
4 Dr Diesel	**9114**	110	300
TEMPO GLX 4			
2 Dr	**9018**	550	1025
4 Dr	**9018**	625	1175
2 Dr Diesel	**9576**	150	350
4 Dr Diesel	**9576**	175	375
TEMPO L 4			
2 Dr	**8333**	300	575
4 Dr	**8333**	375	675
2 Dr Diesel	**8891**	50	225
4 Dr Diesel	**8891**	50	225
THUNDERBIRD 6*			
2 Dr	**10366**	1350	2100
2 Dr Turbo Cpe	**13097**	1325	2050

Refer To Optional Equipment Schedules

Year-Model-Body Type	Original List	Current Whlse	Average Retail
2 Dr Elan	**13394**	1900	2750
2 Dr Fila	**14789**	2100	2950

* For 8 cylinder models add $200 wholesale and $200 retail.

1983 — ALL BODY STYLES

Year-Model-Body Type	Original List	Current Whlse	Average Retail
ESCORT GL	—	350	650
ESCORT GLX	—	400	725
ESCORT GT	—	500	925
ESCORT L	—	275	550
EXP	—	200	400
FAIRMONT FUTURA	—	325	600
LTD	—	775	1500
LTD CROWN VICTORIA	—	1200	1925
MUSTANG	—	875	1600
MUSTANG GT	—	1325	2050
MUSTANG GT CONV	—	2600	3475
MUSTANG GLX CONV	—	2100	2950
THUNDERBIRD	—	1250	1975

LINCOLN

1992

Year-Model-Body Type	Original List	Current Whlse	Average Retail
CONTINENTAL 6			
4 Dr Executive Sdn	**32263**	—	—
4 Dr Signature Series Sdn	**34253**	—	—
ADD FOR:			
Styled Aluminum Wheels (Executive)	**556**	—	—
Cellular Telephone	**459**	—	—
MARK VII 8			
2 Dr Bill Blass Designer Series	**32156**	—	—
2 Dr LSC Series	**32032**	—	—
ADD FOR:			
Special Edit Pkg (LSC)	**680**	—	—
Cellular Telephone	**459**	—	—
TOWN CAR 8			
4 Dr Executive Sdn	**31211**	—	—
4 Dr Signature Series	**34252**	—	—
4 Dr Cartier Designer Series	**36340**	—	—
ADD FOR:			
Jack Nicklaus Spec Edit (Signature)	**1279**	—	—
Vinyl Roof	**800**	—	—
Leather Seat Trim (Executive, Signature)	**570**	—	—
Cellular Telephone (Signature, Designer)	**459**	—	—
Aluminum Wheels (Executive)	**556**	—	—

NOTE: Power windows, power door locks, power seat, tilt steering wheel and cruise control standard on all models.

1991

Year-Model-Body Type	Original List	Current Whlse	Average Retail
CONTINENTAL 6			
4 Dr Executive Sdn	**30335**	16400	19050
4 Dr Signature Series	**32243**	18025	20675
MARK VII 8			
2 Dr LSC Series	**30362**	19075	22125
2 Dr Bill Blass Designer Series	**30485**	19025	22075
TOWN CAR 8			
4 Dr Executive Sdn	**29581**	16850	19500
4 Dr Signature Series	**32540**	18450	21500
4 Dr Cartier Designer Series	**34627**	19500	22550
ADD FOR:			
Special Edit Pkg (Mark VII LSC)	**680**	410	505
Comfort/Conv Pkg (Continental Executive)	**828**	485	590

NOTE: Power anti-lock brakes, air bag, power windows, power door locks and power seat standard on all models.

1990

Year-Model-Body Type	Original List	Current Whlse	Average Retail
CONTINENTAL 6			
4 Dr	**29422**	12950	15275
4 Dr Signature Series	**31346**	14450	16975
MARK VII 8			
2 Dr LSC Series	**29468**	13525	15900
2 Dr Bill Blass Designer Series	**29246**	13475	15800
TOWN CAR 8			
4 Dr	**27986**	14200	16675
4 Dr Signature Series	**30721**	15650	18300
4 Dr Cartier Series	**32809**	16450	19100
ADD FOR:			
Anti-Lock Brakes (Town Car)	**936**	475	575
Comfort/Conv Pkg (Continental Base)	**819**	420	500
(Town Car Base)	**694**	350	425

NOTE: Power brakes, power windows, power door locks and power seat standard on all models. Anti-lock brakes standard on Continental

Refer To Optional Equipment Schedules

Series and Mark VII Series.

1989

Year-Model-Body Type	Original List	Current Whlse	Average Retail
CONTINENTAL 6			
4 Dr	**28032**	9500	10950
4 Dr Signature Series	**29910**	10775	12425
MARK VII 8			
2 Dr LSC Series	**27569**	10675	12325
2 Dr Bill Blass Designer Series	**27569**	10625	12250
TOWN CAR 8			
4 Dr	**25562**	9300	10725
4 Dr Signature Series	**28562**	10575	12200
4 Dr Cartier Series	**29709**	11300	13050
ADD FOR:			
Comfort/Conv Pkg (Town Car Base)	**694**	275	335
(Continental Base)	**819**	365	450
Carriage Roof (Town Car Base)	**1069**	275	350
(Signature Town Car)	**710**	230	280
Electronic Instrument Panel (Town Car)	**822**	275	335

NOTE: Power brakes, power windows, power door locks and power seat standard on all models.

1988

Year-Model-Body Type	Original List	Current Whlse	Average Retail
CONTINENTAL 6			
4 Dr	**26078**	7700	8950
4 Dr Signature Series	**27944**	8800	10175
MARK VII 8			
2 Dr LSC Series	**26380**	8325	9625
2 Dr Bill Blass Designer Series	**26380**	8300	9575
TOWN CAR 8			
4 Dr	**24373**	7475	8675
4 Dr Signature Series	**27374**	8575	9900
4 Dr Cartier Designer Series	**28520**	8400	9700
ADD FOR:			
Comfort/Conv Pkg (Continental Base)	**819**	300	370
Carriage Roof (Base Town Car)	**1069**	190	230
(Signature Town Car)	**710**	190	230
Preferred Equip Pkg (Town Car Base)	**2461**	775	920
Electronic Instrument Panel (Town Car)	**822**	225	275

NOTE: Power brakes, power windows, power door locks and power seat standard on all models.

1987

Year-Model-Body Type	Original List	Current Whlse	Average Retail
CONTINENTAL 8			
4 Dr	**25484**	5200	6125
4 Dr Givenchy Designer Series	**27899**	6225	7250
MARK VII 8			
2 Dr	**23246**	5675	6600
2 Dr Bill Blass Designer Series	**25016**	6700	7800
2 Dr LSC Series	**25016**	6925	8050
TOWN CAR 8			
4 Dr	**22837**	6025	6950
4 Dr Signature Series	**25743**	7025	8150
4 Dr Cartier Designer Series	**27026**	7650	8875
ADD FOR:			
Cambria Carriage Roof (Town Car Base & Signature)	**1069**	150	180
Bayville Carriage Roof (Town Car Signature)	**726**	120	145
Electronic Instrument Panel (Town Car)	**822**	175	215

NOTE: Power windows, power seat, and power brakes standard on all models.

1986

Year-Model-Body Type	Original List	Current Whlse	Average Retail
CONTINENTAL 8			
4 Dr	**24556**	4475	5400
4 Dr Givenchy Designer Series	**26960**	5150	6075
MARK VII 8			
2 Dr	**22399**	5050	5975
2 Dr Bill Blass Designer Series	**23980**	5675	6600
2 Dr LSC Series	**23980**	5775	6700
TOWN CAR 8			
4 Dr	**20764**	4725	5650
4 Dr Signature Series	**23972**	5425	6350
4 Dr Cartier Designer Series	**25235**	5725	6650
ADD FOR:			
Electronic Instrument Panel (Town Car)	**822**	130	155

NOTE: Power windows, power seat, and power brakes standard on all models.

Year-Model-Body Type	Original List	Current Whlse	Average Retail
1985			
CONTINENTAL 8			
4 Dr	**23066**	3550	4450
4 Dr Turbo Diesel	**24321**	3050	3950
4 Dr Valentino Designer Series	**26616**	4150	5075
4 Dr Valentino Designer Series Turbo Diesel	**27388**	3600	4500
4 Dr Givenchy Designer Series	**26321**	4150	5075
4 Dr Givenchy Designer Series Turbo Diesel	**27093**	3600	4500
MARK VII 8			
2 Dr	**22399**	4075	5000
2 Dr Turbo Diesel	**23633**	3500	4400
2 Dr Bill Blass Designer Series	**26659**	4575	5500
2 Dr Bill Blass Designer Turbo Diesel	**27431**	4000	4900
2 Dr Versace Designer Series	**26578**	4575	5500
2 Dr Versace Designer Series Turbo Diesel	**27349**	4000	4900
2 Dr LSC Series	**24332**	4700	5750
2 Dr LSC Series Turbo Diesel	**25104**	3600	4500
TOWN CAR 8			
4 Dr	**19458**	3725	4625
4 Dr Signature Series	**22573**	4425	5350
4 Dr Cartier Designer Series	**24091**	4550	5475
ADD FOR:			
Carriage Roof (Town Car Signature)	**726**	65	80
(Town Car, Town Car Designer)	**1069**	65	80

NOTE: Power windows, power disc brakes, and power seat standard on all models.

Year-Model-Body Type	Original List	Current Whlse	Average Retail
1984			
CONTINENTAL 8			
4 Dr	**21757**	2900	3800
4 Dr Turbo Diesel (6 cyl)	**22991**	2600	3475
4 Dr Valentino Designer Series	**24205**	3000	3900
4 Dr Valentino Designer Series Diesel (6 cyl)	**25440**	2700	3600
4 Dr Givenchy Designer Series	**24230**	3000	3900
4 Dr Givenchy Designer Series Turbo Diesel (6 cyl)	**25464**	2700	3600
MARK VII 8			
2 Dr	**21695**	3025	3925
2 Dr Turbo Diesel (6 cyl)	**22930**	2700	3600
2 Dr Bill Blass Designer Series	**24795**	3225	4125
2 Dr Bill Blass Designer Turbo Diesel (6 cyl)	**26030**	2900	3800
2 Dr Versace Designer Series	**24394**	3225	4125
2 Dr Versace Designer Series Turbo Diesel (6 cyl)	**25628**	2900	3800
2 Dr LSC Series	**23694**	3250	4150
2 Dr LSC Series Turbo Diesel (6 cyl)	**24928**	2975	3875
TOWN CAR 8			
4 Dr	**18059**	2350	3225
4 Dr Signature Series	**20028**	2500	3375
4 Dr Cartier Designer Series	**21694**	2600	3475

NOTE: Power windows, power disc brakes, vinyl roof and power seat standard on all models.

Year-Model-Body Type	Original List	Current Whlse	Average Retail
1983 — ALL BODY STYLES			
CONTINENTAL	—	2200	3025
MARK VI	—	3000	3900
TOWN CAR	—	1850	2700

MERCURY

Year-Model-Body Type	Original List	Current Whlse	Average Retail
1992			
CAPRI 4			
2 Dr Conv	**16001**	—	—
2 Dr XR2 Conv (NA w/auto trans)	**17250**	—	—
ADD FOR:			
Removable Hardtop Roof	**1383**	—	—
Aluminum Wheels	**351**	—	—
COUGAR 6*			
2 Dr LS Cpe	**16460**	—	—

* For 8 cylinder models add $— wholesale and $— retail.

Refer To Optional Equipment Schedules

Year-Model-Body Type	Original List	Current Whlse	Average Retail
COUGAR XR-7 8			
2 Dr XR-7 Cpe	**22054**	—	—
ADD FOR:			
Anti-Lock Brakes (LS)	**695**	—	—
Leather Seat Trim	**515**	—	—
Cast Aluminum Wheels (LS)	**306**	—	—
GRAND MARQUIS 8			
4 Dr GS Sdn	**20216**	—	—
4 Dr LS Sdn	**20644**	—	—
ADD FOR:			
Anti-Lock Brakes	**695**	—	—
Vinyl Roof	**1185**	—	—
Leather Seat Trim	**555**	—	—
Spoke Wheels	**311**	—	—
Cast Aluminum Wheels	**440**	—	—
SABLE 6			
4 Dr GS Sdn	**16418**	—	—
4 Dr LS Sdn	**17368**	—	—
4 Dr GS Wgn	**17396**	—	—
4 Dr LS Wgn	**18395**	—	—
ADD FOR:			
3.8 Liter 6 Cyl Eng	**555**	—	—
Anti-Lock Brakes	**595**	—	—
Leather Seat Trim	**515**	—	—
Aluminum Wheels	**270**	—	—
TOPAZ 4*			
2 Dr GS Sdn	**11892**	—	—
4 Dr GS Sdn	**12058**	—	—
4 Dr LS Sdn	**13437**	—	—

* For 6 cylinder models add $— wholesale and $— retail.

Year-Model-Body Type	Original List	Current Whlse	Average Retail
TOPAZ 6			
2 Dr XR5 Sdn	**14015**	—	—
2 Dr LTS Sdn	**14807**	—	—
ADD FOR:			
Cast Aluminum Wheels	**278**	—	—
TRACER 4			
4 Dr Ntchbk	**11525**	—	—
4 Dr LTS Ntchbk	**13514**	—	—
4 Dr Wgn	**12285**	—	—

NOTE: Power windows standard on Capri, Cougar, Grand Marquis, Sable LS, Topaz LS, XR5 & LTS. Power door locks standard on Topaz LS & LTS. Power seat standard on Topaz LTS. Tilt steering wheel standard on Grand Marquis, Sable, Topaz XR5 & LTS, Tracer LTS. Cruise control standard on Capri, Topaz LS & LTS, Tracer LTS.

1991

Year-Model-Body Type	Original List	Current Whlse	Average Retail
CAPRI 4			
2 Dr Conv	**15239**	8800	10175
2 Dr XR2 Conv (NA w/auto trans)	**16620**	9975	11500
COUGAR 6*			
2 Dr LS Cpe	**15696**	9475	10925

* For 8 cylinder models add $475 wholesale and $475 retail.

Year-Model-Body Type	Original List	Current Whlse	Average Retail
COUGAR XR-7 8			
2 Dr XR-7 Cpe	**20972**	12450	14600
GRAND MARQUIS 8			
4 Dr GS Sdn	**18741**	11475	13250
4 Dr LS Sdn	**19241**	12250	14200
Colony Park GS Wgn	**18918**	11925	13775
Colony Park LS Wgn	**19490**	12700	15025
SABLE 6*			
4 Dr GS Sdn	**15372**	9325	10750
4 Dr LS Sdn	**16215**	10125	11675
4 Dr GS Wgn	**16317**	10050	11600
4 Dr LS Wgn	**17185**	10875	12550

* For models with 231 CID 6 cylinder engine add $300 wholesale and $300 retail.

Year-Model-Body Type	Original List	Current Whlse	Average Retail
TOPAZ 4			
2 Dr GS Sdn	**11492**	6225	7250
4 Dr GS Sdn	**11649**	6325	7350
2 Dr XR5 Sdn	**12490**	6825	7950
4 Dr LS Sdn	**13028**	7075	8225
4 Dr LTS Sdn	**13235**	7400	8600
TRACER 4			
4 Dr Standard Ntchbk	**11138**	6175	7200
4 Dr LTS Ntchbk	**13153**	7425	8625
4 Dr Wgn	**11924**	6550	7625
ADD FOR:			
All Wheel Drive Pkg (Topaz GS)	**1490**	850	1035
(Topaz LTS)	**1380**	850	1035
(Topaz LS)	**1478**	850	1035
Anti-lock Brakes (Cougar LS, Sable)	**985**	545	665
Leather Seats (Cougar LS, Grand Marquis LS, Sable)	**489**	275	335
Formal Coach Vinyl Roof (Grand Marquis)	**726**	300	375
Carrige Roof (Grand Marquis)	**1537**	485	590
Removable Hardtop (Capri)	**1287**	665	815

NOTE: Power brakes standard on all models. Anti-lock brakes standard on Cougar XR7. Air bag standard on Capri, Grand Marquis and

Year-Model-Body Type	Original List	Current Whlse	Average Retail

Sable. Power door locks standard on Capri XR2 and Topaz LS & LTS. Power seat standard on Cougar XR7 and Sable LS. Power windows standard on Capri, Cougar, Grand Marquis, Sable LS and Topaz LS & LTS.

1990

Year-Model-Body Type	Original List	Current Whlse	Average Retail
COUGAR 6			
2 Dr LS Cpe	**15816**	7900	9175
2 Dr XR-7 Cpe	**20808**	10600	12225
GRAND MARQUIS 8			
4 Dr GS Sdn	**17784**	8600	9925
4 Dr LS Sdn	**18284**	9325	10750
Colony Park GS Wgn	**18504**	9000	10400
Colony Park LS Wgn	**19076**	9700	11175
SABLE 6*			
4 Dr GS Sdn	**15065**	6575	7650
4 Dr LS Sdn	**16067**	7275	8450
4 Dr GS Wgn	**16010**	7225	8400
4 Dr LS Wgn	**17038**	7925	9200

* For models with 231 CID 6 cylinder engine add $300 wholesale and $300 retail.

Year-Model-Body Type	Original List	Current Whlse	Average Retail
TOPAZ 4			
2 Dr GS Sdn	**11363**	4825	5750
4 Dr GS Sdn	**11520**	4850	5775
2 Dr XR5 Sdn	**12362**	5350	6275
4 Dr LS Sdn	**12899**	5650	6575
4 Dr LTS Sdn	**13106**	5925	6850
ADD FOR:			
All Wheel Drive Pkg			
(Topaz GS)	**1490**	760	925
(Topaz LTS)	**1380**	760	925
(Topaz LS)	**1478**	760	925
Anti-Lock Brakes (Cougar LS, Sable)	**985**	485	595
Formal Coach Vinyl Roof (Grand Marquis)	**665**	270	330
Leather Upholstery (Cougar, Grand Marquis, Sable)	**489**	215	265

NOTE: Power brakes standard on all models. Power seat standard on Topaz LTS. Power door locks standard on Topaz LS & LTS. Power windows standard on Cougar Series, Grand Marquis Series, Sable LS Topaz LS & LTS. Anti-lock brakes standard on XR-7.

1989

Year-Model-Body Type	Original List	Current Whlse	Average Retail
COUGAR 6			
2 Dr LS Cpe	**15448**	6450	7500
2 Dr XR-7 Cpe	**20165**	8675	10025
GRAND MARQUIS 8			
4 Dr GS Sdn	**16701**	6975	8125
4 Dr LS Sdn	**17213**	7600	8825
Colony Park GS Wgn	**17338**	7300	8475
Colony Park LS Wgn	**17922**	7950	9225
SABLE 6*			
4 Dr GS Sdn	**14101**	5175	6100
4 Dr LS Sdn	**15094**	5825	6750
4 Dr GS Wgn	**14804**	5800	6725
4 Dr LS Wgn	**15872**	6425	7475

* For models with 231 CID 6 cylinder engine add $250 wholesale and $250 retail.

Year-Model-Body Type	Original List	Current Whlse	Average Retail
SCORPIO 6			
Scorpio	**25602**	8100	9350
TOPAZ 4			
2 Dr GS Sdn	**10880**	3575	4475
4 Dr GS Sdn	**11037**	3725	4625
2 Dr XR5 Sdn	**11801**	4075	5000
4 Dr LS Sdn	**12333**	4275	5200
4 Dr LTS Sdn	**12495**	4575	5500
TRACER 4			
2 Dr Htchbk	**9659**	2975	3875
4 Dr Htchbk	**10345**	3125	4025
4 Dr Wgn	**10829**	3225	4125
XR4Ti 4			
XR4Ti	**20238**	5875	6800
ADD FOR:			
Leather Trim (XR4Ti)	**969**	415	505
Touring Pkg (Scorpio)	**2635**	720	880
All Wheel Drive Pkg			
(Topaz GS & LS)	**1441**	645	785
(Topaz LTS)	**1332**	645	785
Anti-Lock Brakes (Cougar)	**985**	340	415
Formal Coach Vinyl Roof (Grand Marquis)	**665**	190	230

NOTE: Power brakes standard on all models. Power windows standard on Topaz LS, Topaz LTS, Sable, Grand Marquis, Cougar, Scorpio and XR4Ti. Power door locks standard on Topaz LS and LTS, Scorpio and XR4Ti.

1988

Year-Model-Body Type	Original List	Current Whlse	Average Retail
COUGAR 6*			
2 Dr LS	**14026**	4775	5700
2 Dr XR-7 (8 cyl)	**16157**	6050	6950

* For 8 cylinder models add $375 wholesale and $375 retail.

Year-Model-Body Type	Original List	Current Whlse	Average Retail
GRAND MARQUIS 8			
4 Dr GS Sdn	**16079**	5375	6300
4 Dr LS Sdn	**16591**	5950	6875
Colony Park GS Wgn	**16428**	5675	6600
Colony Park LS Wgn	**17012**	6250	7275

Refer To Optional Equipment Schedules

MERCURY

Year-Model-Body Type	Original List	Current Whlse	Average Retail
MERKUR SCORPIO 6			
Scorpio	**24598**	5225	6150
MERKUR XR4Ti 4			
XR4Ti	**19492**	4300	5225
SABLE 6			
4 Dr GS Sdn	**13772**	4325	5250
4 Dr LS Sdn	**14765**	4775	5700
4 Dr GS Wgn	**14413**	4825	5750
4 Dr LS Wgn	**15432**	5425	6350
TOPAZ 4			
2 Dr GS Sdn	**10421**	2900	3800
4 Dr GS Sdn	**10578**	3000	3900
2 Dr XR5 Sdn	**11313**	3300	4200
4 Dr LS Sdn	**11846**	3500	4400
4 Dr LTS Sdn	**12023**	3775	4675
TRACER 4			
2 Dr Htchbk	**9438**	2125	2975
4 Dr Htchbk	**9901**	2250	3100
4 Dr Wgn	**10386**	2300	3175
ADD FOR:			
Formal Coach Vinyl Roof (Grand Marquis)	**665**	190	230
Leather Seat Trim (Merkur XR4Ti)	**890**	300	370
Touring Pkg (Merkur Scorpio)	**2465**	490	600

NOTE: Power brakes standard on all models. Power seat standard on Topaz LTS. Power locks standard on Topaz LS and LTS. Power windows standard on Topaz LS and LTS, Sable LS and Grand Marquis Series.

1987

Year-Model-Body Type	Original List	Current Whlse	Average Retail
COUGAR 6*			
2 Dr LS	**13630**	3250	4150
2 Dr XR-7 (8 cyl)	**15660**	4375	5300

* For 8 cylinder models add $350 wholesale and $350 retail.

Year-Model-Body Type	Original List	Current Whlse	Average Retail
GRAND MARQUIS 8			
4 Dr GS Sdn	**15163**	3975	4875
2 Dr LS Sdn	**15478**	4275	5200
4 Dr LS Sdn	**15621**	4425	5350
Colony Park GS Wgn	**15500**	4150	5075
Colony Park LS Wgn	**16029**	4650	5575
LYNX 4			
2 Dr L Htchbk (NA w/auto trans)	**6755**	1375	2125
2 Dr GS Htchbk	**8507**	1550	2400
4 Dr GS Htchbk	**8721**	1650	2500
4 Dr GS Wgn	**9003**	1775	2625
2 Dr XR3 Htchbk (NA w/auto trans)	**9630**	2350	3225
MERKUR XR4Ti 4			
XR4Ti	**18259**	3150	4050
SABLE 6			
4 Dr GS Sdn	**13128**	3225	4125
4 Dr LS Sdn	**14544**	3750	4650
4 Dr GS Wgn	**13692**	3700	4600
4 Dr LS Wgn	**15089**	4225	5150
TOPAZ 4			
2 Dr GS	**9919**	2075	2925
4 Dr GS	**10069**	2150	3000
2 Dr GS Sport	**10574**	2225	3075
4 Dr GS Sport	**10724**	2325	3200
4 Dr LS	**11548**	2425	3300
ADD FOR:			
Electronic Instrument Cluster (Cougar)	**330**	100	120
Formal Coach Vinyl Roof (Grand Marquis)	**665**	150	180

NOTE: Power windows standard on Grand Marquis Series, Sable LS and Topaz LS. Power brakes standard on all models.

1986

Year-Model-Body Type	Original List	Current Whlse	Average Retail
CAPRI 4*			
3 Dr GS	**9603**	1600	2450
3 Dr 5.0 Liter (8 cyl)	**12421**	3500	4400

* For 6 cylinder models add $275 wholesale and $275 retail.

Year-Model-Body Type	Original List	Current Whlse	Average Retail
COUGAR 6*			
2 Dr GS	**12183**	2150	3000
2 Dr LS	**13519**	2675	3575
2 Dr XR-7 (4 cyl)	**15454**	2525	3400

* For 8 cylinder models add $325 wholesale and $325 retail.

Year-Model-Body Type	Original List	Current Whlse	Average Retail
GRAND MARQUIS 8			
2 Dr Sdn	**14242**	3075	3975
4 Dr Sdn	**14266**	3200	4100
2 Dr LS Sdn	**14691**	3450	4350
4 Dr LS Sdn	**14714**	3625	4525
Colony Park Wgn	**14486**	3250	4150
LYNX 4			
2 Dr Htchbk	**6221**	900	1625
2 Dr L Htchbk	**7821**	1100	1825
2 Dr GS Htchbk	**8435**	1325	2050
2 Dr XR3 Htchbk	**8869**	1850	2700
4 Dr L Htchbk	**8035**	1200	1925
4 Dr GS Htchbk	**8649**	1425	2175
4 Dr L Wgn	**8316**	1275	2000
4 Dr GS Wgn	**8930**	1525	2375
MARQUIS 4*			
4 Dr Sdn	**10422**	1275	2000
4 Dr Brougham Sdn	**10810**	1625	2475

Year-Model-Body Type	Original List	Current Whlse	Average Retail
Marquis Wgn (6 cyl)	**11016**	1750	2600
Marquis Brougham Wgn (6 cyl)	**11375**	2100	2950
* For 6 cylinder models add $300 wholesale and $300 retail.			
MERKUR XR4Ti 4			
XR4Ti	**16788**	2375	3250
SABLE 4*			
4 Dr GS	**11462**	2025	2875
* For 6 cylinder models add $325 wholesale and $325 retail.			
SABLE 6			
4 Dr LS Sdn	**13397**	2850	3750
4 Dr GS Wgn	**12599**	2850	3750
4 Dr LS Wgn	**13891**	3175	4075
TOPAZ 4			
2 Dr GS	**9276**	1450	2225
4 Dr GS	**9426**	1500	2350
2 Dr LS	**10415**	1725	2575
4 Dr LS	**10685**	1750	2600
ADD FOR:			
Grand Marquis LS Decor Option	**521**	105	130
"T" Roof (Capri)	**1100**	215	260

NOTE: Power brakes standard on all models. Power windows standard on Capri, Cougar GS & LS, Merkur XR4Ti, Topaz LS and Sable LS.

1985

Year-Model-Body Type	Original List	Current Whlse	Average Retail
CAPRI 4*			
3 Dr GS	**9363**	1200	1925
3 Dr 5.0 Liter (8 cyl)	**11716**	2700	3600
* For 6 cylinder models add $250 wholesale and $250 retail.			
COUGAR 6*			
2 Dr	**11606**	1625	2475
2 Dr LS	**12821**	2100	2950
2 Dr XR-7 (4 cyl)	**14574**	1925	2775
* For 8 cylinder models add $275 wholesale and $275 retail.			
GRAND MARQUIS 8			
2 Dr Sdn	**13358**	2275	3150
4 Dr Sdn	**13423**	2425	3300
2 Dr LS Sdn	**13912**	2600	3475
4 Dr LS Sdn	**13977**	2725	3625
Colony Park Wgn	**13635**	2450	3325
LYNX 4			
3 Dr Htchbk	**6647**	725	1375
3 Dr L Htchbk	**7467**	875	1600
3 Dr GS Htchbk	**7928**	1025	1750
5 Dr L Htchbk	**7681**	950	1675
5 Dr GS Htchbk	**8142**	1125	1850
4 Dr L Wgn	**7805**	1000	1725
4 Dr GS Wgn	**8199**	1175	1900
3 Dr L Diesel Htchbk	**8025**	350	625
3 Dr GS Diesel Htchbk	**8343**	500	925
5 Dr L Diesel Htchbk	**8239**	450	825
5 Dr GS Diesel Htchbk	**8558**	575	1075
4 Dr Diesel Wgn	**8363**	600	1125
4 Dr GS Diesel Wgn	**8609**	550	1025
MARQUIS 4*			
4 Dr Sdn	**9950**	850	1575
4 Dr Brougham Sdn	**10338**	1150	1875
Marquis Wgn (6 cyl)	**10539**	1275	2000
Marquis Wgn w/Brougham Decor Option (6 cyl)	**10899**	1500	2350
* For 6 cylinder models add $200 wholesale and $200 retail.			
MERKUR XR4Ti 4			
XR4Ti	**16788**	1800	2650
TOPAZ 4			
2 Dr GS	**8875**	1000	1725
4 Dr GS	**8875**	1025	1750
2 Dr LS	**10039**	1200	1925
4 Dr LS	**10088**	1200	1925
2 Dr GS Diesel	**9354**	425	775
4 Dr GS Diesel	**9354**	475	875
2 Dr LS Diesel	**10518**	700	1325
4 Dr LS Diesel	**10567**	675	1275
ADD FOR:			
5.0 Liter HO 4 bbl 8 Cyl Engine (Capri GS)	**1257**	130	160
Formal Coach Vinyl Roof (Grand Marquis)	**650**	65	80
"T" Roof (Capri)	**1100**	215	260

NOTE: Power brakes standard on Capri, Cougar, Grand Marquis, Lynx L and GS, Marquis and Topaz. Vinyl top standard on Grand Marquis. Power windows standard on Capri, Cougar, Grand Marquis and Merkur XR4Ti.

1984

Year-Model-Body Type	Original List	Current Whlse	Average Retail
CAPRI 4*			
3 Dr GS	**9133**	875	1600
3 Dr RS (8 cyl)	**10810**	1700	2550
3 Dr RS Turbo	**10994**	1050	1775
* For 6 cylinder models add $200 wholesale and $200 retail.			
COUGAR 6*			
2 Dr	**10711**	1350	2100
2 Dr LS	**11998**	1675	2525
2 Dr XR-7 (4 cyl)	**14272**	1325	2050
* For 8 cylinder models add $200 wholesale and $200 retail.			

Year-Model-Body Type	Original List	Current Whlse	Average Retail
GRAND MARQUIS 8			
2 Dr Sdn	**12308**	1775	2625
4 Dr Sdn	**12372**	1900	2750
2 Dr LS Sdn	**12863**	2000	2850
4 Dr LS Sdn	**12927**	2125	2975
Colony Park Wgn	**12547**	1900	2750
LYNX 4			
3 Dr Htchbk	**7086**	325	600
3 Dr L Htchbk	**7347**	400	725
3 Dr GS Htchbk	**7784**	525	975
3 Dr RS Htchbk	**8854**	750	1475
5 Dr Htchbk	**7293**	375	675
5 Dr L Htchbk	**7522**	475	675
5 Dr GS Htchbk	**7998**	600	1125
5 Dr LTS Htchbk	**9092**	625	1175
4 Dr L Wgn	**7776**	550	1025
4 Dr GS Wgn	**8176**	675	1275
3 Dr L Diesel Htchbk	**7904**	75	250
3 Dr GS Diesel Htchbk	**8342**	125	325
5 Dr L Diesel Htchbk	**8118**	100	300
5 Dr GS Diesel Htchbk	**8557**	225	475
4 Dr L Diesel Wgn	**8334**	150	350
4 Dr GS Diesel Wgn	**8733**	250	500
MARQUIS 4*			
4 Dr Sdn	**9461**	875	1600
4 Dr Brougham Sdn	**9764**	1050	1775
Marquis Wgn (6 cyl)	**9958**	950	1675
Marquis Wgn w/Brougham Decor Option (6 cyl)	**10232**	1175	1900
TOPAZ 4			
2 Dr GS	**8874**	450	825
4 Dr GS	**8874**	550	1025
2 Dr LS	**9277**	550	1025
4 Dr LS	**9277**	650	1225
2 Dr GS Diesel	**9432**	125	325
4 Dr GS Diesel	**9432**	200	400
2 Dr LS Diesel	**9834**	200	400
4 Dr LS Diesel	**9834**	250	500

NOTE: Power brakes standard on Capri, Lynx Wagons, Marquis, Grand Marquis, Topaz and Cougar. Power windows standard on Grand Marquis and Cougar LS.

1983 — ALL BODY STYLES

Year-Model-Body Type	Original List	Current Whlse	Average Retail
CAPRI	—	750	1475
CAPRI RS	—	1275	2000
COUGAR	—	1200	1925
GRAND MARQUIS	—	1325	2050
LN7	—	175	375
LYNX	—	225	475
MARQUIS	—	850	1550
ZEPHYR	—	450	825

OLDSMOBILE

1992

Year-Model-Body Type	Original List	Current Whlse	Average Retail
ACHIEVA 4			
2 Dr S Cpe	**14100**	—	—
4 Dr S Sdn	**14200**	—	—
2 Dr SL Cpe	**15325**	—	—
4 Dr SL Sdn	**15425**	—	—
ADD FOR:			
2.3 Liter 16V 4 Cyl Engine (S)	**410**	—	—
Styled Aluminum Wheels			
(S)	**391**	—	—
(SL)	**218**	—	—
CUSTOM CRUISER 8			
4 Dr Wgn	**20995**	—	—
ADD FOR:			
5.7 Liter 8 Cyl Eng	**250**	—	—
Leather Seat Trim	**515**	—	—
Cast Aluminum Wheels	**330**	—	—
CUTLASS CIERA 4*			
4 Dr S Sdn	**13585**	—	—
4 Dr S Cruiser Wgn	**14690**	—	—
4 Dr SL Sdn (6 cyl)	**16895**	—	—
4 Dr SL Cruiser Wgn (6 cyl)	**17395**	—	—

* For 6 cylinder models add $— wholesale and $— retail.

Year-Model-Body Type	Original List	Current Whlse	Average Retail
ADD FOR:			
Leather Seat Trim (SL)	**515**	—	—
Wire Wheel Discs	**240**	—	—
Styled Aluminum Wheels	**295**	—	—
CUTLASS SUPREME 6			
2 Dr S Cpe	**15695**	—	—
4 Dr S Sdn	**15795**	—	—
2 Dr Conv	**21995**	—	—
2 Dr International Cpe	**21795**	—	—
4 Dr International Sdn	**21895**	—	—
ADD FOR:			
3.4 Liter 6 Cyl Eng			
(S Cpe)	**1285**	—	—
(S Sdn)	**1570**	—	—
Anti-Lock Brakes (S, Conv)	**450**	—	—
Leather Seat Trim			
(S, Conv)	**515**	—	—
(International)	**425**	—	—
Cast Aluminum Wheels	**285**	—	—
EIGHTY-EIGHT ROYALE 6			
4 Dr Sdn	**18495**	—	—
4 Dr LS Sdn	**21395**	—	—

Year-Model-Body Type	Original List	Current Whlse	Average Retail
ADD FOR:			
LSS Pkg (LS)	**1995**	—	—
Anti-Lock Brakes (Base)	**450**	—	—
Electronic Instrument Cluster (LS)	**449**	—	—
Wire Wheel Discs	**240**	—	—
Styled Aluminum Wheels	**274**	—	—
NINETY-EIGHT REGENCY 6			
4 Dr Sdn	**24595**	—	—
NINETY-EIGHT REGENCY ELITE 6			
4 Dr Sdn	**26195**	—	—
NINETY-EIGHT TOURING 6			
4 Dr Sdn	**28995**	—	—
ADD FOR:			
3.8 Liter Supercharged 6 Cyl Eng (Touring)	**1022**	—	—
Electronic Instrument Cluster (Regency, Elite)	**449**	—	—
Leather Seat Trim (Regency, Elite)	**515**	—	—
TORONADO 6			
2 Dr Cpe	**24695**	—	—
2 Dr Trofeo Cpe	**27295**	—	—
ADD FOR:			
Visual Information System	**1295**	—	—
Leather Seat Trim (Base)	**425**	—	—
Mobile Telephone	**995**	—	—

NOTE: Power windows standard on Cutlass Supreme Convertible & International, Eighty-Eight Royale, Ninety-Eight and Toronado. Power door locks standard on Achieva, Cutlass Ciera, Cutlass Supreme International, Eight-Eight Royale LS, Ninety-Eight and Toronado. Power seat standard on Cutlass Ciera SL, Ninety-Eight Elite & Touring and Toronado. Tilt steering wheel standard on Cutlass Supreme International, Eighty-Eight Royale, Custom Cruiser, Ninety-Eight and Toronado. Cruise control standard on Cutlass Supreme International, Eighty-Eight Royale LS, Ninety-Eight and Toronado.

1991

Year-Model-Body Type	Original List	Current Whlse	Average Retail
BRAVADA 6			
4 Dr 4WD Wgn	**23795**	16200	18850
CUSTOM CRUISER 8			
4 Dr Wgn	**20495**	14575	17100
CUTLASS CALAIS 4*			
2 Dr Cpe	**11595**	6900	8025
4 Dr Sdn	**11595**	6900	8025
2 Dr S Cpe	**11795**	7450	8650
4 Dr S Sdn	**12895**	7450	8650
2 Dr SL Cpe	**15095**	8225	9500
4 Dr SL Sdn	**15195**	8225	9500
2 Dr International Cpe	**16295**	9525	10975
4 Dr International Sdn	**16395**	9525	10975

* For models with quad 4 engine (std on SL) add $375 wholesale and $375 retail.

Year-Model-Body Type	Original List	Current Whlse	Average Retail
CUTLASS CIERA 4*			
4 Dr Sdn	**13325**	8225	9500
2 Dr S Cpe	**14225**	8575	9900
4 Dr S Sdn	**13825**	8675	10025
4 Dr S Cruiser Wgn	**14725**	9075	10450
4 Dr SL Sdn (6 cyl)	**15895**	9725	11200
4 Dr SL Cruiser Wgn (6 cyl)	**16595**	10325	11925

* For 6 cylinder models add $450 wholesale and $450 retail.

Year-Model-Body Type	Original List	Current Whlse	Average Retail
CUTLASS SUPREME 4*			
2 Dr Cpe	**14995**	8925	10300
4 Dr Sdn	**15095**	8925	10300
2 Dr SL Cpe (6 cyl)	**16895**	9850	11350
4 Dr SL Sdn (6 cyl)	**16995**	9850	11350
2 Dr International Cpe (6 cyl)	**19695**	11100	12825
4 Dr International Sdn (6 cyl)	**19795**	11100	12825
2 Dr Conv Cpe (6 cyl)	**20995**	—	—

* For 6 cylinder models add $200 wholesale and $200 retail.

Year-Model-Body Type	Original List	Current Whlse	Average Retail
EIGHTY-EIGHT ROYALE 6			
2 Dr Cpe	**17095**	10800	12475
4 Dr Sdn	**17195**	10950	12625
2 Dr Brougham Cpe	**18695**	11800	13625
4 Dr Brougham Sdn	**18795**	15425	18075
NINETY-EIGHT REGENCY 6			
4 Dr Elite Sdn	**23695**	15425	18075
NINETY-EIGHT TOURING SEDAN 6			
4 Dr Sdn	**28595**	17675	20325
TORONADO 6			
2 Dr Cpe	**23795**	13775	16150
2 Dr Trofeo Cpe	**26495**	15650	18300
ADD FOR:			
Anti-lock Brakes (Cutlass Supreme)	**925**	485	595
Leather Pkg (Bravada)	**545**	295	360
(Calais Int., Toronado Base)	**425**	230	280
(Custom Cruiser, Ciera SL Sdn, Cutlass Supreme, Ninety-Eight Elite)	**515**	280	340

NOTE: Power brakes standard on all models. Anti-lock brakes standard on Custom Cruiser,

Refer To Optional Equipment Schedules

Year-Model-Body Type	Original List	Current Whlse	Average Retail

Calais International and Ninety-Eight. Air bag standard on Custom Cruiser, Ninety-Eight and Toronado. Power window standard on Cutlass Supreme Convertible, Ninety-Eight and Toronado. Power door locks standard on Cutlass Supreme International, Ninety-Eight and Toronado. Power seat standard on Custom Cruiser, Ciera SL, Cutlass Supreme International, Ninety-Eight and Toronado.

1990

Year-Model-Body Type	Original List	Current Whlse	Average Retail
CUSTOM CRUISER 8			
4 Dr Wgn	**17595**	8550	9875
CUTLASS CALAIS 4*			
2 Dr Cpe	**11255**	5125	6050
4 Dr Sdn	**11255**	5125	6050
2 Dr S Cpe	**12155**	5650	6575
4 Dr S Sdn	**12255**	5650	6575
2 Dr SL Cpe	**13915**	6350	7400
4 Dr SL Sdn	**14015**	6350	7400
2 Dr International Cpe	**14895**	7500	8700
4 Dr International Sdn	**14995**	7500	8700

* For 6 cylinder models add $300 wholesale and $300 retail.

Year-Model-Body Type	Original List	Current Whlse	Average Retail
CUTLASS CIERA 4*			
4 Dr Sdn	**12800**	5575	6500
2 Dr S Cpe	**13000**	5900	6825
4 Dr S Sdn	**13300**	6000	6925
4 Dr Cruiser Wgn	**14200**	6350	7400
4 Dr SL Sdn (6 cyl)	**14695**	6950	8100
4 Dr SL Cruiser Wgn (6 cyl)	**15295**	7450	8650
2 Dr International Cpe (6 cyl)	**15995**	8175	9450
4 Dr International Sdn (6 cyl)	**16795**	8275	9550

* For 6 cylinder models add $400 wholesale and $400 retail.

Year-Model-Body Type	Original List	Current Whlse	Average Retail
CUTLASS SUPREME 4*			
2 Dr Cpe	**14495**	7000	8150
4 Dr Sdn	**14595**	7000	8150
2 Dr International Cpe	**17995**	8850	10225
4 Dr International Sdn	**17995**	8850	10225
2 Dr SL Cpe (6 cyl)	**16095**	7850	9125
4 Dr SL Sdn (6 cyl)	**16195**	7850	9125

* For 6 cylinder models add $200 wholesale and $200 retail.

Year-Model-Body Type	Original List	Current Whlse	Average Retail
EIGHTY-EIGHT ROYALE 6			
2 Dr Cpe	**15895**	8125	9375
4 Dr Sdn	**15995**	8225	9500
2 Dr Brougham Cpe	**17295**	8975	10375
4 Dr Brougham Sdn	**17395**	9125	10500
NINETY-EIGHT REGENCY 6			
4 Dr Sdn	**19995**	10300	11875
4 Dr Brougham Sdn	**21595**	11225	12975
TORONADO 6			
2 Dr Cpe	**21995**	11275	13025
2 Dr Trofeo Cpe	**24995**	12900	15225
TOURING SEDAN			
4 Dr Sdn	**26795**	13250	15575
ADD FOR:			
Air Bag Supplemental Restraint System (Eighty-Eight, Ninety-Eight)	**850**	390	475
Anti-Lock Brakes (Cutlass Supreme, Eighty-Eight, Toronado Base)	**925**	425	520
Visual Information Center (Toronado)	**1295**	550	670
2.3 Liter Quad 4 Eng (Cutlass Calais S)	**660**	305	370
(Cutlass Calais International)	**400**	185	225
(Cutlass Supreme Base)	**325**	150	180

NOTE: Power brakes standard on all models. Power door locks and power seat standard on Cutlass Supreme International.

1989

Year-Model-Body Type	Original List	Current Whlse	Average Retail
CUSTOM CRUISER 8			
4 Dr Wgn	**16795**	6800	7925
CUTLASS CALAIS 4*			
2 Dr Cpe	**11505**	4175	5100
4 Dr Sdn	**11505**	4175	5100
2 Dr S Cpe	**12585**	4600	5525
4 Dr S Sdn	**12685**	4600	5525
2 Dr SL Cpe	**13585**	4900	5825
4 Dr SL Sdn	**13685**	4900	5825
2 Dr International Cpe	**14910**	6075	6975
4 Dr International Sdn	**15010**	6075	6975

* For models with quad 4 or 6 cylinder engines add $350 wholesale and $350 retail.

Year-Model-Body Type	Original List	Current Whlse	Average Retail
CUTLASS CIERA 4*			
2 Dr Cpe	**12721**	4400	5325
4 Dr Sdn	**13221**	4525	5450
4 Dr Cruiser Wgn	**14563**	4825	5750
2 Dr SL Cpe	**13985**	4900	5825
4 Dr SL Sdn	**14795**	5050	5975
4 Dr SL Cruiser Wgn	**16014**	5525	6450
2 Dr International Cpe (6 cyl)	**15995**	6475	7525
4 Dr International Sdn (6 cyl)	**16795**	6600	7675

Year-Model-Body Type	Original List	Current Whlse	Average Retail
* For 6 cylinder models add $375 wholesale and $375 retail.			
CUTLASS SUPREME 6			
2 Dr Cpe	**14370**	5800	6725
2 Dr SL Cpe	**15270**	6400	7450
2 Dr International Cpe	**16995**	7275	8450
EIGHTY-EIGHT ROYALE 6			
2 Dr Cpe	**15195**	6525	7600
4 Dr Sdn	**15295**	6650	7750
2 Dr Brougham Cpe	**16295**	7225	8400
4 Dr Brougham Sdn	**16395**	7375	8550
NINETY-EIGHT REGENCY 6			
4 Dr Sdn	**19295**	7550	8775
4 Dr Brougham Sdn	**20495**	8325	9625
TORONADO 6			
2 Dr Cpe	**21995**	8625	9950
2 Dr Trofeo Cpe	**24995**	9775	11250
TOURING SEDAN 6			
4 Dr Sdn	**25995**	10075	11625
ADD FOR:			
2.3 Liter Quad 4 Eng (Cutlass Calais)	**660**	250	305
Quad 4 App Pkg (Cutlass Calais S)	**1180**	445	545
Anti-Lock Brakes (Cutlass Supreme, 88, 98, Toronado)	**925**	340	415
Visual Information System (Toronado)	**1295**	455	550

NOTE: Power brakes standard on all models. Power windows, power locks and power seat standard on 98, Touring Sedan and Toronado.

1988

Year-Model-Body Type	Original List	Current Whlse	Average Retail
CUSTOM CRUISER 8			
4 Dr Wgn	**15655**	5425	6350
CUTLASS CALAIS 4*			
2 Dr Cpe	**11485**	3600	4500
4 Dr Sdn	**11485**	3600	4500
2 Dr SL Cpe	**12360**	3900	4800
4 Dr SL Sdn	**12360**	3900	4800
2 Dr International Cpe (quad 4 engine)	**14185**	4700	5625
4 Dr International Sdn (quad 4 engine)	**14185**	4700	5625
* For models with quad 4 or 6 cylinder engines add $300 wholesale and $300 retail.			
CUTLASS CIERA 4*			
2 Dr Cpe	**11770**	3275	4175
4 Dr Sdn	**12431**	3375	4275
4 Dr Cruiser Wgn	**13095**	3625	4525
2 Dr SL Cpe	**12620**	3750	4650
4 Dr Brougham Sdn	**13400**	3850	4750
4 Dr Brougham Cruiser Wgn	**13770**	4100	5025
2 Dr International Cpe (6 cyl)	**14995**	5100	6025
4 Dr International Sdn (6 cyl)	**15825**	5200	6125
* For 6 cylinder models add $325 wholesale and $325 retail.			
CUTLASS SUPREME 6			
2 Dr Cpe	**13621**	4650	5575
2 Dr SL Cpe	**14270**	5125	6050
2 Dr International Cpe	**16259**	5850	6775
CUTLASS SUPREME CLASSIC 8			
2 Dr Cpe	**13938**	4700	5625
2 Dr Brougham Cpe	**14770**	5200	6125
DELTA 88 ROYALE 6			
2 Dr Cpe	**14498**	4900	5825
4 Dr Sdn	**14498**	5025	5950
2 Dr Brougham Cpe	**15451**	5650	6575
4 Dr Brougham Sdn	**15451**	5775	6700
FIRENZA 4			
2 Dr Cpe	**10675**	3075	3975
4 Dr Sdn	**10675**	3175	4075
4 Dr Cruiser Wgn	**11375**	3325	4225
NINETY-EIGHT REGENCY 6			
4 Dr Sdn	**17995**	6025	6950
4 Dr Brougham Sdn	**19371**	6700	7800
TORONADO 6			
2 Dr Cpe	**20598**	6475	7525
2 Dr Trofeo Cpe	**22695**	7175	8325
TOURING SEDAN 6			
4 Dr Sdn	**24470**	8200	9475
ADD FOR:			
Sport Option Pkg (Firenza)	**617**	180	220
Anti-Lock Braking (Ninety-Eight)	**925**	265	325
Deluxe Mobile Telephone (Toronado)	**1795**	175	215

NOTE: Power brakes standard on all models. Power seat standard on Touring Sedan and Toronado Series. Power windows and power door locks standard on Ninety-Eight Series, Touring Sedan and Toronado Series.

1987

Year-Model-Body Type	Original List	Current Whlse	Average Retail
CALAIS 4*			
2 Dr Cpe	**10906**	2600	3475
4 Dr Sdn	**10906**	2600	3475
2 Dr Supreme Cpe	**11562**	2850	3750
4 Dr Supreme Sdn	**11562**	2850	3750

* For 6 cylinder models add $300 wholesale and

Refer To Optional Equipment Schedules

Year-Model-Body Type	Original List	Current Whlse	Average Retail
$300 retail.			
CUSTOM CRUISER 8			
4 Dr Wgn	**14420**	4050	4950
CUTLASS CIERA 4*			
2 Dr 'S' Cpe	**11715**	2600	3475
4 Dr Sdn	**11715**	2675	3575
4 Dr Cruiser	**12208**	2900	3800
2 Dr 'SL' Cpe	**12522**	3000	3900
4 Dr Brougham Sdn	**12522**	3075	3975
4 Dr Brougham Cruiser	**12870**	3275	4175
* For 6 cylinder models add $300 wholesale and $300 retail.			
CUTLASS SUPREME 6*			
2 Dr Cpe	**12314**	3350	4250
4 Dr Sdn	**12314**	3150	4050
2 Dr Brougham Cpe	**13153**	3750	4650
4 Dr Brougham Sdn	**13153**	3550	4450
2 Dr Salon Cpe	**13472**	4075	5000
* For 8 cylinder models add $350 wholesale and $350 retail.			
DELTA 88 ROYALE 6			
2 Dr Cpe	**13639**	3825	4725
4 Dr Sdn	**13639**	3975	4875
2 Dr Brougham Cpe	**14536**	4400	5325
4 Dr Brougham Sdn	**14536**	4550	5475
FIRENZA 4			
2 Dr Cpe	**9931**	2150	3000
2 Dr 'S' Htchbk	**10366**	2225	3075
4 Dr Sdn	**9889**	2225	3075
4 Dr Cruiser Wgn	**10536**	2350	3225
2 Dr 'LC' Cpe	**10804**	2475	3350
2 Dr 'GT' Htchbk (6 cyl)	**12199**	2925	3825
4 Dr 'LX' Sdn	**10572**	2550	3425
NINETY-EIGHT 6			
4 Dr Sdn	**17371**	4250	5175
2 Dr Brougham Cpe	**18388**	4675	5600
4 Dr Brougham Sdn	**18388**	4825	5750
4 Dr Touring Sdn	**24107**	6325	7350
TORONADO 6			
2 Dr Brougham Cpe	**19938**	4800	5725
ADD FOR:			
Calais GT Pkg (Base Calais)	**1350**	400	485
Ciera GT Pkg			
(S Cpe)	**3060**	905	1100
(Base Ciera Sdn)	**3060**	905	1100
Ninety-Eight Grande Premium Interior Pkg (Ninety-Eight Regency)	**975**	290	350
Removable Glass Panels (Cutlass Supreme)	**895**	265	320
3.8 Liter V6 SFI Eng (Cutlass Ciera)	**745**	220	270

NOTE: Power brakes standard on all models. Power seat and power windows standard on Ninety-Eight Regency and Toronado.

1986

Year-Model-Body Type	Original List	Current Whlse	Average Retail
CALAIS 4*			
2 Dr Cpe	**10656**	1875	2725
4 Dr Sdn	**10856**	1875	2725
2 Dr Supreme Cpe	**11050**	2100	2950
4 Dr Supreme Sdn	**11249**	2100	2950
* For 6 cylinder models add $250 wholesale and $250 retail.			
CUSTOM CRUISER 8			
4 Dr Wgn	**13838**	2625	3525
CUTLASS CIERA 4*			
2 Dr LS Cpe	**11921**	1800	2650
4 Dr LS Sdn	**11394**	1900	2750
4 Dr LS Cruiser	**11774**	2100	2950
2 Dr Brougham Cpe	**11420**	2150	3000
4 Dr Brougham Sdn	**11921**	2225	3075
* For 6 cylinder models add $300 wholesale and $300 retail.			
CUTLASS SUPREME 6*			
2 Dr Cpe	**11821**	2350	3225
4 Dr Sdn	**12001**	2175	3025
2 Dr Brougham Cpe	**12554**	2650	3550
4 Dr Brougham Sdn	**12703**	2475	3350
2 Dr Salon Cpe	**12874**	2975	3875
* For 8 cylinder models add $325 wholesale and $325 retail.			
DELTA 88 ROYALE 6			
2 Dr Cpe	**12955**	2875	3775
4 Dr Sdn	**12955**	3025	3925
2 Dr Brougham Cpe	**13667**	3300	4200
4 Dr Brougham Sdn	**13667**	3450	4350
FIRENZA 4			
2 Dr Cpe	**9389**	1725	2575
2 Dr S Htchbk	**9566**	1800	2650
4 Dr Sdn	**9663**	1800	2650
4 Dr Cruiser Wgn	**9889**	1900	2750
2 Dr LC Cpe	**10035**	2000	2850
2 Dr GT Htchbk (6 cyl)	**11232**	2475	3350
4 Dr LX Sdn	**10051**	2100	2950
* For 6 cylinder models add $200 wholesale and $200 retail.			
NINETY-EIGHT 6			
2 Dr Regency Cpe	**16062**	3175	4075
4 Dr Regency Sdn	**16509**	3300	4200
2 Dr Regency Brougham Cpe	**17591**	3700	4600
4 Dr Regency			

Year-Model-Body Type	Original List	Current Whlse	Average Retail
Brougham Sdn	**17509**	3850	4750
TORONADO 6			
2 Dr Brougham Cpe	**19850**	3700	4600
ADD FOR:			
Calais GT Pkg (Base Calais Cpe)	**1350**	290	350
Ciera ES Pkg (Base Ciera Sdn)	**1992**	425	520
Ciera GT Pkg (Base Ciera Cpe)	**3330**	710	865
(Base Ciera Sdn)	**2980**	635	775
Ciera Holiday Cpe Pkg (Ciera Brougham Cpe)	**680**	145	175
Cutlass 442 Pkg (Cutlass Supreme Salon)	**2075**	445	540
ES Sdn Pkg (Base Calais Sdn)	**995**	210	260
Ninety-Eight Grande Premium Interior Pkg (Ninety-Eight Regency Brougham)	**975**	205	255
Removable Glass Panels (Cutlass Supreme)	**895**	190	235
2.8 Liter V6 MPFI Eng (Cutlass Ciera)	**485**	105	125
3.8 Liter V6 SFI Eng (Delta 88 Royale)	**370**	80	95

NOTE: Power windows standard on Ninety-Eight Regency and Toronado. Power seat standard on Toronado. Power brakes standard on all models.

1985

Year-Model-Body Type	Original List	Current Whlse	Average Retail
CALAIS 4*			
2 Dr Cpe	**9739**	1425	2175
2 Dr Supreme Cpe	**10091**	1625	2475
CUTLASS CIERA 4*			
2 Dr LS Cpe	**10243**	1275	2000
4 Dr LS Sdn	**10437**	1250	1975
4 Dr Cruiser	**10805**	1250	1975
2 Dr Brougham Cpe	**10733**	1425	2175
4 Dr Brougham Sdn	**10948**	1525	2375
* For 6 cylinder models add $250 wholesale and $250 retail.			
CUTLASS SUPREME 6*			
2 Dr Cpe	**10743**	1725	2575
4 Dr Sdn	**10910**	1550	2400
2 Dr Brougham Cpe	**11427**	1975	2825
4 Dr Brougham Sdn	**11564**	1775	2625
2 Dr Salon Cpe	**11735**	2175	3025
* For 8 cylinder models add $300 wholesale and $300 retail.			
DELTA 88 6*			
2 Dr Royale Cpe	**11448**	1700	2550
4 Dr Royale Sdn	**11548**	1825	2675
2 Dr Royale Brougham Cpe	**11938**	2075	2925
4 Dr Royale Brougham Sdn	**12043**	2200	3050
4 Dr Brougham LS Sdn (8 cyl)	**14618**	3025	3925
4 Dr Custom Cruiser (8 cyl)	**12610**	2275	3150
* For 8 cylinder models add $375 wholesale and $375 retail.			
FIRENZA 4			
2 Dr S Cpe	**8873**	1225	1950
4 Dr Sdn	**8964**	1300	2025
2 Dr SX Cpe	**9465**	1425	2175
4 Dr LX Sdn	**9325**	1525	2375
4 Dr 2 Seat Wgn	**9183**	1350	2100
4 Dr LX 3 Seat Wgn	**9562**	1600	2450
NINETY-EIGHT 6			
2 Dr Regency Cpe	**15295**	2200	3050
4 Dr Regency Sdn	**15224**	2325	3200
2 Dr Regency Brougham Cpe	**16251**	2600	3475
4 Dr Regency Brougham Sdn	**16181**	2725	3625
TORONADO 8			
2 Dr Brougham Cpe	**17134**	2700	3600
ADD FOR:			
Calais 500 Pkg (Base Calais)	**1595**	210	255
Caliente Pkg (Toronado)	**1970**	260	315
Ciera GT Pkg (Ciera LS Cpe)	**3295**	430	525
Cutlass 442 Pkg (Cutlass Supreme Salon)	**1275**	400	500
ES Pkg (Cutlass Ciera LS Sdn)	**895**	115	145
GT Pkg (Firenza S Cpe)	**1360**	180	220
Holiday Cpe Pkg (Cutlass Ciera Brougham Cpe)	**565**	75	90

NOTE: Power brakes standard on all models. Power windows standard on Delta 88 Brougham LS and Ninety-Eight. Power seat standard on Delta 88 and Ninety-Eight. Power locks standard on Delta 88 Brougham LS and Ninety-Eight.

Refer To Optional Equipment Schedules

Year-Model-Body Type	Original List	Current Whlse	Average Retail
1984			
CUTLASS CIERA 4*			
2 Dr LS Cpe	**9735**	950	1675
4 Dr LS Sdn	**9924**	1050	1775
4 Dr Cruiser Wgn	**10272**	1175	1900
2 Dr Brougham Cpe	**10240**	1150	1875
4 Dr Brougham Sdn	**10442**	1225	1950
* For 6 cylinder models add $150 wholesale and $150 retail.			
CUTLASS SUPREME 6*			
2 Dr Cpe	**10208**	1275	2000
4 Dr Sdn	**10361**	1125	1850
2 Dr Brougham Cpe	**10847**	1500	2350
4 Dr Brougham Sdn	**10977**	1325	2050
2 Dr Calais Cpe	**11106**	1550	2400
* For 8 cylinder models add $200 wholesale and $200 retail.			
DELTA 88 ROYALE 6*			
2 Dr Cpe	**10770**	1175	1900
4 Dr Sdn	**10882**	1300	2025
2 Dr Brougham Cpe	**11239**	1400	2150
4 Dr Brougham Sdn	**11330**	1525	2375
4 Dr Custom Cruiser (8 cyl)	**11669**	1325	2050
4 Dr LS Sdn (8 cyl)	**13854**	1875	2725
* For 8 cylinder models add $300 wholesale and $300 retail.			
FIRENZA 4			
2 Dr S Cpe	**8435**	675	1275
4 Dr Sdn	**8522**	750	1475
4 Dr Cruiser	**8742**	800	1500
2 Dr SX Cpe	**8974**	825	1525
4 Dr LX Sdn	**8870**	900	1625
4 Dr LX Cruiser	**9090**	925	1650
NINETY-EIGHT 8			
2 Dr Regency Cpe	**13962**	1700	2550
4 Dr Regency Sdn	**14139**	1800	2650
4 Dr Regency Brougham Sdn	**15189**	2125	2975
OMEGA 4*			
2 Dr Cpe	**8780**	525	975
4 Dr Sdn	**8978**	600	1125
2 Dr Brougham Cpe	**9069**	700	1325
4 Dr Brougham Sdn	**9250**	750	1475
* For 6 cylinder models add $150 wholesale and $150 retail.			
TORONADO 6*			
2 Dr Brougham Cpe	**16096**	2025	2875
* For 8 cylinder models add $300 wholesale and $300 retail.			

NOTE: Power brakes standard on all models. Power windows standard on Ninety-Eight and Toronado. Vinyl roof standard on Ninety-Eight Brougham.

Year-Model-Body Type	Original List	Current Whlse	Average Retail
1983 — ALL BODY STYLES			
CUTLASS CIERA	—	725	1375
CUTLASS SUPREME	—	925	1650
DELTA 88	—	1100	1825
FIRENZA	—	475	875
NINETY-EIGHT	—	1500	2350
OMEGA	—	425	775
TORONADO	—	1425	2175

PLYMOUTH

Year-Model-Body Type	Original List	Current Whlse	Average Retail
1992			
ACCLAIM 4*			
4 Dr Sdn	**12532**	—	—
* For 6 cylinder models add $— wholesale and $— retail.			
ADD FOR:			
Anti-Lock Brakes	**899**	—	—
Cast Aluminum Wheels	**328**	—	—
LASER 4			
2 Dr Htchbk	**13375**	—	—
2 Dr RS Htchbk	**14915**	—	—
2 Dr RS Turbo Htchbk	**16965**	—	—
2 Dr RS Turbo AWD Htchbk (NA w/auto trans)	**17820**	—	—
ADD FOR:			
Anti-Lock Brakes	**943**	—	—
Alloy Wheels (RS, RS Turbo)	**321**	—	—
SUNDANCE 4			
2 Dr America Htchbk	**9733**	—	—
4 Dr America Sdn	**10131**	—	—
2 Dr Highline Htchbk	**10793**	—	—
4 Dr Highline Sdn	**11193**	—	—
2 Dr Duster Htchbk (6 cyl)	**11439**	—	—
4 Dr Duster Sdn (6 cyl)	**11839**	—	—
ADD FOR:			
2.5 Liter 4 Cyl Eng (Highline)	**286**	—	—
Aluminum Wheels	**328**	—	—

Year-Model-Body Type	Original List	Current Whlse	Average Retail
1991			
ACCLAIM 4 *			
4 Dr Sdn	**11423**	6825	7950
4 Dr LE Sdn	**13752**	7425	8625
* For 6 cylinder models add $425 wholesale and			

Year-Model-Body Type	Original List	Current Whlse	Average Retail
$425 retail.			
ACCLAIM LX 6			
4 Dr Sdn	**15252**	7250	8425
LASER 4			
3 Dr Lftbk Cpe	**13014**	8575	9900
3 Dr RS Lftbk Cpe	**14269**	9250	10650
3 Dr RS Turbo Lftbk Cpe	**15588**	10625	12250
SUNDANCE 4			
3 Dr America Cpe	**9321**	5375	6300
5 Dr America Sdn	**9621**	5475	6400
3 Dr Highline Cpe	**10286**	6175	7200
5 Dr Highline Sdn	**10586**	6275	7300
3 Dr RS Cpe	**11486**	7050	8175
5 Dr RS Sdn	**11812**	7150	8300
ADD FOR:			
Anti-lock Brakes (Acclaim)	**899**	545	665
(Laser ex. Base)	**925**	560	685

NOTE: Power brakes standard on all models. Air bag standard on Acclaim and Sundance.

1990

Year-Model-Body Type	Original List	Current Whlse	Average Retail
ACCLAIM 4*			
4 Dr Sdn	**10931**	5225	6150
4 Dr LE Sdn	**13216**	5800	6725
* For 6 cylinder models add $400 wholesale and $400 retail.			
ACCLAIM LX 6			
4 Dr Sdn	**14670**	5650	6575
HORIZON 4			
4 Dr Htchbk	**8698**	3025	3925
LASER 4			
3 Dr Lftbk Cpe	**12339**	6425	7475
3 Dr RS Lftbk Cpe	**13384**	7025	8150
3 Dr RS Turbo Lftbk Cpe (NA w/auto trans)	**14707**	8450	9750
SUNDANCE 4			
3 Dr Lftbk Cpe	**10156**	4825	5750
5 Dr Lftbk Sdn	**10356**	4925	5850
ADD FOR:			
RS Pkg (Sundance)	**1071**	580	705
2.0 Liter 4 Cyl Eng (Laser)	**873**	470	575
2.5 Liter 4 Cyl Eng (Sundance)	**280**	150	185
2.5 Liter 4 Cyl Turbo Eng (Acclaim)	**700**	380	460
(Sundance)	**552**	300	365

NOTE: Power brakes standard on all models.

1989

Year-Model-Body Type	Original List	Current Whlse	Average Retail
ACCLAIM 4			
4 Dr Sdn	**11231**	4375	5300
4 Dr LE Sdn	**12606**	4825	5750
ACCLAIM LX 6			
4 Dr Sdn	**13970**	5725	6650
GRAN FURY SALON 8			
4 Dr Sdn	**12850**	4050	4950
HORIZON AMERICA 4			
5 Dr Htchbk	**8298**	2350	3225
RELIANT AMERICA 4			
2 Dr Sdn	**9299**	3075	3975
4 Dr Sdn	**9299**	3150	4050
SUNDANCE 4			
3 Dr Lftbk Cpe	**9706**	3625	4525
5 Dr Lftbk Sdn	**9906**	3725	4625
ADD FOR:			
2.5 Liter 4 Cyl Turbo Eng (Acclaim Base & LE)	**678**	310	380
Turbo Engine Pkg (Sundance w/RS Pkg)	**610**	280	340
(Sundance w/Pop Equip Pkg)	**923**	425	515

NOTE: Power brakes standard on all models.

1988

Year-Model-Body Type	Original List	Current Whlse	Average Retail
CARAVELLE 4*			
4 Dr Sdn	**11434**	3025	3925
* For 153 CID 4 cylinder engine models add $100 wholesale and $100 retail.			
CARAVELLE SE 4			
4 Dr Sdn	**12403**	3350	4250
GRAN FURY 8			
4 Dr Sdn	**12127**	3300	4200
GRAN FURY SALON 8			
4 Dr Sdn	**12237**	2900	3800
HORIZON AMERICA 4			
4 Dr Htchbk	**7868**	1775	2625
RELIANT AMERICA 4*			
2 Dr Sdn	**9064**	2450	3325
4 Dr Sdn	**9064**	2525	3400
4 Dr Wgn	**9664**	2925	3825
* For 153 CID 4 cylinder engine models add $100 wholesale and $100 retail.			
SUNDANCE 4*			
2 Dr Lftbk Cpe	**9225**	2750	3650
4 Dr Lftbk Sdn	**9475**	2850	3750
* For 153 CID 4 cylinder engine models add $100 wholesale and $100 retail.			
ADD FOR:			
RS Pkg (Sundance)	**1390**	525	640

Refer To Optional Equipment Schedules

Year-Model-Body Type	Original List	Current Whlse	Average Retail
Turbo Engine Pkg			
(Sundance w/RS Pkg)	**467**	175	215
(Sundance w/o RS Pkg)	**780**	295	360
2.2 Liter 4 Cyl Turbo Eng (Base Caravelle w/o Convenience Pkg)	**399**	150	185
(Base Caravelle w/ Convenience Pkg, Caravelle SE)	**678**	255	310

NOTE: Power brakes standard on Horizon America, Reliant America, Sundance, Caravelle Series and Gran Fury Series.

1987

Year-Model-Body Type	Original List	Current Whlse	Average Retail
CARAVELLE 4*			
4 Dr Sdn	**10595**	1975	2825
CARAVELLE SE 4*			
4 Dr Sdn	**11309**	2225	3075

* For 158 CID 4 cylinder engine models add $100 wholesale and $100 retail.

Year-Model-Body Type	Original List	Current Whlse	Average Retail
GRAN FURY SALON 8			
4 Dr HT	**11435**	2025	2875
HORIZON AMERICA 4			
5 Dr Htchbk	**7214**	1350	2100
RELIANT 4			
2 Dr Sdn	**9430**	1625	2475
4 Dr Sdn	**9430**	1700	2550
RELIANT LE 4			
2 Dr Sdn	**9915**	1925	2775
4 Dr Sdn	**9915**	2025	2875
4 Dr Wgn	**10359**	2325	3200
SUNDANCE 4			
2 Dr Lftbk Cpe	**8822**	2150	3000
4 Dr Lftbk Sdn	**9022**	2225	3075
TURISMO 4			
3 Dr Htchbk	**8614**	1775	2625
ADD FOR:			
Salon Luxury Pkg (Gran Fury)	**545**	160	195
2.2 Liter 4 Cyl Turbo Eng (Caravelle)	**678**	200	245
(Sundance)	**806**	240	290

NOTE: Power brakes standard on all models.

1986

Year-Model-Body Type	Original List	Current Whlse	Average Retail
CARAVELLE 4*			
4 Dr Sdn	**10053**	1350	2100
CARAVELLE SE 4*			
4 Dr Sdn	**10622**	1625	2475

* For 158 CID 4 cylinder engine models add $50 wholesale and $50 retail.

Year-Model-Body Type	Original List	Current Whlse	Average Retail
GRAN FURY SALON 8			
4 Dr HT	**10898**	1475	2300
HORIZON 4			
4 Dr Htchbk	**7719**	900	1625
HORIZON SE 4			
4 Dr Htchbk	**7955**	1225	1950
RELIANT 4			
2 Dr Sdn	**8675**	1175	1900
4 Dr Sdn	**8792**	1275	2000
RELIANT LE 4			
2 Dr Sdn	**9578**	1475	2300
4 Dr Sdn	**9698**	1575	2425
4 Dr Wgn	**10197**	1850	2700
RELIANT SE 4			
2 Dr Sdn	**9130**	1325	2050
4 Dr Sdn	**9250**	1400	2150
4 Dr Wgn	**9677**	1700	2550
TURISMO 4			
2 Dr Htchbk	**8297**	1300	2025
TURISMO 2.2 4			
2 Dr Htchbk	**9129**	1700	2550
ADD FOR:			
Salon Luxury Pkg (Gran Fury)	**545**	115	140
Sun/Sound/Shade Pkg (Turismo 2.2)	**552**	120	145
2.2 Liter 4 Cyl Turbo Eng (Caravelle)	**628**	135	165

NOTE: Power brakes standard on all models.

1985

Year-Model-Body Type	Original List	Current Whlse	Average Retail
CARAVELLE 4*			
4 Dr Sdn	**9764**	1125	1850
GRAN FURY SALON 8			
4 Dr HT	**10470**	1050	1775
HORIZON 4			
4 Dr Htchbk	**7413**	725	1375
HORIZON SE 4			
4 Dr Htchbk	**7643**	975	1700
RELIANT 4			
2 Dr Sdn	**8432**	875	1600
4 Dr Sdn	**8547**	950	1675
RELIANT LE 4			
2 Dr Sdn	**9054**	1150	1875
4 Dr Sdn	**9187**	1250	1975
4 Dr Wgn	**9554**	1450	2225
RELIANT SE 4			
2 Dr Sdn	**8716**	1000	1725
4 Dr Sdn	**8834**	1100	1825
4 Dr Wgn	**9334**	1325	2050
TURISMO 4			
2 Dr Htchbk	**7998**	1050	1775

Year-Model-Body Type	Original List	Current Whlse	Average Retail
TURISMO 2.2 4			
2 Dr Htchbk	**8816**	1375	2125
ADD FOR:			
Salon Luxury Pkg (Gran Fury)	**536**	70	85

NOTE: Power brakes standard on all models.

1984

Year-Model-Body Type	Original List	Current Whlse	Average Retail
GRAN FURY 8			
4 Dr HT	**9961**	650	1225
HORIZON 4			
4 Dr Htchbk	**7236**	250	500
HORIZON SE 4			
4 Dr Htchbk	**7441**	475	875
RELIANT 4			
2 Dr Cpe	**8337**	400	725
4 Dr Sdn	**8449**	475	875
RELIANT CUSTOM 4			
2 Seat Wgn	**9123**	650	1225
RELIANT SPECIAL EDITION 4			
2 Dr Cpe	**8858**	575	1075
4 Dr Sdn	**8984**	650	1225
2 Seat Wgn	**9371**	850	1550
TURISMO 4			
2 Dr Htchbk	**7900**	525	975
TURISMO 2.2 4			
2 Dr Htchbk	**8581**	775	1500

NOTE: Power brakes standard on all models.

1983 — ALL BODY STYLES

Year-Model-Body Type	Original List	Current Whlse	Average Retail
GRAN FURY	—	375	675
HORIZON	—	125	325
RELIANT	—	250	500
RELIANT CUSTOM	—	300	575
RELIANT SPECIAL EDITION	—	325	600
TURISMO	—	300	575

PONTIAC

1992

Year-Model-Body Type	Original List	Current Whlse	Average Retail
BONNEVILLE 6			
4 Dr SE Sdn	**18599**	—	—
4 Dr SSE Sdn	**23999**	—	—
4 Dr SSEi	**28045**	—	—
ADD FOR:			
Anti-Lock Brakes (SE)	**450**	—	—
Leather Seat Trim (SSE)	**1419**	—	—
(SSEi)	**779**	—	—
Cast Aluminum Wheels	**340**	—	—
FIREBIRD 6*			
2 Dr Cpe	**13865**	—	—
2 Dr Conv	**20205**	—	—

* For 8 cylinder models add $— wholesale and $— retail.

Year-Model-Body Type	Original List	Current Whlse	Average Retail
FIREBIRD 8			
2 Dr Formula Cpe	**16735**	—	—
2 Dr Trans Am Cpe	**18635**	—	—
2 Dr Trans Am Conv	**24405**	—	—
2 Dr Trans Am GTA Cpe	**25880**	—	—
ADD FOR:			
5.0 Liter Tuned 8 Cyl Engine (Formula)	**745**	—	—
5.7 Liter 8 Cyl Eng (Formula)	**1045**	—	—
(Trans Am)	**300**	—	—
T-Tops	**914**	—	—
Leather Seat Trim (Trans Am)	**780**	—	—
(GTA)	**475**	—	—
GRAND AM 4			
2 Dr SE Cpe	**13284**	—	—
4 Dr SE Sdn	**13384**	—	—
2 Dr GT Cpe	**15084**	—	—
4 Dr GT Sdn	**15184**	—	—
ADD FOR:			
6 Cyl Engine (SE)	**460**	—	—
Quad 4 Engine (SE)	**410**	—	—
Aluminum Wheels	**300**	—	—
GRAND PRIX 6			
4 Dr LE Sdn	**14890**	—	—
2 Dr SE Cpe	**15390**	—	—
4 Dr SE Sdn	**16190**	—	—
2 Dr GT Cpe	**20340**	—	—
4 Dr STE Sdn	**21635**	—	—
ADD FOR:			
3.4 Liter 6 Cyl Eng	**995**	—	—
Anti-Lock Brakes (LE, SE)	**450**	—	—
Leather Seats	**475**	—	—
Aluminum Wheels	**275**	—	—
LE MANS 4			
2 Dr Value Leader Aerocoupe (NA w/auto trans, power steering or air cond)	**8357**	—	—
2 Dr SE Aerocoupe	**9455**	—	—
4 Dr SE Sdn	**10870**	—	—
SUNBIRD LE 4			
2 Dr Cpe	**10860**	—	—
4 Dr Sdn	**10960**	—	—

Refer To Optional Equipment Schedules

Year-Model-Body Type	Original List	Current Whlse	Average Retail
SUNBIRD SE 4*			
2 Dr Cpe	**11620**	—	—
4 Dr Sdn	**11720**	—	—
2 Dr Conv	**16585**	—	—

* For 6 cylinder models add $— wholesale and $— retail.

Year-Model-Body Type	Original List	Current Whlse	Average Retail
SUNBIRD GT 6			
2 Dr Cpe	**14060**	—	—
ADD FOR:			
Aluminum Wheels	**275**	—	—

NOTE: Power windows standard on Bonneville, Firebird GTA, Grand Prix GT & STE, Sunbird SE Convertible & GT. Power door locks standard on Bonneville, Firebird GTA, Grand Am, Grand Prix GT & STE and Sunbird. Power seat standard on Bonneville SSE & SSEi, Grand Prix GT & STE. Tilt steering wheel standard on Bonneville and Firebird. Cruise control standard on Bonneville SSEi and Firebird GTA.

1991

Year-Model-Body Type	Original List	Current Whlse	Average Retail
6000 LE 4*			
4 Dr Sdn	**13829**	7850	9125

* For 6 cylinder models add $425 wholesale and $425 retail.

Year-Model-Body Type	Original List	Current Whlse	Average Retail
6000 LE 6			
4 Dr Wgn	**16699**	8700	10050
6000 SE 6			
4 Dr Sdn	**18399**	9300	10725
BONNEVILLE 6			
4 Dr LE Sdn	**16834**	10800	12475
4 Dr SE Sdn	**20464**	12275	14225
4 Dr SSE Sdn	**25264**	15825	18475
FIREBIRD 6*			
2 Dr Cpe	**13520**	8000	9300
2 Dr Conv	**19989**	—	—

* For 8 cylinder models add $450 wholesale and $450 retail.

Year-Model-Body Type	Original List	Current Whlse	Average Retail
FIREBIRD 8			
2 Dr Formula Cpe	**16060**	9275	10675
2 Dr Trans Am Cpe	**18060**	11875	13725
2 Dr Trans Am Conv	**23510**	—	—
2 Dr Trans Am GTA Cpe	**24530**	—	—
GRAND AM 4*			
2 Dr Cpe	**11474**	6650	7750
4 Dr Sdn	**11674**	6650	7750
2 Dr LE Cpe	**12424**	7100	8250
4 Dr LE Sdn	**12626**	7100	8250
2 Dr SE Cpe	**16899**	8325	9625
4 Dr SE Sdn	**17099**	8325	9625

* For quad 4 4 cylinder LE models add $200 wholesale and $200 retail.

Year-Model-Body Type	Original List	Current Whlse	Average Retail
GRAND PRIX 4*			
4 Dr LE Sdn	**14294**	9275	10675
2 Dr SE Cpe	**14894**	9700	11175
4 Dr SE Sdn	**15284**	9700	11175

* For 3.1 liter 6 cylinder models add $— wholesale and $— retail.

Year-Model-Body Type	Original List	Current Whlse	Average Retail
GRAND PRIX 6			
2 Dr GT Cpe	**19154**	11450	13225
4 Dr STE Sdn	**19994**	11975	13825
LE MANS 4			
2 Dr Value Leader Aerocoupe (NA w/auto trans or power steering)	**7574**	3925	4825
2 Dr LE Aerocoupe	**9709**	5025	5950
4 Dr LE Sdn	**10159**	5225	6150
SUNBIRD 4			
2 Dr Cpe	**9924**	5825	6750
4 Dr Sdn	**10024**	5925	6850
SUNBIRD LE 4			
2 Dr Cpe	**10684**	6525	7600
4 Dr Sdn	**10784**	6600	7675
2 Dr Conv	**15654**	9750	11225
SUNBIRD SE 4			
2 Dr Cpe	**11934**	7175	8325
SUNBIRD GT 6			
2 Dr Cpe	**13684**	8725	10075
ADD FOR:			
Aero Perf. Pkg (Grand Prix SE & GT Cpes)	**2795**	1675	2070
Anti-lock Brakes (Bonneville LE & SE)	**925**	560	685
Leather Seats (Bonneville SSE)	**779**	470	575
(Firebird Trans Am GTA, Grand Prix GT)	**475**	290	350
Sport Perf. Pkg (Grand Am LE)	**1650**	1000	1220
T-Tops (Firebird)	**920**	560	680

NOTE: Power brakes standard on all models. Anti-lock brakes standard on Bonneville SSE and Grand Am SE. Power seat standard on Bonneville SE & SSE, Grand Prix GT & STE. Power windows and power door locks standard on 6000 SE Sdn, Bonneville SE & SSE, Firebird Trans Am GTA, Grand Am SE, Grand Prix GT & STE.

1990

Year-Model-Body Type	Original List	Current Whlse	Average Retail
6000 LE 4*			
4 Dr Sdn	**12954**	5875	6800

* For 6 cylinder models add $400 wholesale and $400 retail.

Refer To Optional Equipment Schedules

Year-Model-Body Type	Original List	Current Whlse	Average Retail
6000 LE 6			
4 Dr Wgn	**15309**	6600	7675
6000 SE 6			
4 Dr Sdn	**16909**	7150	8300
4 Dr Wgn	**18509**	7500	8700
BONNEVILLE 6			
4 Dr LE Sdn	**15774**	7925	9200
4 Dr SE Sdn	**19144**	9200	10600
4 Dr SSE Sdn	**23994**	12400	14500
FIREBIRD 6*			
2 Dr Cpe	**12640**	6250	7275
* For 8 cylinder Base models add $400 wholesale and $400 retail.			
FIREBIRD 8			
2 Dr Formula Cpe	**15125**	7350	8525
2 Dr Trans Am Cpe	**17025**	8675	11150
2 Dr Trans Am GTA Cpe	**23320**	12150	14025
GRAND AM 4*			
2 Dr LE Cpe	**11804**	5650	6575
4 Dr LE Sdn	**12004**	5650	6575
2 Dr SE Cpe	**15434**	6800	7950
4 Dr SE Sdn	**15734**	6800	7950
* For quad 4 4 cylinder LE models add $300 wholesale and $300 retail.			
GRAND PRIX 4*			
2 Dr LE Cpe	**14564**	6925	8050
4 Dr LE Sdn	**14564**	6925	8050
* For 6 cylinder models add $200 wholesale and $200 retail.			
GRAND PRIX 6			
2 Dr SE Cpe	**18324**	8500	9825
4 Dr STE Sdn	**19179**	9150	10550
2 Dr Turbo SE Cpe	**25560**	—	—
4 Dr Turbo STE Sdn	**23775**	—	—
LE MANS 4			
2 Dr Value Leader Aerocoupe (NA w/auto trans or power steering)	**7683**	2675	3575
2 Dr LE Aerocoupe	**9893**	3650	4550
4 Dr LE Sdn	**10243**	3850	4750
2 Dr GSE Aerocoupe	**11209**	4375	5300
SUNBIRD LE 4			
2 Dr Cpe	**9984**	4950	5875
4 Dr Sdn	**10084**	5050	5975
2 Dr Conv	**15109**	7950	9225
SUNBIRD SE 4			
2 Dr Cpe	**10389**	5200	6125
SUNBIRD GT 4			
2 Dr Cpe	**12909**	6975	8125
ADD FOR:			
All-Wheel Drive Pkg (6000 SE)	**3635**	1965	2400
Anti-Lock Brakes			
(Bonneville LE)	**925**	500	610
(Grand Prix)	**925**	500	610
45/45 Leather Seats (Bonneville SSE)	**779**	420	515
T-Top Roof (Firebird)	**920**	500	605
Turbo Pkg (Sunbird LE Conv)	**1402**	760	925
5.7 Liter V8 EFI Eng			
(Firebird Formula)	**1045**	565	690
(Firebird Trans Am)	**300**	160	200

NOTE: Power brakes standard on Bonneville SSE. Anti-locking brakes standard on Grand Prix Turbo SE & STE. Power windows standard on 6000 SE, Bonneville SE & SSE, Firebird GTA, Grand Am SE, Grand Prix SE, STE, Turbo SE & Turbo STE. Power door locks standard on 6000 SE, Bonneville SE & SSE, Grand Am SE, Grand Prix SE, STE, Turbo SE and Turbo STE.

1989

Year-Model-Body Type	Original List	Current Whlse	Average Retail
6000 LE 4*			
4 Dr Sdn	**12764**	4125	5050
* For 6 cylinder models add $375 wholesale and $375 retail.			
6000 LE 6			
4 Dr Wgn	**14564**	4750	5675
6000 SE 6			
4 Dr Sdn	**16194**	5275	6200
4 Dr Wgn	**17494**	5475	6400
6000 STE 6			
4 Dr Sdn	**22599**	8250	9525
BONNEVILLE 6			
4 Dr LE Sdn	**14829**	6500	7575
4 Dr SE Sdn	**17199**	7500	8700
4 Dr SSE Sdn	**22899**	10125	11675
FIREBIRD 6*			
2 Dr Cpe	**13309**	4925	5850
* For 8 cylinder models add $375 wholesale and $375 retail.			
FIREBIRD 8			
2 Dr Formula Cpe	**14464**	5950	6875
2 Dr Trans Am Cpe	**16514**	8075	9325
2 Dr Trans Am GTA Cpe	**20854**	10250	11825
GRAND AM 4			
2 Dr LE Cpe	**11679**	4725	5650
4 Dr LE Sdn	**11879**	4725	5650
2 Dr SE Cpe	**14865**	5725	6650
4 Dr SE Sdn	**15065**	5725	6650
* For quad 4 4 cylinder models add $300 wholesale and $300 retail.			
GRAND PRIX 6			
2 Dr Cpe	**13975**	5800	6725

Refer To Optional Equipment Schedules

Year-Model-Body Type	Original List	Current Whlse	Average Retail
2 Dr LE Cpe	**14925**	6400	7450
2 Dr SE Cpe	**16639**	7225	8400
LE MANS 4			
2 Dr Value Leader Aerocoupe (NA w/auto trans or power steering)	**6906**	1475	2300
2 Dr LE Aerocoupe	**9338**	2300	3175
4 Dr LE Sdn	**9688**	2475	3350
4 Dr SE Sdn	**11088**	2950	3850
2 Dr GSE Aerocoupe	**10624**	2750	3650
SAFARI 8			
4 Dr Wgn	**15659**	6450	7500
SUNBIRD LE 4			
2 Dr Cpe	**10367**	4250	5175
4 Dr Sdn	**10467**	4350	5275
SUNBIRD SE 4			
2 Dr Cpe	**10617**	4450	5375
SUNBIRD GT 4			
2 Dr Cpe	**12534**	6025	6950
2 Dr Conv	**18034**	8700	10050
ADD FOR:			
2.0 Liter 4 Cyl Turbo Eng (Sunbird SE)	**1434**	660	805
5.0 Liter V8 MFI Eng (Firebird Formula & Trans Am)	**745**	340	415
5.7 Liter V8 MFI Eng (Firebird Formula & Trans Am)	**1045**	480	585
Anti-Lock Brakes (Grand Prix, Bonneville)	**925**	425	520

NOTE: Power brakes standard on all models. Power windows standard on Sunbird Convertible, Firebird GTA, Bonneville SE, Bonneville SSE, 6000 SE and 6000 STE. Power door locks standard on Sunbird Convertible, Firebird GTA, Bonneville SSE, 6000 SE and 6000 STE.

1988

Year-Model-Body Type	Original List	Current Whlse	Average Retail
6000 4*			
4 Dr Sdn	**11974**	3200	4100
4 Dr Wgn	**12414**	3450	4350
6000 LE 4*			
4 Dr Sdn	**12614**	3575	4475
4 Dr Wgn	**13074**	3825	4725

* For 6 cylinder models add $350 wholesale and $350 retail.

Year-Model-Body Type	Original List	Current Whlse	Average Retail
6000 SE 6			
4 Dr Sdn	**13179**	4200	5125
4 Dr Wgn	**14079**	4450	5375
6000 STE 6			
4 Dr Sdn	**18699**	6275	7300
BONNEVILLE 6			
4 Dr LE Sdn	**14099**	4925	5850
4 Dr SE Sdn	**16299**	5775	6700
4 Dr SSE Sdn	**21879**	8275	9550
FIERO 4			
2 Dr Cpe (NA w/power steering)	**10264**	2725	3625
2 Dr Formula Cpe (6 cyl) (NA w/power steering)	**12264**	3875	4775
2 Dr GT Cpe (6 cyl)	**15264**	4900	5825
FIREBIRD 6*			
2 Dr Htchbk Cpe	**12384**	4025	4925

* For 8 cylinder models add $350 wholesale and $350 retail.

Year-Model-Body Type	Original List	Current Whlse	Average Retail
FIREBIRD 8			
2 Dr Formula	**13384**	4775	5700
2 Dr Trans Am	**15384**	6825	7950
2 Dr Trans Am GTA	**19299**	8700	10050
GRAND AM 4*			
2 Dr Cpe	**11034**	3650	4550
4 Dr Sdn	**11234**	3650	4550
2 Dr LE Cpe	**11734**	3950	4850
4 Dr LE Sdn	**11934**	3950	4850
2 Dr SE Cpe (quad 4)	**14034**	4625	5550
4 Dr SE Sdn (quad 4)	**14264**	4625	5550

* For quad 4 4 cylinder models add $275 wholesale and $275 retail.

Year-Model-Body Type	Original List	Current Whlse	Average Retail
GRAND PRIX 6			
2 Dr Cpe	**13314**	4525	5450
2 Dr LE Cpe	**14014**	4975	5900
2 Dr SE Cpe	**15864**	5850	6775
LE MANS 4			
2 Dr Value Leader Aerocoupe (NA w/auto trans or power steering)	**6700**	1275	2000
2 Dr Aerocoupe	**8993**	2050	2900
4 Dr Sdn	**9443**	2225	3075
4 Dr SE Sdn	**10293**	2475	3350
SAFARI 8			
4 Dr Wgn	**14519**	5025	5950
SUNBIRD 4			
4 Dr Sdn	**9972**	3075	3975
SUNBIRD GT 4			
2 Dr Cpe	**11989**	4575	5500
2 Dr Conv	**17289**	7000	8150
SUNBIRD SE 4			
2 Dr Cpe	**10072**	3150	4050
4 Dr Sdn	**10272**	3225	4125
4 Dr Wgn	**10872**	3400	4300
ADD FOR:			
Hatchroof (Firebird)	**920**	345	425
2.0 Liter 4 Cyl Turbo Eng (Grand Am LE)	**1173**	445	540
5.0 Liter V8 MFI Eng			

Year-Model-Body Type	Original List	Current Whlse	Average Retail
(Firebird Formula & Trans Am)	**745**	280	345
5.7 Liter V8 EFI Eng (Firebird Formula & Trans Am)	**1045**	395	480

NOTE: Power brakes standard on all models. Power seat standard on Bonneville SSE. Power windows standard on Sunbird GT, Firebird GTA, Grand Prix LE, Bonneville SE and SSE and 6000 STE. Power door locks standard on Grand Am SE, Firebird GTA, Bonneville SSE and 6000 STE.

1987

Year-Model-Body Type	Original List	Current Whlse	Average Retail
1000 4			
3 Dr Htchbk	**7309**	1125	1850
5 Dr Htchbk	**7449**	1200	1925
6000 4*			
2 Dr Cpe	**11274**	2375	3250
4 Dr Sdn	**11274**	2475	3350
4 Dr Wgn	**11674**	2650	3550
6000 LE 4*			
4 Dr Sdn	**11874**	2750	3650
4 Dr Wgn	**12274**	2975	3875
* For 6 cylinder models add $300 wholesale and $300 retail.			
6000 SE 6			
4 Dr Sdn	**13164**	3325	4225
4 Dr Wgn	**13824**	3550	4450
6000 STE 6			
4 Dr Sdn	**18099**	5200	6125
BONNEVILLE 6			
4 Dr Sdn	**13399**	3950	4850
4 Dr LE Sdn	**14866**	4600	5525
FIERO 4*			
2 Dr Cpe	**9564**	2125	2975
2 Dr Sport Cpe	**11254**	2400	3275
2 Dr SE Cpe	**12504**	2975	3875
2 Dr GT Cpe (6 cyl)	**14754**	4100	5025
* For 6 cylinder models add $325 wholesale and $325 retail.			
FIREBIRD 6*			
2 Dr Cpe	**11624**	2925	3825
* For 8 cylinder models add $300 wholesale and $300 retail.			
FIREBIRD 8			
2 Dr Trans Am	**14524**	4925	5850
GRAND AM 4*			
2 Dr Cpe	**10464**	2675	3575
4 Dr Sdn	**10664**	2675	3575
2 Dr LE Cpe	**11164**	2925	3825
4 Dr LE Sdn	**11364**	2925	3825
2 Dr SE Cpe (6 cyl)	**13334**	3500	4400
4 Dr SE Sdn (6 cyl)	**13574**	3500	4400
* For 6 cylinder models add $300 wholesale and $300 retail.			
GRAND PRIX 6*			
2 Dr Cpe	**11844**	3450	4350
2 Dr LE Cpe	**12574**	3750	4650
2 Dr Brougham Cpe	**13294**	4100	5025
* For 8 cylinder models add $350 wholesale and $350 retail.			
SAFARI 8			
4 Dr Wgn	**13959**	3750	4650
SUNBIRD 4			
4 Dr Sdn	**9211**	2325	3200
4 Dr Wgn	**9741**	2450	3325
SUNBIRD GT 4			
2 Dr Cpe	**11389**	3400	4300
4 Dr Sdn	**11439**	3500	4400
3 Dr Htchbk	**11789**	3500	4400
2 Dr Conv	**16659**	5675	6600
SUNBIRD SE 4			
2 Dr Cpe	**9191**	2450	3325
3 Dr Htchbk	**9711**	2525	3400
2 Dr Conv	**14889**	4725	5650
ADD FOR:			
Formula Opt (Base Firebird)	**1070**	320	360
GTA Opt (Firebird Trans Am)	**2700**	795	970
SE Opt (Bonneville LE)	**940**	275	340
Hatchroof			
(Grand Prix)	**906**	265	325
(Firebird)	**920**	270	330
5.7 Liter V8 Eng (Base Firebird, Firebird, Trans Am)	**1045**	310	375

NOTE: Power brakes standard on all models except 1000. Power locks standard on 6000 STE. Power windows standard on Bonneville, 6000 STE, Bonneville LE and Grand Prix Brougham.

1986

Year-Model-Body Type	Original List	Current Whlse	Average Retail
1000 4			
3 Dr Htchbk	**7209**	900	1625
5 Dr Htchbk	**7349**	900	1625
6000 4*			
2 Dr Cpe	**10560**	1725	2575
4 Dr Sdn	**10740**	1800	2650
4 Dr Wgn	**11120**	2000	2850
6000 LE 4*			
2 Dr Cpe	**11070**	1975	2825
4 Dr Sdn	**11220**	2075	2925
4 Dr Wgn	**11610**	2250	3100

* For 6 cylinder models add $300 wholesale and

Refer To Optional Equipment Schedules

Year-Model-Body Type	Original List	Current Whlse	Average Retail
$300 retail.			
6000 STE 6			
4 Dr Sdn	**16345**	3825	4725
BONNEVILLE 6*			
4 Dr Sdn	**10354**	1875	2725
4 Dr LE Sdn	**11644**	2100	2950
4 Dr Brougham Sdn	**12224**	2350	3225
* For 8 cylinder models add $375 wholesale and $375 retail.			
FIERO 4			
2 Dr Cpe (NA w/auto trans)	**8421**	1300	2025
2 Dr Sport Cpe	**10764**	1600	2450
2 Dr SE Cpe	**11954**	2075	2925
2 Dr GT Cpe (6 cyl)	**14314**	3025	3925
* For 6 cylinder models add $300 wholesale and $300 retail.			
FIREBIRD 4*			
2 Dr Cpe	**10760**	2050	2900
* For 6 cylinder models add $300 wholesale and $300 retail.			
FIREBIRD 6*			
2 Dr SE Cpe	**13210**	2950	3850
* For 8 cylinder models add $300 wholesale and $300 retail.			
FIREBIRD 8			
2 Dr Trans Am	**13940**	4025	4925
GRAND AM 4*			
2 Dr Cpe	**9924**	1925	2775
4 Dr Sdn	**10124**	1925	2775
2 Dr LE Cpe	**10470**	2125	2975
4 Dr LE Sdn	**10670**	2125	2975
2 Dr SE Cpe (6 cyl)	**12474**	2825	3725
4 Dr SE Sdn (6 cyl)	**12724**	2825	3725
* For 6 cylinder models add $250 wholesale and $250 retail.			
GRAND PRIX 6*			
2 Dr Cpe	**11354**	2350	3225
2 Dr LE Cpe	**11914**	2575	3450
2 Dr Brougham Cpe	**12724**	2875	3775
* For 8 cylinder models add $325 wholesale and $325 retail.			
PARISIENNE 6*			
4 Dr Sdn	**12294**	2150	3000
4 Dr Wgn (8 cyl)	**12914**	2625	3525
4 Dr Brougham Sdn	**13094**	2600	3475
* For 8 cylinder models add $400 wholesale and $400 retail.			
SUNBIRD 4			
4 Dr Sdn	**9112**	1600	2450
4 Dr Wgn	**9502**	1675	2525
SUNBIRD GT 4			
2 Dr Cpe	**11069**	2400	3275
4 Dr Sdn	**11119**	2500	3375
3 Dr Htchbk	**11445**	2500	3375
2 Dr Conv	**15904**	4200	5125
SUNBIRD SE 4			
2 Dr Cpe	**9076**	1675	2525
3 Dr Htchbk	**9462**	1750	2600
2 Dr Conv	**14169**	3475	4375
ADD FOR:			
Brougham Landau (Grand Prix Brougham)	**469**	100	120
Driver Enthusiast Pkg (Grand Am)	**699**	150	180
Turbo Engine Pkg (Sunbird except SE Convertible)	**1511**	320	395
(Sunbird SE Convertible)	**1296**	275	335
Hatchroof (Grand Prix)	**931**	200	240
(Firebird)	**895**	190	235
Sport Landau Roof (6000)	**712**	150	185
2.8 Liter V6 EFI Eng (Base 6000, 6000 LE)	**610**	130	160
5.0 Liter V8 Eng (Base Firebird)	**800**	170	210
5.0 Liter HO V8 Eng (Trans Am)	**745**	160	195

NOTE: Power windows standard on 6000 STE, Grand Prix Brougham and Sunbird Convertible. Power brakes standard on 6000 STE, Bonneville, Fiero, Firebird, Grand Am, Grand Prix, Parisienne and Sunbird.

1985

Year-Model-Body Type	Original List	Current Whlse	Average Retail
1000 4			
3 Dr Htchbk	**6860**	550	1025
5 Dr Htchbk	**7080**	650	1225
6000 4*			
2 Dr Cpe	**9839**	1200	1925
4 Dr Sdn	**9999**	1275	2000
4 Dr Wgn	**10349**	1425	2175
6000 LE 4*			
2 Dr Cpe	**10339**	1375	2125
4 Dr Sdn	**10489**	1475	2300
4 Dr Wgn	**10849**	1650	2500
* For 6 cylinder models add $300 wholesale and $300 retail.			
6000 STE 6			
4 Dr Sdn	**15125**	2750	3650
BONNEVILLE 6*			
4 Dr Sdn	**10647**	1550	2400
4 Dr LE Sdn	**10893**	1725	2575
4 Dr Brougham Sdn	**11393**	1925	2775
* For 8 cylinder models add $300 wholesale and			

Year-Model-Body Type	Original List	Current Whlse	Average Retail
$300 retail.			
FIERO 4			
2 Dr Cpe (NA w/auto trans)	**8607**	1075	1800
2 Dr Sport Cpe	**10170**	1375	2125
2 Dr SE Cpe	**11170**	1775	2625
FIERO 6			
2 Dr GT Cpe	**13020**	2550	3425
FIREBIRD 4*			
2 Dr Cpe	**10024**	1200	1925
* For 6 cylinder models add $300 wholesale and $300 retail.			
FIREBIRD 6*			
2 Dr SE Cpe	**12470**	2000	2850
* For 8 cylinder models add $300 wholesale and $300 retail.			
FIREBIRD 8			
2 Dr Trans Am Cpe	**12744**	2875	3775
GRAND AM 4*			
2 Dr Cpe	**9319**	1475	2300
2 Dr LE Cpe	**9829**	1675	2525
* For 6 cylinder models add $200 wholesale and $200 retail.			
GRAND PRIX 6			
2 Dr Cpe	**10509**	1700	2550
2 Dr LE Cpe	**11009**	1900	2750
2 Dr Brougham Cpe	**11745**	2175	3025
* For 8 cylinder models add $300 wholesale and $300 retail.			
PARISIENNE 6*			
4 Dr Sdn	**11497**	1775	2625
4 Dr Wgn (8 cyl)	**12073**	1900	2750
4 Dr Brougham Sdn	**12247**	2175	3025
* For 8 cylinder models add $375 wholesale and $375 retail.			
SUNBIRD 4			
2 Dr Cpe	**8317**	1200	1925
4 Dr Sdn	**8457**	1275	2000
3 Dr Htchbk	**8687**	1275	2000
4 Dr Wgn	**8807**	1325	2050
SUNBIRD LE 4			
2 Dr Cpe	**8905**	1400	2150
4 Dr Sdn	**9105**	1500	2350
4 Dr Wgn	**9435**	1575	2425
2 Dr Conv	**13290**	2850	3750
SUNBIRD SE 4			
2 Dr Cpe	**10549**	1775	2625
4 Dr Sdn	**10719**	1850	2700
3 Dr Htchbk	**11049**	1850	2700
ADD FOR:			
Brougham Landau (Grand Prix)	**469**	60	75
Driver Enthusiast Pkg (Grand Am)	**670**	90	105
Hatch Roof			
(Grand Prix)	**850**	150	200
(Firebird)	**875**	150	200
2.8 Liter V6 Eng			
(6000, 6000 LE)	**435**	60	60
(Fiero SE)	**595**	150	175
5.0 Liter EFI V8 Eng			
(Trans Am)	**695**	100	125
5.0 Liter V8 Eng			
(Base Firebird)	**650**	125	150
(Bonneville, Grand Prix)	**490**	125	150
(Parisienne Sdn)	**340**	150	175
DEDUCT FOR:			
4.3 Liter V6 Diesel Eng			
(6000, 6000 LE)	**335**	40	50

NOTE: Power brakes standard on all models. Power windows standard on 6000 STE and Fiero GT. Power locks standard on 6000 STE.

1984

Year-Model-Body Type	Original List	Current Whlse	Average Retail
1000 4			
3 Dr Htchbk Cpe	**6843**	225	475
5 Dr Htchbk Sdn	**7046**	300	575
2000 4			
2 Dr Cpe	**7933**	700	1325
4 Dr Sdn	**8057**	775	1500
3 Dr Htchbk	**8253**	775	1500
4 Dr Wgn	**8373**	825	1525
2000 LE 4			
2 Dr Cpe	**8479**	875	1600
4 Dr Sdn	**8645**	900	1625
4 Dr Wgn	**8965**	950	1675
2 Dr Convertible	**12691**	1725	2575
2000 SE 4			
2 Dr Cpe	**10034**	1200	1925
4 Dr Sdn	**10200**	1275	2000
3 Dr Htchbk	**10504**	1275	2000
6000 4*			
2 Dr Cpe	**9420**	900	1625
4 Dr Sdn	**9594**	1000	1725
4 Dr Wgn	**9942**	1125	1850
6000 LE 4*			
2 Dr Cpe	**9863**	1050	1775
4 Dr Sdn	**10013**	1150	1875
4 Dr Wgn	**10333**	1275	2000
* For 6 cylinder models add $200 wholesale and $200 retail.			
6000 STE 6			
Sdn	**14428**	1700	2550
BONNEVILLE 6*			
4 Dr Sdn	**9963**	900	1625
4 Dr LE Sdn	**10190**	1025	1750

Refer To Optional Equipment Schedules

Year-Model-Body Type	Original List	Current Whlse	Average Retail
BONNEVILLE BROUGHAM 6*			
4 Dr Sdn	**10667**	1150	1875
* For 8 cylinder models add $200 wholesale and $200 retail.			
FIERO 4			
2 Dr Cpe	**8102**	575	1075
2 Dr Sport Cpe	**9645**	875	1600
2 Dr SE Cpe	**10742**	1150	1875
FIREBIRD 4*			
2 Dr Cpe	**9706**	1325	2050
* For 6 cylinder models add $200 wholesale and $200 retail.			
FIREBIRD 6*			
2 Dr S/E Cpe	**11776**	1775	2625
* For 8 cylinder models add $200 wholesale and $200 retail.			
FIREBIRD 8			
Trans Am	**11826**	2350	3225
GRAND PRIX 6*			
2 Dr	**9977**	1100	1825
2 Dr LE	**10456**	1275	2000
2 Dr Brougham	**11131**	1425	2175
* For 8 cylinder models add $200 wholesale and $200 retail.			
PARISIENNE 6			
4 Dr Sdn	**10712**	1175	1900
4 Dr Wgn (8 cyl)	**11224**	1300	2025
PARISIENNE BROUGHAM 6			
4 Dr Sdn	**11112**	1425	2175
* For 8 cylinder models add $300 wholesale and $300 retail.			
PHOENIX 4*			
2 Dr Cpe	**8451**	450	825
5 Dr Htchbk	**8526**	500	925
PHOENIX LE 4*			
2 Dr Cpe	**9044**	600	1125
5 Dr Htchbk	**9177**	675	1275
* For 6 cylinder models add $175 wholesale and $175 retail.			
PHOENIX SE 6			
2 Dr Cpe	**10217**	1000	1725

NOTE: Power brakes standard on Bonneville, Grand Prix, Firebird, Fiero, 2000 Series, 6000 Series and Phoenix SJ. Power windows standard on Grand Prix Brougham and 6000 STE.

1983 — ALL BODY STYLES

Year-Model-Body Type	Original List	Current Whlse	Average Retail
1000	—	175	375
2000	—	525	975
2000 LE	—	500	925
2000 SE	—	700	1325
2000 SUNBIRD CONV	—	1450	2225
6000	—	800	1500
6000 LE	—	875	1600
6000 STE	—	1275	2000
BONNEVILLE	—	900	1625
BONNEVILLE BROUGHAM	—	1000	1725
FIREBIRD	—	1150	1875
FIREBIRD SE	—	1350	2100
FIREBIRD TRANS AM	—	1850	2700
GRAND PRIX	—	900	1625
GRAND PRIX LJ	—	1025	1750
GRAND PRIX BROUGHAM	—	1150	1875
PARISIENNE	—	1000	1725
PARISIENNE BROUGHAM	—	1250	1975
PHOENIX	—	325	600
PHOENIX LJ	—	425	775
PHOENIX SJ	—	600	1125

SATURN

1992

Year-Model-Body Type	Original List	Current Whlse	Average Retail
SATURN 4			
4 Dr SL Sdn (NA w/power steering or auto trans)	**9220**	—	—
4 Dr SL1 Sdn	**10745**	—	—
4 Dr SL2 Sdn	**12145**	—	—
2 Dr SC Cpe	**13525**	—	—
ADD FOR:			
Anti-Lock Brakes	**595**	—	—
Leather Trim (SL2, SC)	**610**	—	—

NOTE: Tilt steering wheel standard on all models.

1991

Year-Model-Body Type	Original List	Current Whlse	Average Retail
SATURN 4			
4 Dr SL Sdn (NA w/power steering)	**9385**	7675	8900
4 Dr SL1 Sdn	**9985**	8050	9350
4 Dr SL2 Sdn	**11685**	10150	11350
2 Dr SC Cpe	**13165**	11425	12825
ADD FOR:			
Anti-lock Brakes	**895**	545	660

NOTE: Power brakes standard on all models.

ACURA

1992

Year-Model-Body Type	Original List	Current Whlse	Average Retail
INTEGRA 4			
3 Dr RS Htchbk (5 spd)	**14080**	—	—
3 Dr LS Htchbk (5 spd)	**15685**	—	—
3 Dr GS Htchbk (5 spd)	**17855**	—	—
4 Dr RS Sdn (5 spd)	**15005**	—	—
4 Dr LS Sdn (5 spd)	**16435**	—	—
4 Dr GS Sdn (5 spd)	**18395**	—	—
3 Dr GS-R VTEC	**19110**	—	—
ADD FOR:			
Leather Interior (GS)	**500**	—	—
LEGEND 6			
4 Dr Base Sdn (5 spd)	**28000**	—	—
4 Dr L Sdn (5 spd)	**30400**	—	—
2 Dr L Cpe (5 spd)	**31850**	—	—
4 Dr LS Sdn (5 spd)	**34900**	—	—
2 Dr LS Cpe (5 spd)	**36250**	—	—
ADD FOR:			
Leather Interior (L)	**1500**	—	—
NSX 6			
2 Dr Cpe (5 spd)	**65000**	—	—
ADD FOR:			
Auto Trans	**4000**	—	—
VIGOR 5			
4 Dr Sdn (5 spd)	**23665**	—	—
4 Dr GS Sdn (5 spd)	**25650**	—	—

NOTE: Power windows standard on Integra LS, GS & GS-R, Legend, NSX and Vigor. Power door locks standard on Integra LS 4 Dr, GS & GS-R, Legend, NSX and Vigor. Power seat standard on Legend and NSX. Power sunroof standard on Integra LS, GS & GS-R, Legend L & LS, Vigor GS. Tilt steering wheel standard on Integra, Legend, NSX and Vigor. Cruise control standard on Integra LS, GS & GSR, Legend, NSX and Vigor.

1991

Year-Model-Body Type	Original List	Current Whlse	Average Retail
INTEGRA 4			
3 Dr RS Htchbk (5 spd)	**13400**	9500	10950
3 Dr LS Htchbk (5 spd)	**15275**	10575	12200
3 Dr LS Special Htchbk (5 spd)	**15975**	10975	12600
3 Dr GS Htchbk (5 spd)	**17405**	11800	13625
3 Dr GS Htchbk w/Leather Trim (5 spd)	**17905**	12100	13975
4 Dr RS Sdn (5 spd)	**14325**	9675	11150
4 Dr LS Sdn (5 spd)	**16025**	10775	12425
4 Dr GS Sdn (5 spd)	**17945**	12000	13850
4 Dr GS Sdn w/Leather Trim (5 spd)	**18445**	12300	14300
LEGEND 6			
4 Dr Base Sdn (5 spd)	**26800**	19225	22275
4 Dr L Sdn w/Cloth Interior (5 spd)	**28800**	20625	23675
4 Dr L Sdn w/Leather Interior (5 spd)	**30300**	21025	24325
4 Dr LS Sdn (5 spd)	**33400**	23025	26325
2 Dr L Cpe w/Cloth Interior (5 spd)	**30900**	22125	25425
2 Dr L Cpe w/Leather Interior (5 spd)	**32400**	22525	25825
2 Dr LS Cpe (5 spd)	**35500**	24575	27875
NSX 6			
2 Dr Cpe (5 spd)	**61000**	46775	51550
2 Dr Cpe (auto)	**65000**	47500	52350

NOTE: Power brakes standard on all models. Power windows standard on Integra RS, LS and GS, Legend, NSX. Power door locks standard on Integra LS Sedan, LS Special and GS, Legend, NSX. Sunroof standard on Integra LS Hatchback, LS Special and GS, Legend L and LS. Power seat standard on Legend L and LS, NSX.

1990

Year-Model-Body Type	Original List	Current Whlse	Average Retail
INTEGRA 4			
3 Dr RS Sdn (5 spd)	**13450**	8100	9350
4 Dr RS Sdn (5 spd)	**14350**	8300	9575
3 Dr LS Sdn (5 spd)	**14925**	9100	10475
4 Dr LS Sdn (5 spd)	**15745**	9300	10725
3 Dr GS Sdn (5 spd)	**17025**	9850	11350
4 Dr GS Sdn (5 spd)	**17150**	10050	11600
LEGEND 6			
2 Dr Cpe (5 spd)	**24760**	16375	19025
4 Dr Sdn (5 spd)	**22600**	14975	17575
2 Dr L Cpe w/Cloth Interior (5 spd)	**27325**	17425	20075
2 Dr L Cpe w/Leather Interior (5 spd)	**28275**	17675	20325
4 Dr L Sdn w/Cloth Interior (5 spd)	**25900**	16075	18725
4 Dr L Sdn w/Leather Interior (5 spd)	**26850**	16325	18975
2 Dr LS Cpe (5 spd)	**30690**	18725	21775
4 Dr LS Sdn (5 spd)	**29610**	17325	19975

NOTE: Power brakes standard on Integra and Legend. Power windows and power door locks standard on Integra LS 4 Door, Integra GS and Legend. Power seat standard on Legend L and LS. Sunroof standard on Integra LS 3 Door,

Refer To Optional Equipment Schedules

Year-Model-Body Type	Original List	Current Whlse	Average Retail

Integra GS and Legend. Anti-lock brake system standard on Integra GS and Legend L and LS.

1989

Year-Model-Body Type	Original List	Current Whlse	Average Retail
INTEGRA 4			
3 Dr RS Htchbk (5 spd)	**12260**	6350	7400
5 Dr RS Htchbk (5 spd)	**13060**	6550	7625
3 Dr LS Htchbk (5 spd)	**14070**	7025	8150
5 Dr LS Htchbk (5 spd)	**14900**	7200	8350
LEGEND 6			
4 Dr Sdn (5 spd)	**24660**	13000	15325
2 Dr Cpe (5 spd)	**24760**	14300	16800
4 Dr L Sdn w/Cloth Interior (5 spd)	**25900**	14075	16525
4 Dr L Sdn w/Leather Interior (5 spd)	**26850**	14250	16725
2 Dr L Cpe w/Cloth Interior (5 spd)	**27325**	15325	17975
2 Dr L Cpe w/Leather Interior (5 spd)	**28275**	15500	18150
4 Dr LS Sdn (5 spd)	**29160**	14900	17500
2 Dr LS Cpe (5 spd)	**30040**	16200	18850

NOTE: Power brakes standard on Integra and Legend. Power windows and power door locks standard on Ingegra LS 5 Door. Sunroof standard on Integra LS 3 Door.

1988

Year-Model-Body Type	Original List	Current Whlse	Average Retail
INTEGRA 4			
3 Dr RS Htchbk (5 spd)	**10915**	4650	5575
5 Dr RS Htchbk (5 spd)	**11695**	4825	5750
3 Dr LS Htchbk (5 spd)	**12670**	5350	6275
5 Dr LS Htchbk (5 spd)	**13485**	5575	6500
3 Dr LS SE Htchbk (5 spd)	**13670**	5750	6675
LEGEND 6			
4 Dr Sdn (5 spd)	**21535**	9425	10850
2 Dr Cpe (5 spd)	**23675**	10650	12300
4 Dr L Sdn (5 spd)	**25625**	10375	11975
2 Dr L Cpe (5 spd)	**27255**	11625	13425
4 Dr LS Sdn (5 spd)	**28230**	11200	12925
2 Dr LS Cpe (5 spd)	**29085**	12425	14550

NOTE: Power steering standard on all models. Power windows standard on Integra LS 5 Door and Legend. Air conditioning standard on Legend. Electric sunroof standard on Legend L and LS.

1987

Year-Model-Body Type	Original List	Current Whlse	Average Retail
INTEGRA 4			
3 Dr RS Htchbk (5 spd)	**10039**	3500	4400
5 Dr RS Htchbk (5 spd)	**10754**	3700	4600
3 Dr LS Htchbk (5 spd)	**11589**	4075	5000
5 Dr LS Htchbk (5 spd)	**12404**	4250	5175
3 Dr Special LS Htchbk (5 spd)	**12589**	4425	5350
LEGEND 6			
4 Dr Sdn (5 spd)	**20258**	7450	8650
4 Dr Luxury Sdn (5 spd)	**22858**	8225	9500
2 Dr Cpe (5 spd)	**22458**	8600	9925
2 Dr LS Cpe (5 spd)	**—**	9550	10900

1986

Year-Model-Body Type	Original List	Current Whlse	Average Retail
INTEGRA 4			
3 Dr RS Htchbk (5 spd)	**9298**	2875	3775
5 Dr RS Htchbk (5 spd)	**9948**	3050	3950
3 Dr LS Htchbk (5 spd)	**10593**	3325	4225
5 Dr LS Htchbk (5 spd)	**11343**	3525	4425
LEGEND 6			
4 Dr Sdn (5 spd)	**19298**	5925	6850

ALFA ROMEO

1992

Year-Model-Body Type	Original List	Current Whlse	Average Retail
SPIDER 4			
Base Conv	**22259**	—	—
Veloce Conv	**25304**	—	—
ADD FOR:			
Removable Hardtop	**2500**	—	—
Alloy Wheels	**350**	—	—
164 6			
L Sdn	**29490**	—	—
S Sdn	**34990**	—	—
ADD FOR:			
Luxury Pkg	**1950**	—	—

NOTE: Power windows standard on Spider and 164. Power door locks, power seat, power sunroof and cruise control standard on 164.

1991

Year-Model-Body Type	Original List	Current Whlse	Average Retail
SPIDER 4			
Base Convertible	**21945**	12675	15000
Veloce Convertible	**22950**	14375	16875
164 6			
Base Sdn	**24500**	14700	17250

Year-Model-Body Type	Original List	Current Whlse	Average Retail
L Sdn	**27500**	16800	19450
S Sdn	**29500**	17650	20300
ADD FOR:			
Power Leather Seats (164 Base)	**1200**	525	660
Power Recaro Leather Seats (164 S)	**2000**	870	1065

NOTE: Power brakes standard on all models. Power windows standard on 164 and Spider. Power door locks and power seat standard on 164.

1990

Year-Model-Body Type	Original List	Current Whlse	Average Retail
SPIDER 4			
Graduate Convertible (NA w/power steering)	**18590**	10075	11625
Veloce Convertible (NA w/power steering)	**21945**	11750	13575
Quadrifoglio Convertible w/Hardtop (NA w/power steering)	**23950**	12875	15200
ADD FOR:			
Metallic Paint (Veloce, Quadrifoglio)	**275**	80	100

NOTE: Power brakes standard on Spider Series. Power windows standard on Spider Veloce and Spider Quadrifoglio.

1989

Year-Model-Body Type	Original List	Current Whlse	Average Retail
MILANO 6			
Gold Sdn	**18475**	6375	7425
Platinum Sdn (auto)	**22500**	7300	8475
3.0 Liter Sdn	**22700**	7800	9050
SPIDER 4			
Graduate Convertible (NA w/power steering)	**18340**	7400	8600
Veloce Convertible (NA w/power steering)	**21195**	8900	10275
Quadrifoglio Convertible w/Hardtop (NA w/power steering)	**23400**	9825	11325
ADD FOR:			
Metallic Paint (Quadrifoglio)	**275**	70	85

NOTE: Power door locks standard on Milano Series. Power brakes standard on Milano Series and Spider Series. Automatic transmission standard on Milano Platinum. Power windows standard on Milano Series, Spider Veloce and Spider Quadrifoglio.

1988

Year-Model-Body Type	Original List	Current Whlse	Average Retail
MILANO 6			
Gold Sdn	**17550**	4500	5425
Platinum Sdn (auto)	**21450**	5225	6150
Verde Sdn	**21650**	5775	6700
SPIDER 4			
Graduate Convertible	**15950**	6000	6925
Veloce Convertible	**19380**	7325	8500
Quadrifoglio Convertible w/Hardtop	**22440**	8175	9450
ADD FOR:			
Metallic Paint (Veloce, Quadrifoglio)	**275**	70	85
(Milano)	**350**	70	85

NOTE: Air conditioning standard on Spider Quadrifoglio and Milano models. Power windows standard on Spider Veloce, Spider Quadrifoglio and Milano models. Power steering standard on Milano models.

1987

Year-Model-Body Type	Original List	Current Whlse	Average Retail
SPIDER 4			
Graduate Convertible	**14500**	4200	5125
Veloce Convertible	**17195**	5350	6275
Quadrifoglio Convertible w/Hardtop	**21000**	6225	7250
MILANO 6			
Silver Sdn	**15400**	2750	3650
Gold Sdn	**16000**	2875	3775
Platinum Sdn	**20350**	3400	4300
VERDE 6			
Sdn	**19800**	3525	4425
ADD FOR:			
Metallic Paint (Veloce, Quadrifoglio)	**275**	70	85
(Milano, Verde)	**350**	70	85
Leather Seats (Milano Gold)	**—**	150	175

NOTE: Air conditioning standard on Quadrifoglio, Milano and Verde. Power windows standard on Veloce, Quadrifoglio and Milano. Power steering standard on Milano. Sun roof standard on Milano Platinum.

1986

Year-Model-Body Type	Original List	Current Whlse	Average Retail
GRADUATE CONVERTIBLE 4			
Convertible	**14639**	2975	3875
SPIDER VELOCE 4			
Convertible	**17639**	4025	4925

Refer To Optional Equipment Schedules

Year-Model-Body Type	Original List	Current Whlse	Average Retail
QUADRIFOGLIO CONVERTIBLE 4			
Convertible	**19600**	4575	5500
GTV-6 6			
Cpe	**17144**	3225	4125
ADD FOR:			
Leather Seats (GTV-6)	**750**	125	150

NOTE: Power brakes standard on all models. Power windows standard on Spider Veloce and GTV-6. Power steering standard on GTV-6. Air conditioning standard on Quadrifoglio and GTV-6.

1985

Year-Model-Body Type	Original List	Current Whlse	Average Retail
GRADUATE CONVERTIBLE 4			
Convertible	**13495**	2325	3200
GTV-6 6			
Cpe	**16500**	2500	3375
SPIDER VELOCE 4			
Convertible	**16500**	3200	4100
ADD FOR:			
Leather Seats (GTV-6)	**750**	100	125
Fiberglass Hardtop (Spider Veloce)	**1100**	225	275

1984

Year-Model-Body Type	Original List	Current Whlse	Average Retail
GTV-6 6			
Cpe	**19000**	1950	2800
SPIDER VELOCE 4			
Convertible	**16000**	2700	3600

1983

Year-Model-Body Type	Original List	Current Whlse	Average Retail
GTV-6 6			
Cpe	**17995**	1500	2350
SPIDER VELOCE 4			
Convertible	**15495**	2100	2950

AUDI

1992

Year-Model-Body Type	Original List	Current Whlse	Average Retail
80 5			
4 Dr Sdn	**22650**	—	—
4 Dr Quattro 4WD Sdn	**26250**	—	—
ADD FOR:			
CD Changer	**890**	—	—
100 6			
4 Dr Sdn	**27700**	—	—
4 Dr S Sdn	**29900**	—	—
4 Dr CS Sdn	**32900**	—	—
ADD FOR:			
CD Changer (CS)	**790**	—	—
Leather Seat Trim	**1300**	—	—
Cellular Telephone	**990**	—	—
V8 QUATTRO 8			
4 Dr Sdn (auto)	**53100**	—	—

NOTE: Power windows, power door locks and cruise control standard on all models. Power seat and power sunroof standard on 100 S & CS and V8 Quattro. Tilt steering wheel standard on 100 Series and V8 Quattro.

1991

Year-Model-Body Type	Original List	Current Whlse	Average Retail
80 5			
4 Dr Sdn	**20750**	13200	15525
4 Dr Quattro 4WD Sdn	**25200**	9975	11500
90 5			
4 Dr Sdn (auto)	**26250**	16500	19150
4 Dr Quattro 4WD Sdn	**29200**	18000	20650
100 5			
4 Dr Sdn (auto)	**28750**	18675	21725
4 Dr Quattro 4WD Sdn	**31150**	20075	23125
200 5			
4 Dr Turbo Sdn (auto)	**35500**	22025	25325
4 Dr Quattro Turbo 4WD Sdn	**43500**	23475	26775
4 Dr Quattro Turbo 4WD Wgn	**43500**	23825	27125
COUPE QUATTRO 5			
2 Dr Cpe	**31650**	19050	22100
V8 QUATTRO 8			
4 Dr 4WD Sdn	**51500**	31175	24675
ADD FOR:			
Anti-Lock Brakes (80)	**1145**	475	575
Audi-Bose Radio System (100)	**625**	300	350
Leather Seats (90)	**1040**	375	475
(100)	**1300**	375	475

NOTE: Power brakes, power windows and power door locks standard on all models. Power seat standard on 200 and V8 Quattro. Sunroof standard on 90, 100, 200, Coupe Quattro and V8 Quattro.

1990

Year-Model-Body Type	Original List	Current Whlse	Average Retail
80 4			
4 Dr Sdn	**18900**	9675	11150
4 Dr Quattro 4WD Sdn			

Year-Model-Body Type	Original List	Current Whlse	Average Retail
(5 spd)	**22800**	11650	13450
90 5			
4 Dr Sdn	**23990**	12125	14000
4 Dr Quattro 4WD Sdn (5 spd)	**27500**	14125	16575
100 5			
4 Dr Sdn (auto)	**26900**	14475	17000
4 Dr Quattro 4WD Sdn	**29470**	15700	18350
200 5			
4 Dr Turbo Sdn	**33405**	16450	19100
4 Dr Quattro Turbo 4WD Sdn	**35805**	18300	21200
4 Dr Quattro Turbo 4WD Wgn	**36930**	18625	21675
COUPE QUATTRO 5			
2 Dr Cpe	**29750**	15225	17875
V8 QUATTRO 8			
4 Dr Sdn (auto)	**47450**	25925	29250
ADD FOR:			
Anti-Lock Brakes (80)	**1100**	400	475
Audi-Bose Radio System (100)	**600**	200	250
Leather Seats (90)	**1000**	300	350
(100)	**1250**	300	350
Pearlescent Paint (90, Quattro Cpe)	**395**	125	150
(100)	**900**	175	210
(Quattro Sdn)	**450**	175	210

NOTE: Power brakes, power windows, power door locks and anti-lock brake system standard on all models. Sunroof standard on 90, 100, 200, V8 Quattro and Coupe Quattro. Power seat standard on V8 Quattro and 200 Series.

1989

Year-Model-Body Type	Original List	Current Whlse	Average Retail
80 4			
4 Dr Sdn	**19845**	7900	9225
4 Dr Quattro Sdn (5 spd)	**23610**	9850	11350
90 5			
4 Dr Sdn	**25310**	10125	11675
4 Dr Quattro Sdn	**28840**	12025	13900
100 5			
4 Dr E Sdn (auto)	**25230**	9425	10850
4 Dr Sdn	**27750**	9825	11325
4 Dr Wgn	**29250**	10125	11675
4 Dr Quattro Sdn	**31110**	11625	13425
200 5			
4 Dr Turbo Sdn	**34005**	12125	14000
4 Dr Quattro Turbo Sdn	**37905**	13925	16300
4 Dr Quattro Turbo Wgn	**38805**	14225	16700

Year-Model-Body Type	Original List	Current Whlse	Average Retail
ADD FOR:			
Leather Seat Trim (100 ex. E, 200 Turbo Sdn)	**1250**	300	350
(200 Turbo Sdn)	**900**	300	350

NOTE: Power steering, power brakes, power windows and power door locks standard on all models. Sunroof standard on 90, 100 and 200 models.

1988

Year-Model-Body Type	Original List	Current Whlse	Average Retail
80 4			
4 Dr Sdn	**18600**	6200	7225
4 Dr Quattro Sdn	**22700**	7975	9250
90 4			
4 Dr Sdn (auto)	**24330**	8300	9575
90 5			
4 Dr Sdn	**24330**	8300	9575
4 Dr Quattro Sdn	**27720**	9575	11025
5000S 5			
4 Dr Sdn	**22180**	6875	8000
4 Dr Wgn	**23620**	7125	8275
4 Dr Quattro Sdn	**26490**	8550	9875
5000CS 5			
4 Dr Sdn	**30010**	8475	9800
4 Dr Quattro Sdn	**33800**	10125	11675
4 Dr Quattro Wgn	**35250**	10425	12025
ADD FOR:			
Leather Seat Trim (5000S ex. Quattro, 5000CS ex. Quattro)	**1250**	250	300

NOTE: Air conditioning, power steering and power windows standard on all models. Power sunroof standard on 90 and 5000CS.

1987

Year-Model-Body Type	Original List	Current Whlse	Average Retail
4000S 4			
4 Dr Sdn	**15875**	3125	4025
4000CS 5			
4 Dr Quattro Sdn	**19850**	4000	4900
5000S 5			
4 Dr Sdn (110 HP)	**20060**	3850	4750
4 Dr Sdn (130 HP)	**20460**	4000	4900
4 Dr Wgn	**21390**	4100	5025
5000CS 5			
4 Dr Turbo Sdn	**26640**	4850	5775
4 Dr Turbo Special Edition Sdn	**27975**	5125	6050
4 Dr Quattro Turbo Sdn	**31215**	6425	7475

Refer To Optional Equipment Schedules

Year-Model-Body Type	Original List	Current Whlse	Average Retail
4 Dr Quattro Turbo Wgn	**32555**	6650	7750
GT COUPE 5			
2 Dr Cpe	**17580**	3800	4700
ADD FOR:			
Anti-Lock Braking System (5000S, 5000CS ex. Quattro)	**1075**	275	300
Leather Seat Trim (4000CS, GT Cpe)	**1025**	200	250
(5000S, Base 5000CS)	**1185**	200	250

NOTE: Air conditioning standard on 4000S, 4000CS, GT Coupe, 5000S and 5000CS. Sun roof standard on 5000CS. Power door locks standard on 4000S, 4000CS, 5000S and 5000CS. Power steering and power windows standard on 4000S, 4000CS, and GT Coupe. Anti-lock braking system standard on 5000CS Quattro.

1986

Year-Model-Body Type	Original List	Current Whlse	Average Retail
4000S 4			
4 Dr Sdn	**15315**	2425	3300
4000CS 5			
4 Dr Quattro Sdn	**18670**	3100	4000
Commemorative Edition Quattro 4 Dr Sdn	**20365**	3575	4475
5000S 5			
4 Dr Sdn	**18950**	2650	3550
4 Dr Wgn	**20220**	2875	3775
5000CS 5			
4 Dr Turbo Sdn	**25275**	3275	4175
4 Dr Quattro Turbo Sdn	**29345**	4650	5575
4 Dr Quattro Turbo Wgn	**30615**	4850	5775
Commemorative Edition 4 Dr Sdn	**21660**	2750	3650
GT COUPE 5			
2 Dr Cpe	**16535**	2875	3775
Commemorative Edition 2 Dr Cpe	**18525**	3225	4125
ADD FOR:			
Anti-Lock Braking System (5000S, 5000CS)	**995**	175	200

NOTE: Power windows, power brakes, power steering and air conditioning standard on all models. Power seat and sunroof standard on 5000CS Turbo and 5000CS Turbo Quattro. Power locks standard on 4000S, 4000CS Quattro, 5000S, 5000CS Turbo and 5000CS Turbo Quattro.

1985

Year-Model-Body Type	Original List	Current Whlse	Average Retail
4000S 4			
4 Dr Base Sdn	**14330**	1825	2675
4 Dr Quattro Sdn	**17450**	2600	3475
5000S 5			
4 Dr Sdn	**18090**	1875	2725
4 Dr Wgn	**19300**	2050	2900
4 Dr Turbo Sdn (auto)	**23875**	2500	3375
GT COUPE 5			
2 Dr Cpe	**15630**	2175	3025
QUATTRO 5			
2 Dr Cpe	—	—	—
ADD FOR:			
Manual Tilt Seat (GT Coupe)	**495**	50	75
Leather Interior (5000S)	**1085**	125	150
Full Leather Interior (4000S Quattro)	**950**	100	125

NOTE: Power steering standard on 4000S, 5000S, GT Coupe and Quattro. Air conditioning standard on 4000S, GT Coupe and Quattro. Power windows standard on 4000S, 5000S, GT Coupe and Quattro. Power seat standard on 5000S Turbo. Sunroof standard on 5000S Turbo Quattro.

1984

Year-Model-Body Type	Original List	Current Whlse	Average Retail
4000S 4			
2 Dr Sdn	**12750**	1150	1875
4 Dr Sdn	**13340**	1275	2000
4 Dr Quattro Sdn	**16860**	1975	2825
5000S 5			
4 Dr Sdn	**16840**	1675	2525
4 Dr Wgn	**17840**	1625	2475
4 Dr Turbo Sdn (auto)	**22250**	1725	2575
GT COUPE 5			
2 Dr Cpe	**14860**	1500	2350
QUATTRO 5			
2 Dr Cpe	**35000**	—	—

1983 — ALL BODY STYLES

Year-Model-Body Type	Original List	Current Whlse	Average Retail
4000	—	825	1525
4000S	—	900	1625
5000S	—	1075	1800
5000T	—	1225	1950
COUPE	—	1025	1750

BMW

1992

Year-Model-Body Type	Original List	Current Whlse	Average Retail
BMW 4			
318iC 2 Dr Conv	**28870**	—	—
318iS 2 Dr Cpe	**23600**	—	—
318i 4 Dr Sdn	**22900**	—	—
BMW 6			
325i 4 Dr Sdn	**27990**	—	—
325iC 2 Dr Conv	**36320**	—	—
325iS 2 Dr Cpe	**29100**	—	—
525i 4 Dr Sdn	**35600**	—	—
535i 4 Dr Sdn (auto)	**44350**	—	—
M5 4 Dr Sdn	**58600**	—	—
735i 4 Dr Sdn (auto)	**52990**	—	—
735iL 4 Dr Sdn (auto)	**56950**	—	—
BMW 12			
750iL 4 Dr Sdn (auto)	**76500**	—	—
850i 2 Dr Cpe (auto)	**78500**	—	—
ADD FOR:			
Auto Traction Control			
(535i)	**1290**	—	—
(735i, 735iL)	**1290**	—	—
(850i)	**1500**	—	—
Cellular Telephone			
(525i, 535i, M5 735i, 735iL)	**800**	—	—
CD Player (735i, 735iL)	**825**	—	—
Electronic Damping Suspension (850i)	**1470**	—	—
Forged Alloy Wheels (850i)	**1000**	—	—
Leather Seats			
(325i Sdn)	**1100**	—	—
(525i)	**1200**	—	—
Special App Pkg (325iC)	**1850**	—	—
Wood & Leather Pkg (525i Base)	**2040**	—	—

NOTE: Power windows and power door locks standard on all models. Power seats standard on 525, 535, M5, 735, 750 and 850. Sunroof standard on all models except Convertibles. Tilt steering wheel and cruise control standard on all models except 318.

1991

Year-Model-Body Type	Original List	Current Whlse	Average Retail
BMW 4			
318i 4 Dr Sdn	**19900**	14200	16675
318iS 2 Dr Sdn	**21500**	14300	16800
318iC 2 Dr Conv	**28500**	19450	22500
M3 2 Dr Sdn	**35900**	—	—
BMW 6			
325i 2 Dr Sdn	**25600**	17700	20350
325i 4 Dr Sdn	**26400**	17600	20250
325iC 2 Dr Conv	**35700**	24225	27525
325iX 4WD 2 Dr Sdn	**31100**	20350	23400
325iX 4WD 4 Dr Sdn	**31900**	20350	23400
525i 4 Dr Sdn	**34500**	25400	28725
535i 4 Dr Sdn (auto)	**42600**	29100	32425
M5 4 Dr Sdn	**56600**	—	—
735i 4 Dr Sdn (auto)	**50900**	36100	40075
735iL 4 Dr Sdn (auto)	**55000**	37900	42050
BMW 12			
750iL 4 Dr Sdn (auto)	**74000**	48550	53500
850i 2 Dr Sdn (auto)	**73600**	50900	55900
ADD FOR:			
Forged Alloy Wheels (850i)	**1000**	500	600
Leather Seats			
(325i, 325iX)	**950**	475	575
(525i)	**1200**	550	650
Sport Pkg (325i)	**1920**	850	1025
Touring Pkg (325i)	**1665**	725	825

NOTE: Power brakes standard on all models. Power windows and power door locks standard on 3-Series, 5-Series, M3, M5, 7-Series and 8-Series. Sunroof standard on 325iX, M3, M5, 7-Series and 8-Series. Power seat standard on M5, 7-Series and 8-Series.

1990

Year-Model-Body Type	Original List	Current Whlse	Average Retail
BMW 4			
M3 2 Dr Sdn	**34950**	19825	22875
BMW 6			
325i 2 Dr Sdn	**24650**	14750	17325
325i 4 Dr Sdn	**25450**	14650	17200
325iC 2 Dr Conv	**33850**	21050	24200
325iS 2 Dr Sdn	**28950**	16575	19225
325iX 4WD 2 Dr Sdn	**29950**	17300	19950
325iX 4WD 4 Dr Sdn	**30750**	17300	19950
525i 4 Dr Sdn	**33200**	20925	23975
535i 4 Dr Sdn (auto)	**41500**	23975	27275
735i 4 Dr Sdn (auto)	**49000**	28175	31525
735iL 4 Dr Sdn (auto)	**53000**	30000	33350
BMW 12			
750iL 4 Dr Sdn (auto)	**70000**	38225	42425
ADD FOR:			
Cellular Telephone (735)	**1205**	225	275
Leather Interior			
(325i, 325iX)	**895**	350	400
(525)	**1100**	400	450

Refer To Optional Equipment Schedules

Year-Model-Body Type	Original List	Current Whlse	Average Retail

NOTE: Power brakes standard on all BMW models. Power windows and anti-lock brakes standard on 325 Series, M3, 525, 535, 735, 750. Power door locks standard on 325 Series, M3, 750. Power seat standard on 525, 535, 735, 750. Sunroof standard on 325 Series except 325iC, M3, 525, 535, 735, 750.

1989

Year-Model-Body Type	Original List	Current Whlse	Average Retail
BMW 4			
M3 2 Dr Sdn	**34950**	16650	19300
BMW 6			
325i 2 Dr Sdn	**24650**	11925	13775
325i 4 Dr Sdn	**25450**	11800	13625
325iC 2 Dr Conv	**33850**	17900	20550
325is 2 Dr Sdn	**28950**	11500	13350
325iX 4WD 2 Dr Sdn	**29950**	14350	16850
325iX 4WD 4 Dr Sdn	**30750**	14250	16725
525i 4 Dr Sdn (auto)	**37000**	17275	19925
535i 4 Dr Sdn (auto)	**43600**	20250	23300
635CSi 2 Dr Cpe (auto)	**47000**	23750	27050
735i 4 Dr Sdn (auto)	**54000**	22875	26175
735iL 4 Dr Sdn (auto)	**58000**	24675	27975
BMW 12			
750iL 4 Dr Sdn (auto)	**70000**	31125	34600
ADD FOR:			
Hard Top (325iC)	**3500**	1500	1800
Compact Disc (525i, 535, 635CSi, 735i, 735iL, 750iL)	**775**	200	250

NOTE: Power steering, air conditioning, power brakes and power windows standard on all models. Automatic transmission standard on 525i, 535i, 635CSi, 735 Series and 750iL. Sunroof standard on M3, 325 Series except 325iC, 525i, 535i, 635CSi, 735 Series and 750iL. Anti-lock brakes standard on 325 Series, 525i, 535i, 635CSi, 735 and 750iL.

1988

Year-Model-Body Type	Original List	Current Whlse	Average Retail
BMW 4			
M3 2 Dr Sdn	**34800**	14350	16850
BMW 6			
325 2 Dr Sdn	**24350**	9800	11300
325 4 Dr Sdn	**25150**	9725	11200
325i 4 Dr Sdn	**28950**	11250	13000
325i 2 Dr Conv	**32995**	15800	18450
325is 2 Dr Sdn	**28950**	11350	13100
325ix 2 Dr Sdn	**33290**	12075	13950
528e 4 Dr Sdn	**31950**	9875	11375
535i 4 Dr Sdn	**36700**	12500	14700
535is 4 Dr Sdn	**37800**	13100	15425
635CSi 2 Dr Cpe (auto)	**46000**	17900	20550
735i 4 Dr Sdn (auto)	**54000**	17550	20200
750iL 4 Dr Sdn (auto)	**69000**	25425	28750
M5 4 Dr Sdn	**47500**	17850	20500
M6 2 Dr Cpe	**55950**	23650	26950
ADD FOR:			
Leather Upholstery (528e)	**1090**	350	425
Hard Top (325iC)	**3500**	1500	1800

NOTE: Air conditioning, power steering, anti-lock brakes and sunroof standard on all models. Power windows standard on all models except 325 Base.

1987

Year-Model-Body Type	Original List	Current Whlse	Average Retail
BMW 6			
325 2 Dr Sdn	**23180**	7600	9025
325 4 Dr Sdn	**23765**	7600	9025
325es 2 Dr Sdn	**24370**	8000	9650
325e 4 Dr Sdn	**25150**	8000	9650
325is 2 Dr Sdn	**27300**	8850	10225
325i 4 Dr Sdn	**27300**	8750	10100
325i 2 Dr Conv	**31000**	13250	15575
528e 4 Dr Sdn	**28330**	7600	8825
535i 4 Dr Sdn	**33600**	9900	11400
535is 4 Dr Sdn	**35200**	10600	12225
635CSi 2 Dr Cpe	**46965**	15500	18150
735i 4 Dr Sdn (auto)	**42475**	13100	15425
L6 2 Dr Cpe	**49500**	16250	18900
L7 4 Dr Sdn (auto)	**46675**	13850	16225
M6 2 Dr Cpe	**55950**	20425	23475
ADD FOR:			
Leather Upholstery (528e)	**980**	250	300
TRX Wheels & Tires (735i)	**650**	175	200

NOTE: Air conditioning, power steering, power brakes, power windows and sunroof standard on 325 Series, 528e, 535, 635CSi, L6, M6 and 735i. Anti-lock braking system standard on 325 Series, 528e, 635CSi and 735i. Automatic transmission standard on L6.

1986

Year-Model-Body Type	Original List	Current Whlse	Average Retail
BMW 6			
325 2 Dr Sdn	**19955**	6175	7200
325 4 Dr Sdn	**20455**	6075	6975
325es 2 Dr Sdn	**22540**	6650	7750
325e 4 Dr Sdn	**23255**	6575	7650

Year-Model-Body Type	Original List	Current Whlse	Average Retail
524 4 Dr Turbo Diesel Sdn (auto)	**26225**	5100	6025
528e 4 Dr Sdn	**26980**	6475	7525
535i 4 Dr Sdn	**31980**	8400	9700
635CSi 2 Dr Cpe	**43055**	12525	14750
735i 4 Dr Sdn	**39275**	9075	10450
L7 4 Dr Sdn	**44030**	9750	11225
ADD FOR:			
Leather Upholstery			
(325es)	**790**	150	175
(528e)	**1090**	200	250
TRX Wheels & Tires			
(735i)	**850**	150	175

NOTE: Power brakes, power locks, power windows, power steering, air conditioning and sunroof standard on all models. Automatic transmission standard on 524td and L7. Power seat standard on 524td, 528e, 535i, 635CSi, 735i and L7.

1985

Year-Model-Body Type	Original List	Current Whlse	Average Retail
BMW 4			
318i 2 Dr Sdn	**16935**	3875	4775
318i 4 Dr Sdn	**17430**	3875	4775
BMW 6			
325e 2 Dr Sdn	**20970**	5200	6125
325e 4 Dr Sdn	**21105**	5200	6125
524td 4 Dr Sdn (auto)	**24145**	4350	5275
528e 4 Dr Sdn	**24565**	5300	6225
535i 4 Dr Sdn	**30760**	6925	8050
633CSi 2 Dr Cpe	**41315**	10225	11900
735i 4 Dr Sdn	**36880**	7075	8225
ADD FOR:			
Leather Upholstery			
(325e)	**790**	100	125
(528e)	**1090**	125	150
Metallic Paint			
(318i, 325e)	**420**	50	60
TRX Wheels & Tires			
(735i)	**850**	75	100

NOTE: Power steering, air conditioning and power windows standard on all models. Sunroof standard on all models except 318i.

1984

Year-Model-Body Type	Original List	Current Whlse	Average Retail
BMW 4			
318i 2 Dr Sdn	**16935**	3225	4125
BMW 6			
325e 2 Dr Sdn	**20970**	4200	5125
528e 4 Dr Sdn	**24565**	4275	5200
533i 4 Dr Sdn	**30305**	5075	6000
633CSi 2 Dr Cpe	**40705**	8800	10175
733i 4 Dr Sdn	**36335**	6275	7300

1983 — ALL BODY STYLES

Year-Model-Body Type	Original List	Current Whlse	Average Retail
320i	—	2475	3350
528e	—	3550	4450
533i	—	4275	5200
633CSi	—	8050	9300
733i	—	5550	6475

CHALLENGER

1983

Year-Model-Body Type	Original List	Current Whlse	Average Retail
CHALLENGER 4			
2 Dr Luxury HT	**8223**	500	925

COLT

1992

Year-Model-Body Type	Original List	Current Whlse	Average Retail
COLT 4			
3 Dr Htchbk (NA w/power steering)	**8344**	—	—
3 Dr GL Htchbk	**9016**	—	—

1991

Year-Model-Body Type	Original List	Current Whlse	Average Retail
COLT 4			
3 Dr Htchbk (NA w/power steering)	**7919**	3975	4875
3 Dr GL Htchbk	**8815**	4675	5600

NOTE: Power brakes standard on all models.

1990

Year-Model-Body Type	Original List	Current Whlse	Average Retail
COLT 4			
3 Dr Htchbk (NA w/power steering)	**7590**	2950	3825
3 Dr GL Htchbk	**9297**	3550	4450
3 Dr GT Htchbk	**10482**	4225	5125
5 Dr 2WD DL Wgn	**10823**	4575	5500
5 Dr 4WD DL Wgn	**12393**	5625	6550

NOTE: Power brakes standard on all models.

Refer To Optional Equipment Schedules

Year-Model-Body Type	Original List	Current Whlse	Average Retail
1989			
COLT 4			
3 Dr Htchbk (NA w/power steering)	**6951**	1775	2625
3 Dr E Htchbk	**8037**	2200	3050
3 Dr GT Htchbk	**9420**	2725	3625
5 Dr 2WD DL Wgn	**9848**	2950	3850
5 Dr 4WD DL Wgn	**11418**	4000	4900
ADD FOR:			
Cast Aluminum Wheels	**299**	100	125

NOTE: Power brakes standard on all models.

Year-Model-Body Type	Original List	Current Whlse	Average Retail
1988			
COLT 4			
3 Dr Htchbk	**6148**	800	1500
3 Dr E Htchbk	**6845**	1100	1825
4 Dr E Sdn	**8014**	1250	1975
3 Dr DL Htchbk	**8098**	1375	2125
4 Dr DL Sdn	**8466**	1550	2400
5 Dr DL Wgn	**9018**	1725	2575
4 Dr Premier Sdn	**9386**	2000	2850
ADD FOR:			
DL Turbo Pkg	**1271**	400	500
Turbo Pkg (Premier)	**748**	250	300

NOTE: Power brakes standard on all models.

Year-Model-Body Type	Original List	Current Whlse	Average Retail
1987			
COLT 4			
3 Dr Htchbk	**5949**	775	1475
4 Dr Sdn	**7421**	925	1650
3 Dr DL Htchbk	**7255**	1100	1825
4 Dr DL Sdn	**7733**	1200	1925
4 Dr Premier Sdn	**8706**	1575	2425
ADD FOR:			
DL Turbo Pkg	**1248**	325	350
Premier Turbo Pkg	**720**	200	240

NOTE: Power brakes standard on all models.

Year-Model-Body Type	Original List	Current Whlse	Average Retail
1986			
COLT 4			
3 Dr E Htchbk	**5727**	550	1025
4 Dr E Sdn	**6627**	650	1225
3 Dr DL Htchbk	**6604**	950	1675
4 Dr DL Sdn	**6956**	1075	1800
4 Dr Premier Sdn	**7893**	1250	1975
ADD FOR:			
GTS Turbo Pkg (DL)	**1375**	250	300
Premier Turbo Pkg (Premier Sdn)	**664**	200	240

NOTE: Power brakes standard on all models.

Year-Model-Body Type	Original List	Current Whlse	Average Retail
1985			
COLT 4			
3 Dr E Htchbk	**5462**	475	875
5 Dr E Htchbk	**6119**	575	1075
3 Dr DL Htchbk	**6267**	750	1475
4 Dr DL Sdn	**6582**	800	1500
4 Dr Premier Sdn	**7499**	1050	1775
ADD FOR:			
GTS Pkg (DL)	**512**	60	80
GTS Turbo Pkg (DL)	**1580**	175	200
Turbo Pkg (Premier)	**949**	125	150
Technica Pkg (Premier)	**690**	90	100

Year-Model-Body Type	Original List	Current Whlse	Average Retail
1984			
COLT 4			
3 Dr E Htchbk	**5085**	200	400
5 Dr E Htchbk	**5729**	300	575
3 Dr DL Htchbk	**5983**	400	725
5 Dr DL Htchbk	**6119**	475	875

Year-Model-Body Type	Original List	Current Whlse	Average Retail
1983 — ALL BODY STYLES			
COLT 4	—	300	550

CONQUEST

Year-Model-Body Type	Original List	Current Whlse	Average Retail
1989			
CONQUEST 4			
2 Dr TSi Lftbk	**19929**	6125	7125
ADD FOR:			
Leather Seat Trim	**372**	250	300

NOTE: Power brakes, power door locks, tinted glass, power steering and power windows standard.

Year-Model-Body Type	Original List	Current Whlse	Average Retail
1988			
CONQUEST 4			
2 Dr Lftbk	**18683**	4200	5125
ADD FOR:			
Leather Seat Trim	**542**	225	275

Year-Model-Body Type	Original List	Current Whlse	Average Retail
NOTE: Power brakes, power door locks, power steering and power windows standard.			
1987			
CONQUEST 4			
2 Dr Lftbk	**14417**	2750	3650
ADD FOR:			
TSi Intercooler Pkg	**2757**	700	875
NOTE: Power brakes, power door locks, power steering and power windows standard.			
1986			
CONQUEST 4			
2 Dr Lftbk	**13837**	1900	2750
ADD FOR:			
Technica Pkg	**346**	75	90
NOTE: Power steering, power windows and power brakes standard.			
1985			
CONQUEST 4			
2 Dr Lftbk	**12564**	1400	2125
NOTE: Power steering, power windows and power brakes standard.			
1984			
CONQUEST 4			
2 Dr Lftbk	**12149**	1200	1900

DAIHATSU

Year-Model-Body Type	Original List	Current Whlse	Average Retail
1992			
CHARADE (1.0 LITER) 3			
3 Dr SE Htchbk (5 spd) (NA w/power steering)	**7751**	—	—
CHARADE (1.3 LITER) 4			
3 Dr SE Htchbk (5 spd)	**8710**	—	—
4 Dr SE Sdn (5 spd)	**10010**	—	—
4 Dr SX Sdn (auto)	**10951**	—	—
ROCKY 4			
4WD SE Sport Soft Top	**12972**	—	—
4WD SE Sport Hard Top	**13772**	—	—
4WD SX Sport Hard Top	**14772**	—	—
ADD FOR:			
Soft Top Conversion Kit (Hardtop)	**387**	—	—
Alloy Wheels	**550**	—	—
NOTE: Manual sunroof standard on Rocky. Tilt steering wheel standard on Rocky SX.			
1991			
CHARADE (1.0 LITER) 3			
3 Dr SE Htchbk (NA w/power steering)	**7705**	4325	5250
CHARADE (1.3 LITER) 3			
3 Dr SE Htchbk (auto)	**9005**	4800	5725
4 Dr SE Sdn (5 spd)	**9875**	4800	5725
4 Dr SX Sdn (auto)	**11075**	5750	6675
ROCKY 4			
4WD SE Sport Soft Top	**12761**	6925	8050
4WD SE Sport Hard Top	**13561**	7075	8225
4WD Full-Time SE Sport Hard Top	**13981**	7275	8450
4WD SX Sport Hard Top	**14461**	8925	10300
ADD FOR:			
SX Plus Pkg (Rocky)	**1385**	575	675
NOTE: Power brakes standard on all models. Sunroof standard on Rocky.			
1990			
CHARADE (1.0 LITER) 3			
3 Dr SE Htchbk (NA w/power steering)	**7757**	3400	4300
3 Dr SX Htchbk (NA w/power steering)	**8257**	3625	4525
CHARADE (1.3 LITER) 3			
3 Dr SE Htchbk (auto)	**8948**	3850	4850
4 Dr SE Sdn (5 spd)	**9598**	3625	4525
3 Dr SX Htchbk (5 spd)	**8948**	3625	4525
4 Dr SX Sdn (5 spd)	**10131**	3975	4875
ROCKY 4			
4WD SE Sport Soft Top	**12172**	6800	7925
4WD SE Sport Hard Top	**12972**	6925	8050
4WD SX Sport Soft Top	**12872**	7075	8225
4WD SX Sport Hard Top	**13772**	7200	8350
ADD FOR:			
SX Plus Pkg			

Refer To Optional Equipment Schedules

Year-Model-Body Type	Original List	Current Whlse	Average Retail
(Rocky SX)	**1220**	400	500

NOTE: Power brakes standard on all models.

1989

Year-Model-Body Type	Original List	Current Whlse	Average Retail
CHARADE (1.0 LITER) 3			
3 Dr CES Htchbk (NA w/power steering)	**7157**	2075	2925
3 Dr CLS Htchbk (NA w/power steering)	**7657**	2250	3100
3 Dr CLX Htchbk (NA w/power steering)	**8457**	2525	3400
CHARADE (1.3 LITER) 3			
3 Dr CLS Htchbk	**8298**	2375	3250
3 Dr CLX Htchbk	**9617**	2675	3575

NOTE: Power brakes standard on all models.

1988

Year-Model-Body Type	Original List	Current Whlse	Average Retail
CHARADE 3			
3 Dr CLS Htchbk	**6397**	1275	2000
3 Dr CLX Htchbk w/o auto restraint	**7650**	1475	2300
3 Dr CLX Htchbk w/auto restraint	**7725**	1500	2350
3 Dr CSX Htchbk	**9232**	1825	2675

NOTE: Power brakes standard on all models. Air conditioning standard on CSX.

DODGE D-50

1984

Year-Model-Body Type	Original List	Current Whlse	Average Retail
2WD D-50 4			
Custom Pickup	**5767**	1025	1750
Royal Pickup	**6290**	1100	1825
Sport Pickup	**7018**	1150	1875

1983

Year-Model-Body Type	Original List	Current Whlse	Average Retail
2WD D-50 4			
Base Pickup	**5754**	700	1125
Custom Pickup	**6266**	825	1525
Royal Pickup	**7135**	850	1550
Sport Pickup	**7732**	875	1600

GEO

1992

Year-Model-Body Type	Original List	Current Whlse	Average Retail
METRO 3			
2 Dr XFI Htchbk Cpe (NA w/power steering or air cond)	**7300**	—	—
2 Dr Htchbk Cpe (NA w/power steering)	**8020**	—	—
4 Dr Htchbk Sdn (NA w/power steering)	**8420**	—	—
2 Dr LSi Htchbk Cpe (NA w/power steering)	**9220**	—	—
4 Dr LSi Htchbk Sdn (NA w/power steering)	**9620**	—	—
2 Dr LSi Conv (NA w/power steering)	**11020**	—	—
PRIZM 4			
4 Dr Sdn	**11010**	—	—
4 Dr GSi Sdn	**13770**	—	—
STORM 4			
3 Dr 2+2 Sport Cpe	**12075**	—	—
3 Dr Htchbk Cpe	**12845**	—	—
3 Dr GSi Sport Cpe	**14045**	—	—
TRACKER 4			
4WD 2 Dr HT	**13222**	—	—
4WD 2 Dr LSi HT	**14522**	—	—
2WD 2 Dr Conv	**11017**	—	—
4WD 2 Dr Conv	**12822**	—	—
4WD 2 Dr LSi Conv	**13620**	—	—

NOTE: Tilt steering wheel standard on Prizm.

1991

Year-Model-Body Type	Original List	Current Whlse	Average Retail
METRO 3			
2 Dr XFi Htchbk Cpe (NA w/power steering)	**7096**	4000	4900
2 Dr Htchbk Cpe (NA w/power steering)	**7816**	4475	5400
4 Dr Htchbk Sdn (NA w/power steering)	**8016**	4575	5500
2 Dr LSi Htchbk Cpe (NA w/power steering)	**8816**	4825	5750
4 Dr LSi Htchbk Sdn (NA w/power steering)	**9016**	4925	5850
2 Dr LSi Convertible (NA w/power steering)	**10901**	6425	7475
PRIZM 4			
4 Dr Ntchbk Sdn	**10565**	6500	7575
5 Dr Htchbk Sdn	**11180**	6600	7675
4 Dr GSi Ntchbk Sdn	**12940**	7650	8875
5 Dr GSi Htchbk Sdn	**13440**	7750	9000

Year-Model-Body Type	Original List	Current Whlse	Average Retail
STORM 4			
3 Dr 2+2 Sport Cpe	**11415**	6925	8050
2 Dr Htchbk Cpe	**12195**	6975	8125
3 Dr GSi Sport Cpe	**13140**	8100	9350
TRACKER 4			
4WD 2 Dr HT	**12607**	8275	9550
4WD 2 Dr LSi HT	**13907**	9025	10400
2WD 2 Dr Conv	**10321**	6950	8100
4WD 2 Dr Conv	**12207**	8125	9375
4WD 2 Dr LSi Conv	**13317**	8825	10200

NOTE: Power brakes standard on all models.

1990

Year-Model-Body Type	Original List	Current Whlse	Average Retail
METRO 3			
2 Dr XFi Htchbk Cpe (NA w/power steering)	**6966**	2450	3325
2 Dr Htchbk Cpe (NA w/power steering)	**7666**	2625	3525
4 Dr Htchbk Sdn (NA w/power steering)	**7966**	2700	3600
2 Dr LSi Htchbk Cpe (NA w/power steering)	**8466**	3000	3900
4 Dr LSi Htchbk Sdn (NA w/power steering)	**8766**	3075	3975
PRIZM 4			
4 Dr Ntchbk Sdn	**11424**	5150	6075
5 Dr Htchbk Sdn	**11724**	5250	6175
4 Dr GSi Ntchbk Sdn	**12590**	5950	6875
5 Dr GSi Htchbk Sdn	**12975**	6075	6975
STORM 4			
3 Dr 2+2 Sport Cpe	**11080**	5675	6600
3 Dr GSi Sport Cpe	**12340**	6525	7600
TRACKER 4			
2 Dr	**12307**	6925	8050
2 Dr LSi	**13215**	7425	8625
2 Dr Conv	**11997**	6800	7925
2 Dr LSi Conv	**12765**	7250	8425

NOTE: Power brakes standard on all models.

1989

Year-Model-Body Type	Original List	Current Whlse	Average Retail
METRO 3			
2 Dr Htchbk Cpe (NA w/power steering)	**6296**	2050	2900
2 Dr LSi Htchbk Cpe	**7851**	2350	3225
4 Dr LSi Htchbk Sdn	**8151**	2425	3300
SPECTRUM 4			
2 Dr Htchbk Cpe	**8256**	2800	3700
4 Dr Ntchbk Sdn	**8756**	2975	3875
TRACKER 4			
2 Dr HT (NA w/power steering)	**10796**	5075	6000
2 Dr Conv (NA w/power steering)	**10496**	4925	5850
2 Dr LSi Htchbk Cpe (NA w/power steering)	**12796**	5625	6550

HONDA

1992

Year-Model-Body Type	Original List	Current Whlse	Average Retail
ACCORD 4			
2 Dr DX Cpe (5 spd)	**14800**	—	—
4 Dr DX Sdn (5 spd)	**15000**	—	—
2 Dr LX Cpe (5 spd)	**15900**	—	—
4 Dr LX Sdn (5 spd)	**16100**	—	—
5 Dr LX Wgn (5 spd)	**17725**	—	—
2 Dr EX Cpe (5 spd)	**18320**	—	—
4 Dr EX Sdn (5 spd)	**18520**	—	—
5 Dr EX Wgn (5 spd)	**20175**	—	—
CIVIC 4			
3 Dr CX Htchbk (5 spd)	**9400**	—	—
3 Dr DX Htchbk (5 spd)	**11150**	—	—
4 Dr DX Sdn (5 spd)	**12055**	—	—
3 Dr VX Htchbk (5 spd)	**11850**	—	—
3 Dr Si Htchbk (5 spd)	**13200**	—	—
4 Dr LX Sdn (5 spd)	**12885**	—	—
4 Dr EX Sdn (5 spd)	**15075**	—	—
PRELUDE 4			
2 Dr S Cpe (5 spd)	**17950**	—	—
2 Dr Si Cpe (5 spd)	**19550**	—	—
2 Dr Si 4WS Cpe (5 spd)	**21870**	—	—

NOTE: Power windows standard on Civic LX, EX & Si, Accord LX, EX & Prelude. Power door locks standard on Civic LX & EX, Accord LX & EX, Prelude Si. Power sunroof standard on Prelude. Power moonroof standard on Civic EX & Si, Accord EX. Tilt steering wheel standard on Civic DX, LX, EX & Si, Accord and Prelude. Cruise control standard on Civic LX, EX & Si, Accord LX & EX and Prelude.

1991

Year-Model-Body Type	Original List	Current Whlse	Average Retail
ACCORD 4			
2 Dr DX Cpe (5 spd)	**14025**	10125	11675
4 Dr DX Sdn (5 spd)	**14225**	10425	12025
2 Dr LX Cpe (5 spd)	**15175**	11325	13075
4 Dr LX Sdn (5 spd)	**15375**	11425	13200
5 Dr LX Wgn (5 spd)	**17400**	12275	14225
2 Dr EX Cpe (5 spd)	**16895**	12525	14750
4 Dr EX Sdn (5 spd)	**17095**	12825	15150
5 Dr EX Wgn (5 spd)	**19150**	13550	15925
4 Dr SE Sdn (auto)	**19895**	13825	16200

Refer To Optional Equipment Schedules

Year-Model-Body Type	Original List	Current Whlse	Average Retail
CIVIC 4			
3 Dr Htchbk (4 spd)	**8295**	5700	6625
4 Dr Wgn (5 spd)	**11780**	7850	9125
4 Dr 4WD Wgn (6 spd)	**13865**	8600	9925
3 Dr DX Htchbk (5 spd)	**10120**	7250	8425
4 Dr DX Sdn (5 spd)	**10945**	7975	9250
4 Dr LX Sdn (5 spd)	**11955**	8475	9800
4 Dr EX Sdn (5 spd)	**12650**	8875	10250
3 Dr Si Htchbk (5 spd)	**11670**	8000	9300
CRX 4			
2 Dr HF Htchbk (5 spd)	**10600**	7700	8950
2 Dr Htchbk (5 spd)	**10865**	8025	9275
2 Dr Si Htchbk (5 spd)	**12605**	8950	10325
PRELUDE 4			
2 Dr 2.0 Si Cpe (5 spd)	**16595**	12050	13925
2 Dr Si High-Output Cpe (5 spd)	**17445**	12800	15125
2 Dr Si High-Output Cpe w/4 Wheel Steering (5 spd)	**18750**	13200	15525
2 Dr Si High-Output Cpe w/Anti-Lock Brakes (5 spd)	**19000**	13250	15575

NOTE: Power brakes standard on all models. Power windows and power door locks standard on Accord LX and EX, Civic LX Sedan and EX and Prelude Si High-Output. Sunroof standard on Accord EX, Civic Si Hatchback and CRX Si. Power moonroof standard on Prelude.

1990

Year-Model-Body Type	Original List	Current Whlse	Average Retail
ACCORD 4			
2 Dr DX Cpe (5 spd)	**13645**	8625	9950
4 Dr DX Sdn (5 spd)	**13845**	8925	10300
2 Dr LX Cpe (5 spd)	**14695**	9325	10750
4 Dr LX Sdn (5 spd)	**14895**	9625	11100
2 Dr EX Cpe (5 spd)	**16395**	10400	12000
4 Dr EX Sdn (5 spd)	**16595**	10700	12350
CIVIC 4			
3 Dr Htchbk (4 spd)	**7935**	4775	5700
4 Dr Wgn (5 spd)	**11625**	6325	7350
3 Dr DX Htchbk (5 spd)	**9995**	5775	6700
4 Dr DX Sdn (5 spd)	**10740**	6425	7475
4 Dr LX Sdn (5 spd)	**11750**	6925	8050
4 Dr EX Sdn (5 spd)	**12445**	7275	8450
3 Dr Si Htchbk (5 spd)	**11545**	6475	7525
4 Dr 4WD Wgn (6 spd)	**13710**	7025	8150
CRX 4			
2 Dr HF Htchbk (5 spd)	**10445**	6200	7225
2 Dr Htchbk (5 spd)	**10710**	6500	7575
2 Dr Si Htchbk (5 spd)	**12430**	7150	8300
PRELUDE			
2 Dr 2.0 S Cpe (5 spd)	**15145**	9450	10875
2 Dr 2.0 Si Cpe (5 spd)	**16145**	9925	11425
2 Dr Si Cpe (5 spd)	**16965**	10600	12225
2 Dr Si Cpe w/4 Wheel Steering (5 spd)	**18450**	11050	12775
2 Dr Si Cpe w/Anti-Lock Brakes (5 spd)	**18550**	11000	12700

NOTE: Power brakes standard on all models. Power windows standard on Civic LX and EX, Prelude Si High-Output and Prelude Si High-Output w/4 wheel steering. Power door locks standard on Civic LX & EX and Prelude Si High-Output w/4 wheel steering. Sunroof standard on CRX Si. Moonroof standard on Civic Si and Prelude. Anti-lock brakes standard on Prelude Si High-Output w/anti-lock brakes.

1989

Year-Model-Body Type	Original List	Current Whlse	Average Retail
ACCORD 4			
3 Dr DX Htchbk (5 spd)	**12230**	6725	7850
4 Dr DX Sdn (5 spd)	**12770**	7500	8725
2 Dr DX Cpe (5 spd)	**12650**	7200	8375
4 Dr LX Sdn (5 spd)	**14180**	8000	9250
3 Dr LXi Htchbk (5 spd)	**14530**	8025	9275
4 Dr LXi Sdn (5 spd)	**15920**	9075	10450
2 Dr LXi Cpe (5 spd)	**14690**	8525	9850
2 Dr SEi Cpe (5 spd)	**16975**	9300	10725
4 Dr SEi Sdn (5 spd)	**17985**	9775	11250
CIVIC 4			
3 Dr 1.5 Htchbk (4 spd)	**7185**	3950	4850
4 Dr 1.5 Wgn (5 spd)	**10925**	5150	6075
4 Dr 1.5 Wagovan (5 spd)	**10645**	4850	5775
4 Dr 1.6 4WD Wgn (6 spd)	**13010**	5875	6800
3 Dr 1.5 DX Htchbk (5 spd)	**9245**	4800	5725
4 Dr 1.5 DX Sdn (5 spd)	**9990**	5500	6425
3 Dr 1.6 Si Htchbk (5 spd)	**10780**	5450	6375
4 Dr 1.5 LX Sdn (5 spd)	**10950**	5925	6850
CRX 4			
2 Dr 1.5 HF Htchbk (5 spd)	**9695**	5250	6175
2 Dr 1.5 Htchbk (5 spd)	**10110**	5600	6525
2 Dr 1.6 Si Htchbk (5 spd)	**11730**	6400	7425
PRELUDE 4			
2 Dr 2.0 S Cpe (5 spd)	**14945**	7975	9250
2 Dr 2.0 Si Cpe (5 spd)	**16965**	9000	10400
2 Dr 2.0 4WS Si Cpe			

Year-Model-Body Type	Original List	Current Whlse	Average Retail
(5 spd)	**18450**	9300	10725

NOTE: Power brakes standard on all models. Sunroof standard on CRX Si. Moonroof standard on Civic Si Hatchback, Accord LXi Sedan & SEi Sedan and Prelude. Power windows standard on Civic LX Sedan, Prelude Si, Accord LXi Hatchback, Accord LXi Coupe and Accord LX Sedan. Power locks standard on Civic LX Sedan, Accord LX Sedan and Prelude Si 4WS.

1988

Year-Model-Body Type	Original List	Current Whlse	Average Retail
ACCORD 4			
3 Dr DX Htchbk (5 spd)	**11270**	5150	6075
4 Dr DX Sdn (5 spd)	**11800**	5425	6350
4 Dr LX Sdn (5 spd)	**14165**	6375	7400
3 Dr LXi Htchbk (5 spd)	**14510**	6325	7350
4 Dr LXi Sdn (5 spd)	**15880**	7275	8425
CIVIC 4			
3 Dr 1.5 Htchbk (4 spd)	**6515**	2575	3450
4 Dr 1.5 Wgn (5 spd)	**9948**	3475	4375
4 Dr 1.5 Wagovan (5 spd)	**9698**	3200	4100
4 Dr 1.6 4WD Wgn (6 spd)	**11998**	4125	5025
3 Dr 1.5 DX Htchbk (5 spd)	**8540**	3175	4075
4 Dr 1.5 DX Sdn (5 spd)	**9325**	3775	4675
4 Dr 1.5 LX Sdn (5 spd)	**10280**	4300	5225
CRX 4			
3 Dr 1.5 HF Htchbk (5 spd)	**8985**	3550	4450
3 Dr 1.5 DX Htchbk (5 spd)	**9315**	3825	4725
3 Dr 1.5 Si Htchbk (5 spd)	**10950**	4475	5400
PRELUDE 4			
2 Dr 2.0 S Cpe (5 spd)	**13870**	6000	6925
2 Dr 2.0 Si Cpe (5 spd)	**17025**	7400	8575
2 Dr 2.0 4WS Cpe (5 spd)	**18355**	7725	8950

NOTE: Power brakes standard on all models. Power steering on Accord and Prelude Series. Power windows standard on Civic LX, Accord LX and LXi and Prelude Si. Power sunroof standard on Civic CRX Si. Power moonroof standard on Accord LXi Sedan and Prelude S. Air conditioning standard on Accord LX and LXi and Prelude Si. Power door locks standard on Accord LXi Sedan and LX.

1987

Year-Model-Body Type	Original List	Current Whlse	Average Retail
ACCORD 4			
3 Dr DX Htchbk (5 spd)	**10120**	3825	4725
4 Dr DX Sdn (5 spd)	**10795**	4450	5375
4 Dr LX Sdn (5 spd)	**12998**	5075	6000
3 Dr LXi Htchbk (5 spd)	**13160**	4950	5875
4 Dr LXi Sdn (5 spd)	**14680**	5750	6675
CIVIC 4			
3 Dr 1.3 Std Htchbk (4 spd)	**5849**	1975	2825
4 Dr 1.5 Sdn (5 spd)	**8580**	2775	3675
4 Dr 1.5 Wgn (5 spd)	**8455**	2575	3450
4 Dr 1.5 Wagovan (5 spd)	**8200**	2450	3325
4 Dr 1.5 4WD Wgn (6 spd)	**9895**	3175	4075
3 Dr 1.5 DX Htchbk (5 spd)	**7599**	2400	3275
3 Dr 1.5 Si Htchbk (5 spd)	**9035**	2750	3650
CRX 4			
2 Dr 1.5 HF Cpe (5 spd)	**7759**	2850	3750
2 Dr 1.5 Cpe (5 spd)	**8095**	3075	3975
2 Dr 1.5 Si Cpe (5 spd)	**9539**	3600	4500
PRELUDE 4			
2 Dr 1.8 Cpe (5 spd)	**12230**	4900	5825
2 Dr 2.0 Si Cpe (5 spd)	**15245**	6125	7050

NOTE: Power brakes standard on all models. Power windows and air conditioning standard on Accord LX and Prelude Si. Power door locks standard on Accord LX and LXi Sedan. Power steering standard on Civic Automatic Sedan, Civic Wagon, Accord Series and Prelude Series. Sunroof standard on CRX Si. Moonroof standard on Civic Si, Prelude and Accord LXi Sedan.

1986

Year-Model-Body Type	Original List	Current Whlse	Average Retail
ACCORD 4			
3 Dr DX Htchbk (5 spd)	**9195**	2675	3575
3 Dr LXi Htchbk (5 spd)	**12115**	3775	4675
4 Dr DX Sdn (5 spd)	**9998**	3175	4075
4 Dr LX Sdn (5 spd)	**11979**	3875	4775
4 Dr LXi Sdn (5 spd)	**13727**	3900	4800
CIVIC 4			
3 Dr 1.3 Std Htchbk (4 spd)	**5698**	1475	2200
3 Dr 1.5 DX Htchbk (5 spd)	**7094**	1775	2600
3 Dr 1.5 Si Htchbk (5 spd)	**8529**	2150	3000
4 Dr 1.5 Wgn (5 spd)	**7884**	2000	2850

Refer To Optional Equipment Schedules

Year-Model-Body Type	Original List	Current Whlse	Average Retail
4 Dr 1.5 4WD Wgn (6 spd)	**9239**	2425	3275
4 Dr 1.5 Sdn (5 spd)	**7993**	2200	3050
4 Dr Wagovan (5 spd)	**7619**	1825	2675
CRX 4			
2 Dr 1.3 HF Cpe (5 spd)	**7198**	1900	2750
2 Dr 1.5 Cpe (5 spd)	**7523**	2175	3025
2 Dr 1.5 Si Cpe (5 spd)	**8865**	2575	3450
PRELUDE 4			
2 Dr 1.8 Cpe (5 spd)	**11365**	3875	4775
2 Dr 2.0 Si Cpe (5 spd)	**14079**	4775	5700

NOTE: Power locks standard on Accord LX & LXi Sedan. Power steering standard on Accord and Prelude. Power brakes standard on Accord, Civic, CRX and Prelude. Power windows standard on Accord LXi Hatchback, Accord LX Sedan, Accord LXi Sedan and Prelude Si. Air conditioning standard on Accord LX and LXi and Prelude Si. Moonroof standard on Accord LXi Sedan, Civic Si and Prelude Si. Sunroof standard on CRX Si.

1985

Year-Model-Body Type	Original List	Current Whlse	Average Retail
ACCORD 4			
3 Dr Htchbk (5 spd)	**7895**	1900	2750
3 Dr LX Htchbk (5 spd)	**9095**	2375	3250
4 Dr Base Sdn (5 spd)	**8845**	2400	3250
4 Dr LX Sdn (5 spd)	**10295**	2825	3725
4 Dr SE-i (5 spd)	**12945**	3125	4025
CIVIC 4			
2 Dr CRX Si Cpe (5 spd)	**7999**	2100	2950
2 Dr CRX HF Cpe (5 spd)	**6479**	1650	2425
2 Dr CRX Cpe (5 spd)	**6855**	1775	2625
3 Dr Base Htchbk	**5399**	975	1700
3 Dr DX Htchbk (5 spd)	**6529**	1325	2050
3 Dr S Htchbk (5 spd)	**7129**	1575	2325
5 Dr Wgn (5 spd)	**7195**	1475	2200
5 Dr 4WD Wgn (6 spd)	**8649**	1900	2750
4 Dr Sdn (5 spd)	**7295**	1700	2550
PRELUDE 4			
2 Dr Cpe (5 spd)	**10345**	3025	3925

NOTE: Power steering standard on Accord LX Hatchback, Accord Base Sedan and Prelude. Air conditioning standard on Accord LX Sedan and Accord SE-i. Power windows standard on Accord LX Sedan. Moonroof standard on Accord SE-i and Prelude.

1984

Year-Model-Body Type	Original List	Current Whlse	Average Retail
ACCORD 4			
3 Dr Htchbk (5 spd)	**7699**	1400	2150
4 Dr Sdn (5 spd)	**8549**	1700	2550
3 Dr LX Htchbk (5 spd)	**8849**	1525	2375
4 Dr LX Sdn (5 spd)	**9949**	1800	2650
CIVIC 4			
2 Dr 1.3 CRX Cpe	**6149**	1025	1750
2 Dr 1.5 CRX Cpe	**6599**	1300	2025
3 Dr Base Htchbk	**5249**	675	1275
3 Dr 1.5 DX Htchbk	**6299**	925	1650
3 Dr 1.5 S Htchbk	**6849**	1050	1775
5 Dr 1.5 Wgn	**6999**	1075	1800
4 Dr 1.5 Sdn	**7099**	1175	1900
PRELUDE 4			
2 Dr Cpe (5 spd)	**9995**	2250	3100

1983 — ALL BODY STYLES

Year-Model-Body Type	Original List	Current Whlse	Average Retail
ACCORD	—	975	1700
ACCORD SEDAN	—	1150	1875
CIVIC 1300	—	275	550
CIVIC 1500	—	575	1075
PRELUDE	—	1825	2675

HYUNDAI

1992

Year-Model-Body Type	Original List	Current Whlse	Average Retail
ELANTRA 4			
4 Dr Base Sdn (5 spd)	**10125**	—	—
4 Dr GLS Sdn (5 spd)	**10919**	—	—
EXCEL 4			
3 Dr Base Htchbk (4 spd)	**8010**	—	—
3 Dr GS Htchbk (5 spd)	**8654**	—	—
4 Dr Base Sdn (4 spd)	**9110**	—	—
4 Dr GL Sdn (5 spd)	**9554**	—	—
SCOUPE 4			
2 Dr Base Cpe (5 spd)	**10189**	—	—
2 Dr LS Cpe (5 spd)	**10794**	—	—
SONATA 4			
4 Dr Base Sdn (5 spd)	**12000**	—	—
4 Dr GLS Sdn (5 spd)	**13995**	—	—
SONATA 6			
4 Dr Base Sdn (auto)	**13540**	—	—
4 Dr GLS Sdn (auto)	**15535**	—	—

NOTE: Power windows and tilt steering wheel standard on Scoupe LS, Elantra GLS and Sonata. Power door locks standard on Elantra

Year-Model-Body Type	Original List	Current Whlse	Average Retail

GLS and Sonata. Power seat standard on Scoupe LS and Elantra GLS.

1991

Year-Model-Body Type	Original List	Current Whlse	Average Retail
EXCEL 4			
3 Dr Base Htchbk (4 spd)	**7770**	4250	5175
3 Dr GS Htchbk (5 spd)	**8740**	4650	5575
4 Dr Base Sdn (4 spd)	**8905**	4500	5425
4 Dr GL Sdn (5 spd)	**9610**	4950	5875
4 Dr GLS Sdn (5 spd)	**9815**	5275	6200
SCOUPE 4			
2 Dr Base Cpe (5 spd)	**9605**	6225	7250
2 Dr LS Cpe (5 spd)	**10620**	6775	7875
SONATA 4			
4 Dr Base Sdn (5 spd)	**11725**	7400	8600
4 Dr GLS Sdn (5 spd)	**13450**	8200	9475
SONATA 6			
4 Dr Sdn (auto)	**13195**	8400	9700
4 Dr GLS Sdn (auto)	**14920**	9150	10550

NOTE: Power brakes standard on all models. Power windows standard on Scoupe LS and Sonata GLS. Power door locks standard on Sonata GLS.

1990

Year-Model-Body Type	Original List	Current Whlse	Average Retail
EXCEL 4			
3 Dr Base Htchbk (4 spd) (NA w/power steering)	**6969**	2775	3675
3 Dr GS Htchbk (5 spd)	**8329**	3200	4100
5 Dr GL Htchbk (5 spd) (NA w/power steering)	**8669**	3325	4225
4 Dr Base Sdn (4 spd) (NA w/power steering)	**8069**	3025	3925
4 Dr GL Sdn (5 spd) (NA w/power steering)	**8949**	3425	4325
4 Dr GLS Sdn (5 spd)	**9514**	3850	4750
SONATA 4			
4 Dr Base Sdn (5 spd)	**11114**	5500	6425
4 Dr GLS Sdn (5 spd)	**13129**	6200	7225
SONATA 6			
4 Dr Base Sdn (auto)	**12504**	5925	6850
4 Dr GLS Sdn (auto)	**14519**	7025	8150
ADD FOR:			
Leather Pkg (Sonata GLS)	**575**	200	250

NOTE: Power brakes standard on all models. Power windows and power door locks standard on Sonata GLS.

1989

Year-Model-Body Type	Original List	Current Whlse	Average Retail
EXCEL 4			
3 Dr L Htchbk (4 spd)	**7014**	1700	2550
4 Dr L Sdn (4 spd)	**7739**	1925	2775
3 Dr GL Htchbk (5 spd)	**8239**	2075	2925
5 Dr GL Htchbk (5 spd)	**8439**	2200	3050
4 Dr GL Sdn (5 spd)	**8689**	2275	3150
5 Dr GLS Htchbk (5 spd)	**8844**	2375	3250
4 Dr GLS Sdn (5 spd)	**8994**	2475	3350
3 Dr GS Htchbk (5 spd)	**8944**	2425	3300
SONATA 4			
4 Dr Sdn (5 spd)	**10770**	3925	4825
4 Dr GLS Sdn (5 spd)	**12770**	4475	5400

NOTE: Power brakes standard on all models. Power windows and power door locks standard on Sonata GLS.

1988

Year-Model-Body Type	Original List	Current Whlse	Average Retail
EXCEL 4			
3 Dr L Htchbk (4 spd)	**5395**	725	1375
4 Dr L Sdn (4 spd)	**5995**	825	1525
3 Dr GL Htchbk (5 spd)	**6495**	950	1675
5 Dr GL Htchbk (5 spd)	**6745**	1100	1825
4 Dr GL Sdn (5 spd)	**6895**	1200	1925
5 Dr GLS Htchbk (5 spd)	**7495**	1250	1975
4 Dr GLS Sdn (5 spd)	**7645**	1325	2050
3 Dr GS Htchbk (5 spd)	**7595**	1300	2025

NOTE: Power brakes standard on all models.

1987

Year-Model-Body Type	Original List	Current Whlse	Average Retail
EXCEL 4			
3 Dr Htchbk (4 spd)	**5195**	475	875
5 Dr Htchbk (4 spd)	**5495**	625	1175
3 Dr GL Htchbk (5 spd)	**6095**	700	1325
5 Dr GL Htchbk (5 spd)	**6395**	850	1550
4 Dr GL Sdn (5 spd)	**6545**	900	1625
3 Dr GLS Htchbk (5 spd)	**6795**	825	1525
5 Dr GLS Htchbk (5 spd)	**7095**	925	1650
4 Dr GLS Sdn (5 spd)	**7245**	1025	1750

NOTE: Power brakes standard on all models.

1986

Year-Model-Body Type	Original List	Current Whlse	Average Retail
EXCEL 4			
3 Dr Htchbk (4 spd)	**5270**	400	725

Year-Model-Body Type	Original List	Current Whlse	Average Retail
5 Dr Htchbk (4 spd)	**5470**	450	825
3 Dr GL Htchbk (5 spd)	**6170**	500	925
5 Dr GL Htchbk (5 spd)	**6370**	650	1225
4 Dr GL Sdn (5 spd)	**6520**	750	1475
3 Dr GLS Htchbk (5 spd)	**6395**	600	1125
5 Dr GLS Htchbk (5 spd)	**6595**	750	1475
4 Dr GLS Sdn (5 spd)	**6745**	850	1550

INFINITI

1992

Year-Model-Body Type	Original List	Current Whlse	Average Retail
G20 4			
4 Dr Sdn (5 spd)	**19100**	—	—
ADD FOR:			
Leather Seat Trim	**1000**	—	—
M30 6			
2 Dr Cpe (auto)	**25500**	—	—
2 Dr Conv (auto)	**33700**	—	—
Q45 8			
4 Dr Sdn (auto)	**44000**	—	—
4 Dr Full Active Suspension Sdn (auto)	**48500**	—	—
ADD FOR:			
Touring Pkg	**2800**	—	—
Traction Control Pkg	**1500**	—	—

NOTE: Power windows, power door locks, tilt steering wheel, and cruise control standard on all models. Power seat and power sunroof standard on M30, J30 and Q45.

1991

Year-Model-Body Type	Original List	Current Whlse	Average Retail
G20 4			
4 Dr Sdn (5 spd)	**17750**	12625	14950
M30 6			
2 Dr Cpe	**24500**	15300	17950
2 Dr Conv	**31000**	—	—
Q45 8			
4 Dr Performance Luxury Sdn	**40000**	28525	31875
4 Dr Full Active Suspension Sdn	**45000**	30325	33725
ADD FOR:			
Q45 Touring Pkg	**2800**	1200	1350

NOTE: Power brakes, power windows and power door locks standard on all models. Power seat standard on Q45. Sunroof standard on M30 and Q45.

1990

Year-Model-Body Type	Original List	Current Whlse	Average Retail
M30 6			
2 Dr Cpe	**23500**	12500	14700
2 Dr Conv	—	—	—
Q45 8			
4 Dr Sdn	**38000**	23900	27200
ADD FOR:			
Q45 Touring Pkg	**2500**	680	830

NOTE: Power brakes, power windows, power door locks, sunroof, power seat and anti-lock brakes standard on all models.

ISUZU

1992

Year-Model-Body Type	Original List	Current Whlse	Average Retail
2WD S PICKUPS (2.3 LITER) 4			
Std Bed (5 spd)	**9624**	—	—
Long Bed (5 spd)	**10674**	—	—
2WD S PICKUPS (2.6 LITER) 4			
Std Bed (5 spd)	**10394**	—	—
1 Ton Long Bed (5 spd)	**11629**	—	—
Spacecab (5 spd)	**11714**	—	—
2WD LS PICKUPS (2.6 LITER) 4			
Spacecab (5 spd)	**13899**	—	—
4WD S PICKUP (3.1 LITER) 6			
Std Bed (5 spd)	**13289**	—	—
2WD AMIGO S (2.3 LITER) 4			
Sport Utility (5 spd)	**12414**	—	—
2WD AMIGO S (2.6 LITER) 4			
Sport Utility (5 spd)	**13104**	—	—
2WD AMIGO XS (2.6 LITER) 4			
Sport Utility (5 spd)	**13479**	—	—
2WD RODEO (2.6 LITER) 4			
S Sport Utility (5 spd)	**14191**	—	—
2WD RODEO (3.1 LITER) 6			
S Sport Utility (5 spd)	**14806**	—	—
XS Sport Utility (5 spd)	**15579**	—	—
LS Sport Utility (5 spd)	**16889**	—	—
TROOPER 6			
4WD S 4 Dr (5 spd)	**19650**	—	—
4WD LS 4 Dr (5 spd)	**24250**	—	—
ADD FOR:			
Anti-lock Brakes (LS)	**1100**	—	—
STYLUS 4			
S Sdn (5 spd)	**10479**	—	—
RS Sdn (5 spd)	**11499**	—	—

NOTE: Tilt steering wheel standard on LS Pickup and Rodeo LS. Cruise control, power windows and power door locks standard on Trooper LS.

1991

Year-Model-Body Type	Original List	Current Whlse	Average Retail
2WD S PICKUPS (2.3 LITER) 4			
Std Bed (5 spd)	**9244**	5925	6850
Long Bed (5 spd)	**10274**	6075	6975
2WD S PICKUPS (2.6 LITER) 4			
Std Bed (5 spd)	**9974**	6125	7125
Long Bed (auto)	**11454**	6650	7750
1 Ton Long Bed (5 spd)	**11129**	6275	7300
Spacecab (5 spd)	**10949**	6525	7600
2WD LS PICKUPS (2.6 LITER) 4			
Spacecab (5 spd)	**13299**	7500	8700
4WD S PICKUP (3.1 LITER) 6			
Std Bed (5 spd)	**12479**	7650	8875
4WD LS PICKUP (3.1 LITER) 6			
Std Bed (5 spd)	**15099**	8650	10000
TROOPER 4			
4WD S 4 Dr (5 spd)	**14849**	10675	12325
TROOPER 6			
4WD S 4 Dr (5 spd)	**15349**	11075	12800
4WD SE 4 Dr (5 spd)	**16599**	11850	13675
4WD XS 4 Dr (5 spd)	**16419**	11650	13450
4WD LS 4 Dr (5 spd)	**18569**	12800	15125
2WD AMIGO S (2.3 LITER) 4			
Sport Utility (5 spd)	**11084**	7275	8450
2WD AMIGO S (2.6 LITER) 4			
Sport Utility (5 spd)	**11734**	7475	8675
2WD AMIGO XS (2.6 LITER) 4			
Sport Utility (5 spd)	**12434**	7875	9150
IMPULSE 4			
XS Cpe (5 spd)	**12799**	8200	9475
RS Cpe (5 spd)	**15599**	9825	11325
XS Htchbk (5 spd)	**13349**	—	—
2WD RODEO 4			
S Sport Utility (5 spd)	**13834**	10275	11850
2WD RODEO 6			
S Sport Utility (5 spd)	**14409**	10675	12325
XS Sport Utility (5 spd)	**15049**	11375	13150
LS Sport Utility (5 spd)	**16619**	12025	13900
STYLUS 4			
S Sdn (5 spd)	**10159**	6275	7300
XS Sdn (5 spd)	**12049**	7275	8450
ADD FOR:			
Sport Pkg			
(Impulse XS)	**1195**	650	800
(Impulse RS)	**1850**	1000	1175
(Stylus XS)	**1295**	700	875

NOTE: Power brakes standard on all models.

1990

Year-Model-Body Type	Original List	Current Whlse	Average Retail
2WD S PICKUPS (2.3 LITER) 4			
Std Bed (5 spd)	**8989**	4425	5350
Long Bed (5 spd)	**9819**	4550	5475
2WD S PICKUPS (2.6 LITER)			
Std Bed (5 spd)	**9619**	4600	5525
Spacecab (5 spd)	**10624**	4925	5850
Long Bed (auto)	**11039**	4950	5875
1 Ton Long Bed (5 spd)	**10744**	4725	5650
2WD XS PICKUP (2.3 LITER) 4			
Std Bed (5 spd)	**9529**	4675	5600
2WD XS PICKUP (2.6 LITER) 4			
Spacecab (5 spd)	**11254**	4875	5800
2WD LS PICKUPS (2.6 LITER) 4			
Std Bed (5 spd)	**11554**	5275	6200
Spacecab (5 spd)	**12784**	5850	6775
4WD XS PICKUP (2.6 LITER) 4			
Std Bed (5 spd)	**12834**	6075	6975
TROOPER 4			
4WD S 4 Dr (5 spd)	**14559**	9750	11225
4WD RS 2 Dr (5 spd)	**16199**	10125	11675
TROOPER 6			
4WD S 4 Dr (5 spd)	**14809**	10125	11675
4WD XS 4 Dr (5 spd)	**15649**	10650	12300
4WD LS 4 Dr (5 spd)	**17749**	11050	12775
2WD AMIGO S (2.3 LITER)			
Sport Utility (5 spd)	**10744**	5950	6875
2WD AMIGO S (2.6 LITER)			
Sport Utility (5 spd)	**11344**	6125	7125
2WD AMIGO XS (2.6 LITER)			
Sport Utility (5 spd)	**11739**	6425	7475
IMPULSE 4			
XS Cpe (5 spd)	**12749**	6425	7475
ADD FOR:			
Aluminum Wheel Pkg			
(Amigo, Trooper S)	**900**	250	305
(Trooper XS & LS)	**700**	195	240
(4WD S Pickup)	**700**	175	220
(4WD LS Pickup)	**400**	175	220
Rear Seat			
(Trooper S & XS)	**420**	175	200
(Trooper LS)	**520**	175	200
Sport Pkg (Impulse)	**1195**	500	625

NOTE: Power brakes standard on all models.

1989

Year-Model-Body Type	Original List	Current Whlse	Average Retail
2WD S PICKUPS (2.3 LITER) 4			
Std Bed (5 spd)	**8749**	3225	4125
Long Bed (5 spd)	**9339**	3325	4225
2WD S PICKUPS (2.6 LITER) 4			
Std Bed (5 spd)	**9129**	3375	4275
Spacecab (5 spd)	**10379**	3925	4825
Long Bed (auto)	**10429**	3875	4775
1-Ton Long Bed (5 spd)	**10579**	3525	4425

Refer To Optional Equipment Schedules

ISUZU

Year-Model-Body Type	Original List	Current Whlse	Average Retail
2WD XS PICKUP (2.3 LITER) 4			
Std Bed (5 spd)	**9259**	3450	4350
2WD XS PICKUP (2.6 LITER) 4			
Spacecab (5 spd)	**10949**	4150	5075
2WD LS PICKUPS (2.6 LITER) 4			
Std Bed (5 spd)	**11094**	4025	4925
Spacecab (5 spd)	**12294**	4475	5400
4WD XS PICKUPS (2.6 LITER) 4			
Std Bed (5 spd)	**11694**	4900	5825
TROOPER II 4			
4WD S 4 Dr (5 spd)	**14184**	8175	9450
4WD XS 4 Dr (5 spd)	**14999**	8525	9850
4WD LS 4 Dr (5 spd)	**16689**	8775	10125
4WD RS 2 Dr (5 spd)	**15749**	8300	9575
TROOPER II 6			
4WD S 4 Dr (5 spd)	**14434**	8475	9800
4WD LS 4 Dr (5 spd)	**17409**	9075	10450
2WD AMIGO S (2.3 LITER) 4			
Sport Utility	**10259**	5100	6025
2WD AMIGO S (2.6 LITER) 4			
Sport Utility	**10829**	5225	6150
2WD AMIGO XS (2.6 LITER) 4			
Sport Utility	**11529**	5475	6400
I-MARK 4			
3 Dr S Htchbk (5 spd)	**8864**	2525	3400
4 Dr S Sdn (5 spd)	**9264**	2700	3600
3 Dr XS Htchbk (5 spd)	**10044**	2975	3875
4 Dr XS Sdn (5 spd)	**10244**	3100	4000
4 Dr RS Turbo Sdn (5 spd)	**10239**	3675	4575
3 Dr RS Turbo Htchbk (5 spd)	**10039**	3650	4550
4 Dr LS Turbo Sdn (5 spd)	**12049**	3875	4775
IMPULSE 4			
2 Dr Htchbk (5 spd)	**14329**	5325	6250
2 Dr Turbo Htchbk (5 spd)	**16329**	5900	6825
ADD FOR:			
Recaro Pkg (I-Mark RS)	**1200**	450	550
Sunsport Pkg (I-Mark S Htchbk)	**1200**	450	550
Rear Seat (Trooper II)	**420**	125	150

1988½

Year-Model-Body Type	Original List	Current Whlse	Average Retail
I-MARK 4			
3 Dr S Htchbk (5 spd)	**7659**	1425	2175
4 Dr S Sdn (5 spd)	**8009**	1575	2425
3 Dr XS Htchbk (5 spd)	**9029**	1700	2550
4 Dr XS Sdn (5 spd)	**9219**	2000	2850
3 Dr RS Turbo Htchbk (5 spd)	**9829**	2150	3000
4 Dr LS Turbo Sdn (5 spd)	**11189**	2225	3075

1988

Year-Model-Body Type	Original List	Current Whlse	Average Retail
2WD S PICKUP (2.3 LITER) 4			
Std Bed (5 spd)	**7199**	2000	2850
Long Bed (5 spd)	**7729**	2100	2950
2WD S PICKUP (2.6 LITER) 4			
Std Bed (5 spd)	**7649**	2075	2925
1 Ton Long Bed (5 spd)	**8999**	2275	3150
2WD LS PICKUP (2.6 LITER) 4			
Std Bed (5 spd)	**10249**	2775	3675
Spacecab (5 spd)	**11399**	3100	4000
TROOPER II 4			
4WD S 2 Dr (5 spd)	**11909**	5675	6600
4WD S 4 Dr (5 spd)	**12639**	6025	6950
4WD XS 2 Dr (5 spd)	**12909**	6000	6925
4WD XS 4 Dr (5 spd)	**13439**	6325	7350
4WD LS 4 Dr (5 spd)	**14799**	6550	7625
4WD Limited (5 spd)	**14499**	7275	8450
4WD LX Limited (5 spd)	**15399**	7050	8175
I-MARK 4			
3 Dr S Htchbk (5 spd)	**7629**	1350	2100
4 Dr S Sdn (5 spd)	**7979**	1525	2375
3 Dr XS Htchbk (5 spd)	**8999**	1675	2525
4 Dr XS Sdn (5 spd)	**9189**	1800	2650
3 Dr Turbo Htchbk (5 spd)	**10669**	2050	2900
4 Dr Turbo Sdn (5 spd)	**10859**	2000	2850
IMPULSE 4			
2 Dr Htchbk (5 spd)	**14109**	3175	4075
2 Dr Turbo Htchbk (5 spd)	**16079**	3600	4500

NOTE: Power brakes standard on all models. Sunroof standard on I-Mark Turbo, Impulse and LS Pickup. Air conditioning standard on Impulse. Power steering standard on Impulse, Trooper II, 4WD S Pickup, 1 Ton S Pickup and LS Pickup. Power windows standard on Impulse and Trooper II LX Limited. Power door locks standard on Impulse and Trooper II LX Limited.

1987

Year-Model-Body Type	Original List	Current Whlse	Average Retail
2WD PICKUP (GAS) 4			
Std Bed (4 spd)	**6399**	1200	1925
Std Bed (5 spd)	**6649**	1250	1975
Long Bed (5 spd)	**6899**	1225	1950
Spacecab (5 spd)	**7849**	1475	2300
LS Std Bed (5 spd)	**8699**	1675	2525
LS Spacecab (5 spd)	**10199**	2000	2850
2WD PICKUP (DIESEL) 4			
MPG Std Bed (4 spd)	**7469**	675	1275
MPG Std Bed (5 spd)	**7469**	725	1375

Refer To Optional Equipment Schedules

Year-Model-Body Type	Original List	Current Whlse	Average Retail
Long Bed (5 spd)	**7719**	775	1500
LS Spacecab Turbo (5 spd)	**11519**	—	—
4WD PICKUP (DIESEL) 4			
Long Bed Turbo (5 spd)	**10739**	2300	3175
TROOPER II 4			
4WD Dlx 2 Dr (5 spd)	**10979**	3800	4700
4WD Dlx 4 Dr (5 spd)	**11399**	4050	4950
4WD LS 4 Dr (5 spd)	**13199**	4375	5300
4WD Dlx 2 Dr Turbo Diesel (5 spd)	**12899**	3525	4425
4WD Dlx 4 Dr Turbo Diesel (5 spd)	**13319**	3825	4725
4WD LS 4 Dr Turbo Diesel (5 spd)	**15119**	4175	5100
I-MARK 4			
2 Dr S Htchbk (5 spd)	**7229**	750	1475
4 Dr S Ntchbk (5 spd)	**7569**	850	1550
2 Dr Htchbk (5 spd)	**8369**	1000	1725
4 Dr Ntchbk (5 spd)	**8549**	1175	1900
2 Dr RS Turbo Htchbk (5 spd)	**10149**	1400	2150
4 Dr RS Turbo Ntchbk (5 spd)	**10329**	1475	2300
IMPULSE 4			
2 Dr Turbo Cpe (5 spd)	**14859**	2475	3350

NOTE: Power brakes, power windows and power door locks standard on all models. Air conditioning standard on Impulse. Sun roof standard on I-Mark Turbo and Spacecab Pickup. Power steering standard on I-Mark Turbo, Impulse, Trooper II Series, Spacecab Pickup, Deluxe Pickup and LS Pickup.

1986

Year-Model-Body Type	Original List	Current Whlse	Average Retail
2WD PICKUP (GAS) 4			
Std Bed (4 spd)	**6326**	850	1550
Long Bed (5 spd)	**6816**	975	1700
Dlx Std Bed (5 spd)	**7366**	1100	1825
Dlx Long Bed (5 spd)	**7616**	1175	1900
Dlx Spacecab (5 spd)	**8399**	1350	2100
LS Std Bed (5 spd)	**8149**	1100	1825
LS Spacecab (5 spd)	**9499**	1600	2450
2WD PICKUP (DIESEL) 4			
MPG Plus Std Bed (4 spd)	**7336**	625	1175
Long Bed (5 spd)	**7586**	700	1325
Dlx Long Bed Turbo (5 spd)	**8669**	1225	1950
Dlx Spacecab Turbo (5 spd)	**9619**	1325	2050
LS Spacecab Turbo (5 spd)	**10719**	1350	2225
4WD PICKUP (DIESEL) 4			
Dlx Std Bed Turbo (5 spd)	**10846**	1900	2750
TROOPER II			
4WD Dlx 2 Dr (5 spd)	**10389**	2575	3450
4WD Dlx 4 Dr (5 spd)	**10809**	2750	3650
4WD LS (5 spd)	**11649**	2925	3825
4WD Dlx 2 Dr Turbo Diesel (5 spd)	**12309**	2625	3525
4WD Dlx 4 Dr Turbo Diesel	**12729**	2750	3650
4WD LS Turbo Diesel (5 spd)	**13509**	2875	3775
I-MARK 4			
2 Dr S Htchbk (5 spd)	**7249**	650	1225
2 Dr Htchbk (5 spd)	**8059**	750	1475
4 Dr Ntchbk (5 spd)	**8169**	825	1525
4 Dr S Ntchbk (5 spd)	**7439**	700	1325
IMPULSE 4			
2 Dr S Cpe (5 spd)	**10979**	1600	2450
2 Dr Cpe (5 spd)	**12279**	1775	2625
2 Dr Turbo Cpe (5 spd)	**14439**	1875	2725
ADD FOR:			
Leather Pkg (Turbo Impulse)	**780**	150	175

NOTE: Power windows and air conditioning standard on Impulse series. Power locks standard on Impulse Turbo. Power steering standard on Impulse series, Trooper II and LS Pickup, Power brakes standard on I-Mark, Impulse, Trooper II Deluxe and Pickups. Sunroof standard on LS Spacecab Pickup.

1985

Year-Model-Body Type	Original List	Current Whlse	Average Retail
2WD PICKUP (GAS)			
Std Bed (4 spd)	**5942**	675	1275
Dlx Std Bed (5 spd)	**6519**	825	1525
Dlx Std Bed w/Bucket Seats (5 spd)	**6669**	825	1525
LS Std Bed (5 spd)	**7295**	750	1475
LS Std Bed w/Bucket Seats (5 spd)	**7345**	775	1500
Base Long Bed (4 spd)	**6097**	750	1475
Dlx Long Bed (5 spd)	**6674**	775	1500
Dlx Long Bed w/Bucket Seats (5 spd)	**6824**	800	1500
LS Long Bed (5 spd)	**7450**	825	1525
LS Long Bed w/Bucket Seats (5 spd)	**7500**	850	1550
2WD PICKUP (DIESEL)			
Base Std Bed (4 spd)	**6707**	325	600
Base Std Bed (5 spd)	**6707**	325	600

Refer To Optional Equipment Schedules

Year-Model-Body Type	Original List	Current Whlse	Average Retail
Dlx Std Bed (5 spd)	**7284**	525	950
Dlx Std Bed w/Bucket Seats (5 spd)	**7434**	550	975
Base Long Bed (5 spd)	**6862**	425	775
Dlx Long Bed (5 spd)	**7439**	650	1225
Dlx Long Bed w/Bucket Seats (5 spd)	**7589**	675	1275
LS Long Bed (5 spd)	**8215**	825	1525
LS Long Bed w/Bucket Seats (5 spd)	**8265**	850	1550
TROOPER II 4			
4WD Utility (4 spd)	**8933**	2075	2925
I-MARK (GAS) 4			
4 Dr Dlx Sdn (5 spd)	**7020**	625	1175
2 Dr Htchbk (5 spd)	**7384**	525	975
IMPULSE 4			
2 Dr Cpe (5 spd)	**11048**	1400	2150
ADD FOR:			
Decor Pkg (Trooper II)	**815**	75	100

NOTE: Power steering, power windows, air conditioning and power door locks standard on Impulse. Power brakes standard on all models.

1984

Year-Model-Body Type	Original List	Current Whlse	Average Retail
2WD PICKUP (GAS) 4			
Std Bed (4 spd)	**5942**	475	875
Dlx Std Bed (5 spd)	**6519**	600	1125
Dlx Std Bed w/Bucket Seats (5 spd)	**6669**	600	1125
LS Std Bed (5 spd)	**7295**	600	1125
LS Std Bed w/Bucket Seats (5 spd)	**7345**	600	1125
Base Long Bed w/Bucket Seats (4 spd)	**6097**	550	1025
Dlx Long Bed (5 spd)	**6674**	650	1225
Dlx Long Bed w/Bucket Seats (5 spd)	**6824**	650	1225
LS Long Bed (5 spd)	**7450**	650	1225
LS Long Bed w/Bucket Seats (5 spd)	**7500**	650	1225
2WD PICKUP (DIESEL) 4			
Base Std Bed (4 spd)	**6707**	300	525
Base Std Bed (5 spd)	**6707**	300	525
Dlx Std Bed (5 spd)	**7284**	350	575
Dlx Std Bed w/Bucket Seats (5 spd)	**7434**	350	575
Base Long Bed w/Bucket Seats (5 spd)	**6862**	425	850
Dlx Long Bed (5 spd)	**7439**	450	875
Dlx Long Bed w/Bucket Seats (5 spd)	**7589**	450	875
LS Long Bed (5 spd)	**8215**	475	900
LS Long Bed w/Bucket Seats (5 spd)	**8265**	475	900
I-MARK (GAS) 4			
4 Dr Dlx Sdn (5 spd)	**6770**	300	575
I-MARK (DIESEL) 4			
4 Dr Dlx Sdn (5 spd)	**7620**	200	425
2 Dr Cpe (4 spd)	**6955**	150	350
IMPULSE 4			
2 Dr Cpe (5 spd)	**10498**	1050	1775
TROOPER 4			
4WD Utility (4 spd)	**8933**	1725	2575

1983 — ALL BODY STYLES

Year-Model-Body Type	Original List	Current Whlse	Average Retail
2WD PICKUP (GAS)	—	200	350
2WD PICKUP (DIESEL)	—	95	300
4WD PICKUP (GAS)	—	800	1475
4WD PICKUP (DIESEL)	—	250	500
I-MARK (GAS)	—	100	300
I-MARK (DIESEL)	—	75	225
IMPULSE	—	750	1475

JAGUAR

1992

Year-Model-Body Type	Original List	Current Whlse	Average Retail
XJ 6			
Base Sdn (auto)	**44500**	—	—
Sovereign Sdn (auto)	**49500**	—	—
Vanden Plas Sdn (auto)	**54500**	—	—
Majestic Sdn (auto)	**59500**	—	—
XJS 12			
Base Cpe (auto)	**60500**	—	—
Conv (auto)	**67500**	—	—

NOTE: Tilt steering wheel, cruise control, power windows, power door locks and power seat standard on all models. Power sunroof standard on Sovereign, Vanden Plas and Majestic.

1991

Year-Model-Body Type	Original List	Current Whlse	Average Retail
XJ 6			
Base Sdn (auto)	**43000**	25250	28575
Sovereign Sdn (auto)	**47800**	27625	30975
Vanden Plas Sdn (auto)	**52800**	29600	32950
XJS 12			
Base Cpe (auto)	**49900**	31900	35475
Conv (auto)	**59900**	40300	44600

NOTE: Power windows, power door locks, power seat and power brakes standard on all models. Sunroof standard on XJ6 Sovereign and Vanden Plas models.

Year-Model-Body Type	Original List	Current Whlse	Average Retail
1990			
XJ 6			
Base Sdn (auto)	**39700**	19700	22750
Sovereign Sdn (auto)	**43000**	21625	24925
Vanden Plas Sdn (auto)	**48000**	23275	26575
Vanden Plas Majestic Sdn (auto)	**53000**	24925	28250
XJS 12			
Base Cpe (auto)	**48000**	25000	28325
Conv (auto)	**57000**	34650	38525
Collection Rouge Cpe (auto)	**51000**	—	—

NOTE: Power windows, power door locks, and anti-lock power brakes standard on all models. Power sunroof standard on XJ6 Sovereign and Vanden Plas models.

Year-Model-Body Type	Original List	Current Whlse	Average Retail
1989			
XJ 6			
Sdn (auto)	**44000**	16850	19500
Vanden Plas Sdn (auto)	**48000**	18050	20700
XJS 12			
Cpe (auto)	**48000**	18350	21300
Conv (auto)	**57000**	28325	31675

NOTE: Power brakes, power door locks and power windows standard on all models. Power sunroof standard on XJ6.

Year-Model-Body Type	Original List	Current Whlse	Average Retail
1988			
XJ 6			
Sdn (auto)	**43500**	12350	14400
Vanden Plas Sdn (auto)	**47500**	13300	15625
XJS 12			
Cpe (auto)	**44500**	13000	15325
XJ-SC 12			
Cabriolet (auto)	**50450**	17900	20550

NOTE: Air conditioning, power brakes, power door locks, power steering, power sunroof, automatic transmission, power windows, and anti-lock brake system standard.

Year-Model-Body Type	Original List	Current Whlse	Average Retail
1987			
XJ 6			
Sdn (auto)	**37500**	10025	11575
Vanden Plas Sdn (auto)	**41500**	10925	12600
XJS 12			
Cpe (auto)	**39700**	11625	13425
XJ-SC 12			
Cabriolet (auto)	**44850**	16250	18900

NOTE: Air conditioning, power brakes, power door locks, power steering, power sunroof, automatic transmission and power windows standard.

Year-Model-Body Type	Original List	Current Whlse	Average Retail
1986			
XJ 6			
Sdn (auto)	**33900**	8050	9300
Vanden Plas Sdn (auto)	**37400**	8900	10275
XJS 12			
Cpe (auto)	**37800**	9150	10550

NOTE: Power locks, power windows, power brakes, automatic transmission, power steering and air conditioning standard on all models. Sunroof standard on XJ6 series.

Year-Model-Body Type	Original List	Current Whlse	Average Retail
1985			
XJ 6			
Sdn (auto)	**32250**	7125	8275
Vanden Plas Sdn (auto)	**35550**	7850	9125
XJS 12			
Cpe (auto)	**36000**	8450	9750

NOTE: Air conditioning, power steering, power brakes, power windows, and automatic transmission standard on all models. Sunroof standard on XJ.

Year-Model-Body Type	Original List	Current Whlse	Average Retail
1984			
XJ 6			
Sdn (auto)	**31100**	6425	7475
Vanden Plas Sdn (auto)	**34200**	6925	8050
XJS 12			
Cpe (auto)	**34700**	7875	9150

NOTE: Air conditioning, power steering, power brakes, power windows, and automatic transmission standard on all models. Sunroof standard on XJ.

Year-Model-Body Type	Original List	Current Whlse	Average Retail
1983			
XJ 6			
Sdn (auto)	**31111**	5675	6600
Vanden Plas Sdn (auto)	**34226**	6075	6975
XJS 12			
Cpe (auto)	**34606**	7425	8625

Refer To Optional Equipment Schedules

LEXUS

Year-Model-Body Type	Original List	Current Whlse	Average Retail
1992			
ES 300 6			
4 Dr Sdn (5 spd)	**26550**	—	—
ADD FOR:			
Leather Pkg	**1200**	—	—
CD Player	**900**	—	—
LS 400 8			
4 Dr Sdn (auto)	**44300**	—	—
ADD FOR:			
Memory System	**800**	—	—
Air Susp System	**1500**	—	—
Traction Control Pkg	**1700**	—	—
CD Player	**900**	—	—
SC 300 6			
2 Dr Sport Cpe (5 spd)	**32700**	—	—
ADD FOR:			
Leather Pkg	**1700**	—	—
Traction Control System	**1600**	—	—
Premium Sound System	**1000**	—	—
CD Player	**900**	—	—
SC 400 8			
2 Dr Sport Cpe (auto)	**39400**	—	—
ADD FOR:			
Traction Control System	**1600**	—	—
Premium Sound System	**1000**	—	—
CD Player	**900**	—	—

NOTE: Tilt steering wheel, cruise control, power windows, power door locks and power seats standard on all models.

Year-Model-Body Type	Original List	Current Whlse	Average Retail
1991			
ES 250 6			
4 Dr Sdn (5 spd)	**21500**	15250	17900
LS 400 8			
4 Dr Sdn (auto)	**39000**	29725	33075
ADD FOR:			
Leather Pkg (ES 250)	**950**	345	420
(LS 400)	**1400**	510	625
Lexus/Nakamachi Radio Equip (LS 400)	**1000**	350	425
Traction Control System (LS 400)	**1600**	300	1100

NOTE: Power brakes, power windows and power door locks standard on all models. Power seat standard on LS 400.

Year-Model-Body Type	Original List	Current Whlse	Average Retail
1990			
ES 250 6			
4 Dr Sdn (5 spd)	**21050**	12400	14500
LS 400 8			
4 Dr Sdn (auto)	**35000**	25575	28900
4 Dr Sdn w/Luxury Group (auto)	**39400**	26950	30000
ADD FOR:			
Air Suspension System (LS 400)	**1500**	700	900
Leather Pkg (ES 250)	**950**	385	470
(LS 400)	**1400**	450	550
Lexus/Nakamachi Radio Equip (LS 400)	**1000**	250	325
Traction Control System (LS 400)	**1600**	750	875

NOTE: Anti-lock power brakes, power windows and power door locks standard on all models. Power seat standard on LS 400. Moonroof standard on LS 400 w/luxury group.

MAZDA

Year-Model-Body Type	Original List	Current Whlse	Average Retail
1992			
323 4			
3 Dr Base Htchbk (5 spd)	**8289**	—	—
3 Dr SE Htchbk (5 spd)	**10239**	—	—
626 4			
4 Dr DX Sdn (5 spd)	**14525**	—	—
4 Dr LX Sdn (5 spd)	**15645**	—	—
ADD FOR:			
Leather Pkg	**1000**	—	—
Anti-lock Brakes (DX, LX)	**950**	—	—
(ES)	**800**	—	—
CD Player (ES)	**700**	—	—
Aluminum Wheels (LX)	**425**	—	—
MX-3 4			
3 Dr Htchbk (5 spd)	**12280**	—	—
MX-3 6			
3 Dr GS Htchbk (5 spd)	**15080**	—	—
ADD FOR:			
Anti-lock Brakes	**900**	—	—
Aluminum Wheels (Base)	**425**	—	—
MX-5 MIATA 4			
2 Dr Conv (5 spd)	**16170**	—	—
2 Dr Black/Tan Conv (5 spd)	**17880**	—	—
ADD FOR:			
Anti-lock Brakes	**900**	—	—

Year-Model-Body Type	Original List	Current Whlse	Average Retail
Detachable Hardtop	**1500**	—	—
CD Player	**600**	—	—
MX-6 4			
2 Dr DX Cpe (5 spd)	**14315**	—	—
2 Dr LX Cpe (5 spd)	**15635**	—	—
2 Dr GT Cpe (5 spd)	**17955**	—	—
ADD FOR:			
Anti-lock Brakes	**1000**	—	—
CD Player	**700**	—	—
Aluminum Wheels (LX)	**425**	—	—
929 6			
4 Dr Sdn (auto)	**28500**	—	—
ADD FOR:			
Leather Seat Trim	**1300**	—	—
Premium Pkg	**3200**	—	—
CD Player	**700**	—	—
PROTEGE 4			
4 Dr DX Sdn (5 spd)	**11669**	—	—
4 Dr LX Sdn (5 spd)	**12839**	—	—
ADD FOR:			
Aluminum Wheels	**425**	—	—
MPV 4			
2WD Van (auto)	**14979**	—	—
2 WD Wgn/Van (auto)	**17149**	—	—
2WD Wgn (auto)	**18569**	—	—
MPV 6			
2WD Wgn (auto)	**19349**	—	—
4WD Wgn (auto)	**22219**	—	—
ADD FOR:			
Touring Pkg	**570**	—	—
CD Player	**699**	—	—
NAVAJO 6			
2WD DX Sport Utility (5 spd)	**16590**	—	—
4WD DX Sport Utility (5 spd)	**18390**	—	—
2WD LX Sport Utility (5 spd)	**18645**	—	—
4WD LX Sport Utility (5 spd)	**20445**	—	—
ADD FOR:			
Leather Pkg	**3770**	—	—
B2200 2WD PICKUPS 4			
Short Bed (5 spd)	**10130**	—	—
Long Bed (5 spd)	**10845**	—	—
Cab Plus (5 spd)	**10590**	—	—
ADD FOR:			
LE-5 Luxury Pkg	**850**	—	—
SE-5 Sport Pkg	**650**	—	—
B2600i 2WD PICKUPS 4			
Short Bed (5 spd)	**10185**	—	—
Cab Plus (5 spd)	**11570**	—	—
B2600i 4WD PICKUPS 4			
Short Bed (5 spd)	**12620**	—	—
Cab Plus (5 spd)	**14120**	—	—
ADD FOR:			
LE-5 Luxury Pkg	**850**	—	—
SE-5 Sport Pkg	**750**	—	—

NOTE: Tilt steering wheel standard on MX-3 GS, 626, MX-6, 929 and MPV. Cruise control standard on Protege LX, 626 LX, MX-6 LX & GT and 929. Power windows standard on Protege LX, 626 LX, MX-6 LX & GT, MX-5 Miata Black/Tan, 929 and Navajo LX. Power door locks standard on Protege LX, 626 LX, MX-6 LX & GT, 929 and Navajo LX.

1991

Year-Model-Body Type	Original List	Current Whlse	Average Retail
323 4			
3 Dr Base Htchbk (5 spd)	**8444**	5650	6575
3 Dr SE Htchbk (5 spd)	**9494**	6275	7300
626 4			
4 Dr DX Sdn (5 spd)	**14095**	8700	10050
4 Dr LX Sdn (5 spd)	**15215**	9525	10975
5 Dr LX Htchbk (5 spd)	**15615**	9725	11200
4 Dr LE Sdn (5 spd)	**16545**	10125	11675
5 Dr GT Htchbk (5 spd)	**17215**	10600	12225
MX-5 MIATA 4			
2 Dr Conv (5 spd)	**16475**	11950	13800
2 Dr Special Edit. Conv (5 spd)	**19249**	13075	15400
MX-6 4			
2 Dr DX Cpe (5 spd)	**13895**	8950	10325
2 Dr LX Cpe (5 spd)	**15215**	9750	11225
2 Dr LE Cpe (5 spd)	**16545**	10125	11675
2 Dr GT Cpe (5 spd)	**17535**	10650	12300
929 6			
4 Dr Sdn (auto)	**23850**	14650	17200
4 Dr S Sdn (auto)	**25350**	15425	18075
PROTEGE 4			
4 Dr DX Sdn (5 spd)	**11044**	7050	8175
4 Dr LX Sdn (5 spd)	**12194**	7875	9150
4 Dr 4WD Sdn (5 spd)	**12484**	8000	9300
RX-7 ROTARY			
2 Dr Base Cpe (5 spd)	**20000**	13225	15550
2 Dr Conv (5 spd)	**28150**	17925	20575
2 Dr Turbo Cpe (5 spd)	**27100**	16025	18675
MPV 4			
Van (auto)	**13674**	—	—
Wgn/Van (5 spd)	**14994**	—	—
Wgn (5 spd)	**16394**	12025	13900
MPV 6			
2WD Wgn (auto)	**17874**	13075	15400

Refer To Optional Equipment Schedules

Year-Model-Body Type	Original List	Current Whlse	Average Retail
NAVAJO 6			
2 Dr 4WD Sport Utility (5 spd)	**18810**	14000	16375
B2200 2WD PICKUPS 4			
Short Bed (5 spd)	**9794**	6275	7300
Long Bed (5 spd)	**10454**	6400	7450
Cab Plus (5 spd)	**11314**	6875	8000
B2600i 2WD PICKUPS 4			
Short Bed (5 spd)	**10029**	6575	7650
Cab Plus (5 spd)	**11279**	7125	8275
ADD FOR:			
Detachable Hardtop (MX-5 Miata)	**1400**	600	700
Leather Pkg (929 Base)	**900**	325	400
(929 S)	**1150**	325	400
Luxury Pkg (929 Base)	**1400**	510	625
(929 S)	**1600**	580	700

NOTE: Power brakes standard on all models. Power door locks standard on 626 LX, 626 GT, 626 LE, 929, MX-6 LX, MX-6 LE, MX-6 GT, Protege LX and RX-7. Power windows standard on 626 LX, 626 GT, 626 LE, 929, MX-5 Miata, MX-6 LX, MX-6 LE, MX-6 GT, Navajo, Protege LX and RX-7. Power seat standard on 929. Moonroof standard on 626 LE, 929 and MX-6 LE.

1990

Year-Model-Body Type	Original List	Current Whlse	Average Retail
323 4			
3 Dr Base Htchbk (5 spd)	**7634**	4400	5325
3 Dr SE Htchbk (5 spd)	**9364**	4850	5775
626 4			
4 Dr DX Sdn (5 spd)	**13269**	7650	8875
4 Dr LX Sdn (5 spd)	**14139**	8400	9700
5 Dr LX Touring Sdn (5 spd)	**14939**	8600	9925
5 Dr GT Turbo Touring Sdn (5 spd)	**16509**	9275	10675
MX-5 MIATA 4			
2 Dr Conv (5 spd)	**15740**	10575	12200
MX-6 4			
2 Dr DX Cpe (5 spd)	**13089**	7850	9125
2 Dr LX Cpe (5 spd)	**14579**	8600	9925
2 Dr GT Turbo Cpe (5 spd)	**16839**	9275	10675
2 Dr 4WS Turbo Cpe (5 spd)	**18039**	9725	11200
929 6			
4 Dr Sdn (auto)	**23300**	12700	15025
4 Dr S Sdn (auto)	**24800**	13300	15625
RX-7 ROTARY			
2 Dr GTU Cpe (5 spd)	**18739**	11375	13150
2 Dr GTUs Cpe (5 spd)	**20180**	11375	13150
2 Dr GXL Cpe (5 spd)	**22330**	12575	14850
2 Dr GXL 2+2 Cpe (5 spd)	**22830**	12800	15125
2 Dr Turbo Cpe (5 spd)	**26530**	13700	16075
2 Dr Conv (5 spd)	**26530**	15700	18350
PROTEGE 4			
4 Dr SE Sdn (5 spd)	**10574**	5600	6525
4 Dr LX Sdn (5 spd)	**11334**	6275	7300
4 Dr 4WD Sdn (5 spd)	**12474**	6425	7475
MPV 4			
Van (5 spd)	**12548**	8900	10275
Wgn/Van (5 spd)	**14548**	—	—
Wgn (5 spd)	**15793**	10625	12250
MPV 6			
2WD Wgn (auto)	**17243**	11250	13000
4WD Wgn (5 spd)	**19743**	12700	15025
B2200 2WD PICKUPS 4			
Short Bed (5 spd)	**9009**	4750	5675
Long Bed (5 spd)	**9659**	4850	5775
Cab Plus (5 spd)	**10409**	5300	6225
B2600i 2WD PICKUPS 4			
SE-5 Short Bed (5 spd)	**10238**	5050	5975
LE-5 Short Bed (5 spd)	**10538**	5200	6125
SE-5 Cab Plus (5 spd)	**11638**	5650	6575
LE-5 Cab Plus (5 spd)	**11938**	5825	6750
B2600i 4WD PICKUPS 4			
Short Bed (5 spd)	**11879**	6475	7525
ADD FOR:			
Anti-Lock Braking System (626 LX)	**1150**	315	385
(626 GT)	**1000**	275	335
(MX-6 GT & 4WS)	**1000**	275	335
(MX-6 LX)	**1150**	315	385
(929 Base)	**1000**	275	335
Detachable Hardtop (MX-5 Miata)	**1100**	305	370
Leather Seat Trim (RX-7 GXL)	**850**	235	285
(RX-7 Turbo)	**1000**	275	335
(929)	**880**	245	295
LE-5 Luxury Pkg (2WD Short Bed & Cab Plus Pickups)	**779**	210	255
(4WD Pickups)	**879**	245	295
SE-5 Sport Pkg (2WD Short Bed & Cab Plus Pickups)	**479**	130	160
(4WD Pickups)	**579**	160	200

NOTE: Power brakes standard on all models. Anti-lock brakes standard on RX-7 Turbo, 929 S and MPV. Sunroof standard on RX-7 GXL and Turbo. Moonroof standard on MX-6 4WS and 929

Year-Model-Body Type	Original List	Current Whlse	Average Retail

Series. Power windows standard on 626 LX, MX-6 LX, MX-6 GT, MX-6 4WS, RX-7 Convertible, RX-7 GXL, RX-7 Turbo and 929 Series. Power door locks standard on Protege LX, 626 LX, MX-6 LX, MX-6 GT, MX-6 4WS, RX-7 Convertible, RX-7 GXL, RX-7 Turbo and 929 Series.

1989½

Year-Model-Body Type	Original List	Current Whlse	Average Retail
B2600i 4WD PICKUPS 4			
Short Bed (5 spd)	**11653**	5075	6000
SE-5 Short Bed (5 spd)	**12153**	5400	6325
SE-5 Cab Plus (5 spd)	**13893**	5900	6825
LX Cab Plus (5 spd)	**14528**	6075	6975
ADD FOR:			
4x4 Pkg (B2600i LX)	**430**	220	260

NOTE: Power brakes standard on all models.

1989

Year-Model-Body Type	Original List	Current Whlse	Average Retail
323 4			
3 Dr Base Htchbk (4 spd) (NA w/radio)	**7459**	3100	4000
4 Dr Base Sdn (5 spd)	**8909**	3550	4450
3 Dr SE Htchbk (5 spd)	**8659**	3550	4450
4 Dr SE Sdn (5 spd)	**10059**	3975	4875
4 Dr LX Sdn (5 spd)	**11259**	4425	5350
3 Dr GTX Turbo Htchbk (5 spd)	**14459**	6875	8000
626 4			
4 Dr DX Sdn (5 spd)	**12699**	5950	6875
4 Dr LX Sdn (5 spd)	**14199**	6600	7675
5 Dr LX Touring Sdn (5 spd)	**14399**	6800	7925
5 Dr Turbo Touring Sdn (5 spd)	**16049**	6650	7750
929 6			
4 Dr Sdn (auto)	**22900**	9675	11150
MX-6 4			
2 Dr DX Cpe (5 spd)	**12649**	6100	7000
2 Dr LX Cpe (5 spd)	**14099**	6725	7825
2 Dr GT Turbo Cpe (5 spd)	**16299**	7375	8550
2 Dr 4WS Turbo Cpe (5 spd)	**17499**	7775	9025
MPV 4			
Van (5 spd)	**12048**	7225	8400
Wgn/Van (5 spd)	**14048**	—	—
Wgn (5 spd)	**14898**	8775	10125
MPV 6			
2WD Wgn (5 spd)	**15598**	9250	10650
2WD Wgn (auto)	**16348**	11125	12850
RX-7 ROTARY			
2 Dr GTU 2-Seater (5 spd)	**18159**	8850	10225
2 Dr GTUS 2-Seater (5 spd)	**20459**	8850	10225
2 Dr Conv (5 spd)	**26459**	13100	15425
2 Dr GXL 2-Seater (5 spd)	**21600**	9775	11250
2 Dr GXL 2+2 (5 spd)	**22100**	9975	11500
2 Dr Turbo 2-Seater (5 spd)	**25950**	10875	12550
B2200 2WD PICKUPS 4			
Short Bed (5 spd)	**9049**	3550	4450
Long Bed (5 spd)	**9549**	3675	4575
Cab Plus (5 spd)	**10549**	3975	4875
SE-5 Short Bed (5 spd)	**9449**	3800	4700
SE-5 Long Bed (5 spd)	**9949**	3925	4825
SE-5 Cab Plus (5 spd)	**10849**	4225	5150
LX Short Bed (5 spd)	**10824**	4100	5000
LX Cab Plus (5 spd)	**11824**	4700	5625
ADD FOR:			
Anti-Lock Braking System (MX-6 GT, 626 Turbo, 929)	**1000**	300	350
Leather Power Seat (929, RX-7 GXL ex. Conv)	**880**	300	350
(RX-7 Turbo ex. Conv)	**1000**	300	350

NOTE: Power brakes standard on all models. Power windows and power door locks standard on 929, MX-6 LX, MX-6 GT, MX-6 4WS, RX-7 Convertible, RX-7 GXL and RX-7 Turbo. Sunroof standard on RX-7 GXL and RX-7 Turbo.

1988

Year-Model-Body Type	Original List	Current Whlse	Average Retail
323 4			
3 Dr Htchbk (4 spd)	**6149**	1775	2625
4 Dr Sdn (5 spd)	**7299**	2100	2950
5 Dr Wgn (5 spd)	**7999**	2175	3025
3 Dr SE Htchbk (5 spd)	**7149**	2025	2875
4 Dr SE Sdn (5 spd)	**7999**	2325	3200
4 Dr LX Sdn (5 spd)	**9299**	2700	3600
4 Dr GT Turbo Sdn (5 spd)	**11799**	3625	4525
3 Dr GTX Htchbk (5 spd)	**12999**	5075	6000
626 4			
4 Dr DX Sdn (5 spd)	**10999**	4125	5050
4 Dr LX Sdn (5 spd)	**12899**	4550	5475
5 Dr LX Touring Sdn (5 spd)	**13099**	4725	5650
4 Dr Turbo Sdn (5 spd)	**14549**	5025	5950

Year-Model-Body Type	Original List	Current Whlse	Average Retail
5 Dr Turbo Touring Sdn (5 spd)	**14749**	5225	6150
4 Dr Turbo 4WS Sdn (auto)	**17799**	5775	6700
MX-6 4			
2 Dr DX Cpe (5 spd)	**11099**	4225	5150
2 Dr LX Cpe (5 spd)	**12999**	4650	5575
2 Dr GT Turbo Cpe (5 spd)	**15099**	5125	6050
RX-7 ROTARY			
2 Dr Conv (5 spd)	**21550**	9925	11425
2 Dr Conv w/Opt Pkg (5 spd)	**24050**	—	—
2 Dr SE Cpe (5 spd)	**16150**	5975	6900
2 Dr SE 2+2 Cpe (5 spd)	**16650**	6175	7200
2 Dr GTU Cpe (5 spd)	**18150**	6275	7300
2 Dr GXL Cpe (5 spd)	**20050**	6925	8050
2 Dr GXL 2+2 Cpe (5 spd)	**20550**	7125	8275
2 Dr Turbo Cpe (5 spd)	**22750**	7700	8950
929 6			
4 Dr Sdn (5 spd)	**19850**	6625	7700
4 Dr Sdn (auto)	**19850**	7500	8700
B2200 2WD PICKUPS 4			
Short Bed (5 spd)	**7549**	2375	3250
Long Bed (5 spd)	**8049**	2475	3350
Cab Plus (5 spd)	**8849**	2750	3650
SE-5 Short Bed (5 spd)	**7849**	2650	3525
SE-5 Long Bed (5 spd)	**8349**	2775	3675
SE-5 Cab Plus (5 spd)	**9149**	3375	4275
LX Short Bed (5 spd)	**9449**	2975	3875
LX Cab Plus (5 spd)	**10499**	3375	4275
B2600 4WD PICKUPS 4			
Short Bed (5 spd)	**10199**	3825	4725
Long Bed (5 spd)	**10699**	3950	4850
Cab Plus (5 spd)	**11599**	4275	5200
SE-5 Short Bed (5 spd)	**10699**	4025	4925
SE-5 Long Bed (5 spd)	**11199**	4150	5075
SE-5 Cab Plus (5 spd)	**12099**	4400	5325
LX Short Bed (5 spd)	**12399**	4425	5350
LX Long Bed (5 spd)	**12899**	4450	5375
LX Cab Plus (5 spd)	**13449**	4850	5775
ADD FOR:			
Anti-Lock Braking System (929)	**1650**	225	275
(MX-6 GT, RX-7 Turbo)	**1395**	225	275
Leather Power Seat (929)	**1275**	250	300

NOTE: Power brakes standard on all models. Air conditioning standard on RX-7 GXL and Turbo, 929. Power windows standard on 626 LX, 626 Turbo and 626 4WS, MX-6 LX, MX-6 GT, RX-7 Convertible and 929. Power door locks standard on 626 LX, 626 Turbo, 626 4WS, MX-6 LX, MX-6 GT and 929. Power steering standard on 323 GTX, 626, MX-6, RX-7 Series except Turbo, 929, 4WD Standard Pickup, SE-5 Pickup and LX Pickup.

1987

Year-Model-Body Type	Original List	Current Whlse	Average Retail
323 4			
3 Dr Htchbk (4 spd)	**6099**	1400	2150
4 Dr Wgn (5 spd)	**8399**	2075	2925
3 Dr SE Htchbk (5 spd)	**6699**	1600	2450
3 Dr Dlx Htchbk (5 spd)	**7799**	1775	2625
4 Dr Dlx Sdn (5 spd)	**8299**	2050	2900
4 Dr Dlx Wgn (5 spd)	**8999**	2175	3025
4 Dr Lux Sdn (5 spd)	**8999**	2275	3150
626 4			
4 Dr Dlx Sdn (5 spd)	**10149**	2850	3750
2 Dr Dlx Cpe (5 spd)	**10199**	2950	3850
4 Dr Lux Sdn (5 spd)	**11949**	3225	4125
2 Dr Lux Cpe (5 spd)	**12149**	3300	4200
5 Dr Lux Touring Sdn (5 spd)	**12649**	3400	4300
4 Dr GT Turbo Sdn (5 spd)	**13399**	3650	4550
2 Dr GT Turbo Cpe (5 spd)	**13699**	3750	4650
5 Dr GT Turbo Touring Sdn (5 spd)	**14299**	3850	4750
RX-7 ROTARY			
2 Dr Cpe (5 spd)	**14399**	3875	4775
2 Dr 2+2 Cpe (5 spd)	**14899**	4025	4925
2 Dr Sport Cpe (5 spd)	**16649**	4150	5075
2 Dr SE Cpe (5 spd)	**15199**	4025	4925
2 Dr 2+2 SE Cpe (5 spd)	**15699**	4150	5075
2 Dr GXL Cpe (5 spd)	**18669**	4650	5575
2 Dr 2+2 GXL Cpe (5 spd)	**19199**	4825	5750
2 Dr Turbo Cpe (5 spd)	**20799**	5275	6200
B2200 2WD PICKUPS 4			
Std Short Bed	**6799**	1750	2600
Std Long Bed	**7299**	1850	2700
Std Cab Plus	**8299**	2075	2925
SE-5 Short Bed	**7299**	1925	2775
SE-5 Long Bed	**7799**	2000	2850
SE-5 Cab Plus	**8799**	2200	3050
LX Short Bed	**8699**	2200	3050
LX Long Bed	**9199**	2275	3150
LX Cab Plus	**9749**	2525	3400
B2600 2WD PICKUPS 4			
LX Short Bed	**9049**	2275	3150
LX Long Bed	**9549**	2375	3250
LX Cab Plus	**10099**	2650	3550

Year-Model-Body Type	Original List	Current Whlse	Average Retail
B2600 4WD PICKUPS 4			
Std Short Bed	**9499**	2875	3775
Std Long Bed	**9999**	2975	3875
Std Cab Plus	**10999**	3250	4150
SE-5 Short Bed	**9999**	3050	3950
SE-5 Long Bed	**10499**	3150	4050
SE-5 Cab Plus	**11499**	3450	4350
ADD FOR:			
Leather Pkg (RX-7 GXL except 2+2)	**730**	150	175
(RX-7 GXL 2+2)	**930**	150	175

NOTE: Power brakes standard on all models. Air conditioning and sunroof standard on RX-7 GXL and RX-7 Turbo. Power windows standard on 626 Luxury, RX-7 GXL and RX-7 Turbo. Power door locks standard on 626 Luxury. Power steering standard on 626 Luxury, RX-7 Sport, RX-7 GXL and 4WD Pickups. AM/FM stereo radio standard on Base RX-7, 2WD LX Pickups and 4WD LX Pickups.

1986

Year-Model-Body Type	Original List	Current Whlse	Average Retail
323 4			
3 Dr Htchbk (4 spd)	**6160**	975	1700
3 Dr Dlx Htchbk (5 spd)	**7760**	1275	2000
4 Dr Dlx Sdn (5 spd)	**8260**	1350	2100
3 Dr Lux Htchbk (5 spd)	**8460**	1475	2300
4 Dr Luxury Sdn (5 spd)	**8860**	1525	2375
626 4			
4 Dr Dlx Sdn (5 spd)	**9660**	1900	2750
2 Dr Dlx Cpe (5 spd)	**9910**	1900	2750
4 Dr Luxury Sdn (5 spd)	**11045**	2350	3200
2 Dr Lux Cpe (5 spd)	**11345**	2250	3100
5 Dr Lux Touring Sdn (5 spd)	**11945**	2400	3275
4 Dr GT Turbo Sdn (5 spd)	**12695**	2675	3575
2 Dr GT Turbo Cpe (5 spd)	**12995**	2775	3675
5 Dr GT Turbo Touring Sdn (5 spd)	**13595**	2875	3775
RX-7 ROTARY			
2 Dr Cpe (5 spd)	**13595**	2950	3850
2 Dr 2+2 Cpe (5 spd)	**14095**	2950	3850
2 Dr GXL Cpe (5 spd)	**18445**	3550	4450
2 Dr GXL 2+2 Cpe (5 spd)	**18945**	3675	4575
B2000 PICKUPS 4			
Std Short Bed	**6295**	1325	2050
Std Long Bed	**6495**	1425	2175
SE-5 Short Bed	**6990**	1425	2175
SE-5 Long Bed	**7190**	1500	2350
LX Short Bed	**7895**	1700	2550
LX Long Bed	**8095**	1775	2625
Std Cab Plus	**7695**	1600	2450
SE-5 Cab Plus	**8095**	1675	2525
LX Cab Plus	**8995**	1975	2825
ADD FOR:			
Leather Pkg (RX-7 GXL except 2+2)	**720**	125	150
Luxury Pkg (RX-7 GXL 2+2)	**900**	125	150
Sport Pkg (RX-7 Base 2-Seater)	**1550**	200	250

NOTE: Power locks standard on 626 Luxury. Power windows and power steering standard on 626 Luxury and RX-7 Series. Sunroof standard on RX-7 Series. Power brakes standard on 323 Series, 626 Series and B2000 Pickups.

1985

Year-Model-Body Type	Original List	Current Whlse	Average Retail
626 4			
2 Dr Dlx Cpe (5 spd)	**9170**	1400	2150
2 Dr Lux Cpe (5 spd)	**10595**	1800	2650
4 Dr Dlx Sdn (5 spd)	**8820**	1400	2150
4 Dr Luxury Sdn (5 spd)	**10245**	1800	2650
4 Dr Lux Touring Sdn (5 spd)	**11245**	1875	2725
4 Dr Diesel Lux Sdn (5 spd)	**10795**	1100	1825
GLC 4			
3 Dr Base Htchbk (4 spd)	**5195**	625	1175
3 Dr Dlx Htchbk (5 spd)	**6420**	800	1500
3 Dr Lux Htchbk (5 spd)	**7120**	1000	1725
4 Dr Dlx Sdn (5 spd)	**7020**	975	1700
4 Dr Luxury Sdn (5 spd)	**7720**	1100	1825
RX-7 ROTARY			
2 Dr S Cpe (5 spd)	**10945**	2150	3000
2 Dr GS Cpe (5 spd)	**11845**	2375	3250
2 Dr GSL Cpe (5 spd)	**13645**	2625	3525
2 Dr GSL-SE Cpe (5 spd)	**15645**	2925	3825
ADD FOR:			
Leather Pkg (RX-7)	**720**	100	125

NOTE: Power steering, power windows and power locks standard on 626 Luxury. Air conditioning standard on RX-7 GSL-SE. Sunroof standard on RX-7 GSL and GSL-SE.

Refer To Optional Equipment Schedules

Year-Model-Body Type	Original List	Current Whlse	Average Retail
1984			
626 4			
2 Dr Dlx Cpe (5 spd)	**8615**	1275	2000
2 Dr Lux Cpe (5 spd)	**9845**	1500	2350
4 Dr Dlx Sdn (5 spd)	**8215**	1225	1950
4 Dr Lux Sdn (5 spd)	**9445**	1450	2225
4 Dr Lux Touring Sdn (5 spd)	**10395**	1600	2450
B2000 PICKUPS 4			
Base Short Bed	**5945**	725	1375
Long Bed	**6145**	800	1500
Sport SE-5 Short Bed	**6145**	800	1500
Sport SE-5 Long Bed	**6345**	875	1600
Sport Short Bed	**6745**	825	1525
Sport Long Bed	**6945**	925	1650
SE-5 Short Bed	**6145**	775	1500
SE-5 Long Bed	**6445**	875	1600
B2200 PICKUPS 4			
Diesel Short Bed	**6695**	375	675
Diesel Long Bed	**6895**	400	725
GLC 4			
3 Dr Base Htchbk (4 spd)	**4995**	450	825
3 Dr Dlx Htchbk (5 spd)	**6175**	600	1125
3 Dr Lux Htchbk (5 spd)	**6775**	725	1375
4 Dr Dlx Sdn (5 spd)	**6725**	725	1375
4 Dr Lux Sdn (5 spd)	**7375**	850	1550
RX-7 ROTARY			
2 Dr S Cpe (5 spd)	**10195**	1725	2575
2 Dr GS Cpe (5 spd)	**11295**	1950	2800
2 Dr GSL Cpe (5 spd)	**13095**	2150	3000
2 Dr GSL-SE Cpe (5 spd)	**15095**	2325	3200

1983 — ALL BODY STYLES

Year-Model-Body Type	Original List	Current Whlse	Average Retail
626	—	825	1525
B2000 PICKUPS	—	600	1125
B2200 PICKUPS	—	125	325
GLC	—	450	825
RX-7 ROTARY	—	1725	2575

MERCEDES-BENZ

Year-Model-Body Type	Original List	Current Whlse	Average Retail
1992			
190 E 4			
2.3 4 Dr Sdn (5 spd)	**28950**	—	—
2.6 4 Dr Sdn (5 spd)	**34000**	—	—
ADD FOR:			
Leather Seat Trim	**1550**	—	—
300 D 5			
4 Dr Turbo Sdn (auto)	**42950**	—	—
300 E 6			
2.6 4 Dr Sdn (auto)	**42950**	—	—
3.0 4 Dr Sdn (auto)	**49500**	—	—
3.0 4Matic 4 Dr Sdn (auto)	**57100**	—	—
300 CE 6			
2 Dr Cpe (auto)	**60400**	—	—
300 TE 6			
4Matic 5 Dr Wgn (auto)	**61100**	—	—
5 Dr Wgn (auto)	**53900**	—	—
300 SD 6			
4 Dr Turbo Sdn (auto)	**69400**	—	—
300 SE 6			
4 Dr Sdn (auto)	**69400**	—	—
300 SL 6			
2 Dr Cpe/Rdstr (5 spd)	**82500**	—	—
ADD FOR:			
Leather Seat Trim (300 D, 300 E w/2.6 liter eng, 300 TE)	**1550**	—	—
Four Place Seating Pkg	**5120**	—	—
400 E 8			
4 Dr Sdn (auto)	**55800**	—	—
400 SE 8			
4 Dr Sdn (auto)	**77900**	—	—
ADD FOR:			
Four Place Seating Pkg	**5120**	—	—
500 E 8			
4 Dr Sdn (auto)	**79200**	—	—
500 SL 8			
2 Dr Cpe/Rdstr (auto)	**97500**	—	—
500 SEL 8			
4 Dr Sdn (auto)	**93500**	—	—
ADD FOR:			
Four Place Seating Pkg	**5120**	—	—
600 SEL 12			
4 Dr Sdn (auto)	**127800**	—	—
ADD FOR:			
Four Place Seating Pkg	**3900**	—	—

NOTE: Cruise control, power windows, power door locks and power seat standard on all models. Tilt steering wheel standard on 300 Series models with 3.0 liter engine, 400 Series, 500 Series and 600 SEL.

Year-Model-Body Type	Original List	Current Whlse	Average Retail
1991			
190 E 4			
2.3 4 Dr Sdn (5 spd)	**28050**	19400	22450
2.3 4 Dr Sdn (auto)	**28950**	20175	23225
190 E 6			
2.6 4 Dr Sdn (5 spd)	**32800**	21875	25175
2.6 4 Dr Sdn (auto)	**33700**	22650	25950
300 D 5			
2.5 4 Dr Turbo Sdn (auto)	**41000**	29050	32400
300 E 6			
2.6 4 Dr Sdn (auto)	**41000**	29150	32500
4 Dr Standard Sdn (auto)	**47200**	32825	36500
4Matic 4 Dr Sdn (auto)	**54150**	36200	40175
300 SE 6			
4 Dr Sdn (auto)	**53900**	40025	44300
300 SEL 6			
4 Dr Sdn (auto)	**57800**	42625	47175
300 CE 6			
2 Dr Cpe (auto)	**57350**	39375	43700
300 SL 6			
2 Dr Cpe/Rdstr (5 spd)	**77500**	56000	61375
2 Dr Cpe/Rdstr (auto)	**78500**	54500	59725
300 TE 6			
5 Dr Standard Wgn (auto)	**51150**	35875	39825
4Matic 5 Dr Wgn (auto)	**57900**	39200	43500
350 SD 6			
4 Dr Turbo Sdn (auto)	**53900**	39600	44075
350 SDL 6			
4 Dr Turbo Sdn (auto)	**57800**	42100	46350
420 SEL 8			
4 Dr Sdn (auto)	**63600**	45025	49625
500 SL 8			
2 Dr Cpe/Rdstr (auto)	**89300**	66000	71675
560 SEL 8			
4 Dr Sdn (auto)	**75100**	50575	55425
560 SEC 8			
2 Dr Cpe (auto)	**82900**	56925	62400
ADD FOR:			
Leather Seats (190 E)	**1495**	540	660
(300 D 2.5, 300 E 2.6, 300 TE)	**1495**	540	660
Velour Seats (190 E)	**1495**	540	660
(300 D 2.5, 300 E 2.6, 300 TE)	**1475**	540	660
Four Place Seating (350 SDL, 300 SEL, 420 SEL)	**3080**	1185	1445
(560 SEL)	**2390**	1120	1370
Rear Facing Third Seat (300 TE)	**1120**	405	495

NOTE: Power brakes, power door locks and power windows standard on all models. Power seat standard on 190 E 2.6, 300 Series, 420 Series and 500 Series. Power sunroof standard on 560 Series.

Year-Model-Body Type	Original List	Current Whlse	Average Retail
1990			
190 E 6			
2.6 4 Dr Sdn (5 spd)	**31600**	18625	21675
2.6 4 Dr Sdn (auto)	**32500**	19350	22400
300 D 6			
2.5 4 Dr Turbo Sdn (auto)	**39700**	23975	27275
300 E 6			
2.6 4 Dr Sdn (auto)	**39950**	23875	27175
4 Dr Sdn (auto)	**45950**	27225	30550
4Matic 4 Dr Sdn (auto)	**52550**	30675	34100
300 CE 6			
2 Dr Cpe (auto)	**55700**	33975	37775
300 TE 6			
5 Dr Wgn (auto)	**49650**	30175	33550
4Matic 5 Dr Wgn (auto)	**56250**	33575	37325
300 SE 6			
4 Dr Sdn (auto)	**52950**	30550	33975
300 SEL 6			
4 Dr Sdn (auto)	**56800**	32850	36525
300 SL 6			
2 Dr Cpe/Rdstr (5 spd)	**72500**	56975	62450
2 Dr Cpe/Rdstr (auto)	**73500**	55925	61300
350 SD 6			
4 Dr Turbo Sdn (auto)	**52950**	—	—
350 SDL 6			
4 Dr Turbo Sdn (auto)	**56800**	32175	35775
420 SEL 8			
4 Dr Sdn (auto)	**62500**	35850	39800
560 SEL 8			
4 Dr Sdn (auto)	**73800**	40300	44600
560 SEC 8			
2 Dr Cpe (auto)	—	46150	50850
500 SL 8			
2 Dr Cpe/Rdstr (auto)	**83500**	63925	69425
ADD FOR:			
Electric Front Seats (190 E, 500 SL)	**505**	150	175
Leather Seats (190 E)	**1460**	400	490
Velour Seats (190 E)	**1440**	400	490
Third Facing Rear Seat (300 TE, 300 TE 4Matic)	**1095**	300	350
Four Place Seating (420 SEL)	**3005**	700	900
(560 SEL)	**2330**	640	780

NOTE: Anti-lock power brakes, power windows,

Refer To Optional Equipment Schedules

power door locks and power seat standard on all models. Sunroof standard on 560 SEL and 560 SEC.

Year-Model-Body Type	Original List	Current Whlse	Average Retail
1989			
190 D 5			
2.5 4 Dr Sdn (auto)	**30980**	14150	16600
190 E 6			
2.6 4 Dr Sdn (5 spd)	**31590**	16800	19450
2.6 4 Dr Sdn (auto)	**32500**	16800	19450
260 E 6			
2.6 4 Dr Sdn (auto)	**39200**	19475	22525
300 E 6			
4 Dr Sdn (auto)	**44850**	22550	25850
300 CE 6			
2 Dr Cpe (auto)	**53880**	28525	31875
300 TE 6			
4 Dr Wgn (auto)	**48210**	25100	28425
300 SE 6			
4 Dr Sdn (auto)	**51400**	23950	27250
300 SEL 6			
4 Dr Sdn (auto)	**55100**	26050	29375
420 SEL 8			
4 Dr Sdn (auto)	**61210**	29500	32850
560 SEL 8			
4 Dr Sdn (auto)	**64230**	33900	37700
560 SEC 8			
2 Dr Cpe (auto)	**79840**	38975	43250
560 SL 8			
2 Dr Cpe/Rdstr (auto)	**72280**	38250	42450
ADD FOR:			
Electric Front Bucket Seats (190 Series, 260 E)	**950**	190	230
Electric 4 Place Seating (300 SEL, 420 SEL)	**2835**	560	685
(560 SEL)	**2175**	430	525
Leather Seats (190 Series, 260 E, 300 E, 300 TE)	**1425**	275	335
Velour Seats (190 Series, 260 E, 300 E, 300 TE)	**1405**	275	335
Third Facing Rear Seat (300 TE)	**1070**	210	260

NOTE: Power brakes, power windows and power door locks standard on all models. Power sunroof standard on 560 SEL Sedan and 560 SEC Coupe.

Year-Model-Body Type	Original List	Current Whlse	Average Retail
1988			
190 D 5			
2.5 4 Dr Sdn (auto)	**29960**	12100	13975
190 E 4			
2.3 4 Dr Sdn	**29190**	13150	15500
2.3 4 Dr Sdn (auto)	**29960**	13800	16175
190 E 6			
2.6 4 Dr Sdn	**33500**	14400	16900
2.6 4 Dr Sdn (auto)	**34260**	14950	17550
260 E 6			
2.6 4 Dr Sdn	**37845**	15950	18600
2.6 4 Dr Sdn (auto)	**38760**	16550	19200
300 E 6			
4 Dr Sdn	**43365**	18250	21100
4 Dr Sdn (auto)	**44400**	18850	21900
300 CE 6			
2 Dr Cpe (auto)	**53340**	24475	27775
300 TE 6			
4 Dr Wgn (auto)	**47730**	21275	24575
300 SE 6			
4 Dr Sdn (auto)	**49900**	20425	23475
300 SEL 6			
4 Dr Sdn (auto)	**53490**	22250	25550
420 SEL 8			
4 Dr Sdn (auto)	**59080**	25250	28575
560 SEL 8			
4 Dr Sdn (auto)	**69760**	29275	32625
560 SEC 8			
2 Dr Cpe (auto)	**77065**	34600	38475
560 SL 8			
2 Dr Cpe/Rdstr (auto)	**62110**	33100	36800
ADD FOR:			
Anti-Lock Brake System (190 D, 190 E)	**1685**	400	475
Electric Front Bucket Seats (190 Series, 260 E)	**920**	175	200
Electric 4 Place Seating (300 SEL, 420 SEL)	**2750**	700	850
(560 SEL)	**2110**	600	750
Leather Seats (190 Series, 260 E, 300 E, 300 TE)	**1425**	300	350
Velour Seats (190 Series, 260 E, 300 E, 300 TE)	**1405**	300	350

NOTE: Power steering, power door locks, power brakes, air conditioning and power windows standard on all models. Power sun roof standard on 560 SEC and 560 SEL.

Year-Model-Body Type	Original List	Current Whlse	Average Retail
1987			
190 D 5			
2.5 4 Dr Sdn	**28450**	9600	11050
2.5 4 Dr Sdn (auto)	**29200**	10125	11675
2.5 4 Dr Turbo-diesel Sdn (auto)	**32110**	10525	12150
190 E 4			
2.3 4 Dr Sdn	**28450**	10775	12425
2.3 4 Dr Sdn (auto)	**29200**	11325	13075
2.3-16 4 Dr Sdn	**42670**	15800	18450
2.3-16 4 Dr Sdn (auto)	**43420**	16350	19000
190 E 6			
2.6 4 Dr Sdn (auto)	**33390**	12150	14025
260 E 6			
2.6 4 Dr Sdn (auto)	**37180**	14300	16800
300 D 6			
4 Dr Turbo-diesel Sdn (auto)	**42570**	14900	17500
300 TD 6			
4 Dr Turbo-diesel Wgn (auto)	**45790**	16725	19375
300 E 6			
4 Dr Sdn (auto)	**42570**	16050	18700
300 SDL 6			
4 Dr Turbo-diesel Sdn (auto)	**50650**	20000	23050
420 SEL 8			
4 Dr Sdn (auto)	**56050**	20825	23875
560 SEL 8			
4 Dr Sdn (auto)	**66260**	24300	27600
560 SEC 8			
2 Dr Cpe (auto)	**73260**	29400	32750
560 SL 8			
2 Dr Cpe/Rdstr (auto)	**59580**	28525	31875
ADD FOR:			
Anti-Lock Brake System (190 D except Turbo, 190 E)	**1635**	375	425
Electric Left Front Seat (190 D, 190 E, 260)	**465**	125	150
Electric 4 Place Seating (560 SEL)	**2050**	500	600
(420)	**2670**	600	700
Leather Seats (190 D, 190 E, 260, 300 D, 300 E, 300 TD)	**1385**	250	300
Velour Seats (190 D, 190 E, 260, 300 D, 300 E, 300 TD)	**1365**	250	300

NOTE: Power steering, power locks, power brakes, air conditioning and power windows standard on all models. Power sun roof standard on 560 SEC and 560 SEL.

Year-Model-Body Type	Original List	Current Whlse	Average Retail
1986			
190 D 5			
2.5 4 Dr Sdn	**25080**	7650	8875
2.5 4 Dr Sdn (auto)	**25710**	8100	9350
190 E 4			
2.3 4 Dr Sdn	**25080**	8800	10175
2.3 4 Dr Sdn (auto)	**25710**	9250	10650
2.3-16 4 Dr Sdn	**36820**	13600	15975
2.3-16 4 Dr Sdn (auto)	**37450**	14050	16500
300 E 6			
4 Dr Sdn	**25870**	13100	15475
4 Dr Sdn (auto)	**36710**	13600	15975
300 SDL 6			
4 Dr Turbo-diesel (auto)	**43800**	16050	18700
420 SEL 8			
4 Dr Sdn (auto)	**47720**	16850	19500
560 SEL 8			
4 Dr Sdn (auto)	**56390**	19950	23000
560 SEC 8			
2 Dr Cpe (auto)	**62110**	24900	28225
560 SL 8			
2 Dr Cpe/Rdstr (auto)	**51000**	25350	28675
ADD FOR:			
Anti-Lock Brake System (190 D, 190 E)	**1405**	200	250
Electric Left Front Seat (190 D, 190 E)	**1265**	150	175
Electric 4 Place Seating (420 SEL)	**2300**	400	500
(560 SEL)	**1760**	350	450
Leather Seats (190 D, 190 E, 300 E)	**1190**	200	250
Velour Seats (190 D, 190 E, 300 E)	**1170**	200	250

NOTE: Power steering, power locks, power brakes, air conditioning and power windows standard on all models.

Year-Model-Body Type	Original List	Current Whlse	Average Retail
1985			
190 D 4			
4 Dr Sdn	**22930**	6025	6950
4 Dr Sdn (auto)	**23510**	6425	7475
190 E 4			
4 Dr Sdn	**22850**	7250	8425
4 Dr Sdn (auto)	**23430**	7650	8875
300 D 5			
2 Dr Turbo-diesel Cpe (auto)	**35220**	10425	12025
4 Dr Turbo-diesel Sdn (auto)	**31940**	8850	10225
300 SD 5			
4 Dr Turbo-diesel Sdn			

Year-Model-Body Type	Original List	Current Whlse	Average Retail
(auto)	**39500**	11875	13725
300 TD 5			
4 Dr Turbo-diesel Wgn (auto)	**35310**	10125	11675
380 SE 8			
4 Dr Sdn (auto)	**42730**	13450	15775
380 SL 8			
2 Dr Cpe/Rdstr (auto)	**43820**	20625	23675
500 SEC 8			
2 Dr Cpe (auto)	**56800**	18125	20850
500 SEL 8			
4 Dr Sdn (auto)	**51200**	15300	17950
ADD FOR:			
Rear Facing Third Seat (300 TD)	**834**	100	125
Leather Seats (190 E, 190 D, 300 D, 300 TD, 300 CD)	**1083**	150	175
(300 SD, 380 SE)	**1124**	150	175
(380 SL)	**853**	150	175
Velour Seats (190 E, 190 D, 300 D, 300 TD, 300 CD)	**1073**	150	175
(300 SD, 380 SE)	**1117**	150	175

1984

Year-Model-Body Type	Original List	Current Whlse	Average Retail
190 D 4			
4 Dr Sdn	**22930**	5125	6050
4 Dr Sdn (auto)	**23510**	5500	6425
190 E 4			
4 Dr Sdn	**22850**	6175	7200
4 Dr Sdn (auto)	**23430**	6525	7600
300 D 5			
2 Dr Turbo-diesel Cpe (auto)	**35220**	8875	10250
4 Dr Turbo-diesel Sdn (auto)	**31940**	7425	8625
300 SD 5			
4 Dr Turbo-diesel Sdn (auto)	**39500**	11075	12800
300 TD 5			
4 Dr Turbo-diesel Wgn (auto)	**35310**	8750	10100
380 SE 8			
4 Dr Sdn (auto)	**42730**	12225	14175
380 SL 8			
2 Dr Cpe/Rdstr (auto)	**43830**	19575	22625
500 SEC 8			
2 Dr Cpe (auto)	**56800**	18125	20850
500 SEL 8			
4 Dr Sdn (auto)	**51200**	14150	16600

1983

Year-Model-Body Type	Original List	Current Whlse	Average Retail
240 D 4			
4 Dr Sdn	**22470**	4950	5875
4 Dr Sdn (auto)	**23800**	5150	6075
300 D 5			
2 Dr Turbo-diesel Cpe (auto)	**33750**	8025	9275
4 Dr Turbo-diesel Sdn (auto)	**30530**	6800	7925
300 SD 5			
4 Dr Sdn (auto)	**37970**	9675	11150
300 TD 5			
4 Dr Turbo-diesel Wgn (auto)	**33850**	7725	8975
380 SEC 8			
Cpe (auto)	**53570**	17025	19675
380 SEL 8			
4 Dr Sdn (auto)	**47870**	12875	15200
380 SL 8			
2 Dr Cpe/Rdstr (auto)	**43030**	18275	21150

MITSUBISHI

1992

Year-Model-Body Type	Original List	Current Whlse	Average Retail
2WD TRUCKS 4			
Mighty Max (5 spd)	**9509**	—	—
Mighty Max Macrocab (5 spd)	**10839**	—	—
Mighty Max 1-Ton (5 spd)	**10609**	—	—
4WD TRUCKS 6			
Mighty Max (5 spd)	**13519**	—	—
ADD FOR:			
Special Edit Pkg	**454**	—	—
3000 GT 6			
2 Dr Base Htchbk (5 spd)	**21739**	—	—
2 Dr SL Htchbk (5 spd)	**27289**	—	—
2 Dr VR-4 Htchbk (5 spd)	**34150**	—	—
ADD FOR:			
Anti-Lock Brakes (Base)	**1130**	—	—
Leather & Vinyl Seat Trim	**1120**	—	—
DIAMANTE 6			
4 Dr Base Sdn (auto)	**21489**	—	—
4 Dr LS Sdn (auto)	**26450**	—	—
ADD FOR:			
Euro Handling Pkg	**1670**	—	—

Year-Model-Body Type	Original List	Current Whlse	Average Retail
Leather Seat Pkg	**1741**	—	—
Alloy Wheels (Base)	**388**	—	—
ECLIPSE 4			
3 Dr 1.8 Liter Base Cpe (5 spd)	**12463**	—	—
3 Dr 1.8 Liter GS Cpe (5 spd)	**13476**	—	—
3 Dr 2.0 Liter GS Cpe (5 spd)	**14436**	—	—
3 Dr GS Turbo Cpe (5 spd)	**17269**	—	—
3 Dr GSX 4WD Turbo Cpe (5 spd)	**19029**	—	—
ADD FOR:			
Leather Pkg	**435**	—	—
Anti-Lock Brakes	**943**	—	—
Alloy Wheels	**321**	—	—
EXPO 4			
3 Dr LRV Lftbk (5 spd)	**12271**	—	—
3 Dr LRV Sport Lftbk (5 spd)	**13290**	—	—
3 Dr LRV Sport AWD Lftbk (5 spd)	**15190**	—	—
4 Dr Base Lftbk (5 spd)	**14324**	—	—
4 Dr SP Lftbk (5 spd)	**15284**	—	—
4 Dr SP AWD Lftbk (5 spd)	**16614**	—	—
ADD FOR:			
Anti-Lock Brakes	**924**	—	—
Alloy Wheels	**291**	—	—
GALANT 4			
4 Dr Base Sdn (5 spd)	**13368**	—	—
4 Dr LS Sdn (auto)	**16041**	—	—
4 Dr GS Sport Sdn (5 spd)	**16441**	—	—
4 Dr GSX 4WD Sport Sdn (auto)	**19041**	—	—
4 Dr GSR Sport Sdn (5 spd)	**17991**	—	—
4 Dr VR-4 4WD Turbo Sport Sdn (5 spd)	**23100**	—	—
ADD FOR:			
Anti-Lock Brakes (GSR, GSX)	**924**	—	—
Alloy Wheels (LS, GS, GSX)	**294**	—	—
MIRAGE 4			
3 Dr VL Htchbk (4 spd)	**8735**	—	—
3 Dr Base Htchbk (5 spd)	**9550**	—	—
3 Dr Special Edit Htchbk (5 spd)	**9094**	—	—
4 Dr Base Sdn (5 spd)	**10580**	—	—
4 Dr LS Sdn (5 spd)	**11304**	—	—
4 Dr GS Sdn (5 spd)	**12472**	—	—
ADD FOR:			
Alloy Wheels	**285**	—	—
MONTERO 6			
4WD 4 Dr Base (5 spd)	**19924**	—	—
4WD 4 Dr RS (5 spd)	**21089**	—	—
4WD 4 Dr LS (auto)	**24560**	—	—
4WD 4 Dr SR (auto)	**23985**	—	—
ADD FOR:			
Leather Pkg	**1213**	—	—
Anti-Lock Brakes (SR)	**1188**	—	—
PRECIS 4			
3 Dr Base Htchbk (4 spd)	**8068**	—	—

NOTE: Tilt steering wheel standard on Mirage GS, Expo, Eclipse, Galant, Diamante, 3000 GT, Pickups and Montero. Cruise control standard on Eclipse GS Turbo & GSX, Galant LS, GS, GSX, GSR & VR-4, Diamante LS, 3000 GT SL & VR-4, Montero LS & SR. Power windows and power door locks standard on Galant LS, GS, GSX, GSR & VR-4, Diamante, 3000 GT and Montero LS & SR. Power seat standard on Galant LS, GS, GSX, GSR & VR-4, Diamante and 3000 GT SL & VR-4.

1991

Year-Model-Body Type	Original List	Current Whlse	Average Retail
2WD TRUCKS 4			
Mighty Max (5 spd)	**8969**	5775	6700
Mighty Max Macrocab (5 spd)	**10199**	6325	7350
Mighty Max 1-Ton (5 spd)	**9969**	5800	6725
4WD TRUCKS 6			
Mighty Max (5 spd)	**12689**	8050	9300
3000 GT 4			
2 Dr Base Htchbk (5 spd)	**19059**	14725	17275
2 Dr Base Htchbk (auto)	**19859**	15375	18025
2 Dr SL Htchbk (5 spd)	**24749**	17825	20475
2 Dr VR-4 4WD Twin-Turbo Htchbk (5 spd)	**30800**	—	—
ECLIPSE 4			
3 Dr Base Htchbk (5 spd)	**11932**	8625	9950
3 Dr GS Htchbk (5 spd)	**12700**	9225	10625
3 Dr GS DOHC Htchbk			

Refer To Optional Equipment Schedules

Year-Model-Body Type	Original List	Current Whlse	Average Retail
(5 spd)	**13600**	9725	11200
3 Dr GS DOHC Turbo Htchbk (5 spd)	**15910**	10575	12200
3 Dr GSX DOHC Turbo Htchbk (5 spd)	**17570**	12225	14175
GALANT 4			
4 Dr Base Sdn (5 spd)	**12355**	8425	9725
4 Dr LS Sdn (auto)	**14781**	9650	11125
4 Dr GS Sport Sdn (5 spd)	**15061**	9825	11325
4 Dr GSR Sport Sdn (5 spd)	**17371**	10775	12425
4 Dr 4WD GSX Sport Sdn (auto)	**17761**	—	—
4 Dr 4WD VR-4 Turbo Sport Sdn (5 spd)	**21000**	—	—
MIRAGE 4			
3 Dr VL Htchbk (4 spd) (NA w/power steering)	**8165**	5375	6300
3 Dr Standard Htchbk (5 spd)	**8907**	6025	6950
4 Dr Base Sdn (5 spd)	**9837**	6200	7225
4 Dr LS Sdn (5 spd)	**10407**	6475	7525
4 Dr GS Sdn (5 spd)	**11772**	7075	8225
MONTERO 6			
4WD 4 Dr Base (5 spd)	**16805**	12125	14000
4WD 4 Dr RS (auto)	**17985**	12875	15200
4WD 4 Dr LS (5 spd)	**19609**	13825	16200
PRECIS 4			
3 Dr Base Htchbk (4 spd) (NA w/power steering)	**7522**	4075	5000
3 Dr RS Htchbk (5 spd)	**8418**	4300	5225
ADD FOR:			
Anti-Lock Brakes (Eclipse GS DOHC Turbo, Galant GS & GSX)	**924**	525	600
Leather Pkg (3000GT)	**1120**	625	725
(Eclipse GSX)	**427**	250	300

NOTE: Power brakes standard on all models. Power door locks standard on 3000GT SL & VR-4, Eclipse, Galant except Base, Montero LS and Pickups. Power windows standard on 3000GT SL and VR-4, Galant except Base and Montero LS. Power seat standard on Galant VR-4.

1990

Year-Model-Body Type	Original List	Current Whlse	Average Retail
2WD TRUCKS 4			
Mighty Max (5 spd)	**8969**	4525	5450
Mighty Max Macrocab (5 spd)	**9909**	4975	5900
Mighty Max 1-Ton (5 spd)	**9969**	4775	5700
VAN/WAGON 4			
Van (auto)	**11950**	6425	7475
Wagon (auto)	**17134**	9125	10500
Wagon w/LS Pkg (auto)	**18005**	9850	11350
ECLIPSE 4			
3 Dr Htchbk (5 spd)	**11871**	7175	8325
3 Dr GS Htchbk (5 spd)	**12560**	7675	8900
3 Dr GS DOHC Htchbk (5 spd)	**13490**	8025	9275
3 Dr GS DOHC Turbo Htchbk (5 spd)	**15450**	8675	10025
3 Dr GSX DOHC Turbo Htchbk (5 spd)	**17260**	10350	11950
GALANT 4			
4 Dr Sdn (5 spd)	**12343**	7225	8400
4 Dr LS Sdn (auto)	**14777**	8175	9450
4 Dr GS Sport Sdn (5 spd)	**16477**	8900	10275
4 Dr 4WD GSX Sport Sdn (5 spd)	**17171**	9575	11025
MIRAGE 4			
3 Dr VL Htchbk (4 spd) (NA w/power steering)	**8012**	3950	4850
3 Dr Htchbk (5 spd)	**8875**	4575	5500
3 Dr RS Htchbk (5 spd)	**9824**	4800	5725
3 Dr EXE Spec Edit (5 spd)	**8339**	4200	5125
4 Dr Sdn (5 spd)	**9595**	4750	5675
4 Dr EXE Spec Edit (5 spd)	**9509**	4825	5750
MONTERO 6			
4WD 2 Dr SP (5 spd)	**15086**	10275	11850
4WD 2 Dr Sport (auto)	**16219**	10900	12575
4WD 4 Dr (5 spd)	**16835**	11125	12850
4WD 4 Dr RS (5 spd)	**18949**	11625	13425
4WD 4 Dr LS (auto)	**20309**	12675	15000
PRECIS 4			
3 Dr Htchbk (4 spd)	**7212**	2800	3700
3 Dr RS Htchbk (5 spd)	**8312**	3225	4125
SIGMA 6			
4 Dr Lux Sdn (auto)	**17879**	9400	10825
ADD FOR:			
Anti-Lock Brakes (Galant GS & GSX Sport, Sigma)	**1495**	500	575
Eurotech Pkg (Sigma)	**2042**	600	725
Leather Pkg (Eclipse GSX)	**427**	175	225
(Sigma)	**816**	225	275

NOTE: Power windows standard on Galant LS, GS & GSX, Sigma, Van/Wagon LS, Montero LS & RS. Power door locks standard on Galant LS, GS & GSX, Sigma, Van/Wagon Series and Montero Series.

Year-Model-Body Type	Original List	Current Whlse	Average Retail
1989			
2WD TRUCKS 4			
Mighty Max (5 spd)	**8861**	3025	3925
Mighty Max Macrocab Ext. Cab (5 spd)	**10071**	3475	4375
Mighty Max 1-Ton (5 spd)	**9841**	3250	4150
Mighty Max Sport Short Bed (5 spd)	**9751**	3425	4325
Mighty Max Sport Long Bed (5 spd)	**10341**	3550	4450
SPX Macrocab Ext. Cab (5 spd)	**11654**	4175	5100
4WD TRUCKS 4			
SPX Short Bed (5 spd)	**13289**	4175	5100
VAN/WAGON 4			
L Cargo Van (auto)	**11950**	4250	5175
Wgn (auto)	**17134**	6500	7575
Wgn w/LS Pkg (auto)	**18005**	6900	8025
GALANT 4			
4 Dr Sdn (5 spd)	**11761**	5150	6075
4 Dr LS Sdn (auto)	**14369**	6075	6975
4 Dr GS Sdn (5 spd)	**16059**	6550	7625
MIRAGE 4			
3 Dr VL Htchbk (5 spd)	**9158**	2900	3800
4 Dr VL Sdn (5 spd)	**9818**	3075	3975
3 Dr Htchbk (5 spd)	**10048**	3075	3975
4 Dr Sdn (5 spd) (NA w/power steering)	**9956**	3350	4250
4 Dr LS Sdn (5 spd)	**11505**	3675	4575
3 Dr Turbo Spt Htchbk (5 spd)	**13265**	4050	4950
MONTERO 6			
4WD 2 Dr SP (5 spd) (4 cyl)	**13109**	7275	8450
4WD 2 Dr SP (5 spd)	**14759**	7500	8700
4WD 2 Dr Sport (auto)	**16209**	8275	9550
4 Dr Sport (5 spd) (6 cyl)	**17909**	8775	10125
4 Dr LS Sport (auto)	**19199**	9750	11225
PRECIS 4			
3 Dr Htchbk (4 spd) (NA w/power steering)	**6019**	2050	2900
3 Dr RS Htchbk (5 spd) (NA w/power steering)	**7244**	2400	3275
3 Dr LS Htchbk (5 spd)	**8594**	2600	3475
5 Dr LS Htchbk (5 spd)	**8109**	2750	3650
SIGMA 6			
4 Dr Sdn (auto)	**17069**	6925	8075
STARION 4			
ESI Turbo 2+2 Cpe (5 spd)	**19859**	7150	8300
ADD FOR:			
Anti-Lock Brakes (Galant, Sigma)	**1495**	450	525
Eurotech Pkg (Sigma)	**2042**	500	625
Leather Seats (Starion)	**626**	175	225
(Sigma)	**816**	200	250

NOTE: Power brakes standard on all models. Power door locks standard on Galant LS & GS, Sigma, Starion, Montero Series and Van/Wagon. Power windows standard on Galant LS & GS, Sigma, Starion and LS Van/Wagon.

Year-Model-Body Type	Original List	Current Whlse	Average Retail
1988			
2WD TRUCKS 4			
Mighty Max (5 spd)	**6999**	1825	2675
Mighty Max Macrocab (5 spd)	**8109**	2150	3000
Mighty Max 1-Ton (5 spd)	**8159**	1975	2825
Mighty Max Sport Short Bed (5 spd)	**7919**	2175	3025
Mighty Max Sport Long Bed (5 spd)	**8469**	2250	3100
Mighty Max SPX Macrocab (5 spd)	**9589**	2750	3650
4WD TRUCKS			
SPX (5 spd)	**11469**	3725	4625
VAN/WAGON 4			
Cargo Van (auto)	**10789**	2600	3475
Cargo Van w/Converter Conv Pkg (auto)	**11549**	2850	3750
Wgn (auto)	**14269**	4125	5050
Wgn w/LS Pkg (auto)	**15789**	4525	5450
CORDIA 4			
2 Dr L Sport Htchbk	**10829**	2225	3075
GALANT SIGMA 6			
4 Dr Luxury Sdn	**16129**	5125	6050
MIRAGE 4			
4 Dr Sdn	**8619**	1775	2625
2 Dr Turbo Sport Htchbk	**9239**	2025	2875
MONTERO 4			
3 Dr SP (5 spd)	**11929**	4625	5550
3 Dr Sport (5 spd)	**14259**	5125	6050
PRECIS 4			
3 Dr Htchbk	**5395**	900	1625
3 Dr RS Htchbk	**6499**	1125	1850
3 Dr LS Htchbk	**7249**	1350	2100
5 Dr LS Htchbk	**7499**	1500	2350
STARION 4			
ESI Turbo 2+2 Cpe (5 spd)	**17129**	5225	6150
ESI-R Turbo 2+2 Cpe (5 spd)	**19789**	6300	7325

Refer To Optional Equipment Schedules

Year-Model-Body Type	Original List	Current Whlse	Average Retail
TREDIA 4			
4 Dr L Sdn	**10039**	2125	2975
4 Dr LS Sdn (auto)	**11109**	2425	3300
4 Dr Turbo Sdn (5 spd)	**10949**	2675	3575
ADD FOR:			
Eurotech Pkg (Galant Sigma)	**1920**	400	500
Leather Seats (Galant Sigma)	**753**	200	250
(Starion ESI-R)	**563**	175	200

NOTE: Air conditioning standard on Galant Sigma and Starion ESI-R. Power windows standard on Tredia LS, Tredia Turbo, Galant Sigma, Starion Series, Converter Convenience Van and LS Wagon. Power door locks standard on Tredia LS, Tredia Turbo, Galant Sigma, Starion ESI-R and Van/Wagon Series. Power steering standard on Tredia Series, Cordia Series, Galant Sigma, Starion Series, LS Wagon, Mighty Max Pickups except 2WD Base and Montero Series. Power brakes standard on all models.

1987

Year-Model-Body Type	Original List	Current Whlse	Average Retail
2WD TRUCKS 4			
Mighty Max (5 spd)	**6499**	900	1625
Mighty Max 1-Ton (5 spd)	**7329**	1075	1800
Mighty Max Sport Short Bed (5 spd)	**7299**	1225	1950
Mighty Max Sport Long Bed (5 spd)	**7589**	1325	2050
SPX (5 spd)	**7779**	1425	2175
4WD TRUCKS 4			
Mighty Max Long Bed (5 spd)	**9569**	2075	2925
VAN/WAGON 4			
Cargo Van (auto)	**9839**	1825	2675
Cargo Van w/Converter Conv Pkg (auto)	**10529**	2000	2850
Wgn (auto)	**13099**	3000	3900
Wgn w/LS Pkg (auto)	**14649**	3325	4225
CORDIA 4			
2 Dr L Sport Htchbk	**9999**	1850	2700
2 Dr L Sport Htchbk (auto)	**10439**	2150	3000
2 Dr Turbo Sport Htchbk	**11619**	2100	2950
GALANT 4			
4 Dr Luxury Sdn	**14339**	3200	4100
MIRAGE 4			
2 Dr Base Htchbk	**5969**	950	1675
4 Dr Base Sdn	**8069**	1250	1975
2 Dr L Htchbk	**7479**	1150	1875
2 Dr Turbo Sport Htchbk	**8479**	1325	2050
MONTERO 4			
4WD 3 Dr (5 spd)	**10089**	3350	4250
4WD 3 Dr Sport (5 spd)	**12399**	3700	4600
PRECIS 4			
3 Dr Htchbk	**5195**	575	1075
3 Dr LS Htchbk	**6499**	975	1700
5 Dr LS Htchbk	**6799**	1125	1850
STARION 4			
LE Turbo 2+2 Cpe (5 spd)	**15959**	4025	4925
ESI-R Turbo 2+2 Cpe (5 spd)	**18479**	4650	5575
TREDIA 4			
4 Dr L Sdn	**9699**	1550	2400
4 Dr LS Sdn (auto)	**10749**	1800	2650
4 Dr Turbo Sdn (5 spd)	**10589**	1775	2625
ADD FOR:			
ECS Pkg (Galant)	**670**	175	200
Leather Seat Trim (Galant LS)	**669**	150	200
(Starion LE)	**389**	125	150

NOTE: Power brakes standard on all models. Air conditioning standard on Galant and Starion. Power door locks standard on Galant, Starion Series, Van, LS Wagon. Power windows standard on Tredia LS, Galant, Starion Series, Converter Convenience Van and LS Wagon. Power steering standard on Mirage Turbo w/automatic transmission, Tredia Series, Cordia Series, Galant, Starion Series, LS Wagon and Mighty Max Sport Pickup.

1986

Year-Model-Body Type	Original List	Current Whlse	Average Retail
2WD TRUCKS 4			
Mighty Max (5 spd)	**6208**	625	1175
Mighty Max Sport (5 spd)	**6668**	825	1525
SPX (5 spd)	**7458**	975	1700
CORDIA 4			
2 Dr L Sport Htchbk	**9319**	1100	1825
2 Dr Turbo Sport Htchbk	**10799**	1275	2000
GALANT 4			
4 Dr Luxury Sdn (auto)	**13899**	2250	3100
MIRAGE 4			
2 Dr Base Htchbk	**6152**	600	1125
2 Dr L Htchbk	**7352**	750	1475
2 Dr L Htchbk (auto)	**7752**	900	1625
2 Dr Turbo Htchbk	**8636**	900	1625
2 Dr Turbo Htchbk			

Year-Model-Body Type	Original List	Current Whlse	Average Retail
(auto)	**9226**	1000	1725
MONTERO 4			
4WD 3 Dr (5 spd)	**9588**	2700	3600
4WD 3 Dr w/Sport Group (5 spd)	**10599**	2875	3775
STARION 4			
LE Turbo 2+2 Cpe (5 spd)	**15209**	2725	3625
ESI-R Turbo Cpe (5 spd)	**17569**	3100	4000
TREDIA 4			
4 Dr Base Sdn	**8150**	875	1600
4 Dr L Sdn	**9079**	975	1700
4 Dr LS Sdn (auto)	**10279**	1300	2025
4 Dr Turbo Sdn	**10089**	1175	1900
ADD FOR:			
ECS Pkg (Galant)	**670**	125	150
Sport Group (Montero)	**865**	175	200
Leather/Digital Pkg (Starion LE)	**640**	100	125
Off-Road Pkg (4WD Pickup)	**474**	100	125

NOTE: Power brakes standard on all models. Power locks, power windows, automatic transmission and air conditioning standard on Galant and Starion Series. Power steering standard on Mirage Turbo, Cordia Series, Galant, Starion Series, Montero and 4WD Mighty Max.

1985

Year-Model-Body Type	Original List	Current Whlse	Average Retail
2WD TRUCKS 4			
Mighty Max (4 spd)	**5948**	475	875
SP (5 spd)	**6868**	725	1375
SP Turbodiesel (5 spd)	**7798**	525	975
SPX (5 spd)	**7239**	800	1500
SPX Turbodiesel (5 spd)	**8109**	625	1175
CORDIA 4			
2 Dr L Htchbk	**8449**	750	1475
2 Dr Turbo Htchbk	**9959**	925	1650
GALANT 4			
4 Dr Luxury Sdn (auto)	**11989**	1775	2625
MIRAGE 4			
2 Dr Base Htchbk	**5389**	425	775
2 Dr L Htchbk	**6576**	600	1125
2 Dr LS Htchbk	**7056**	725	1375
2 Dr Turbo Htchbk	**8076**	775	1500
MONTERO 4			
4WD 3 Dr (5 spd)	**9955**	2200	3050
STARION 4			
LS Turbo 2+2 Cpe (5 spd)	**12629**	1500	2350
LE Turbo 2+2 Cpe (5 spd)	**14869**	1850	2700
LE Turbo 2+2 Cpe (auto)	**15409**	1975	2825
ES Turbo 2+2 Cpe (5 spd)	**14489**	1975	2825
TREDIA 4			
4 Dr Base Sdn	**7112**	550	1025
4 Dr L Sdn	**8189**	675	1275
4 Dr Turbo Sdn	**9279**	800	1500
ADD FOR:			
Sport Group (Montero)	**770**	75	100
ECS Pkg (Galant)	**910**	100	125
LS Pkg (Tredia L)	**760**	100	125
(Cordia L)	**699**	100	125

NOTE: Power steering standard on Cordia, Tredia L, Tredia Turbo, Starion, Galant, Montero, 2WD SPX Truck and 4WD Trucks. Air conditioning standard on Starion LE, Starion ES and Galant. Power windows standard on Starion and Galant. Power brakes standard on all models. Power door locks standard on Starion LE and Galant. Automatic transmission standard on Galant.

1984

Year-Model-Body Type	Original List	Current Whlse	Average Retail
2WD TRUCKS 4			
Mighty Max (4 spd)	**5841**	325	600
SP (5 spd)	**6941**	475	875
SP Turbodiesel (5 spd)	**7861**	275	550
SPX (5 spd)	**7839**	600	1125
SPX Turbodiesel (5 spd)	**8819**	400	725
CORDIA 4			
2 Dr Base Sport Htchbk	**7482**	475	875
2 Dr L Sport Htchbk	**8179**	600	1125
2 Dr LS Sport Htchbk	**9419**	700	1325
2 Dr Turbo Sport Htchbk	**9809**	775	1500
MONTERO 4			
4WD 3 Dr Base (5 spd)	**9778**	1775	2625
4WD 3 Dr Sport (5 spd)	**10309**	1875	2725
STARION 4			
LS Turbo 2+2 Cpe (5 spd)	**12509**	1225	1950
LE Turbo 2+2 Cpe (5 spd)	**14279**	1425	2175
ES Turbo 2+2 Cpe (5 spd)	**14559**	1600	2450
TREDIA 4			
4 Dr Base Sdn	**7040**	325	600
4 Dr L 4+4 Sdn	**7879**	425	775
4 Dr LS 4+4 Sdn	**9019**	525	975

Refer To Optional Equipment Schedules

Year-Model-Body Type	Original List	Current Whlse	Average Retail
4 Dr Turbo Sdn	**9349**	600	1125
1983 — ALL BODY STYLES			
MIGHTY MAX	—	125	325
2WD S TRUCKS	—	225	475
2WD SP TRUCKS	—	250	500
2WD SPX TRUCKS	—	350	625
4WD S TRUCKS	—	725	1375
4WD SP TRUCKS	—	475	875
4WD SPX TRUCKS	—	750	1475
CORDIA	—	300	575
MONTERO	—	1100	1825
STARION	—	750	1475
TREDIA	—	150	350

NISSAN

Year-Model-Body Type	Original List	Current Whlse	Average Retail
1992			
2WD PICKUPS 4			
2 Dr Reg Cab	**10260**	—	—
2 Dr King Cab	**11605**	—	—
2WD PICKUPS 6			
2 Dr Reg Cab Long Bed	**11710**	—	—
2 Dr SE King Cab	**14585**	—	—
4WD PICKUPS 4			
2 Dr Reg Cab	**13185**	—	—
2 Dr King Cab	**14845**	—	—
4WD PICKUPS 6			
2 Dr SE King Cab	**16700**	—	—
ADD FOR:			
Chrome Pkg	**825**	—	—
Power Plus Pkg (SE 2WD)	**1540**	—	—
(SE 4WD)	**2109**	—	—
240SX 4			
2 Dr Base Cpe	**15365**	—	—
2 Dr SE Cpe	**17840**	—	—
2 Dr Base Fstbk	**16115**	—	—
2 Dr SE Fstbk	**18285**	—	—
2 Dr LE Fstbk	**19320**	—	—
ADD FOR:			
Anti-Lock Brakes	**995**	—	—
Handling Pkg	**500**	—	—
300ZX 6			
2-Seater Cpe w/o T-Bar Roof	**29705**	—	—
2-Seater Cpe w/T-Bar Roof	**31815**	—	—
2+2 Cpe w/T-Bar Roof	**33090**	—	—
Turbo Cpe w/T-Bar Roof	**36610**	—	—
ADD FOR:			
Leather Pkg	**1075**	—	—
Bose Radio System (models w/o T-bar roof)	**700**	—	—
MAXIMA 6			
4 Dr GXE Sdn (auto)	**20425**	—	—
4 Dr SE Sdn	**21490**	—	—
ADD FOR:			
Anti-Lock Brakes	**995**	—	—
Leather Seat Trim (GXE)	**1000**	—	—
(SE)	**1400**	—	—
NX 4			
3 Dr 1600 Cpe	**12770**	—	—
3 Dr 2000 Cpe	**14530**	—	—
ADD FOR:			
Anti-Lock Brakes	**700**	—	—
T-Bar Roof	**900**	—	—
2WD PATHFINDER 6			
XE Sport	**18805**	—	—
4WD PATHFINDER 6			
XE Sport	**20515**	—	—
SE Sport	**22735**	—	—
ADD FOR:			
Leather Seat Trim	**1000**	—	—
Power Pkg	**1050**	—	—
Sport/Power Pkg	**2000**	—	—
SENTRA 4			
2 Dr E Sdn	**9795**	—	—
4 Dr E Sdn	**11200**	—	—
2 Dr XE Sdn	**11530**	—	—
4 Dr XE Sdn	**12215**	—	—
2 Dr SE Sdn	**12210**	—	—
2 Dr SE-R Sdn	**13465**	—	—
4 Dr GXE Sdn	**13265**	—	—
ADD FOR:			
Anti-Lock Brakes	**700**	—	—
STANZA 4			
4 Dr XE Sdn	**13225**	—	—
4 Dr GXE Sdn (auto)	**17465**	—	—
4 Dr SE Sdn	**17090**	—	—
ADD FOR:			
Anti-Lock Brakes	**995**	—	—

NOTE: Tilt steering wheel standard on Sentra, Stanza, 240SX, NX, Maxima, Pathfinder and SE Pickup. Cruise control, power windows and power door locks standard on Sentra GXE, Stanza GXE & SE, 240SX SE & LE, Maxima, 300ZX and Pathfinder SE. Power seat standard on 300ZX.

Year-Model-Body Type	Original List	Current Whlse	Average Retail
1991			
2WD PICKUPS 4			
2 Dr Std Short Bed	**9710**	6625	7700
2 Dr Std King Cab	**11015**	7225	8400
2WD PICKUPS 6			
2 Dr Std Long Bed	**10780**	7300	8475
2 Dr SE King Cab	**13955**	8725	10075
240SX 4			
2 Dr Base Cpe	**14945**	11250	13000
2 Dr SE Cpe	**16200**	12200	14100
3 Dr Base Fstbk	**15200**	11350	13100
3 Dr SE Fstbk	**16390**	12300	14300
3 Dr LE Fstbk	**18170**	13250	15575
300ZX 6			
Base 2-Seater Cpe	**28175**	20575	23625
Turbo 2-Seater Cpe	**34570**	23650	26950
2+2 Cpe	**31270**	22075	25375
MAXIMA 6			
4 Dr GXE Sdn (auto)	**19375**	13325	15650
4 Dr SE Sdn	**20495**	14250	16725
NX 4			
3 Dr 1600 Cpe	**12390**	—	—
3 Dr 2000 Cpe	**13820**	—	—
2WD PATHFINDER 6			
XE Sport	**17485**	13525	15900
4WD PATHFINDER 6			
SE Sport	**21205**	16425	19075
SENTRA 4			
2 Dr E Sdn (power steering available only w/auto trans)	**9140**	7075	8225
4 Dr E Sdn (power steering available only w/auto trans)	**10075**	7200	8350
2 Dr XE Sdn	**10380**	7625	8850
4 Dr XE Sdn	**11065**	7750	9000
2 Dr SE Sdn	**10960**	7725	8975
2 Dr SE-R Sdn	**11370**	8500	9825
4 Dr GXE Sdn	**12485**	9075	10450
STANZA 4			
4 Dr XE Sdn	**13680**	9800	11300
4 Dr GXE Sdn	**15825**	10900	12575
ADD FOR:			
Leather Pkg (300ZX Std & Turbo 2-Seater)	**1300**	405	495
(300ZX 2+2)	**1500**	465	570
(Maxima, Pathfinder SE)	**1000**	320	390
Luxury Pkg (Maxima GXE)	**1900**	600	730
T-Bar Roof (NX 2000)	**900**	460	550
Sport/Power Pkg (Pathfinder XE)	**1050**	330	405
(Pathfinder SE)	**2000**	630	770

NOTE: Power brakes standard on all models. Power door locks and power windows standard on 240SX SE & LE, 300ZX, Maxima, Pathfinder SE, Sentra GXE and Stanza GXE. Power seat standard on 240SX SE & LE. Power sunroof standard on Maxima SE.

Year-Model-Body Type	Original List	Current Whlse	Average Retail
1990			
2WD PICKUPS 4			
2 Dr E Reg Cab	**9289**	5050	5975
2 Dr E King Cab	**10574**	5650	6575
2WD PICKUPS 6			
2 Dr E Reg Cab	**10349**	5700	6625
2 Dr SE King Cab	**13424**	7075	8225
VAN 4			
7-Passenger XE	**14799**	8075	9325
7-Passenger GXE (auto)	**17449**	9225	10625
240SX 4			
2 Dr XE Cpe	**14074**	8700	10050
3 Dr SE Fstbk	**14324**	8850	10225
300ZX 6			
GS Htchbk Cpe	**27900**	16400	19050
GS 2+2 Htchbk Cpe	**29100**	16800	19450
Turbo Htchbk Cpe	**33000**	19125	22175
AXXESS 4			
XE Wgn	**14849**	8300	9575
SE Wgn (auto)	**16749**	9075	10450
MAXIMA 6			
4 Dr GXE Sdn (auto)	**17899**	11350	13100
4 Dr SE Sdn	**18949**	12175	14050
2WD PATHFINDER 6			
XE Sport	**14855**	11075	12800
4WD PATHFINDER 6			
SE 2 Dr Sport	**21814**	14025	16400
SE 4 Dr Sport	**20149**	14475	17000
PULSAR NX 4			
2 Dr XE Htchbk Cpe	**13074**	7325	8500
SENTRA 4			
2 Dr Sdn (NA w/power steering)	**8224**	4625	5550
2 Dr XE Sdn	**9774**	5500	6425
4 Dr XE Sdn	**10374**	5625	6550
4 Dr XE Wgn	**11124**	5875	6800
2 Dr XE Htchbk Cpe	**11824**	6325	7350
2 Dr SE Htchbk Cpe	**13124**	6775	7875
STANZA 4			
4 Dr XE Sdn	**12875**	7550	8775
4 Dr GXE Sdn	**14975**	8500	9825
ADD FOR:			
Anti-Lock Braking System (240SX SE)	**995**	270	330
Convenience/Sport Pkg (240SX XE)	**2300**	630	765

Refer To Optional Equipment Schedules

Year-Model-Body Type	Original List	Current Whlse	Average Retail
(240SX SE)	**2100**	575	700
Sport Pkg (240SX)	**1150**	315	385
Electronic Equipment Pkg (300ZX ex. Turbo)	**1600**	440	535
(300ZX Turbo)	**900**	250	305
(Maxima GXE)	**1550**	420	515
Leather Trim Pkg (300ZX GS 2-Seater)	**1000**	275	335
(300ZX GS 2+2)	**1200**	330	405
(Maxima)	**950**	260	315
Luxury Pkg (Maxima GXE)	**1900**	520	635
SE Sport Pkg (Maxima SE)	**995**	270	330
Power Plus Pkg (2WD V6 SE King Cab Pickup)	**1540**	420	515
(4WD V6 SE King Cab Pickup)	**2109**	580	705

NOTE: Power brakes standard on all models. Anti-lock brakes standard on 300ZX Series. Power windows standard on Stanza GXE, Axxess SE, Maxima Series, 300ZX Series, Van GXE and Pathfinder SE. Power door locks standard on Stanza GXE, Axxess Series, Maxima Series, 300ZX Series, Van GXE and Pathfinder SE. Sunroof standard on Sentra SE, Axxess SE and Maxima SE.

1989

Year-Model-Body Type	Original List	Current Whlse	Average Retail
2WD PICKUP 4			
2 Dr E Reg Bed	**8689**	3575	4475
2 Dr E King Cab	**9974**	4150	5075
2 Dr Special Reg Cab	**10089**	4025	5000
2 Dr Special King Cab	**10974**	4625	5550
2WD PICKUP 6			
2 Dr E Reg Bed	**10089**	4225	5150
2 Dr Special Reg Cab	**11089**	4725	5650
2 Dr SE King Cab	**13024**	5550	6475
240SX 4			
2 Dr XE Cpe	**13249**	7425	8625
3 Dr SE Fstbk	**13499**	7575	8800
300ZX 6			
GS Htchbk Cpe	**23449**	10475	12100
GS 2+2 Htchbk Cpe	**24649**	10625	12250
Turbo Htchbk Cpe	**25949**	11275	13025
MAXIMA 6			
4 Dr GXE Sdn (auto)	**17499**	9275	10675
4 Dr SE Sdn	**18549**	9875	11375
2WD PATHFINDER 6			
XE Sport	**16224**	8950	10325
4WD PATHFINDER 6			
SE Sport	**20499**	11375	13150
PULSAR NX 4			
2 Dr XE Htchbk Cpe	**12824**	5875	6800
2 Dr SE Htchbk Cpe	**13824**	6350	7400
SENTRA 4			
2 Dr Sdn	**7824**	2850	3750
2 Dr E Sdn	**9074**	3600	4500
4 Dr E Sdn	**9624**	3700	4600
2WD E Wgn	**10324**	4000	4900
2 Dr XE Sdn	**10774**	4000	4900
4 Dr XE Sdn	**11424**	4100	5025
2 Dr XE Cpe	**11824**	4400	5325
2WD XE Wgn	**11874**	4325	5250
4WD XE Wgn	**12424**	4975	5900
2 Dr SE Cpe	**13124**	4750	5675
STANZA 4			
4 Dr E Ntchbk Sdn	**13198**	5675	6600
4 Dr GXE Ntchbk Sdn	**15074**	6200	7225
ADD FOR:			
Convenience/Sport Pkg (240SX SE)	**2100**	415	505
Sport Pkg (240SX SE)	**1150**	230	280
(Pathfinder SE)	**2000**	395	480
Anti-Lock Braking System (240SX SE)	**1450**	285	345
(Maxima SE)	**1450**	285	345
Electronic Equipment Pkg (Maxima GXE)	**1550**	305	375
(300ZX)	**1375**	270	330
Luxury Pkg (Maxima GXE)	**1900**	375	460
Power Plus Pkg (2WD XE Pathfinder)	**1700**	335	410
(4WD XE Pathfinder)	**1900**	375	460
(2WD SE Pickup)	**1390**	275	335
(4WD SE Pickup)	**1959**	385	470
Leather Seat Trim (Maxima SE)	**1450**	285	345
(300ZX ex. 2+2, 300ZX Turbo)	**1055**	205	250
(300ZX GS 2+2)	**1215**	240	290

NOTE: Power brakes standard on all models. Sunroof standard on Maxima SE and Sentra SE. Power windows and power door locks standard on 300ZX Series, Maxima Series, Pathfinder SE and Stanza GXE.

1988

Year-Model-Body Type	Original List	Current Whlse	Average Retail
2WD PICKUP 4			
2 Dr Std Reg Bed	**7349**	2375	3250
2 Dr E Reg Bed	**7724**	2700	3600
2 Dr E Long Bed	**8424**	2800	3700

Year-Model-Body Type	Original List	Current Whlse	Average Retail
2 Dr E King Cab	**8724**	3075	3975
2 Dr XE King Cab	**10174**	3625	4525
2WD PICKUP 6			
2 Dr E HD Long Bed	**9249**	3325	4225
2 Dr SE King Cab	**11324**	4225	5150
4WD PICKUP 6			
2 Dr E Reg Bed	**11224**	4650	5575
2 Dr SE Reg Bed	**12874**	4975	5900
PATHFINDER 6			
XE Sport Utility	**15299**	8675	9975
SE Sport Utility	**17349**	9300	10700
VAN 4			
7-Passenger XE	**14599**	4750	5675
7-Passenger GXE (auto)	**16849**	5175	6100
200SX 4			
2 Dr XE Ntchbk	**12349**	3875	4775
2 Dr XE Htchbk	**12599**	4025	4925
200SX 6			
2 Dr SE Htchbk	**15399**	4650	5575
300ZX 6			
GS Htchbk Cpe	**21199**	8375	9675
GS 2+2 Htchbk Cpe	**22349**	8475	9800
Turbo Htchbk Cpe	**23699**	8975	10375
Limited Turbo Htchbk Cpe	**24699**	9400	10825
MAXIMA 6			
4 Dr GXE Sdn (auto)	**17449**	7025	8150
4 Dr GXE Wgn (auto)	**18699**	6925	8050
4 Dr SE Sdn (5 spd)	**17699**	6925	8050
4 Dr SE Special Edit. (5 spd)	**18699**	7075	8225
PULSAR NX 4			
3 Dr XE Htchbk	**11649**	3850	4750
2 Dr XE Sportbak	**12199**	4050	4950
3 Dr SE Htchbk Cpe	**12999**	4300	5225
2 Dr SE Sportbak	**13549**	4475	5400
SENTRA 4			
2 Dr Std Sdn	**6499**	1625	2475
2 Dr E Sdn	**7449**	2200	3050
3 Dr E Htchbk Sdn	**7349**	2200	3050
4 Dr E Sdn	**8649**	2275	3150
2WD E Wgn	**9099**	2450	3325
2 Dr XE Sdn	**9149**	2650	3550
4 Dr XE Sdn	**9749**	2725	3625
2WD XE Wgn	**10049**	2925	3825
2 Dr XE Cpe	**9999**	3000	3900
4WD XE Wgn	**10849**	3525	4425
4 Dr GXE Sdn	**10349**	2850	3750
2 Dr SE Cpe	**11249**	3150	4050
STANZA 4			
4 Dr E Ntchbk Sdn	**11249**	3750	4650
2WD XE Wgn	**12349**	3975	4875
4WD XE Wgn	**13899**	4575	5500
4 Dr GXE Ntchbk Sdn	**13199**	4175	5100

Year-Model-Body Type	Original List	Current Whlse	Average Retail
ADD FOR:			
Electronic Pkg			
(300ZX)	**1300**	125	150
(Maxima GXE Sdn)	**845**	115	140
Desert Runner Pkg			
(4WD Pickup)	**3000**	400	490
Sport Pkg			
(2WD Pickup)	**750**	100	120
(4WD Pickup)	**1300**	175	210
(Pathfinder XE)	**900**	120	145
(Pathfinder SE)	**2000**	270	325
Leather Trim Pkg			
(Maxima GXE)	**785**	105	130
(300ZX)	**1100**	145	180
Suede Trim (Maxima SE)	**785**	105	130

NOTE: Power brakes standard on all models. Power windows standard on Stanza GXE, 200SX SE, Maxima Series, 300ZX Series, Van GXE and Pathfinder SE. Air conditioning standard on Maxima Series, 300ZX Series and Vans. Power door locks standard on Stanza GXE, Maxima Series, Van GXE and Pathfinder SE. Sunroof standard on Sentra SE, Maxima GXE Wagon, Maxima SE and Maxima Special Edition. Power steering standard on Sentra E with automatic transmission, Sentra XE, Sentra GXE, Sentra SE, Stanza Series, Pulsar NX Series, 200SX Series, Maxima Series, 300ZX Series, Vans, Pathfinder Pickup E V6, Pickup XE and Pickup SE.

1987

Year-Model-Body Type	Original List	Current Whlse	Average Retail
2WD PICKUP 4			
2 Dr Std Reg Bed	**6999**	2050	2900
2 Dr E Reg Bed	**7399**	2200	3050
2 Dr E Long Bed	**8199**	2275	3150
2 Dr E King Cab	**8899**	2525	3400
2 Dr XE Long Bed	**9249**	2725	3625
2 Dr XE King Cab	**9949**	2975	3875
2WD PICKUP 6			
2 Dr HD Long Bed	**9449**	2575	3450
2 Dr SE Std Reg Bed	**10349**	2925	3825
2 Dr SE Std King Cab	**11499**	3275	4175
PATHFINDER 4			
E Sport Utility	**12899**	6225	7250
PATHFINDER 6			
XE Sport Utility	**14899**	6875	8000
SE Sport Utility	**16299**	7225	8400
VAN 4			
7-Passenger XE	**12849**	3625	4525
7-Passenger GXE (auto)	**15099**	4075	5000
200SX 4			
2 Dr XE Ntchbk	**11649**	3025	3925

Refer To Optional Equipment Schedules

Year-Model-Body Type	Original List	Current Whlse	Average Retail
3 Dr XE Htchbk	**11899**	3100	4000
200SX 6			
3 Dr SE Htchbk	**15199**	3775	4675
300ZX 6			
GS Htchbk Cpe w/o T-Bar Roof	**18999**	6175	7200
GS Htchbk Cpe w/T-Bar Roof	**20449**	6475	7525
GS 2+2 Htchbk Cpe w/T-Bar Roof	**21599**	6550	7625
Turbo Htchbk Cpe w/T-Bar Roof	**22699**	7050	8175
Turbo Htchbk Cpe w/Limited Slip Differential	**22949**	7075	8225
MAXIMA 6			
4 Dr GXE Sdn (auto)	**16799**	5275	6200
4 Dr GXE Wgn (auto)	**17999**	5175	6100
4 Dr SE Sdn (5 spd)	**16999**	5250	6175
4 Dr SE Sdn (auto)	**17749**	5650	6575
PULSAR NX 4			
3 Dr XE Htchbk Cpe	**11399**	3075	3975
3 Dr SE Htchbk Cpe	**12599**	3375	4275
SENTRA 4			
2 Dr Std Sdn	**6399**	1250	1975
2 Dr E Sdn	**7599**	1750	2600
3 Dr E Htchbk Sdn	**7499**	1675	2525
4 Dr E Sdn	**8349**	1850	2700
2WD E Wgn	**8799**	2000	2850
2 Dr XE Sdn	**8849**	2100	2950
3 Dr XE Htchbk Sdn	**8699**	2025	2875
4 Dr XE Sdn	**9449**	2175	3025
2WD XE Wgn	**9749**	2300	3175
4WD XE Wgn	**10499**	2800	3700
2 Dr XE Cpe	**9699**	2400	3275
4 Dr GXE Sdn	**10049**	2350	3225
2 Dr SE Cpe	**10899**	2775	3675
STANZA 4			
4 Dr E Ntchbk Sdn	**10949**	3225	4125
5 Dr XE Htchbk Sdn	**12049**	3250	4150
2WD XE Wgn	**11949**	3400	4300
4WD XE Wgn	**13499**	3950	4850
4 Dr GXE Ntchbk Sdn	**12899**	3625	4525
ADD FOR:			
Electronic Pkg			
(300ZX)	**1300**	105	130
(Maxima GXE Sdn)	**825**	100	125
Leather Trim Pkg			
(Maxima GXE Sdn)	**750**	100	125
Sport/Power Pkg			
(2WD SE Pickup, Pathfinder SE)	**1950**	160	195
(4WD SE Pickup)	**2350**	195	240
Sportbak Rear Canopy			
(Pulsar NX)	**925**	225	275

NOTE: Power brakes standard on all models. Air conditioning standard on Maxima Series and 300ZX Series. Power door locks standard on Stanza GXE, Maxima Series and 300ZX Series. Power windows standard on Stanza GXE, Maxima Series, 200SX SE, 300ZX Series and Van GXE. Sunroof standard on Sentra SE, 200SX SE, Maxima GXE Wagon and Maxima SE. Power steering standard on Sentra E with automatic transmission, Sentra XE, Sentra GXE, Sentra SE, Stanza Series, Pulsar NX Series, 200SX Series, Maxima Series, 300ZX Series, Van Series, Pathfinder Series, HD Pickups and XE Pickups.

1986½

Year-Model-Body Type	Original List	Current Whlse	Average Retail
2WD PICKUP 4			
2 Dr Std Reg Bed	**6299**	1700	2550
2 Dr E Reg Bed	**6949**	1900	2750
2 Dr E Long Bed	**7249**	2025	2875
2 Dr E King Cab	**8049**	2225	3075
2 Dr HD Long Bed	**8549**	2100	2950
2 Dr XE Long Bed	**8199**	2325	3200
2 Dr XE King Cab	**8999**	2525	3400
2 Dr SE Reg Bed	**9399**	2525	3400
2 Dr SE King Cab	**10499**	2650	3525

1986

Year-Model-Body Type	Original List	Current Whlse	Average Retail
2WD PICKUP 4			
2 Dr Std Reg Bed	**6199**	1450	2225
2 Dr Std King Cab	**7699**	1725	2575
2 Dr Dlx Reg Bed	**7599**	1800	2650
2 Dr ST Reg Bed	**8639**	1975	2825
2 Dr Std Long Bed	**6549**	1550	2400
2 Dr ST Long Bed	**8799**	2075	2925
2 Dr Dlx King Cab	**8219**	2000	2850
2 Dr ST King Cab	**9259**	1925	2775
4WD PICKUP 4			
2 Dr Dlx Long Bed	**9619**	2800	3700
200SX 4			
2 Dr E Ntchbk	**9899**	2225	3075
2 Dr E Htchbk	**10199**	2300	3175
2 Dr XE Ntchbk	**11299**	2325	3200
2 Dr XE Htchbk	**11899**	2425	3300
2 Dr Turbo Htchbk	**13549**	2475	3350
300ZX 4			
2 Dr Cpe w/o T-Bar Roof	**17999**	4675	5600
2 Dr Cpe w/T-Bar Roof	**18999**	4900	5925
2 Dr 2+2 Cpe w/T-Bar Roof	**20149**	4975	6025

Year-Model-Body Type	Original List	Current Whlse	Average Retail
2 Dr Turbo Cpe w/T-Bar Roof	**20999**	5350	6275
MAXIMA 6			
4 Dr SE Sdn	**14459**	3750	4650
4 Dr GL Sdn (auto)	**14459**	3775	4675
4 Dr GL Wgn (auto)	**15399**	3675	4575
PULSAR 4			
2 Dr Cpe	**9099**	1475	2300
SENTRA 4			
2 Dr Std Sdn	**5649**	725	1375
2 Dr MPG Diesel Sdn	**7449**	650	1225
2 Dr Dlx Sdn	**6969**	1100	1825
4 Dr Dlx Sdn	**7169**	1175	1900
4 Dr Dlx Wgn	**7699**	1300	2025
2 Dr XE Sdn	**7649**	1450	2225
4 Dr XE Sdn	**7849**	1550	2400
2 Dr XE Htchbk	**8169**	1600	2450
4 Dr XE Wgn	**8379**	1725	2575
2 Dr SE Htchbk	**9109**	1675	2525
STANZA 4			
4 Dr GL Ntchbk	**10069**	1850	2700
4 Dr XE Wgn	**10799**	1925	2775
4 Dr 4WD E Wgn	**11429**	2275	3150
4 Dr 4WD XE Wgn	**12099**	2375	3250
ADD FOR:			
Electronic Pkg (Maxima)	**600**	50	75
Leather Pkg (Maxima)	**600**	75	100

NOTE: Power brakes standard on all models. Power windows standard on Stanza GL, Maxima, 200SX SE and 300ZX. Sunroof standard on Sentra SE, Maxima Wagon, Maxima SE and 200SX Turbo. Power locks standard on Stanza GL, Maxima and 300ZX. Automatic transmission standard on Maxima and 300ZX. Power steering standard on Sentra XE, Sentra SE, Stanza, Maxima, 200SX E, 300ZX, Deluxe Pickups and ST Pickups.

1985

Year-Model-Body Type	Original List	Current Whlse	Average Retail
2WD PICKUP 4			
2 Dr Std Reg Bed	**5999**	1225	1950
2 Dr Dlx Reg Bed	**7295**	1475	2300
2 Dr ST Reg Bed	**8295**	1700	2550
2 Dr Std Long Bed	**6299**	1325	2050
2 Dr ST Long Bed	**8445**	1775	2625
2 Dr Std King Cab	**7395**	1500	2350
2 Dr Dlx King Cab	**7895**	1725	2575
2 Dr ST King Cab	**8895**	1825	2675
4WD PICKUP 4			
2 Dr Dlx Long Bed	**9245**	2400	3275
200SX 4			
2 Dr Dlx Ntchbk	**8999**	1925	2775
2 Dr XE Ntchbk	**10249**	2075	2925
3 Dr Dlx Htchbk	**9199**	2000	2850
3 Dr XE Htchbk	**10749**	2125	2975
3 Dr Turbo Htchck	**12349**	2150	3000
300ZX 6			
2 Seater Cpe	**17199**	3425	4325
2+2 Cpe	**18399**	3525	4425
2 Dr Turbo Cpe	**19699**	3825	4725
MAXIMA 6			
4 Dr SE Sdn	**13499**	3175	4075
4 Dr GL Wgn (auto)	**14399**	3250	4150
4 Dr GL Sdn (auto)	**13499**	3200	4100
PULSAR 4			
2 Dr Cpe	**8249**	1200	1925
SENTRA 4			
2 Dr Std Sdn	**5499**	625	1175
2 Dr Dlx Sdn	**6649**	825	1525
2 Dr MPG Diesel Sdn	**7099**	525	975
2 Dr XE Sdn	**7299**	1100	1825
4 Dr Dlx Sdn	**6849**	925	1650
4 Dr XE Sdn	**7499**	1200	1925
4 Dr Dlx Wgn	**7349**	1125	1850
4 Dr XE Wgn	**7999**	1275	2000
3 Dr XE Htchbk	**7799**	1200	1925
3 Dr SE Htchbk	**8699**	1300	2025
STANZA 4			
4 Dr XE Htchbk	**8949**	1225	1950
4 Dr GL Sdn	**9549**	1325	2050
ADD FOR:			
ST Pkg (Dlx King Cab)	**1000**	75	100
Electronic Pkg (300ZX)	**1200**	75	100
Leather Pkg (300ZX)	**1200**	75	100

NOTE: Power steering standard on Pulsar, Stanza, 200SX, Sentra XE, Maxima, 300ZX, 2WD Deluxe Pickups and 2WD ST Pickups. Air conditioning and power windows standard on Maxima and 300ZX. Power seat standard on Maxima and 300ZX. Sunroof standard on Pulsar and Maxima. Power brakes standard on all models. Power door locks standard on Maxima and 300ZX. Automatic transmission standard on Maxima.

1984

Year-Model-Body Type	Original List	Current Whlse	Average Retail
200SX 4			
2 Dr Dlx Ntchbk	**8699**	1450	2250
2 Dr XE Ntchbk	**9949**	1625	2475
3 Dr Dlx Htchbk	**8899**	1575	2425
3 Dr XE Htchbk	**10249**	1700	2550
3 Dr Turbo Htchck	**11949**	1700	2550
300ZX 6			
2 Seater Cpe	**16199**	2675	3575
2+2 Cpe	**17399**	2800	3700

Year-Model-Body Type	Original List	Current Whlse	Average Retail
2 Seater Turbo Cpe	**18699**	2875	3775
50th Anniversary Edit. Turbo	**25999**	3325	4225
2WD PICKUP 4			
2 Dr Std Reg Bed MPG	**5999**	1200	1925
2 Dr Std Reg Bed	**5999**	1200	1925
2 Dr Dlx Reg Bed	**7195**	1325	2050
2 Dr Sport Truck Reg Bed	**8145**	1325	2050
2 Dr Dlx Long Bed	**7345**	1375	2125
2 Dr HD Dlx Long Bed	**7445**	1400	2150
2 Dr Std King Cab MPG	**6895**	1325	2050
2 Dr Dlx King Cab	**7795**	1550	2400
2 Dr Dlx Diesel King Cab	**8635**	1225	1950
2 Dr XE King Cab	**8895**	1575	2425
MAXIMA 4			
4 Dr Sdn	**11899**	1825	2675
4 Dr Wgn (auto)	**13299**	1775	2625
PULSAR 4			
2 Dr NX Cpe	**8099**	925	1650
SENTRA 4			
2 Dr Std Sdn	**5399**	450	825
2 Dr Dlx Sdn	**6549**	700	1325
4 Dr Dlx Sdn	**6749**	775	1500
4 Dr Dlx Wgn	**7249**	875	1600
2 Dr MPG Sdn	**6999**	450	825
2 Dr XE Sdn	**7199**	875	1600
4 Dr XE Sdn	**7399**	900	1625
4 Dr XE Wgn	**7899**	1025	1750
2 Dr XE Htchbk Cpe	**7699**	950	1675
STANZA 4			
2 Dr XE Htchbk	**8649**	975	1700
4 Dr XE Htchbk	**8849**	1050	1775
4 Dr GL Sdn	**9449**	1200	1925

1983 — ALL BODY STYLES

Year-Model-Body Type	Original List	Current Whlse	Average Retail
200SX	—	825	1525
280-ZX	—	1825	2675
PICKUP	—	825	1525
MAXIMA GL	—	1200	1925
PULSAR	—	450	825
SENTRA	—	350	625
STANZA	—	650	1225

PEUGEOT

1991

Year-Model-Body Type	Original List	Current Whlse	Average Retail
405 4			
DL 4 Dr Sdn	**15490**	—	—
S 4 Dr Sdn	**17990**	—	—
Mi16 4 Dr Sdn	**21990**	—	—
DL 4 Dr Sportswagon	**16180**	—	—
S 4 Dr Sportswagon	**18785**	—	—
505 4			
DL 2.2i 5 Dr Wgn	**18950**	—	—
SW8 2.2i 5 Dr Wgn	**20800**	—	—
SW8 5 Dr Turbo Wgn (auto)	**26300**	—	—

NOTE: Power brakes and power door locks standard on all models. Power windows standard on 405 S and Mi16, 505 SW8 2.2i and Turbo SW8. Power seat standard on 405 Mi16. Power sunroof standard on 405 Mi16.

1990

Year-Model-Body Type	Original List	Current Whlse	Average Retail
405 4			
DL 4 Dr Sdn	**15390**	5675	6600
S 4 Dr Sdn	**17700**	6425	7475
Mi16 4 Dr Sdn	**21990**	7925	9200
DL 5 Dr Sportswagon	**15990**	6075	6975
S 5 Dr Sportswagon	**18495**	6875	8000
505 4			
S 2.2i 4 Dr Sdn	**19945**	—	—
S V6 4 Dr Sdn	**22485**	—	—
DL 2.2i 5 Dr Wgn	**18590**	—	—
SW8 2.2i 5 Dr Wgn	**20400**	—	—
5 Dr Turbo Wgn (auto)	**25940**	—	—
SW8 5 Dr Turbo Wgn (auto)	**26100**	—	—

NOTE: Power brakes and power door locks standard on all models. Anti-lock power brakes standard on 405 Mi16. Sunroof standard on 505 S 2.2i and 505 S V6. Power seat standard on 405 Mi16. Moonroof standard on 405 S Sedan and 405 Mi16 Sedan. Power windows standard on 405 S, 405 Mi16, 505 SW8 2.2i and 505 Turbo Wagon.

1989

Year-Model-Body Type	Original List	Current Whlse	Average Retail
405 4			
DL 4 Dr Sdn	**14500**	3400	4300
S 4 Dr Sdn	**17700**	4175	5100
Mi 16 4 Dr Sdn (6 cyl)	**20700**	5350	6275
505 4			
DL 4 Dr Wgn	**17590**	4225	5150
S 4 Dr Sdn	**19295**	4975	5900
S 4 Dr Sdn (6 cyl)	**21435**	5550	6475
SW8 5 Dr Wgn	**19995**	5300	6225
STX 4 Dr Sdn (6 cyl)	**25895**	7525	8725

Year-Model-Body Type	Original List	Current Whlse	Average Retail
4 Dr Turbo Sdn	**26335**	7675	8900
5 Dr Turbo Wgn (auto)	**25540**	7975	9250
SW8 5 Dr Turbo Wgn (auto)	**25695**	8150	9425
ADD FOR:			
Leather Package (405 S)	**1300**	200	225
(505 Turbo Sdn)	**960**	200	225

NOTE: Power brakes and power door locks standard on all models. Power moonroof standard on 405 S and 405 Mi16. Sunroof standard on 505 Series except DL. Power windows standard on 405 S, 405 Mi16, 505 S, 505 SW8, 505 STX, 505 Turbo and 505 SW8 Turbo.

1988

505 4

Year-Model-Body Type	Original List	Current Whlse	Average Retail
DL 4 Dr Sdn	**15950**	2500	3375
DL 4 Dr Wgn	**16975**	2750	3650
GLS 4 Dr Sdn	**18290**	3475	4375
GLS 5 Dr Wgn	**18475**	3750	4650
SW8 5 Dr Wgn	**19200**	4100	5025
GLX 4 Dr Sdn	**20425**	4000	4900
STI 4 Dr Sdn (auto)	**20890**	4425	5350
STX 4 Dr Sdn	**24690**	5275	6200
S 4 Dr Turbo Sdn	**25330**	5275	6200
S 5 Dr Wgn (auto)	**24330**	6075	6975
ADD FOR:			
Leather Upholstery (505 STI, STX & S)	**950**	175	200

NOTE: Power steering and power brakes standard on all models. Power windows standard on 505 GLS, 505 SW8, 505 GLX and 505 STI. Sunroof standard on 505 GLS Sedan, 505 SW8 Sedan, 505 GLX and 505 STI.

1987

505 4

Year-Model-Body Type	Original List	Current Whlse	Average Retail
GL 4 Dr Sdn	**14160**	1825	2675
Liberte 4 Dr Sdn (auto)	**16100**	2075	2925
Liberte 5 Dr Wgn (auto)	**17100**	2275	3150
GLS 4 Dr Sdn	**16170**	2250	3100
STI 4 Dr Sdn	**18870**	2575	3450
STI 4 Dr Sdn (6 cyl)	**21100**	3000	3900
STX 4 Dr Sdn	**23750**	3625	4525
4 Dr Turbo Sdn	**18990**	2825	3725
5 Dr Turbo Wgn	**20200**	3075	3975
S 4 Dr Turbo Sdn	**23100**	3625	4525
S 5 Dr Turbo Wgn	**22750**	3875	4775
GLS 4 Dr Turbodiesel Sdn (auto)	**18550**	—	—
GLS 5 Dr Turbodiesel Wgn (auto)	**19450**	—	—
ADD FOR:			
Anti-Lok Braking System (505 STI w/6 Cyl)	**1300**	300	350
Leather Upholstery (505 STI w/4 Cyl, 505 S Turbo)	**380**	110	135

NOTE: Power steering and power brakes standard on all models. Power windows standard on 505 Liberte, 505 GLS, 505 STI, 505 STX, 505 Turbo, 505 Turbo S and 505 GSL Turbo-diesel Wagon. Sunroof standard on 505 Liberte Sedan, 505 STI, 505 STX, 505 Turbo, 505 S Turbo and 505 GLS Turbo-diesel. Air conditioning standard on 505 GL, 505 GLS, 505 STI w/6 cyl, 505 STX, 505 Turbo, 505 S Turbo and 505 GLS Turbo-diesel.

1986

505 4

Year-Model-Body Type	Original List	Current Whlse	Average Retail
GL 4 Dr Sdn	**12895**	875	1600
S 4 Dr Sdn	**16245**	1575	2425
STI 4 Dr Sdn	**17295**	1825	2675
GL 4 Dr Wgn	**13495**	1050	1775
S 4 Dr Wgn	**17445**	1775	2625
4 Dr Turbo Sdn	**19345**	2125	2975
4 Dr Turbo Wgn (auto)	**20495**	2600	3475
ADD FOR:			
Leather Upholstery (505 S Gasoline, Turbo Gasoline Sdn & Wgn)	**750**	100	125

NOTE: Power brakes and power steering standard on all models. Power windows and air conditioning standard on all models except 505 GL. Sunroof standard on all models except wagons and 505 GL Sedan. Automatic transmission standard on 505 GL Turbodiesel Wagon and 505 S Turbodiesel Wagon.

1985

505 4

Year-Model-Body Type	Original List	Current Whlse	Average Retail
GL 4 Dr Sdn	**11900**	775	1500

Refer To Optional Equipment Schedules

Year-Model-Body Type	Original List	Current Whlse	Average Retail
S 4 Dr Sdn	**15580**	1275	2000
STI 4 Dr Sdn	**16630**	1450	2225
GL 4 Dr Wgn	**12440**	1125	1850
S 4 Dr Wgn	**16695**	1425	2175
4 Dr Turbo Sdn	**18150**	1600	2450
GL 4 Dr Turbodiesel Sdn	**13220**	600	1125
S 4 Dr Turbodiesel Sdn	**16900**	900	1625
STI 4 Dr Turbodiesel Sdn	**17950**	1100	1825
GL 4 Dr Turbodiesel Wgn	**13860**	775	1500
S 4 Dr Turbodiesel Wgn	**17965**	1075	1800
ADD FOR:			
Metallic Paint (505 GL)	**350**	45	55
Leather Upholstery (505 S Wgn)	**675**	90	110

NOTE: Power brakes and power steering standard on all models. Power windows and air conditioning standard on all models except 505 GL. Sunroof standard on all models except wagons and 505 GL Sedan. Automatic transmission standard on 505 GL Turbodiesel Wagon and 505 S Turbodiesel Wagon.

1984

Year-Model-Body Type	Original List	Current Whlse	Average Retail
505 4			
GL 4 Dr Sdn	**11300**	525	975
GL 4 Dr Wgn	**11990**	600	1125
GL 4 Dr Turbodiesel Sdn	**12800**	200	400
GL 4 Dr Turbodiesel Wgn (auto)	**13680**	275	550
S 4 Dr Sdn	**14845**	825	1525
S 4 Dr Wgn	**16095**	900	1625
S 4 Dr Turbodiesel Sdn	**16345**	475	875
S 4 Dr Turbodiesel Wgn (auto)	**17695**	550	1025
STI 4 Dr Sdn	**15800**	1050	1775
STI 4 Dr Turbodiesel Sdn	**17300**	725	1375
604 4			
4 Dr Turbodiesel Sdn	**20885**	675	1275

1983

Year-Model-Body Type	Original List	Current Whlse	Average Retail
504 4			
Diesel 4 Dr Wgn	**12085**	110	300
505 4			
4 Dr Sdn	**11865**	375	675
Diesel 4 Dr Sdn	**12575**	110	300
Turbodiesel 4 Dr Sdn	**14445**	110	300
604 4			
Turbodiesel 4 Dr Sdn	**19780**	525	975

PORSCHE

1992

Year-Model-Body Type	Original List	Current Whlse	Average Retail
911 CARRERA 2 6			
2 Dr Cpe (5 spd)	**63900**	—	—
2 Dr Cpe (Tiptronic)	**67050**	—	—
2 Dr Targa (5 spd)	**65500**	—	—
2 Dr Targa (Tiptronic)	**68650**	—	—
2 Dr Cabriolet (5 spd)	**72900**	—	—
2 Dr Cabriolet (Tiptronic)	**76050**	—	—
2 Dr American Rdstr Cabriolet (5 spd)	**87900**	—	—
2 Dr American Rdstr Cabriolet (Tiptronic)	**91050**	—	—
911 CARRERA 4 6			
2 Dr Cpe (5 spd)	**75780**	—	—
2 Dr Targa (5 spd)	**77380**	—	—
2 Dr Cabriolet (5 spd)	**84780**	—	—
911 TURBO COUPE 6			
2 Dr Cpe (5 spd)	**98875**	—	—
ADD FOR:			
5-Spoke Wheels	**1352**	—	—
Hardtop Roof (Cabriolet)	**9670**	—	—
CD Player	**755**	—	—
968 4			
2 Dr Cpe (6 spd)	**39850**	—	—
2 Dr Cpe (Tiptronic)	**43000**	—	—
2 Dr Cabriolet (6 spd)	**51000**	—	—
2 Dr Cabriolet (Tiptronic)	**54150**	—	—
ADD FOR:			
5-Spoke Turbo Wheels	**1352**	—	—
Special Chassis	**1976**	—	—
CD Player	**1250**	—	—

NOTE: Power windows and power door locks standard on all models. Cruise control and power seat standard on 911 Carrera, 911 American Roadster, 911 Turbo Coupe and 968. Power sunroof standard on 911 Carrera 2 Coupe and 968 Coupe.

Year-Model-Body Type	Original List	Current Whlse	Average Retail
1991			
911 CARRERA 2 6			
2 Dr Cpe (5 spd)	**61915**	44525	49275
2 Dr Cpe (Tiptronic)	**64925**	45725	50500
2 Dr Targa (5 spd)	**63445**	45475	50125
2 Dr Targa (Tiptronic)	**66455**	46700	51475
2 Dr Cabriolet (5 spd)	**70690**	49875	54950
2 Dr Cabriolet (Tiptronic)	**73695**	50775	55650
911 CARRERA 4 6			
2 Dr Cpe (5 spd)	**73440**	50075	54875
2 Dr Targa (5 spd)	**74970**	50850	55725
2 Dr Cabriolet (5 spd)	**82215**	55875	61250
911 TURBO COUPE 6			
2 Dr Cpe (5 spd)	**95000**	—	—
928 8			
2 Dr S4 Cpe (auto)	**77500**	50125	54925
2 Dr GT (5 spd)	**77500**	50925	55825
944 S2 4			
2 Dr Cpe (5 spd)	**43350**	28025	31375
2 Dr Cabriolet (5 spd)	**50350**	31800	35350
ADD FOR:			
Hardtop Roof (911 Cabriolet)	**8582**	5350	6520

NOTE: Power brakes, power door locks, power windows, power seat and sunroof standard on all models.

Year-Model-Body Type	Original List	Current Whlse	Average Retail
1990			
911 CARRERA 2 6			
2 Dr Cpe (5 spd)	**58500**	38425	42650
2 Dr Cpe (Tiptronic)	**61280**	39425	43750
2 Dr Targa (5 spd)	**59900**	39075	43375
2 Dr Targa (Tiptronic)	**62680**	40200	44500
2 Dr Cabriolet (5 spd)	**66800**	43825	48525
2 Dr Cabriolet (Tiptronic)	**69580**	44925	49725
911 CARRERA 4 6			
2 Dr Cpe (5 spd)	**69500**	43475	48125
2 Dr Targa (5 spd)	**70900**	44075	48800
2 Dr Cabriolet (5 spd)	**77800**	47600	52450
928S 8			
2 Dr Cpe (5 spd)	**74545**	41875	46350
2 Dr Cpe (auto)	**74545**	42725	47300
944 S2 4			
2 Dr Cpe (5 spd)	**41900**	23400	26700
2 Dr Cabriolet (5 spd)	**48600**	26950	30275

NOTE: Power windows, power door locks and anti-lock power brakes standard on all models. Power seat standard on 911 and 944. Sunroof standard on 911 Coupe, 944 Coupe and 928.

Year-Model-Body Type	Original List	Current Whlse	Average Retail
1989			
911 6			
Cpe (5 spd)	**51205**	32200	35800
Targa (5 spd)	**52435**	32850	36525
Cabriolet (5 spd)	**59200**	36450	40450
Speedster (5 spd)	**65480**	47625	52475
Turbo Cpe (5 spd)	**70975**	42725	47300
Turbo Targa (5 spd)	**77065**	44050	48775
Turbo Cabriolet (5 spd)	**85060**	46275	51000
928S 4			
Cpe (auto)	**74545**	35275	39150
944 4			
Cpe (5 spd)	**33245**	14800	17375
Cpe (auto)	**34215**	15050	17700
S Cpe (5 spd)	**41900**	16650	19300
Turbo Cpe (5 spd)	**44900**	18650	21700
ADD FOR:			
930 Slant Nose Pkg (911)	**29555**	—	—
930 Turbo Look (911)	**14218**	—	—

NOTE: Power brakes, sunroof and power windows standrd on all models. Power door locks standard on 911 Series.

Year-Model-Body Type	Original List	Current Whlse	Average Retail
1988			
911 6			
5 Spd Cpe	**45895**	25675	29000
5 Spd Targa	**48230**	26375	29700
5 Spd Cabriolet	**52895**	29725	33075
4 Spd Turbo Cpe	**68670**	39075	43375
4 Spd Turbo Targa	**77065**	39450	43800
4 Spd Turbo Cabriolet	**85060**	43450	48100
924S 4			
5 Spd Cpe	**26560**	6700	7800
Cpe (auto)	**27660**	6800	7925
928S 8			
Cpe (auto)	**69680**	28575	31925
944 4			
5 Spd Cpe	**30995**	11075	12800
Cpe (auto)	**32115**	11275	13025
5 Spd S Cpe	**36830**	12275	14225
5 Spd Turbo Cpe	**39765**	12025	13900
ADD FOR:			
Turbo Look (911 Non-Turbo)	**13970**	—	—
Turbo Pkg (944S)	**5510**	2080	2535
Anti-Lock Brake System (944)	**2368**	895	1090
Special Edit. Pkg (924S)	**918**	345	420
(911 Non-Turbo Cpe)	**3819**	1440	1775

Refer To Optional Equipment Schedules

Year-Model-Body Type	Original List	Current Whlse	Average Retail
(911 Non-Turbo Targa, 911 Non-Turbo Cabriolet)	**2411**	910	1110
(944)	**2486**	940	1145

NOTE: Air conditioning and power windows standard on 924S, 944 Series, 911 Series and 928S. Power locks standard on 944 Series. Sunroof standard on 911 Turbo Coupe and 928. Power steering standard on 924S, 944 Series and 928. Power brakes standard on 924S, 944 Series and 911 Series.

1987

Year-Model-Body Type	Original List	Current Whlse	Average Retail
911 6			
5 Spd Cpe	**41440**	22850	26150
5 Spd Targa	**43590**	23400	26700
5 Spd Cabriolet	**47895**	26725	30050
5 Spd Turbo Cpe	**63295**	35450	39350
5 Spd Turbo Targa	**71035**	35850	39800
5 Spd Turbo Cabriolet	**78415**	42200	46725
924S 4			
5 Spd Cpe	**24408**	4825	5750
Cpe (auto)	**25523**	4950	5875
928S 8			
Cpe (auto)	**63520**	23350	26650
944 4			
5 Spd Cpe	**28338**	8950	10325
Cpe (auto)	**29453**	9050	10425
5 Spd S Cpe	**31348**	9700	11175
5 Spd Turbo Cpe	**36798**	11725	13550
ADD FOR:			
Forged Alloy Wheels			
(944 ex. Turbo)	**3191**	940	1150
(944 Turbo)	**2255**	665	810
Pressure Cast Magnesium Wheels			
(944 ex. Turbo)	**2655**	785	955
(944 Turbo)	**1744**	515	630
16" Forged Alloy Wheels (944 ex. Turbo)	**2139**	630	770

NOTE: Air conditioning and power windows standard on 911 Series, 928S, 924S and 944 Series. Power steering standard on 924S, 928S and 944 Series. Sunroof and power door locks standard on 911 Turbo and 928S.

1986

Year-Model-Body Type	Original List	Current Whlse	Average Retail
911 6			
5 Spd Cpe	**34632**	20700	23750
5 Spd Targa	**36157**	21200	24500
5 Spd Cabriolet	**39407**	24075	27375
5 Spd Turbo Cpe	**53475**	32075	35675
928S 8			
5 Spd Cpe	**51900**	15675	18325
Cpe (auto)	**51900**	15825	18475
944 4			
5 Spd Cpe	**25157**	7300	8475
Cpe (auto)	**25657**	7400	8600
5 Spd Turbo Cpe	**30457**	9550	11000

NOTE: Power windows, power brakes, power steering and air conditioning standard on all models. Automatic transmission standard on 928S and 944. Power locks, sunroof and power seat standard on 928S.

1985

Year-Model-Body Type	Original List	Current Whlse	Average Retail
911 CARRERA 6			
5 Spd Cpe	**31950**	18025	20675
5 Spd Targa	**33450**	18625	21675
5 Spd Cabriolet	**36450**	21350	24650
928S 8			
5 Spd Cpe	**50000**	13700	16075
Cpe (auto)	**50000**	13975	16350
944 4			
5 Spd Htchbk	**22950**	6025	6950
Htchbk (auto)	**23450**	6125	7125

NOTE: Power steering standard on 928 and 944. Air conditioning and power windows standard on all models. Power seat standard on 928. Sunroof standard on 944.

1984

Year-Model-Body Type	Original List	Current Whlse	Average Retail
911 CARRERA 6			
5 Spd Cpe	**32550**	16875	19525
5 Spd Targa	**34050**	17475	20125
5 Spd Cabriolet	**37050**	19275	22325
928S 8			
5 Spd Cpe	**44600**	12425	14550
Cpe (auto)	**44600**	12625	14950
944 4			
5 Spd Htchbk	**22040**	5050	5975
Htchbk (auto)	**22540**	5175	6100

1983

Year-Model-Body Type	Original List	Current Whlse	Average Retail
911 SC 6			
5 Spd Cpe	**30745**	15725	18375
911 SC TARGA 6			
5 Spd Rdstr	**32245**	16025	18675
5 Spd Cabriolet	**35245**	18325	21250

Year-Model-Body Type	Original List	Current Whlse	Average Retail
928S 8			
5 Spd Cpe	**43795**	11900	13750
944 4			
5 Spd Cpe	**19775**	4225	5150
Htchbk (auto)	**19475**	4225	5150

RANGE ROVER

1992

Year-Model-Body Type	Original List	Current Whlse	Average Retail
RANGER ROVER 8			
4WD Standard Rover	**38900**	—	—
4WD County Rover	**44500**	—	—
ADD FOR:			
LSE Sport & Trim Pkg	**4000**	—	—

NOTE: Tilt steering wheel, cruise control, power windows, power door locks, power seat and power sunroof standard on all models.

1991

Year-Model-Body Type	Original List	Current Whlse	Average Retail
RANGE ROVER 8			
4WD Hunter Rover	**36500**	—	—
4WD Standard Rover	**43000**	29250	33025
4WD County SE Rover	**47300**	30550	34325

NOTE: Power brakes, power door locks and power windows standard on all models. Power seat standard on Standard and County SE. Sunroof standard on County SE.

1990

Year-Model-Body Type	Original List	Current Whlse	Average Retail
RANGE ROVER 8			
4WD Base Rover	**38025**	24750	28075
4WD County Rover	**40125**	25550	28875
ADD FOR:			
Premium Radio (Range Rover County)	**1600**	500	575

NOTE: Power door locks, power windows, anti-lock power brakes and power seat standard.

1989

Year-Model-Body Type	Original List	Current Whlse	Average Retail
RANGE ROVER 8			
4WD Base Rover	**36600**	20275	23325
4WD County Rover	**43100**	22150	25450
ADD FOR:			
Leather Interior (Base Rover)	**1125**	475	525

NOTE: Power brakes, power windows and power door locks standard on all models. Power sunroof standard on County Rover.

1988

Year-Model-Body Type	Original List	Current Whlse	Average Retail
RANGE ROVER 8			
4WD Rover	**34400**	15575	18225
ADD FOR:			
Leather Interior	**1125**	400	475

NOTE: Air conditioning, power brakes, power steering, automatic transmission and power windows standard.

1987

Year-Model-Body Type	Original List	Current Whlse	Average Retail
RANGE ROVER 8			
4WD Rover	**30825**	13000	15325
ADD FOR:			
Leather Interior	**1025**	275	325

NOTE: Air conditioning, power disc brakes, power door locks, power steering, automatic transmission, power windows and AM/FM stereo cassette radio standard.

RENAULT

1986

Year-Model-Body Type	Original List	Current Whlse	Average Retail
SPORTWAGON 4			
Sportwagon	**10199**	600	1125
Sportwagon Touring Edit.	**12024**	700	1325

NOTE: Power brakes, power steering and air conditioning standard on Sportwagon. Power locks and power windows standard on Sportwagon Touring Edition.

1985

Year-Model-Body Type	Original List	Current Whlse	Average Retail
FUEGO 4			
Fuego Cpe	**9295**	400	725
SPORTWAGON 4			
Sportwagon	**9895**	400	725
Sportwagon Touring Edit.	**11700**	500	925

NOTE: Power steering standard on Fuego and Sportwagon. Air conditioning standard on Sportwagon. Power brakes standard on Fuego

Refer To Optional Equipment Schedules

and Sportwagon. Power windows and power door locks standard on Sportwagon Touring Edition.

Year-Model-Body Type	Original List	Current Whlse	Average Retail
1984			
FUEGO 4			
Fuego Cpe Fuel Inj.	**8995**	150	350
Fuego Turbo Cpe	**11395**	150	350
SPORTWAGON 4			
Sportwagon	**9595**	110	300
Sportwagon Touring Edit.	**11350**	200	400
1983 — ALL BODY STYLES			
18i	—	75	225
FUEGO	—	75	225
LE CAR	—	75	225

SAAB

Year-Model-Body Type	Original List	Current Whlse	Average Retail
1992			
900 4			
3 Dr Htchbk	**19880**	—	—
4 Dr Sdn	**20495**	—	—
3 Dr S Htchbk	**23980**	—	—
4 Dr S Sdn	**24595**	—	—
2 Dr S Conv	**31360**	—	—
3 Dr Turbo Htchbk	**29360**	—	—
2 Dr Turbo Conv	**36230**	—	—
9000 4			
5 Dr Htchbk	**25465**	—	—
5 Dr S Htchbk	**28795**	—	—
4 Dr CD Sdn (auto)	**30950**	—	—
5 Dr Turbo Htchbk	**36945**	—	—
4 Dr CD Turbo Sdn (5 spd or auto)	**37615**	—	—
CD Griffin Edition Sdn (auto)	**42195**	—	—

NOTE: Power windows and power door locks standard on all models. Cruise control standard on 900 S & Turbo, 9000 S, 9000 CD, 9000 Turbo, Turbo CD & Turbo CD Griffin Edition. Power seat standard on 900 S Convertible & Turbo, 9000 CD, 9000 Turbo, Turbo CD & Turbo CD Griffin Edition.

Year-Model-Body Type	Original List	Current Whlse	Average Retail
1991			
900 4			
3 Dr Htchbk	**18295**	12050	13925
4 Dr Sdn	**18815**	12150	14025
S 3 Dr Htchbk	**22445**	14025	16400
S 4 Dr Sdn	**22995**	14125	16575
Turbo 3 Dr Htchbk	**26295**	16150	18775
Turbo 2 Dr Conv	**33295**	22350	25650
SPG Turbo 3 Dr Htchbk	**29295**	17300	19950
S Conv	**29495**	19575	22600
9000 4			
5 Dr Htchbk	**22895**	16100	18750
S 5 Dr Htchbk	**26995**	16925	19575
CD 4 Dr Sdn	**28995**	17250	19900
Turbo 5 Dr Htchbk	**32995**	20350	23400
CD Turbo 4 Dr Sdn	**33995**	21375	24675

NOTE: Power brakes and power door locks standard on all models. Power windows standard on 900 S, 900 Turbo, 900 Turbo SPG and 9000. Power seat standard on 900 Turbo Convertible, 9000 CD, 9000 Turbo Hatchback and 9000 Turbo CD. Power sunroof standard on 900 S, 900 Turbo, 900 Turbo SPG, 9000 S, 9000 CD, 9000 Turbo Hatchback and 9000 Turbo CD.

Year-Model-Body Type	Original List	Current Whlse	Average Retail
1990			
900 4			
3 Dr Htchbk	**16995**	9975	11500
4 Dr Sdn	**17515**	10075	11625
S 3 Dr Htchbk	**20995**	11775	13600
S 4 Dr Sdn	**21545**	11875	13725
Turbo 3 Dr Htchbk	**25495**	13950	16325
Turbo 4 Dr Sdn	**26045**	14050	16500
2 Dr Conv	**32995**	20025	23075
SPG Turbo 3 Dr Htchbk	**28995**	14800	17275
9000 4			
S 5 Dr Htchbk	**25495**	14250	16725
S 4 Dr Sdn	**25995**	14725	17275
Turbo 5 Dr Htchbk	**32495**	17450	20100
CD Turbo 4 Dr Sdn	**32995**	17950	20600
ADD FOR:			
Leather Package (9000 S Htchbk, 9000 S Sdn)	**1995**	400	500

NOTE: Anti-lock power brakes standard on all models. Power windows and sunroof standard on 900 S, 900 Turbo and 900 SPG. Power door locks standard on 900 Series, 900 Turbo and 900 SPG.

Year-Model-Body Type	Original List	Current Whlse	Average Retail
1989			
900 4			
3 Dr Htchbk	**16995**	7400	8600
4 Dr Sdn	**17515**	7500	8700
S 3 Dr Htchbk	**19695**	8750	10100
S 4 Dr Sdn	**20245**	8850	10225
Turbo 3 Dr Htchbk	**23795**	10375	11975
Turbo 4 Dr Sdn	**24345**	10475	12100
Turbo Convertible	**32095**	16500	19150
SPG 3 Dr Htchbk	**26895**	11325	12950
9000 4			
S 5 Dr Htchbk	**24445**	11075	12800
Turbo 5 Dr Sdn	**30795**	12500	14700
Turbo CD 4 Dr Sdn w/Cloth Interior	**30895**	13000	15325
Turbo CD 4 Dr Sdn w/Leather Interior	**31995**	13700	16075
ADD FOR:			
Leather Package (900 Turbo Htchbk & Sdn)	**1295**	350	425
(9000S)	**1595**	350	425
Air Bag Restraint System (9000 Turbo)	**895**	375	450

NOTE: Power brakes and power door locks standard on all models. Sunroof and power windows standard on all models except 900 Base.

Year-Model-Body Type	Original List	Current Whlse	Average Retail
1988			
900 4			
3 Dr Sdn	**15432**	5725	6650
4 Dr Sdn	**15935**	5825	6750
S 3 Dr Sdn	**19280**	6625	7700
S 4 Dr Sdn	**19783**	6700	7800
Turbo 3 Dr Sdn	**22655**	8000	9300
Turbo Convertible	**30632**	13525	15900
9000 4			
S 5 Dr Sdn	**24037**	7125	8275
Turbo 5 Dr Sdn	**28985**	8300	9575
ADD FOR:			
Leather Package (900 Turbo, 9000 S)	**1151**	335	380
Special Performance Group (900 Turbo)	**2960**	800	900

NOTE: Air conditioning, power steering, power brakes and power locks standard on all models. Sunroof and power windows standard on all models except 900 Base.

Year-Model-Body Type	Original List	Current Whlse	Average Retail
1987			
900 4			
3 Dr Sdn	**14395**	4225	5150
4 Dr Sdn	**14805**	4325	5250
S 3 Dr Sdn	**17935**	4875	5800
S 4 Dr Sdn	**18345**	4975	5900
Turbo 3 Dr Sdn	**20815**	5800	6725
Turbo Convertible	**27115**	11425	13200
9000 4			
5 Dr Sdn	**22245**	5425	6350
Turbo 5 Dr Sdn	**26025**	6325	7350
ADD FOR:			
Leather Package (900 Turbo)	**1030**	250	300
(9000 S)	**1030**	250	300
Special Performance Group (900 Turbo)	**2680**	700	775

NOTE: Air conditioning, power steering, power brakes and power door locks standard on 900, 900 S, 900 Turbo, 9000 S and 9000 Turbo. Power windows and sunroof standard on 900 S, 900 Turbo, 9000 S and 9000 Turbo).

Year-Model-Body Type	Original List	Current Whlse	Average Retail
1986			
900 4			
3 Dr Sdn	**12585**	2550	3425
4 Dr Sdn	**12985**	2625	3525
S 2 Dr Sdn	**15795**	3000	3900
S 3 Dr Sdn	**16095**	3100	4000
S 4 Dr Sdn	**16495**	3175	4075
Turbo 3 Dr Sdn	**18895**	3975	4875
Turbo Convertible	**25390**	9700	11175
9000 4			
Turbo 5 Dr Sdn	**22145**	4275	5200
ADD FOR:			
Metallic Paint	**395**	75	100
Special Black Paint	**395**	85	105
Exclusive Appointment Pkg (900 Turbo)	**1360**	250	300
Leather Package (900 Turbo)	**1800**	200	225
Special Performance Group (900 Turbo)	**2820**	600	675

NOTE: Power brakes standard on all models. Power steering and air conditioning standard on 900 Series and 900 Turbo. Sunroof standard on 900 S and 900 Turbo. Power locks standard on 900 Series. Power windows standard on 900 S, 900 Turbo and 9000 Turbo.

Refer To Optional Equipment Schedules

Year-Model-Body Type	Original List	Current Whlse	Average Retail
1985			
900 4			
3 Dr Sdn	**11850**	1950	2800
4 Dr Sdn	**12170**	2050	2900
S 3 Dr Sdn	**15040**	2475	3350
S 4 Dr Sdn	**15510**	2575	3450
Turbo 3 Dr Sdn	**18150**	3125	4025
Turbo 4 Dr Sdn	**18620**	3225	4125
ADD FOR:			
Exclusive Appointment Pkg (900 Turbo)	**1330**	150	175
Special Performance Group (900 Turbo)	**2860**	375	460

NOTE: Power steering, power brakes and air conditioning standard on all models. Power windows and sunroof standard on 900 S and 900 Turbo.

Year-Model-Body Type	Original List	Current Whlse	Average Retail
1984			
900 4			
3 Dr Sdn	**11110**	1475	2300
4 Dr Sdn	**11420**	1550	2400
S 3 Dr Sdn	**13850**	1800	2650
S 4 Dr Sdn	**14310**	1900	2750
Turbo 3 Dr Sdn	**16940**	2400	3275
Turbo 4 Dr Sdn	**17400**	2475	3350

Year-Model-Body Type	Original List	Current Whlse	Average Retail
1983 — ALL BODY STYLES			
900	—	1125	1850
900 S	—	1025	1750
900 TURBO	—	1350	2100

SAPPORO

Year-Model-Body Type	Original List	Current Whlse	Average Retail
1983			
SAPPORO 4			
2 Dr Luxury Cpe	**8323**	525	975

STERLING

Year-Model-Body Type	Original List	Current Whlse	Average Retail
1991			
827 6			
Si (5 spd)	**26500**	—	—
SLi (auto)	**28500**	—	—
SL (auto)	**28500**	—	—

NOTE: Power brakes, power door locks, power windows, power seat and power moonroof standard on all models.

Year-Model-Body Type	Original List	Current Whlse	Average Retail
1990			
827 6			
S (5 spd)	**23550**	10450	12100
Si (5 spd)	**26500**	11050	12800
SL (5 spd)	**28500**	11425	13200
SLi (auto)	**28500**	11550	13350
Oxford Edition (auto)	—	11550	13350
ADD FOR:			
Anti-Lock Braking System (S)	**1250**	650	725
Leather Seat Trim (S)	**1150**	400	475

NOTE: Power windows, power door locks and moonroof standard on all models. Anti-lock power brakes standard on 827Si, 827SL, 827SLi and Oxford Edition.

Year-Model-Body Type	Original List	Current Whlse	Average Retail
1989			
827 6			
S (5 spd)	**23300**	8075	9350
SL (auto)	**29675**	9425	10850
SLi (auto)	**29675**	9425	10850
LE (auto)	**30150**	9725	11200
ADD FOR:			
Anti-Lock Brakes (S)	**1225**	400	450
Leather Seats (S)	**1100**	300	375

NOTE: Power brakes, power windows, power door locks and power moonroof standard on all models.

Year-Model-Body Type	Original List	Current Whlse	Average Retail
1988			
825 6			
S (5 spd)	**20804**	5275	6200
SL (auto)	**25995**	6600	7675
ADD FOR:			
Anti-Lock Braking System (S)	**1150**	300	350
Leather Seat Trim (S)	**1025**	225	275

NOTE: Air conditioning, power brakes, power door locks, power steering, power windows and electric moonroof standard on all models.

Year-Model-Body Type	Original List	Current Whlse	Average Retail
1987			
825 6			
S (5 spd)	**19000**	3350	4250
SL (auto)	**23900**	4400	5325
ADD FOR:			
Anti-Lock Braking System (S)	**940**	275	325
Leather Trim (S)	**950**	200	225

NOTE: Air conditioning, power disc brakes, power door locks, electric moonroof, power steering and power windows standard on all models. Power seats and anti-lock braking system standard on 825SL.

SUBARU

Year-Model-Body Type	Original List	Current Whlse	Average Retail
1992			
JUSTY 3			
3 Dr Htchbk (5 spd) (NA w/power steering or radio)	**6945**	—	—
3 Dr GL Htchbk (5 spd)	**8349**	—	—
5 Dr GL 4WD Htchbk (5 spd) (NA w/power steering)	**9249**	—	—
ADD FOR:			
On-Demand 4WD (GL 3 Dr)	**800**	—	—
LEGACY 4			
4 Dr L Sdn (5 spd)	**14564**	—	—
5 Dr L Wgn (5 spd)	**15064**	—	—
4 Dr LS Sdn (auto)	**19649**	—	—
5 Dr LS Wgn (auto)	**20149**	—	—
4 Dr LSi (auto)	**21049**	—	—
4 Dr Sport 4WD Turbo Sdn (5 spd)	**21645**	—	—
ADD FOR:			
Anti-Lock Brakes (L)	**1100**	—	—
Full-Time 4WD			
(L Sdn)	**1100**	—	—
(L Wgn)	**1600**	—	—
(LS, LSi)	**1500**	—	—
LOYALE 4			
4 Dr Sdn (5 spd)	**10049**	—	—
5 Dr Wgn (5 spd)	**10899**	—	—
ADD FOR:			
On-Demand 4WD (Sdn)	**1350**	—	—
(Wgn)	**1500**	—	—
SVX 6			
2 Dr Cpe (auto)	**26250**	—	—
ADD FOR:			
Touring Pkg	**3000**	—	—

NOTE: Tilt steering wheel standard on Loyale, Legacy and SVX. Cruise control standard on Legacy LS, LSi, LE 4WD & Sport 4WD and SVX. Power windows and power door locks standard on SVX. Moonroof standard on Legacy LS, LSi, LE 4WD & Sport 4WD.

Year-Model-Body Type	Original List	Current Whlse	Average Retail
1991			
JUSTY 3			
2 Dr Htchbk (5 spd) (NA w/power steering)	**6295**	4025	4925
2 Dr GL Htchbk (5 spd) (NA w/power steering)	**7699**	4600	5525
5 Dr GL 4WD Htchbk (5 spd) (NA w/power steering)	**8599**	5450	6375
LEGACY 4			
4 Dr L Sdn (5 spd)	**12924**	8375	9675
5 Dr L Wgn (5 spd)	**13524**	8675	10025
4 Dr LS Sdn (5 spd)	**17324**	10275	11850
5 Dr LS Wgn (5 spd)	**17924**	10575	12200
4 Dr LSi Sdn (auto)	**19024**	—	—
4 Dr Sport 4WD Turbo Sdn (5 spd)	**19224**	11575	13375
LOYALE 4			
4 Dr Sdn (5 spd)	**9499**	6850	7975
5 Dr Wgn (5 spd)	**10499**	7150	8300
XT GL 4			
2 Dr Cpe (5 spd)	**13438**	8450	9750
XT6 6			
2 Dr Cpe (auto)	**17478**	10250	11825
ADD FOR:			
Full Time 4WD			
(XT6 w/manual trans)	**840**	450	550
(XT6 w/auto trans)	**1610**	550	650
(Legacy L Sdn)	**1280**	650	750
(Legacy L Wgn, Legacy LSi)	**1300**	650	750
(Legacy LS Sdn)	**1500**	650	750
(Legacy LS Wgn)	**1400**	650	750
On-Demand 4WD			
(Justy GL)	**800**	325	400
(Loyale)	**1500**	600	700
Anti-Lock Braking System (Legacy L)	**895**	450	550

NOTE: Power brakes standard on all models. Power door locks and power windows standard on Legacy L, Loyale, XT and XT6. Power moonroof standard on Legacy LS, LSi and Legacy Sport Sedan.

Refer To Optional Equipment Schedules

SUBARU

Year-Model-Body Type	Original List	Current Whlse	Average Retail
1990			
JUSTY 3			
2 Dr DL Htchbk (5 spd) (NA w/power steering)	**5866**	2525	3400
2 Dr GL Htchbk (5 spd) (NA w/power steering)	**7251**	2975	3875
5 Dr GL 4WD Htchbk (5 spd) (NA w/power steering)	**8156**	3725	4625
LEGACY 4			
4 Dr Sdn (5 spd)	**11299**	6675	7775
5 Dr Wgn (5 spd)	**11849**	6975	8625
4 Dr L Sdn (5 spd)	**13494**	7425	8625
5 Dr L Wgn (5 spd)	**14044**	7700	8950
4 Dr LS Sdn (5 spd)	**14699**	7675	8900
5 Dr LS Wgn (5 spd)	**15249**	7950	9225
LOYALE 4			
4 Dr Sdn (5 spd)	**9299**	5050	5975
3 Dr Cpe (5 spd)	**9599**	5000	5925
5 Dr Wgn (5 spd)	**9999**	5325	6250
5 Dr Touring Wgn	**10699**	5500	6425
ADD FOR:			
Full Time 4WD			
(Loyale Sdn & Wgn)	**3750**	650	725
(Loyale Touring Wgn)	**3400**	650	725
(Loyale Cpe)	**4100**	650	725
(Legacy L)	**1200**	600	700
(Legacy LS)	**1800**	600	700
On Demand 4WD			
(Justy GL)	**700**	300	375
(Loyale Cpe)	—	600	675
(Loyale Sdn)	—	600	675
(Loyale Wgn)	—	600	675
Anti-Lock Braking System (Legacy LS)	**1095**	400	475

NOTE: Power brakes standard on all models. Power windows standard on Legacy L and Legacy LS. Power door locks standard on Loyale Coupe, Legacy L and Legacy LS. Sunroof standard on Legacy LS.

Year-Model-Body Type	Original List	Current Whlse	Average Retail
1989			
DL 4			
4 Dr Sdn (5 spd)	**9731**	3625	4525
3 Dr Cpe (5 spd)	**10031**	3525	4425
4 Dr Wgn (5 spd)	**10181**	3850	4750
GL 4			
3 Dr Htchbk (5 spd)	**8596**	2950	3850
4 Dr Sdn (5 spd)	**11521**	4225	5150
3 Dr Cpe (5 spd)	**11821**	4175	5100
4 Dr Wgn (5 spd)	**11971**	4450	5375
4 Dr Touring Wgn (5 spd)	**12171**	4550	5475
4 Dr Turbo Sdn (auto)	**12521**	4575	5500
4 Dr Turbo Wgn (auto)	**12971**	5100	6025
2 Dr XT Cpe (5 spd)	**13071**	5300	6225
GL-10 4			
4 Dr Sdn (auto)	**16401**	4725	5650
4 Dr Wgn (auto)	**16851**	4950	5875
4 Dr Touring Wgn (auto)	**16851**	5175	6100
JUSTY 3			
2 Dr DL Htchbk (5 spd)	**5866**	2225	3075
2 Dr GL Htchbk (5 spd)	**7251**	2500	3375
2 Dr RS 4WD Htchbk (5 spd)	**8351**	3100	4000
RX 4			
3 Dr 4WD Cpe (5 spd)	**16361**	5300	6225
XT 6			
2 Dr Cpe (auto)	**17111**	6700	7800
ADD FOR:			
4WD (DL, GL)	—	500	600
(XT 6)	—	375	450

NOTE: Power brakes standard on all models. Power windows standard on GL except Hatchback, GL-10, RX and XT-6. Power door locks standard on GL Turbo Sedan and Turbo Wagon, GL-10, RX and XT-6. Sunroof standard on GL-10.

Year-Model-Body Type	Original List	Current Whlse	Average Retail
1988			
DL 4			
4 Dr Sdn (5 spd)	**9748**	2300	3175
3 Dr Cpe (5 spd)	**10048**	2250	3100
4 Dr Wgn (5 spd)	**10198**	2500	3375
2 Dr XT Cpe (5 spd)	**10413**	2275	3150
GL 4			
3 Dr Htchbk (5 spd)	**8693**	1975	2825
4 Dr Sdn (5 spd)	**11393**	2850	3750
3 Dr Cpe (5 spd)	**11693**	2800	3700
4 Dr Wgn (5 spd)	**11843**	3050	3950
2 Dr XT Cpe (5 spd)	**12915**	3100	4000
GL-10 4			
4 Dr Sdn (auto)	**14928**	3600	4500
4 Dr Wgn (auto)	**15378**	3925	4825
JUSTY 3			
2 Dr Htchbk (5 spd)	**6088**	775	1500
2 Dr GL Htchbk (5 spd)	**7213**	900	1625
2 Dr RS 4WD Htchbk (5 spd)	**8213**	1500	2350
RX 4			
4 Dr 4WD Turbo Sdn (5 spd)	**15913**	4500	5425
3 Dr 4WD Turbo Cpe (5 spd)	**15913**	4450	5375

Year-Model-Body Type	Original List	Current Whlse	Average Retail
XT-6 6			
2 Dr Cpe (auto)	**16663**	4450	5375
ADD FOR:			
Full Time 4WD (GL-10)	**2600**	475	550
(XT6)	**1600**	250	300
On-Demand 4WD			
(Justy GL, GL Htchbk, DL Wgn)	**600**	225	275
(GL Wgn w/Turbo Eng)	**2450**	475	550
Turbo Engine (GL-10)	**1550**	475	550

NOTE: Power brakes standard on all models. Power steering standard on DL Series, GL Series except Hatchback, GL-10 Series, RX Series and XT-6. Power door locks standard on GL Series except Hacthback, RX Series and XT-6. Sunroof standard on GL-10 Series. Air conditioning standard on GL-10 Series, RX Series and XT-6. Power windows standard on GL Series except Hatchback, GL-10 Series, RX Series and XT-6.

1987½

Year-Model-Body Type	Original List	Current Whlse	Average Retail
DL 4			
2 Dr XT Cpe (5 spd)	**9531**	1675	2525
GL 4			
2 Dr XT Cpe (5 spd)	**11653**	2200	3075
2 Dr 4WD XT Cpe (5 spd)	**12728**	2700	3600
GL-10 4			
2 Dr XT Cpe (auto)	**14264**	3000	3900
2 Dr 4WD Turbo XT Cpe (5 spd)	**16224**	3400	4300
RX 4			
3 Dr 4WD Turbo Cpe (5 spd)	**14153**	3300	4200
ADD FOR:			
Turbo Engine			
(GL XT 2 Dr Cpe)	**1863**	550	670
(GL-10 XT 2 Dr w/man trans)	**735**	215	265
(GL-10 XT 2 Dr Cpe w/auto trans)	**1285**	380	465

NOTE: Power steering standard on GL, GL-10 and RX. Power brakes standard on all models. Air conditioning standard on GL-10 and RX. Power windows standard on RX. Power door locks and sunroof standard on GL-10.

1987

Year-Model-Body Type	Original List	Current Whlse	Average Retail
DL 4			
4 Dr Sdn (5 spd)	**8908**	1775	2625
3 Dr Cpe (5 spd)	**9208**	1650	2500
4 Dr Wgn (5 spd)	**9308**	1875	2725
GL 4			
3 Dr Htchbk (5 spd)	**7688**	1275	2000
4 Dr Sdn (5 spd)	**9938**	2050	2900
3 Dr Cpe (5 spd)	**10238**	2000	2850
4 Dr Wgn (5 spd)	**10338**	2225	3075
3 Dr 4WD Htchbk (4 spd)	**8393**	1775	2625
4 Dr 4WD Sdn (5 spd)	**10408**	2525	3400
3 Dr 4WD Cpe (5 spd)	**10708**	2475	3350
4 Dr 4WD Wgn (5 spd)	**10808**	2700	3600
4 Dr 4WD Brat (4 spd)	**8453**	1275	2000
GL-10 4			
4 Dr Sdn (auto)	**12448**	2725	3625
4 Dr Wgn (auto)	**12848**	2875	3775
4 Dr 4WD Turbo Sdn (5 spd)	**15168**	3100	4000
4 Dr 4WD Turbo Wgn (5 spd)	**14788**	3275	4175
JUSTY 3			
2 Dr DL Htchbk (5 spd)	**5366**	475	875
2 Dr GL Htchbk (5 spd)	**6166**	575	1075
RX 4			
4 Dr 4WD Turbo Sdn (5 spd)	**13933**	3150	4050
STANDARD 4			
3 Dr 4WD Htchbk (4 spd)	**7355**	325	600
ADD FOR:			
Turbo Engine	**—**	350	425

NOTE: Power brakes standard on Standard Series, DL Series, GL Series, GL-10 Series, RX and Brat. Power windows, power door locks and air conditioning standard on GL-10 Series and RX. Sunroof standard on GL-10 4WD. Power steering standard on GL Coupe, Sedan and Wagon, RX and GL-10 Series.

1986

Year-Model-Body Type	Original List	Current Whlse	Average Retail
BRAT 4			
2 Dr 4WD (4 spd)	**8235**	875	1600
DL 4			
2 Dr XT Cpe (5 spd)	**9192**	925	1650
4 Dr Sdn (5 spd)	**8168**	1025	1750
4 Dr Wgn (5 spd)	**8490**	1150	1875
4 Dr 4WD Wgn (5 spd)	**9080**	1475	2300
GL SERIES 4			
2 Dr XT Cpe (5 spd)	**11030**	1450	2225
3 Dr Htchbk (5 spd)	**7509**	700	1325
3 Dr 4WD Htchbk (4 spd dual range)	**8174**	1150	1875
4 Dr Sdn (5 spd)	**8803**	1275	2000

Refer To Optional Equipment Schedules

Year-Model-Body Type	Original List	Current Whlse	Average Retail
4 Dr 4WD Sdn (5 spd dual range)	**10013**	1650	2500
4 Dr Wgn (5 spd)	**9125**	1450	2225
4 Dr Wgn (5 spd dual range)	**9715**	1700	2550
GL-10 SERIES			
2 Dr XT Turbo Cpe (5 spd)	**13930**	1925	2825
2 Dr 4WD Turbo Cpe (5 spd)	**14925**	2400	3275
4 Dr Sdn (auto)	**12080**	1775	2625
4 Dr Turbo Sdn (5 spd)	**12811**	1900	2750
4 Dr 4WD Turbo Sdn (5 spd)	**13806**	2175	3025
4 Dr Wgn (auto)	**12262**	1900	2750
4 Dr Turbo Wgn (5 spd)	**12997**	1950	2800
4 Dr 4WD Turbo Wgn (5 spd)	**13587**	2200	3050
4 Dr 4WD Turbo Wgn (auto)	**14412**	2375	3250
RX 4			
4 Dr 4WD Turbo Sdn (5 spd)	**12643**	2400	3275
STANDARD SERIES 4			
3 Dr Htchbk (4 spd)	**5379**	250	500

NOTE: Power brakes standard on all models. Power windows, power locks and air conditioning standard on GL-10 and RX Turbo Sedan. Sunroof standard on GL-10. Power steering standard on GL XT Coupe, GL-10 and RX Turbo Sedan.

1985

Year-Model-Body Type	Original List	Current Whlse	Average Retail
BRAT 4			
2 Dr GL 4WD (4 spd)	**7783**	750	1475
DL SERIES 4			
4 Dr Sdn (4 spd)	**7109**	825	1525
4 Dr Sdn (5 spd)	**7208**	825	1525
4 Dr Wgn	**7509**	975	1700
4 Dr 4WD Wgn	**8059**	1300	2025
2 Dr XT Cpe (5 spd)	**7889**	950	1550
GL SERIES 4			
3 Dr Htchbk	**6924**	700	1325
3 Dr 4WD Htchbk	**7474**	1025	1750
4 Dr Sdn	**7758**	1050	1775
4 Dr 4WD Sdn (auto)	**9281**	1525	2375
4 Dr 4WD Turbo Sdn (5 spd)	**11453**	1725	2575
5 Dr Wgn	**8059**	1150	1875
5 Dr 4WD Wgn	**8609**	1425	2175
5 Dr 4WD Turbo Wgn (auto)	**11917**	1825	2675
2 Dr XT Cpe (5 spd)	**9899**	1250	1975
RX 4 — *Schedule C*			
4 Dr 4WD Turbo Sdn	**11031**	1850	2700
STANDARD SERIES 4 — *Schedule C*			
3 Dr Htchbk	**4989**	225	475
ADD FOR:			
GL-10 Pkg (GL Sdn)	**2419**	300	365
(GL Wgn)	**2290**	300	365
GL-10T Pkg (GT Sdn)	**2869**	375	425
(GL Wgn)	**2740**	375	425

NOTE: Power steering, power door locks and power windows standard on GL Turbo. Air conditioning standard on GL Turbo and RX. Power brakes standard on all models.

1984

Year-Model-Body Type	Original List	Current Whlse	Average Retail
BRAT 4			
2 Dr GL 4WD	**8043**	400	725
2 Dr Turbo 4WD (auto)	**10413**	475	875
DL SERIES 4			
3 Dr Htchbk	**6398**	300	575
4 Dr Sdn	**6935**	475	875
2 Dr HT	**7051**	575	1075
4 Dr Wgn	**7174**	600	1125
4 Dr 4WD Wgn	**7723**	925	1650
GL SERIES 4			
3 Dr Htchbk	**7129**	475	875
3 Dr 4WD Htchbk	**7678**	850	1550
2 Dr HT	**7727**	725	1375
2 Dr 4WD Turbo HT (auto)	**11338**	1025	1750
4 Dr Sdn	**7534**	625	1175
4 Dr 4WD Sdn (auto)	**8955**	975	1700
4 Dr Wgn	**7773**	750	1475
4 Dr 4WD Wgn	**8322**	1100	1825
4 Dr 4WD Turbo Wgn (auto)	**10578**	1200	1925
STANDARD SERIES 4			
3 Dr Htchbk	**5393**	110	300

1983 — ALL BODY STYLES

Year-Model-Body Type	Original List	Current Whlse	Average Retail
BRAT	—	250	500
DL SERIES	—	200	400
GL SERIES	—	325	600
STANDARD SERIES	—	100	275

SUZUKI

Year-Model-Body Type	Original List	Current Whlse	Average Retail
1992			
SAMURAI 4			
2WD JA Soft Top (NA w/power steering)	**6399**	—	—
4WD JL Soft Top (NA w/power steering)	**8299**	—	—
SIDEKICK 4			
2WD JS-Plus 2 Dr Soft Top (NA w/power steering)	**10799**	—	—
4WD JX 2 Dr Soft Top	**12139**	—	—
4WD JX LTD 2 Dr Soft Top	**13299**	—	—
4WD JX 4 Dr Hard Top	**12649**	—	—
4WD JLX 4 Dr Hard Top	**13849**	—	—
4WD JLX LTD 4 Dr Hard Top	**15199**	—	—
SWIFT 4			
3 Dr GA Htchbk	**6999**	—	—
3 Dr GT Htchbk	**9699**	—	—
4 Dr GA Sdn	**7799**	—	—
4 Dr GS Sdn	**9199**	—	—

NOTE: Tilt steering wheel, power door locks and power windows standard on Sidekick JLX & JLX Limited Edition.

Year-Model-Body Type	Original List	Current Whlse	Average Retail
1991			
SAMURAI 4			
2WD JA Soft Top (NA w/power steering)	**5999**	3925	4825
2WD JS Soft Top (NA w/power steering)	**6999**	4325	5250
4WD JL Soft Top (NA w/power steering)	**8299**	5525	6450
SIDEKICK 4			
2WD JS 2 Dr Soft Top (NA w/power steering)	**10299**	7200	8350
4WD JX 2 Dr Soft Top	**11799**	8475	9800
4WD JX 4 Dr Hard Top	**11999**	8625	9950
4WD JLX 4 Dr Hard Top	**12999**	9275	10675
SWIFT 4			
GA 3 Dr Htchbk	**6699**	3800	4700
GT 3 Dr Htchbk	**9399**	5050	5975
GA 4 Dr Sdn	**7499**	3925	4825
GS 4 Dr Sdn	**8599**	4425	5350

NOTE: Power brakes standard on all models. Power windows standard on Sidekick JLX.

Year-Model-Body Type	Original List	Current Whlse	Average Retail
1990			
SAMURAI 4			
Soft Top (NA w/power steering)	**7999**	4225	5150
SIDEKICK 4			
2WD JS Soft Top	**9999**	5225	6150
4WD JX Soft Top	**10799**	6200	7225
4WD JX Hard Top	**11099**	6350	7400
4WD JLX Hard Top	**12499**	6850	7975
4WD JLX Soft Top	**12299**	6700	7800
SWIFT 4			
GA 3 Dr Htchbk	**6399**	2925	3825
GA 4 Dr Sdn	**7399**	3050	3950
GL 3 Dr Htchbk	**6799**	3075	3975
GL 4 Dr Sdn	**7899**	3225	4125
GS 4 Dr Sdn	**8599**	3525	4425
GT 3 Dr Htchbk	**9399**	4125	5050
GLX 3 Dr Htchbk	**7799**	3100	4000
ADD FOR:			
Sport/Convenience Pkg B (Sidekick JX)	**528**	285	350

NOTE: Power brakes standard on all models.

Year-Model-Body Type	Original List	Current Whlse	Average Retail
1989			
SAMURAI STANDARD PLUS 4			
Soft Top (NA w/power steering)	**9774**	2875	3775
Hard Top (NA w/power steering)	**9874**	3000	3900
SIDEKICK 4			
Std Convertible 2 Passenger (NA w/power steering)	**8995**	3825	4725
Deluxe Convertible 2 Passenger (NA w/power steering)	**11660**	4900	5825
Deluxe Convertible 4 Passenger (NA w/power steering)	**12215**	5175	6100
Deluxe Hardtop 2 Passenger (auto) (NA w/power steering)	**13160**	5575	6500
Deluxe Hardtop 4 Passenger (auto) (NA w/power steering)	**13679**	5775	6700
Custom Convertible 2 Passenger (auto) (NA w/power steering)	**13260**	5400	6325

Year-Model-Body Type	Original List	Current Whlse	Average Retail
Custom Convertible			
4 Passenger (auto)			
(NA w/power steering)	**13959**	5625	6550
Custom Hardtop			
2 Passenger (auto)	**14260**	5625	6550
Custom Hardtop			
4 Passenger (auto)	**14939**	5875	6800
SWIFT 4			
GLX 5 Dr Htchbk (auto)	**7495**	2450	3325
GTi 3 Dr Htchbk	**8995**	2850	3750

NOTE: Power brakes standard on all models. Power windows standard on Sidekick Custom Hardtop. Power door locks standard on Sidekick Custom Hardtop and Swift.

1988½

Year-Model-Body Type	Original List	Current Whlse	Average Retail
SAMURAI 4			
Std Convertible	**7995**	2875	3775
Std Hardtop	**8095**	3025	3925
Deluxe Convertible			
2-Seater	**8695**	3250	4150
Deluxe Hardtop			
2-Seater	**8725**	3500	4400
Deluxe Convertible			
4-Seater	**8945**	3450	4350
Deluxe Hardtop			
4-Seater	**8995**	3700	4600
ADD FOR:			
Fiberglass Hardtop	**1395**	525	640

NOTE: Power brakes standard on all models.

1988

Year-Model-Body Type	Original List	Current Whlse	Average Retail
SAMURAI 4			
Std Convertible	**7995**	2400	3275
Std Hardtop	**8095**	2550	3425
Deluxe Convertible			
2-Seater	**8695**	2700	3600
Deluxe Hardtop			
2-Seater	**8725**	2775	3675
Deluxe Convertible			
4-Seater	**8945**	2725	3625
Deluxe Hardtop			
4-Seater	**8995**	2800	3700
ADD FOR:			
Fiberglass Hardtop	**1395**	525	640

NOTE: Power brakes standard on all models.

1987

Year-Model-Body Type	Original List	Current Whlse	Average Retail
SAMURAI 4			
Convertible Truck	**6695**	1950	2800
Hardtop Truck	**6900**	2075	2925
JA Std Convertible	**7495**	2000	2850
JA Std Hardtop	**7495**	2100	2950
JX Deluxe Convertible	**8545**	2100	2950
JX Deluxe Hardtop	**8665**	2200	3050
JX Deluxe II			
Convertible	**8635**	2150	3000
JX Deluxe II Hardtop	**8795**	2250	3100
ADD FOR:			
Automatic Hub Set	**250**	75	90
Fiberglass Hardtop	**1395**	410	500

NOTE: Power front disc brakes standard on all models.

1986

Year-Model-Body Type	Original List	Current Whlse	Average Retail
SAMURAI 4			
Convertible Truck	**6456**	1525	2375
Hardtop Truck	**6856**	1600	2450
Base Convertible	**6951**	1600	2450
Base Hardtop	**7121**	1725	2575
JX Deluxe Convertible	**7375**	1650	2500
JX Deluxe Hardtop	**7530**	1825	2675
JX Deluxe II			
Convertible	**8115**	1775	2625
JX Deluxe II Hardtop	**8275**	1875	2725
ADD FOR:			
Fiberglass Hardtop	**1399**	300	365
Automatic Hub Set	**210**	45	55

NOTE: Power front disc brakes standard on all models. Air conditioning standard on JX Deluxe II models.

TOYOTA

1992

Year-Model-Body Type	Original List	Current Whlse	Average Retail
2WD 4RUNNER SR5 6			
4 Dr (auto)	**20758**	—	—
4WD 4RUNNER SR5 4			
4 Dr (5 spd)	**19918**	—	—
4 Dr 4WDemand			
(5 spd)	**20118**	—	—
4WD 4RUNNER SR5 6			
2 Dr (5 spd)	**22098**	—	—
4 Dr 4WDemand			
(5 spd)	**21618**	—	—

Year-Model-Body Type	Original List	Current Whlse	Average Retail
ADD FOR:			
Leather Pkg	1390	—	—
Sports Pkg (4 Dr Models)	440	—	—
Aluminum Wheels	490	—	—
2WD PICKUPS 4			
Std Short Bed (5 spd)	10338	—	—
Dlx Short Bed (5 spd)	11278	—	—
Dlx Long Bed (5 spd)	11808	—	—
Dlx Xtracab (5 spd)	12708	—	—
2WD PICKUPS 6			
Dlx Xtracab (5 spd)	13538	—	—
SR5 Xtracab (5 spd)	15188	—	—
1-Ton (5 spd)	13148	—	—
4WD PICKUPS 4			
Dlx Short Bed (5 spd)	14488	—	—
Dlx Short Bed 4WDemand (5 spd)	14688	—	—
Dlx Long Bed (5 spd)	15098	—	—
Dlx Long Bed 4WDemand (5 spd)	15298	—	—
Dlx Xtracab (5 spd)	15928	—	—
Dlx Xtracab 4WDemand (5 spd)	16128	—	—
4WD PICKUPS 6			
Dlx Short Bed (5 spd)	15378	—	—
Dlx Long Bed (5 spd)	15958	—	—
Dlx Xtracab (5 spd)	16788	—	—
SR5 Xtracab (5 spd)	17548	—	—
CAMRY 4			
4 Dr Dlx Sdn	15818	—	—
4 Dr LE Sdn (auto)	17498	—	—
4 Dr XLE Sdn (auto)	19428	—	—
5 Dr Dlx Wgn (auto)	17768	—	—
5 Dr LE Wgn (auto)	18798	—	—
CAMRY 6			
4 Dr Dlx Sdn (auto)	17328	—	—
4 Dr LE Sdn (auto)	19228	—	—
4 Dr SE Sdn (5 spd)	18528	—	—
4 Dr XLE Sdn (auto)	21178	—	—
5 Dr LE Wgn (auto)	20528	—	—
ADD FOR:			
Anti-Lock Brakes	1245	—	—
Leather Seat Trim	950	—	—
Aluminum Alloy Wheels	420	—	—
CELICA 4			
2 Dr ST Spt Cpe	14788	—	—
2 Dr GT Spt Cpe	17248	—	—
2 Dr GT Lftbk	17388	—	—
2 Dr GT Conv	22208	—	—
2 Dr GT-S Lftbk	19118	—	—
2 Dr All-Trac Turbo Lftbk	23998	—	—
ADD FOR:			
Anti-Lock Brakes			
(GT, GT-S)	1360	—	—
(All-Trac)	1130	—	—
Leather Pkg (GT)	1420	—	—
Aluminum Alloy Wheels	420	—	—
COROLLA 4			
4 Dr Std Sdn	11128	—	—
4 Dr Dlx Sdn	12148	—	—
4 Dr Dlx Wgn	12838	—	—
5 Dr All-Trac Wgn	14508	—	—
4 Dr LE Sdn (auto)	13798	—	—
ADD FOR:			
Aluminum Alloy Wheels	410	—	—
CRESSIDA 6			
4 Dr Sdn (auto)	24428	—	—
ADD FOR:			
Anti-Lock Brakes	1130	—	—
LAND CRUISER 6			
4 Dr Wgn (auto)	27548	—	—
ADD FOR:			
Third Rear Seat	800	—	—
MR2 4			
2 Dr Cpe	19128	—	—
2 Dr Cpe w/T-Bar Roof	20128	—	—
2 Dr Turbo Cpe	21748	—	—
2 Dr Turbo Cpe w/T-Bar Roof	22688	—	—
ADD FOR:			
Anti-Lock Brakes	1130	—	—
Leather Pkg (Base)	1750	—	—
(Turbo)	1275	—	—
Aluminum Alloy Wheels (Base)	400	—	—
PASEO 4			
2 Dr Cpe	11558	—	—
ADD FOR:			
Aluminum Alloy Wheels	455	—	—
PREVIA 4			
2WD Dlx	19358	—	—
4WD Dlx	22188	—	—
2WD LE (auto)	22748	—	—
4WD LE (auto)	25518	—	—
ADD FOR:			
Anti-Lock Brakes	1405	—	—
Third Seat (Dlx)	600	—	—
SUPRA 6			
2 Dr Lftbk	26290	—	—
2 Dr Turbo Lftbk	29900	—	—
2 Dr Turbo Lftbk w/Sport Roof	30960	—	—
ADD FOR:			
Anti-Lock Brakes (Base)	1130	—	—

Refer To Optional Equipment Schedules

Year-Model-Body Type	Original List	Current Whlse	Average Retail
Leather Seat Pkg	**1100**	—	—
Sports Pkg (Base)	**795**	—	—
(Turbo)	**360**	—	—
TERCEL 4			
2 Dr Std Sdn (NA w/power steering)	**8208**	—	—
2 Dr DX Sdn	**10158**	—	—
4 Dr DX Sdn	**10258**	—	—
4 Dr LE Sdn (auto)	**11388**	—	—

NOTE: Tilt steering wheel standard on Corolla LE, Camry, Celica GT, GT-S & All-Trac, Supra, MR2, Cressida, Previa, 4Runner V6 and Land Cruiser. Cruise control standard on Camry LE & XLE, Celica All-Trac, Supra, Cressida and Previa. Power windows and power door locks standard on Camry LE & XLE, Celica All-Trac, Supra, Cressida, Previa LE and Land Cruiser. Moonroof standard on Camry XLE.

1991

Year-Model-Body Type	Original List	Current Whlse	Average Retail
2WD 4RUNNER SR5 4			
4 Dr (auto)	**16488**	13025	15350
2WD 4RUNNER SR5 6			
4 Dr (auto)	**19013**	13525	15900
4WD 4RUNNER SR5 4			
2 Dr (5 spd)	**17308**	13425	15750
4 Dr (5 spd)	**17298**	13925	16300
4WD 4RUNNER SR5 6			
2 Dr (5 spd)	**20293**	13925	16300
4 Dr 4WDemand (5 spd)	**19793**	14475	17000
2WD PICKUPS 4			
Std Short Bed (5 spd)	**9738**	6475	7525
Dlx Short Bed (5 spd)	**10558**	6925	8050
Dlx Long Bed (5 spd)	**11088**	7050	8175
Dlx Std Xtracab Short Bed (5 spd)	**11798**	7700	8900
2WD PICKUPS 6			
Dlx Xtracab Short Bed (5 spd)	**12578**	8100	9400
SR5 Xtracab Short Bed (5 spd)	**14308**	8675	10025
1-Ton (5 spd)	**12368**	7350	8525
4WD PICKUPS 6			
Dlx Short Bed (5 spd)	**14138**	9200	10600
Dlx Long Bed (5 spd)	**14698**	9300	10725
CAMRY 4			
4 Dr Sdn	**13353**	9300	10725
4 Dr Dlx Sdn	**14043**	9975	11500
4 Dr LE Sdn (auto)	**16103**	11375	13150
4 Dr Dlx All-Trac 4WD Sdn (auto)	**16713**	11475	13250
4 Dr LE All-Trac 4WD Sdn (auto)	**18093**	12125	14000
5 Dr Dlx Wgn (auto)	**15513**	11075	12800
CAMRY 6			
4 Dr Dlx Sdn	**15323**	10375	11950
4 Dr LE Sdn (auto)	**17668**	11725	13550
5 Dr LE Wgn (auto)	**18458**	12225	14175
CELICA 4			
2 Dr ST Spt Cpe	**13623**	9725	11200
2 Dr GT Spt Cpe	**15293**	10750	12400
2 Dr GT Conv	**20153**	13975	16350
2 Dr GT Lftbk	**15543**	10825	12500
2 Dr GT-S Lftbk	**17758**	11900	13750
2 Dr All-Trac Turbo Lftbk	**22498**	13950	16325
COROLLA 4			
4 Dr Std Sdn	**10383**	7075	8225
4 Dr Dlx Sdn	**11383**	7550	8775
4 Dr LE Sdn	**12403**	8200	9475
4 Dr Dlx Wgn	**12053**	7875	9150
5 Dr 4WD Dlx All-Trac Wgn	**13753**	8625	9950
2 Dr SR5 Spt Cpe	**12923**	8400	9700
2 Dr GT-S Spt Cpe	**14513**	9400	10825
CRESSIDA 6			
4 Dr Lux Sdn (auto)	**22698**	15675	18325
LAND CRUISER			
4 Dr Wgn (auto)	**24378**	18625	21675
MR2 4			
2 Dr Cpe	**16873**	11950	13800
2 Dr Cpe w/T-Bar Roof	**17823**	12525	14750
2 Dr Turbo Cpe	**20203**	13025	15350
2 Dr Turbo Cpe w/T-Bar Roof	**21103**	13575	15950
PREVIA 4			
2WD Dlx	**16448**	12725	15050
2WD LE (auto)	**19598**	14950	17550
SUPRA 6			
2 Dr Lftbk	**24320**	16025	18675
2 Dr Turbo Lftbk	**27790**	17375	20025
2 Dr Turbo Lftbk w/Sport Roof	**28810**	17975	20625
TERCEL			
2 Dr Std Sdn (NA w/power steering)	**7553**	4975	5900
2 Dr DX Sdn	**9213**	6175	7200
4 Dr DX Sdn	**9313**	6275	7300
4 Dr LE Sdn	**10483**	6925	8050
ADD FOR:			
Leather/Power Seat Pkg			
(Camry LE)	**1080**	500	575
(Celica GT-S)	**1530**	600	675
(Celica GT Cpe)	**1830**	600	675
(Celica All-Trac Turbo)	**950**	600	675
(Cressida)	**1585**	600	675

Year-Model-Body Type	Original List	Current Whlse	Average Retail
Leather Trim Pkg			
(MR2 Base)	**1710**	375	450
(MR2 Turbo)	**1235**	375	450
(Supra)	**1010**	400	475
Dual Sunroofs			
(Previa LE 2WD)	**1370**	650	750

NOTE: Power brakes standard on all models. Power door locks standard on Camry LE 6 cylinder, Celica All-Trac Turbo, Cressida, Previa LE and Supra. Power windows standard on Camry LE 6 cylinder, Celica All-Trac Turbo, Cressida and Supra.

1990

Year-Model-Body Type	Original List	Current Whlse	Average Retail
2WD 4RUNNER SR5 4			
4 Dr (auto)	**16783**	11425	13200
2WD 4RUNNER SR5 6			
4 Dr (auto)	**18393**	11800	13625
4WD 4RUNNER SR5 4			
2 Dr (5 spd)	**17208**	11950	13800
4WD 4RUNNER SR5 6			
2 Dr (5 spd)	**18788**	12325	14350
2WD PICKUPS 4			
Std Short Bed (4 spd)	**9288**	4950	5875
Dlx Short Bed (5 spd)	**9878**	5400	6325
Dlx Long Bed (5 spd)	**10408**	5550	6475
Dlx Xtracab (5 spd)	**11048**	5950	6875
SR5 Long Bed (5 spd)	**10998**	6075	6975
SR5 Xtracab (5 spd)	**11998**	6525	7600
2WD PICKUPS 6			
Dlx Long Bed (5 spd)	**11408**	5925	6850
Dlx Xtracab (5 spd)	**12048**	6350	7400
SR5 Xtracab (5 spd)	**13778**	6900	8025
1-Ton Long Bed (5 spd)	**12048**	6200	7225
4WD PICKUPS 4			
SR5 Short Bed (5 spd)	**13228**	7700	8950
4WD PICKUPS 6			
Dlx Short Bed (5 spd)	**13468**	7450	8650
SR5 Short Bed (5 spd)	**15448**	8025	9275
CAMRY 4			
4 Dr Sdn	**12743**	7775	9025
4 Dr Dlx Sdn	**13543**	8375	9675
4 Dr All Trac Sdn	**15323**	9050	10425
5 Dr Wgn (auto)	**14923**	9250	10650
4 Dr LE Sdn (auto)	**15483**	9650	11125
4 Dr LE All Trac Sdn (auto)	**17473**	10325	11925
CAMRY 6			
4 Dr Dlx Sdn	**14028**	8825	10200
5 Dr Dlx Wgn (auto)	**15408**	9700	11175
4 Dr LE Sdn (auto)	**17078**	10075	11625
5 Dr LE Wgn (auto)	**17868**	10475	12100
CELICA 4			
2 Dr ST Spt Cpe	**13093**	8050	9300
2 Dr GT Spt Cpe	**14763**	8950	10325
2 Dr GT Lftbk	**15013**	9050	10425
2 Dr GT-S Lftbk	**17258**	9875	11375
2 Dr 4WD All Trac Turbo Lftbk	**21998**	11875	13725
COROLLA 4			
4 Dr Std Sdn	**10103**	5650	6575
4 Dr Dlx Sdn	**10843**	6000	6925
5 Dr Dlx Wgn	**11483**	6325	7350
4 Dr Dlx All Trac Sdn	**12113**	6700	7800
5 Dr 4WD Dlx All Trac Wgn	**13193**	7025	8150
4 Dr LE Sdn	**11703**	6525	7600
2 Dr SR5 Spt Cpe	**12423**	6825	7950
5 Dr 4WD SR5 All Trac Wgn	**14013**	7800	9050
2 Dr GT-S Spt Cpe	**14013**	7775	9025
CRESSIDA			
4 Dr Lux Sdn (auto)	**21498**	12800	15125
LAND CRUISER 6			
4 Dr Wgn (auto)	**20898**	14850	17425
SUPRA 6			
2 Dr Lftbk	**22860**	13550	15925
2 Dr Lftbk w/Sport Roof	**23930**	14050	16500
2 Dr Turbo Lftbk	**25200**	14625	17175
2 Dr Turbo Lftbk w/Sport Roof	**26220**	15100	17750
TERCEL 4			
3 Dr Base Lftbk (NA w/power steering)	**7433**	4425	5350
3 Dr EZ Lftbk (NA w/power steering)	**6698**	3775	4675
2 Dr Std Cpe	**8813**	4425	5350
3 Dr Std Lftbk	**8753**	4650	5575
2 Dr Dlx Cpe	**9973**	5250	6175
ADD FOR:			
Anti-Lock Braking System	—	500	600
Leather/Power Seat Pkg	—	375	425

NOTE: Power brakes standard on all models. Anti-lock brakes standard on 4Runner 6 Cylinder. Power windows standard on Camry LE 6 Cylinder, Celica All-Trac, Supra Series, Cressida and 4Runner. Power door locks standard on Camry LE 6 Cylinder, Celica All-Trac, Supra Series and Cressida.

1989

Year-Model-Body Type	Original List	Current Whlse	Average Retail
4RUNNER 4			
Dlx 2 Pass (5 spd)	**14478**	9400	10825
Dlx 5 Pass (5 spd)	**16458**	9800	11300
SR5 2 Pass (5 spd)	**18413**	10600	12225

Refer To Optional Equipment Schedules

Year-Model-Body Type	Original List	Current Whlse	Average Retail
Dlx 2 Pass V6 (5 spd)	**16083**	9775	11250
SR5 5 Pass V6 (5 spd)	**19223**	10775	12425
2WD PICKUPS 4			
Std Short Bed (4 spd)	**8488**	4050	4950
Dlx Short Bed (5 spd)	**9198**	4425	5350
Dlx Long Bed (5 spd)	**9728**	4450	5375
Dlx Xtracab (5 spd)	**10438**	4850	5775
SR5 Long Bed (5 spd)	**10478**	5025	5950
SR5 Xtracab (5 spd)	**11478**	5425	6350
2WD PICKUPS 6			
Dlx Long Bed (5 spd)	**10858**	4750	5675
Dlx Xtracab (5 spd)	**11498**	5250	6175
SR5 Xtracab (5 spd)	**12788**	5825	6750
1-Ton Long Bed (5 spd)	**11218**	5100	6025
4WD PICKUPS 4			
SR5 Short Bed (5 spd)	**12708**	6425	7475
SR5 Short Bed w/4WD Demand (5 spd)	**12908**	6575	7650
4WD PICKUPS 6			
Dlx Short Bed (5 spd)	**12918**	6175	7200
SR5 Short Bed (5 spd)	**14458**	6700	7800
CAMRY 4			
4 Dr Sdn	**12613**	6125	7125
4 Dr Dlx Sdn	**13453**	6600	7675
4 Dr Dlx All Trac Sdn	**15233**	7275	8450
5 Dr Wgn	**14143**	6900	8025
4 Dr LE Sdn (auto)	**15453**	7825	9075
4 Dr LE All Trac Sdn (auto)	**17443**	8525	9850
5 Dr LE Wgn (auto)	**16233**	8125	9375
CAMRY 6			
4 Dr Dlx Sdn	**14763**	6925	8050
5 Dr Dlx Wgn (auto)	**16203**	7375	8550
4 Dr LE Sdn (auto)	**16428**	8000	9300
5 Dr LE Wgn	**17218**	8300	9575
CELICA 4			
2 Dr ST Spt Cpe	**12603**	6075	6975
2 Dr GT Spt Cpe	**14203**	6725	7825
2 Dr GT Lftbk	**14453**	6825	7950
2 Dr GT Convertible	**19113**	9800	11300
2 Dr GT-S Spt Cpe	**16348**	7650	8875
2 Dr GT-S Lftbk	**16698**	7750	9000
2 Dr 4WD All Trac Turbo Lftbk	**21838**	9550	11000
COROLLA 4			
4 Dr Dlx Sdn	**10403**	4825	5750
5 Dr Dlx Wgn	**10993**	5325	6250
4 Dr Dlx All Trac Sdn (5 spd)	**11843**	5600	6525
4 Dr Dlx All Trac 4WD Wgn	**12703**	5850	6775
4 Dr LE Sdn	**11413**	5400	6325
2 Dr SR5 Spt Cpe	**11953**	5500	6425
4 Dr SR5 All Trac 4WD Wgn	**14163**	6525	7600
2 Dr GT-S Spt Cpe	**13723**	6325	7350
CRESSIDA 6			
4 Dr Luxury Sdn (auto)	**21498**	11000	12700
LAND CRUISER 6			
4 Dr Wgn (auto)	**21788**	12200	14100
MR2 4			
2 Dr Cpe	**14593**	7225	8400
2 Dr Cpe w/T-Bar Roof	**16063**	7800	9050
2 Dr Supercharged Cpe w/T-Bar Roof	**18423**	8475	9800
SUPRA 6			
2 Dr Lftbk	**22360**	10725	12375
2 Dr Lftbk w/Sport Roof	**23430**	11250	13000
2 Dr Turbo Lftbk	**24700**	11475	13250
2 Dr Turbo Lftbk w/Sport Roof	**25720**	12025	13900
TERCEL 4			
3 Dr Base Lftbk (NA w/power steering)	**7273**	3275	4175
3 Dr EZ Lftbk (NA w/power steering)	**6538**	2800	3700
2 Dr Std Cpe	**8533**	3350	4250
3 Dr Std Lftbk	**8373**	3625	4525
2 Dr Dlx Cpe	**9593**	3925	4825
3 Dr Dlx Lftbk	**9493**	3825	4725
5 Dr Dlx Lftbk	**9733**	3925	4825
VANS 4			
Dlx Van	**15663**	6475	7525
Window	**11418**	4750	5675
Panel	**11118**	4500	5425
LE Van	**16958**	7125	8275
4WD Deluxe Van	**17848**	7425	8625
4WD Panel (auto)	**14018**	6125	7125
4WD LE Van (auto)	**18448**	8725	10075
ADD FOR:			
Anti-Lock Braking System	—	400	475
Leather Seat Trim			
(Camry 2WD LE)	**1080**	495	605
(Celica GT-S)	**1550**	710	870
(Celica All-Trac)	**1160**	535	650
(Supra)	**1010**	465	565
(Cressida)	**905**	415	505
Leather/Power Seat Pkg	**1240**	350	400

NOTE: Power brakes standard on all models. Power steering standard on Camry, Celica, Cressida, Land Cruiser, Supra, 4WD Van, LE Van, Corolla SR5 All-Trac, 4Runner Deluxe 6 Cylinder, 4Runner SR5. Power windows standard on Cressida and Supra. Power door locks standard on Cressida, Supra and LE Van. Air conditioning standard on Camry LE V6, Cressida and Supra.

Year-Model-Body Type	Original List	Current Whlse	Average Retail
1988			
4RUNNER 4			
Dlx 2 Pass (5 spd)	**13618**	7875	9150
Dlx 5 Pass (5 spd)	**14278**	8225	9500
SR5 2 Pass (5 spd)	**14718**	8525	9850
SR5 2 Pass V6 (5 spd)	**15528**	8825	10200
SR5 5 Pass V6 (5 spd)	**16698**	9675	11150
2WD PICKUP 4			
Std Short Bed (4 spd)	**7698**	2600	3475
Std Short Bed (5 spd)	**8078**	2625	3525
Std Long Bed (5 spd)	**8608**	2700	3600
Std Xtracab Long Bed (5 spd)	**9068**	3025	3925
Dlx Long Bed (5 spd)	**8818**	2925	3825
Dlx Xtracab Long Bed (5 spd)	**9358**	3325	4225
SR5 Xtracab (5 spd)	**10758**	3675	4575
SR5 Xtracab Turbo (5 spd)	**11918**	3950	4850
1-Ton Long Bed (5 spd)	**9478**	2850	3750
4WD PICKUP 4			
Std Short Bed V6 (5 spd)	**11808**	4175	5100
Dlx Long Bed V6 (5 spd)	**12628**	4575	5500
Dlx Xtracab V6 (5 spd)	**12858**	4850	5775
SR5 Short Bed (5 spd)	**12598**	4600	5525
SR5 Short Bed V6 (5 spd)	**13408**	4875	5800
SR5 Xtracab V6 (5 spd)	**13898**	5375	6300
CAMRY 4			
4 Dr Sdn	**11248**	4550	5475
4 Dr Dlx Sdn	**12098**	5025	5950
4 Dr 4WD Dlx Sdn	**13828**	5675	6600
5 Dr Wgn	**12788**	5250	6175
4 Dr LE Sdn (auto)	**14438**	6075	6975
4 Dr 4WD LE Sdn	**15488**	6175	7200
5 Dr LE Wgn (auto)	**15208**	6325	7350
CAMRY 6			
4 Dr Dlx Sdn	**13148**	5325	6250
5 Dr Dlx Wgn	**14568**	5650	6575
4 Dr LE Sdn (auto)	**15998**	6325	7350
5 Dr LE Wgn (auto)	**16788**	6625	7700
CELICA 4			
2 Dr ST Spt Cpe	**11548**	4300	5225
2 Dr GT Spt Cpe	**13288**	4825	5750
2 Dr GT Lftbk	**13538**	4900	5825
2 Dr GT Convertible	**18248**	7425	8625
2 Dr GT-S Spt Cpe	**15298**	5675	6600
2 Dr GT-S Lftbk	**15648**	5750	6675
2 Dr 4WD Turbo Lftbk	**20698**	7300	8475
COROLLA 4			
4 Dr Dlx Sdn	**8998**	3325	4225
5 Dr Dlx Wgn	**9548**	3575	4475
4 Dr 4WD Wgn	**10948**	4225	5150
4 Dr LE Sdn	**10248**	3750	4650
2 Dr SR5 Spt Cpe	**10348**	3825	4725
4 Dr 4WD SR5 Wgn	**12418**	4650	5575
2 Dr GT-S Spt Cpe	**12478**	4525	5450
3 Dr FX Lftbk	**7948**	2150	3000
3 Dr FX-16 Lftbk	**9978**	2775	3675
3 Dr FX-16 Gt-S Lftbk	**10968**	3225	4125
CRESSIDA 6			
4 Dr Luxury Sdn (auto)	**20998**	8275	9550
LAND CRUISER 6			
4 Dr Wgn (auto)	**20398**	9050	10425
MR2 4			
2 Dr Cpe	**13458**	4875	5800
2 Dr Cpe w/T-Bar Roof	**14808**	5225	6150
2 Dr Supercharged Cpe w/T-Bar Roof	**17068**	5825	6750
SUPRA 6			
2 Dr Lftbk	**21740**	8125	9375
2 Dr Lftbk w/Sport Roof	**22780**	8525	9850
2 Dr Turbo Lftbk	**24210**	8775	10125
2 Dr Turbo Lftbk w/Sport Roof	**25200**	9150	10550
TERCEL 4			
3 Dr EZ Lftbk	**6148**	1750	2600
2 Dr Std Cpe	**7148**	2200	3050
3 Dr Std Lftbk	**6988**	2125	2975
3 Dr Std Cpe (auto)	**7458**	2425	3300
2 Dr Dlx Cpe	**8238**	2600	3475
3 Dr Dlx Lftbk	**8088**	2525	3400
5 Dr Sdn	**8328**	2725	3625
5 Dr Lftbk (auto)	**8798**	2850	3750
4 Dr 4WD Dlx Wgn	**10698**	3325	4225
4 Dr 4WD SR5 Wgn	**11718**	3800	4700
VANS 4			
Dlx Van	**13198**	3975	4875
Window	**10808**	2975	3875
Panel	**10508**	2775	3675
LE Van	**15258**	4550	5475
4WD Panel	**12928**	3575	4475
4WD LE Van	**17328**	5425	6350

NOTE: Power brakes stanard on all models. Power windows standard on Celica 4WD, Supra Series and Cressida Series. Power door locks standard on Celica 4WD, Supra Series, Cressida Series and Van LE. Power steering standard on Corolla FX16, Corolla FX16 GT-S, Camry Series, Celica Series, Supra Series, Cressida Series, Van 4WD, Van Deluxe, Van LE, Pickup SR5, 4Runner SR5 and Land Cruiser. Air conditioning standard on Camry LE with V6 engine, Supra Series and Cressida Series.

Refer To Optional Equipment Schedules

Year-Model-Body Type	Original List	Current Whlse	Average Retail
1987½			
TERCEL 4			
2 Dr Std Cpe	**6738**	1650	2500
2 Dr Dlx Cpe (auto)	**8298**	2325	3200

NOTE: Power front disc brakes standard.

Year-Model-Body Type	Original List	Current Whlse	Average Retail
1987			
4RUNNER 4			
Dlx (5 spd)	**12998**	6500	7575
SR5 2 Pass (5 spd)	**14548**	6950	8100
SR5 Wgn (5 spd)	**15248**	7325	8500
SR5 Turbo (auto)	**18698**	7925	9200
2WD PICKUP 4			
Std Short Bed (4 spd)	**6998**	1950	2800
Std Short Bed (5 spd)	**7378**	1975	2825
Std Long Bed (5 spd)	**7898**	2025	2875
Xtracab Long Bed (5 spd)	**8498**	2275	3150
Dlx Long Bed (5 spd)	**8245**	2250	3100
Dlx Xtracab Long Bed (5 spd)	**8778**	2550	3425
SR5 Xtracab (5 spd)	**10188**	2850	3750
SR5 Xtracab Turbo (5 spd)	**12488**	3050	3950
1-Ton Long Bed (5 spd)	**8898**	2100	2950
4WD PICKUP 4			
Std Short Bed Turbo (5 spd)	**11638**	3375	4275
SR5 Short Bed (5 spd)	**11988**	3825	4725
CAMRY 4			
4 Dr Sdn	**10798**	3425	4325
4 Dr Dlx Sdn	**11448**	4050	4950
5 Dr Dlx Wgn	**12138**	4050	4950
4 Dr LE Sdn (auto)	**13798**	4725	5650
5 Dr LE Wgn (auto)	**14568**	4975	5900
CELICA 4			
2 Dr ST Spt Cpe	**10948**	3325	4225
2 Dr GT Spt Cpe	**12638**	3825	4725
2 Dr GT Lftbk	**12888**	3925	4825
2 Dr GT Convertible	**17598**	6200	7225
2 Dr GT-S Spt Cpe	**14648**	4525	5450
2 Dr GT-S Lftbk	**15368**	4625	5550
COROLLA 4			
4 Dr Dlx Sdn	**8478**	2525	3400
5 Dr Dlx Lftbk (auto)	**9408**	3000	3900
4 Dr LE Sdn	**9628**	2850	3750
2 Dr SR5 Spt Cpe	**9998**	2925	3825
2 Dr GT-S Spt Cpe	**10998**	3475	4375
3 Dr FX Lftbk	**7878**	1575	2425
3 Dr FX-16 Lftbk	**9678**	2150	3000
3 Dr FX-16 Gt-S Lftbk	**10668**	2575	3450
CRESSIDA 6			
4 Dr Lux Sdn (5 spd or auto)	**20250**	6575	7650
4 Dr Lux Wgn (auto)	**20310**	6775	7875
LAND CRUISER 6			
4 Dr Wgn	**18148**	7050	8175
4 Dr Wgn w/o Rear Seat	**17448**	6850	7975
MR2 4			
2 Dr Cpe	**12848**	3725	4625
2 Dr Cpe w/T-Bar Roof	**14038**	4025	4925
SUPRA 6			
2 Dr Lftbk	**20890**	6875	8000
2 Dr Lftbk w/Sport Roof (auto)	**22660**	7275	8450
2 Dr Turbo Lftbk	**23210**	7450	8650
2 Dr Turbo Lftbk w/Sport Roof	**24210**	7775	9025
TERCEL 4			
3 Dr EZ Lftbk	**5848**	1275	2000
3 Dr Lftbk	**6328**	1550	2400
3 Dr Dlx Lftbk	**7638**	1900	2750
5 Dr Dlx Lftbk (auto)	**8338**	2175	3025
5 Dr Dlx Wgn	**8898**	2025	2875
4 Dr 4WD Dlx Wgn	**10138**	2450	3325
4 Dr 4WD SR5 Wgn	**11208**	2750	3650
VANS 4			
Dlx Van	**12338**	2750	3650
Window	**9948**	2175	3025
Panel	**9648**	1975	2825
LE Van (auto)	**14998**	3725	4625
4WD Panel	**12018**	2500	3375
4WD LE Van	**16428**	4000	4900
ADD FOR:			
Sports Pkg (Supra)	**700**	200	250
(Celica GT-S)	**800**	235	290
Leather Pkg (MR2)	**760**	225	275
(Cressida Sdn)	**760**	225	275

NOTE: Power brakes standard on all models. Air conditioning standard on Cressida and Supra. Power windows standard on Cressida, Supra and 4Runner. Power door locks standard on Cressida, Van LE, SR5 Turbo Pickup and Supra. Sunroof standard on Corolla FX-16 GT-S. Power steering standard on Corolla FX-16, Camry, Celica, Cressida, Van LE, SR5 Pickup, 4Runner, Supra and Land Cruiser.

Year-Model-Body Type	Original List	Current Whlse	Average Retail
1986			
4RUNNER 4			
Std (5 spd)	**12398**	4525	5450
Dlx (auto)	**13778**	5100	6025
SR5 (5 spd)	**14578**	5375	6300

Year-Model-Body Type	Original List	Current Whlse	Average Retail
SR5 Turbo Diesel (auto)	**17678**	5225	6150
2WD PICKUPS			
Std Short Bed (4 spd)	**6298**	1675	2525
Std Long Bed (5 spd)	**7128**	1775	2625
Dlx Long Bed (5 spd)	**7438**	2000	2850
Dlx Xtracab Long Bed (5 spd)	**8168**	2175	3025
SR5 Long Bed (5 spd)	**9188**	2525	3400
SR5 Xtracab (5 spd)	**9388**	2725	3625
SR5 Xtracab Turbo (5 spd)	**11868**	2625	3525
1-Ton Long Bed (5 spd)	**8088**	2000	2850
4WD PICKUPS			
Std Short Bed Turbo (5 spd)	**10738**	2550	3425
SR5 Short Bed (5 spd)	**11438**	3275	4175
SR5 Xtracab Turbo (auto)	**14838**	3725	4625
CAMRY 4			
4 Dr Dlx Sdn	**10198**	2600	3475
4 Dr Turbo-diesel Dlx Sdn (auto)	**12208**	2550	3425
4 Dr LE Sdn	**11738**	3050	3950
5 Dr LE Lftbk (auto)	**12758**	3450	4350
CELICA 4			
2 Dr ST Spt Cpe	**10098**	2300	3175
2 Dr GT Spt Cpe	**11398**	2850	3750
2 Dr GT Lftbk	**11648**	2950	3850
2 Dr GT-S Spt Cpe	**13348**	3325	4225
2 Dr GT-S Lftbk	**13698**	3425	4325
COROLLA 4			
4 Dr Dlx Sdn	**7798**	1925	2775
5 Dr Dlx Lftbk	**8158**	2000	2850
4 Dr LE Sdn	**8818**	2225	3075
4 Dr LE LTD Sdn (auto)	**10778**	2625	3525
2 Dr GT-S Spt Cpe	**10198**	2700	3600
2 Dr GT-S Lftbk	**10378**	2700	3600
2 Dr SR5 Spt Cpe	**9108**	2300	3175
2 Dr SR5 Lftbk	**9288**	2300	3175
CRESSIDA 6			
4 Dr Lux Sdn	**18280**	4950	5875
4 Dr Lux Wgn (auto)	**18340**	5200	6125
LAND CRUISER 6			
4 Dr Wgn	**16548**	5600	6525
MR2 4			
2 Dr Cpe	**12548**	2725	3625
SUPRA 6			
2 Dr Lftbk	**16558**	5150	6075
1986.5 SUPRA 6			
2 Dr Lftbk	**17990**	5625	6550
2 Dr Sport Lftbk	**18790**	5800	6725
TERCEL 4			
3 Dr Std Lftbk	**5798**	1025	1750
3 Dr Dlx Lftbk	**7038**	1275	2000
5 Dr Dlx Lftbk	**7188**	1350	2100
5 Dr Dlx Wgn	**7888**	1450	2225
5 Dr Dlx 4WD Wgn (auto)	**9018**	1800	2650
5 Dr SR5 4WD Wgn	**9948**	2075	2925
VANS 4			
Dlx Van	**11148**	2000	2850
LE Van (auto)	**13538**	2575	3450
Cargo Van	**8998**	1425	2175
ADD FOR:			
Leather Pkg (MR2)	**730**	155	190
(Celica GT-S)	**770**	165	200
(Cressida Sdn)	**670**	145	175
Luxury Pkg (Cargo Van)	**800**	170	210
Sports Pkg (Cressida)	**670**	145	175
Converter Pkg (Cargo Van)	**295**	150	200

NOTE: Power brakes standard on Camry Deluxe, Corolla Series, Tercel Series, Celica Series, MR2, Supra, Cressida, Vans, 4Runner and Pickups. Air conditioning and power windows standard on Cressida and Supra. Power locks standard on Corolla LE Sedan, Corolla SR5, Corolla GTS, Supra, Cressida and LE Van. Power steering standard on Camry Series, Corolla Deluxe diesel models, Corolla LE, Corolla SR5, Corolla GT-S, Celica GT, Celica GT-S, Supra, Cressida, LE Van, SR5 4Runner and SR5 4WD Pickups.

1985

Year-Model-Body Type	Original List	Current Whlse	Average Retail
4RUNNER 4			
Std (5 spd)	**10668**	3725	4625
Dlx (auto)	**12068**	4250	5175
SR5 (5 spd)	**12568**	4400	5325
PICKUP 4			
Std (4 spd)	**5998**	1375	2125
Long Bed (5 spd)	**6498**	1475	2300
Dlx Long Bed (5 spd)	**6898**	1675	2525
Dlx Xtracab (5 spd)	**7288**	1850	2700
SR5 Std Bed (5 spd)	**8098**	1800	2650
SR5 Long Bed (5 spd)	**8268**	1900	2750
SR5 Xtracab (5 spd)	**8448**	2050	2900
SR5 Xtracab Turbo (auto)	**10378**	1975	2825
Dlx Long Bed Diesel (5 spd)	**7648**	1275	2000
Dlx Long Bed Turbo-diesel (5 spd)	**7888**	1425	2175
Dlx Xtracab Std Bed Turbodiesel (5 spd)	**8788**	1475	2300
1-Ton Long Bed (5 spd)	**7338**	1550	2400

Refer To Optional Equipment Schedules

Year-Model-Body Type	Original List	Current Whlse	Average Retail
CAMRY 4			
4 Dr Dlx Sdn	**9248**	1975	2825
4 Dr LE Sdn (auto)	**10898**	2500	3375
5 Dr Dlx Lftbk (auto)	**10288**	2175	3025
5 Dr LE Lftbk (auto)	**11248**	2550	3425
4 Dr Dlx Turbodiesel Sdn	**10998**	1500	2350
CELICA 4			
2 Dr ST Spt Cpe	**8449**	2050	2900
2 Dr GT-S Spt Cpe	**11199**	2775	3675
2 Dr GT Spt Cpe	**10099**	2350	3225
2 Dr GT-S Lftbk	**11549**	2850	3750
2 Dr GT Lftbk	**9989**	2400	3275
2 Dr GT-S Convertible	**17669**	5100	6025
COROLLA 4			
4 Dr Dlx Sdn	**7163**	1550	2400
4 Dr LE Sdn	**7738**	1750	2600
4 Dr LE LTD Sdn (auto)	**9258**	2050	2900
5 Dr Dlx Lftbk	**7423**	1625	2475
5 Dr LE Lftbk (auto)	**8358**	1800	2650
4 Dr Dlx Diesel Sdn (auto)	**7898**	1225	1950
5 Dr Dlx Diesel Lftbk (5 spd)	**7788**	1250	1975
2 Dr SR5 Spt Cpe	**8058**	1800	2650
2 Dr SR5 Lftbk	**8238**	1800	2650
2 Dr GT-S Spt Cpe	**9298**	2125	2975
2 Dr GT-S Lftbk	**9538**	2125	2975
CRESSIDA 6			
4 Dr Lux Sdn	**15690**	3875	4775
4 Dr Lux Wgn (auto)	**15750**	3975	4875
LAND CRUISER 6			
4 Dr Wgn	**14570**	4475	5400
MR2 4			
2 Dr Cpe	**10999**	2200	3050
SUPRA 6			
2 Dr Lftbk	**16558**	3625	4525
2 Dr L Lftbk (auto)	**16558**	3425	4325
TERCEL 4			
3 Dr Lftbk	**5573**	800	1500
3 Dr Dlx Lftbk	**6563**	1025	1750
5 Dr Dlx Lftbk	**6713**	1100	1825
5 Dr Dlx Wgn	**7143**	1175	1900
5 Dr Dlx 4WD Wgn (auto)	**8433**	1775	2625
5 Dr SR5 4WD Wgn	**8778**	1825	2675
VAN WAGON 4			
Dlx Wgn	**10013**	1625	2475
LE Wgn	**11348**	1900	2750
Cargo Wgn	**9198**	1075	1800
ADD FOR:			
Leather Seat Pkg	**—**	75	100
Leather Sport Seats (Supra L)	**700**	90	110
Converter Pkg (Cargo Van)	**1300**	150	200

NOTE: Power brakes standard on all models. Power steering standard on Corolla LE, Corolla SR5 Sport, Corolla GT-S, Camry except Sdn, Celica GT, Celica GT-S, Supra, Cressida, LE Van and 4Runner. Air conditioning standard on Celica GT-S, Supra and Cressida. Power windows standard on Supra and Cressida.

1984

Year-Model-Body Type	Original List	Current Whlse	Average Retail
PICKUP 4			
Std Short Bed (4 spd)	**5998**	1050	1775
Std Long Bed (5 spd)	**6298**	1125	1850
Std Long Bed (4 spd)	**6728**	1125	1850
Dlx Long Bed (5 spd)	**7268**	1300	2025
Dlx Extra Cab (5 spd)	**7508**	1375	2125
SR5 Short Bed (5 spd)	**8308**	1325	2050
SR5 Long Bed (5 spd)	**8478**	1375	2125
SR5 Extra Cab (5 spd)	**8548**	1475	2300
Dlx Long Bed Diesel (5 spd)	**7868**	875	1600
¾ Ton Long Bed (5 spd)	**6998**	1100	1825
Dlx 4WD Long Bed Diesel (5 spd)	**7868**	1450	2225
CAMRY 4			
4 Dr Dlx Sdn	**8498**	1325	2050
5 Dr Dlx Lftbk (auto)	**9448**	1450	2225
4 Dr Dlx Turbodiesel Sdn	**9598**	975	1700
4 Dr LE Sdn (auto)	**10498**	1675	2525
5 Dr LE Lftbk (auto)	**10848**	1725	2575
CELICA 4			
2 Dr ST Spt Cpe	**8334**	1325	2050
2 Dr GT Spt Cpe	**9149**	1550	2400
2 Dr GT Lftbk	**9499**	1625	2475
2 Dr GT-S Spt Cpe	**10919**	1850	2700
2 Dr GT-S Lftbk	**11269**	1900	2750
COROLLA 4			
4 Dr Dlx Sdn	**7018**	1150	1875
4 Dr Dlx Diesel Sdn (auto)	**7938**	750	1475
5 Dr Dlx Lftbk	**7268**	1250	1975
5 Dr Dlx Diesel Lftbk	**7818**	850	1550
4 Dr LE Sdn	**7498**	1300	2025
2 Dr SR5 HT	**7898**	1375	2125
2 Dr SR5 Lftbk	**8078**	1350	2100
CRESSIDA 6			
4 Dr Lux Sdn	**14259**	2175	3025
4 Dr Lux Wgn (auto)	**14819**	2175	3025
LAND CRUISER 6			
4 Dr Wgn	**14218**	3250	4150

Year-Model-Body Type	Original List	Current Whlse	Average Retail
STARLET 4			
3 Dr Lftbk	**6168**	750	1475
SUPRA 6			
2 Dr L Lftbk (auto)	**15438**	2575	3450
2 Dr Lftbk (5 spd)	**16088**	2600	3475
TERCEL 4			
3 Dr Lftbk	**5248**	775	1500
3 Dr Dlx Lftbk	**6418**	875	1600
5 Dr Dlx Lftbk	**6608**	900	1625
5 Dr Dlx Wgn	**7008**	925	1650
5 Dr Dlx 4WD Wgn	**8288**	1175	1900
3 Dr SR5 Lftbk	**6968**	1025	1750
5 Dr SR5 4WD Wgn	**8528**	1300	2025
VAN WAGON 4			
Dlx Wgn	**9698**	1150	1875
Dlx LE Wgn	**10948**	1350	2100

1983 — ALL BODY STYLES

Model	Original List	Current Whlse	Average Retail
HALF TON PICKUPS	—	825	1525
4WD PICKUPS	—	1325	2050
¾ TON PICKUPS	—	850	1550
CAMRY	—	1275	2000
CELICA	—	1250	1975
COROLLA	—	875	1600
COROLLA TERCEL	—	650	1225
CRESSIDA	—	1775	2625
LAND CRUISER	—	2475	3350
STARLET	—	400	725
SUPRA	—	1950	2800

VISTA

1992

Year-Model-Body Type	Original List	Current Whlse	Average Retail
VISTA 4			
5 Dr 2WD Wgn	**12331**	—	—
5 Dr 4WD Wgn	**14403**	—	—
5 Dr 2WD SE Wgn	**12894**	—	—
ADD FOR:			
Anti-Lock Brakes	**913**	—	—

NOTE: Tilt steering wheel standard on 4WD models.

1991

Year-Model-Body Type	Original List	Current Whlse	Average Retail
VISTA 4			
5 Dr 2WD Wgn	**13367**	7175	8325
5 Dr 4WD Wgn	**14334**	7625	8850

NOTE: Power brakes standard on all models.

1990

Year-Model-Body Type	Original List	Current Whlse	Average Retail
VISTA 4			
5 Dr 2WD Wgn	**12628**	5575	6500
5 Dr 4WD Wgn	**13595**	6075	6975

NOTE: Power brakes standard on all models.

1989

Year-Model-Body Type	Original List	Current Whlse	Average Retail
VISTA 4			
5 Dr 2WD Wgn	**12789**	4200	5125
5 Dr 4WD Wgn	**13840**	4650	5575

NOTE: Power brakes and tinted glass standard on all models. Power steering standard on Vista 4WD.

1988

Year-Model-Body Type	Original List	Current Whlse	Average Retail
VISTA 4			
5 Dr 2WD Wgn	**11461**	2700	3600
5 Dr 4WD Wgn	**12775**	3375	4275
ADD FOR:			
Custom Pkg (2WD)	**433**	165	200
(4WD)	**359**	165	200

NOTE: Power brakes standard on all models. Power steering standard on Vista 4WD model.

1987

Year-Model-Body Type	Original List	Current Whlse	Average Retail
VISTA 4			
5 Dr 2WD Wgn	**10644**	2175	3025
5 Dr 4WD Wgn	**11888**	2675	3575

NOTE: Power brakes and tinted glass standard on all models.

1986

Year-Model-Body Type	Original List	Current Whlse	Average Retail
VISTA 4			
5 Dr 2WD Wgn	**9577**	1800	2650
5 Dr 4WD Wgn	**10701**	2375	3250
ADD FOR:			
Custom Pkg (2WD)	**298**	65	80
(4WD)	**257**	55	65

NOTE: Power brakes standard on all models.

1985

Year-Model-Body Type	Original List	Current Whlse	Average Retail
VISTA 4			
5 Dr Wgn	**8721**	1575	2425

Refer To Optional Equipment Schedules

Year-Model-Body Type	Original List	Current Whlse	Average Retail
ADD FOR:			
Custom Pkg	**292**	40	45

NOTE: Power brakes and tinted glass standard.

1984

Year-Model-Body Type	Original List	Current Whlse	Average Retail
VISTA 4			
5 Dr Wgn	**8115**	1275	2000

NOTE: Power brakes and tinted glass standard.

VOLKSWAGEN

1992

Year-Model-Body Type	Original List	Current Whlse	Average Retail
CABRIOLET 4			
2 Dr Conv (5 spd)	**18215**	—	—
2 Dr Carat Conv (5 spd)	**19845**	—	—
CORRADO 4			
2 Dr Cpe (5 spd)	**19860**	—	—
2 Dr SLC Cpe (5 spd)	**22170**	—	—
ADD FOR:			
Anti-Lock Brakes (Base)	**835**	—	—
Leather Seat Trim	**770**	—	—
FOX 4			
2 Dr Sdn (4 spd) (NA w/power steering)	**8335**	—	—
4 Dr GL Sdn (NA w/power steering)	**9335**	—	—
GOLF 4			
2 Dr GL Htchbk (5 spd)	**11255**	—	—
4 Dr GL Htchbk (5 spd)	**11565**	—	—
GTI 4			
2 Dr Htchbk (5 spd)	**12460**	—	—
2 Dr 16V Htchbk	**15455**	—	—
JETTA 4			
4 Dr GL Sdn (5 spd)	**12720**	—	—
4 Dr GL ECO Diesel Sdn (5 spd)	**13030**	—	—
4 Dr Carat Sdn (5 spd)	**13915**	—	—
4 Dr GLI Sdn (5 spd)	**16550**	—	—
ADD FOR:			
Anti-Lock Brakes	**835**	—	—
Alloy Wheels (GL)	**395**	—	—
PASSAT 4			
4 Dr CL Sdn (5 spd)	**16350**	—	—
4 Dr GL Sdn (5 spd)	**17810**	—	—
4 Dr GL Wgn (5 spd)	**18240**	—	—

Year-Model-Body Type	Original List	Current Whlse	Average Retail
ADD FOR:			
Anti-Lock Brakes	**835**	—	—
Leather Seat Trim	**770**	—	—
Cast Alloy Wheels	**395**	—	—
Forged Alloy Wheels	**625**	—	—

NOTE: Tilt steering wheel standard on Corrado, GTi and Jetta. Cruise control standard on Cabriolet Carat and Corrado. Power windows standard on Cabriolet and Corrado. Power door locks standard on Jetta Carat & GLi.

1991

Year-Model-Body Type	Original List	Current Whlse	Average Retail
CABRIOLET 4			
2 Dr Convertible (5 spd)	**17400**	11600	13400
2 Dr Carat Convertible (5 spd)	**18960**	11800	13625
2 Dr Etienne Aigner Convertible (5 spd)	**19260**	12000	13850
CORRADO 4			
2 Dr Cpe (5 spd)	**19100**	12250	14200
FOX 4			
2 Dr Sdn (4 spd) (NA w/power steering)	**8515**	5300	6225
4 Dr GL Sdn (5 spd) (NA w/power steering)	**9705**	6200	7225
GOLF 4			
2 Dr GL Htchbk (5 spd)	**10720**	6900	8025
4 Dr GL Htchbk (5 spd)	**11020**	7000	8150
GTI 4			
2 Dr Htchbk (5 spd)	**11990**	7675	8900
2 Dr 16V Htchbk (5 spd)	**14680**	9575	11025
JETTA 4			
2 Dr GL Sdn (5 spd)	**11795**	7850	9125
4 Dr GL Sdn (5 spd)	**12095**	8025	9275
4 Dr GL Diesel Sdn (5 spd)	**12095**	7425	8625
4 Dr ECO Diesel Sdn (5 spd)	**12395**	7675	8900
4 Dr Carat Sdn (5 spd)	**13220**	8325	9625
4 Dr GLI Sdn (5 spd)	**15720**	10575	12200
PASSAT 4			
4 Dr GL Sdn (5 spd)	**15590**	11425	13200
4 Dr GL Wgn (5 spd)	**16010**	11600	13400
VANAGON 4			
Base 7-Seater (4 spd)	**16365**	10225	11800
GL 7-Seater (4 spd)	**17855**	12300	14300
Carat 7-Seater (4 spd)	**19555**	13450	15775
Multi-Van 7-Seater (4 spd)	**22035**	—	—
GL Camper (4 spd)	**22625**	15325	17975

Year-Model-Body Type	Original List	Current Whlse	Average Retail
ADD FOR:			
Leather Upholstery (Corrado, Passat)	**740**	460	560

NOTE: Power brakes standard on all models. Power door locks standard on Corrado, Jetta Carat, Vanagon Carat and Multi-Van. Power windows standard on Cabriolet, Corrado, Jetta Carat, Vanagon Carat and Multi-Van.

1990

Year-Model-Body Type	Original List	Current Whlse	Average Retail
CABRIOLET 4			
2 Dr Convertible (5 spd)	**16310**	9925	11425
2 Dr Best Seller Convertible (5 spd)	**17005**	10125	11675
2 Dr Boutique Convertible (5 spd)	**17565**	10325	11925
CORRADO 4			
2 Dr Cpe (5 spd)	**17900**	10200	11775
FOX 4			
2 Dr Sdn (NA w/power steering)	**8370**	4175	5100
2 Dr GL Sport Sdn (NA w/power steering)	**9740**	4950	5875
4 Dr GL Sdn (NA w/power steering)	**9455**	4850	5775
2 Dr GL Wgn (NA w/power steering)	**9695**	4875	5800
GOLF 4			
2 Dr GL Htchbk (5 spd)	**10075**	5375	6300
4 Dr GL Htchbk (5 spd)	**10375**	5500	6425
GTI 4			
2 Dr Htchbk (5 spd)	**11100**	6150	7150
JETTA 4			
2 Dr GL Sdn (5 spd)	**11100**	6600	7675
4 Dr GL Sdn (5 spd)	**11400**	6775	7875
4 Dr GL Diesel Sdn (5 spd)	**11600**	5775	6700
4 Dr Carat Sdn (5 spd)	**12095**	7150	8300
4 Dr GLI Sdn (5 spd)	**15005**	9150	10550
PASSAT 4			
4 Dr GL Sdn (5 spd)	**15070**	9575	11025
4 Dr GL Wgn (auto)	**16185**	10325	11925
VANAGON 4			
Base 7-Seater (4 spd)	**15460**	7500	8700
GL 7-Seater (4 spd)	**16840**	9500	10950
Carat 7-Seater (auto)	**19020**	11025	12650
Multi-Van 7-Seater (4 spd)	**20780**	12550	14800
GL Camper (4 spd)	**21340**	12350	14400
ADD FOR:			
Anti-Lock Braking System (Corrado, Jetta, Passat)	**835**	450	550
Leather Upholstery (Corrado, Passat)	**710**	385	470

NOTE: Power brakes standard on all models. Power windows standard on Cabriolet, Corrado, Vanagon Carat, Vanagon Multi-Van and GL Syncro Camper. Power door locks standard on Corrado, Jetta Carat, Vanagon Carat, Vanagon Multi-Van and GL Syncro Camper.

1989

Year-Model-Body Type	Original List	Current Whlse	Average Retail
CABRIOLET 4			
2 Dr Convertible (5 spd)	**16310**	8950	10325
2 Dr Best Seller Convertible (5 spd)	**17005**	9125	10500
2 Dr Best Seller Wolfsburg LTD Edit Convertible (5 spd)	**17005**	9275	10675
2 Dr Boutique Convertible (5 spd)	**17565**	9450	10875
FOX 4			
2 Dr Sdn (4 spd) (NA w/power steering)	**8035**	3050	3950
2 Dr GL Sdn (4 spd) (NA w/power steering)	**8865**	3400	4300
4 Dr GL Sdn (4 spd) (NA w/power steering)	**9065**	3575	4475
2 Dr GL Wgn (4 spd) (NA w/power steering)	**9295**	3600	4500
2 Dr GL Spt Sdn (5 spd) (NA w/power steering)	**9340**	3625	4525
4 Dr GL Spt Sdn (5 spd) (NA w/power steering)	**9540**	3800	4700
2 Dr GL Wolfsburg LTD Edit Sdn (5 spd) (NA w/power steering)	**9920**	3950	4850
GOLF 4			
2 Dr Htchbk (5 spd)	**10025**	4225	5150
2 Dr GL Htchbk (5 spd)	**10730**	4550	5475
4 Dr GL Htchbk (5 spd)	**10940**	4650	5575
4 Dr GL Wolfsburg LTD Edit Htchbk (5 spd)	**11515**	4850	5775
GTI 4			
2 Dr Htchbk (5 spd)	**15040**	6825	7950
JETTA 4			
2 Dr Sdn (5 spd)	**11295**	5250	6175
4 Dr Sdn (5 spd)	**11515**	5450	6375
4 Dr Diesel Sdn (5 spd)	**11715**	4800	5725
4 Dr GL Sdn (5 spd)	**12575**	5850	6775
4 Dr GL Wolfsburg LTD Edit Sdn (5 spd)	**12975**	6050	6975
4 Dr GLI Sdn (5 spd)	**14770**	7425	8625
4 Dr GLI Wolfsburg			

Refer To Optional Equipment Schedules

VOLKSWAGEN

Year-Model-Body Type	Original List	Current Whlse	Average Retail
LTD Edit Sdn (5 spd)	**17575**	7625	8850
4 Dr Carat Sdn (5 spd)	**15140**	6375	7425
VANAGON GL 4			
7-Seater (4 spd)	**18690**	8325	9625
Carat 7-Seater (4 spd)	**21010**	9450	10875
Carat Wolfsburg LTD Edit 7-Seater (4 spd)	**20545**	9600	11050
GL Camper (4 spd)	**23265**	11000	12700
ADD FOR:			
Anti-Lock Brakes (Jetta)	**995**	350	425

NOTE: Power brakes standard on all models. Sunroof and power door locks standard on Jetta GLI Wolfsburg LTD Edition and Jetta Carat. Power windows standard on Jetta GLI Wolfsburg LTD Edition, Jetta Carat, Vanagon Carat and Vanagon LTD Edition.

1988

Year-Model-Body Type	Original List	Current Whlse	Average Retail
CABRIOLET 4			
2 Dr Convertible (5 spd)	**14750**	6875	8000
2 Dr Best Seller Convertible (5 spd)	**15425**	7075	8225
2 Dr Boutique Convertible (5 spd)	**16390**	7250	8425
FOX 4			
2 Dr Sdn (4 spd)	**6290**	1475	2300
4 Dr GL Sdn (4 spd)	**7280**	1925	2775
2 Dr GL Wgn (4 spd)	**7380**	1950	2800
GOLF 4			
2 Dr Htchbk (5 spd)	**7990**	2200	3050
2 Dr GL Htchbk (5 spd)	**8695**	2500	3375
4 Dr GL Htchbk (5 spd)	**8905**	2625	3525
2 Dr GT Htchbk (5 spd)	**10175**	3150	4050
4 Dr GT Htchbk (5 spd)	**10385**	3225	4125
GTI 4			
2 Dr Htchbk (5 spd)	**12995**	4650	5575
JETTA 4			
2 Dr Sdn (5 spd)	**9195**	3650	4550
4 Dr Sdn (5 spd)	**9415**	3775	4675
4 Dr GL Sdn (5 spd)	**10590**	3950	4850
4 Dr GLI Sdn (5 spd)	**14080**	5450	6375
4 Dr Carat Sdn (5 spd)	**14570**	4275	5200
QUANTUM 5			
4 Dr GL Sdn (5 spd)	**17975**	5350	6275
4 Dr GL Wgn (5 spd)	**18375**	5375	6300
4 Dr GL Syncro Wgn (5 spd)	**21205**	6000	6925
SCIROCCO 4			
2 Dr Cpe (5 spd)	**14440**	5050	5975
VANAGON 4			
GL 7-Seater (4 spd)	**16590**	5425	6350
GL Wolfsburg 7-Seater (4 spd)	**18990**	6075	6975
GL Camper (4 spd)	**21690**	7900	9175
ADD FOR:			
Weekender Pkg (Vanagon GL)	**295**	110	135
Leather Interior (Scirocco)	**685**	200	250

NOTE: Power brakes standard on all models. Power steering standard on GTI, Jetta GL, Jetta GLI 16-Valve, Jetta Carat, Cabriolet, Scirocco, Quantum and Vanagon. Power door locks and sunroof standard on Quantum. Air conditioning standard on Jetta Carat and Quantum.

1987

Year-Model-Body Type	Original List	Current Whlse	Average Retail
CABRIOLET 4			
2 Dr Convertible (5 spd)	**13750**	5350	6275
2 Dr Wolfsburg Convertible (5 spd)	**15350**	5075	6000
FOX 4			
2 Dr Sdn (4 spd)	**5690**	950	1675
4 Dr GL Sdn (4 spd)	**6490**	1375	2125
2 Dr GL Wgn (4 spd)	—	1375	2125
GOLF 4			
2 Dr GL Htchbk (5 spd)	**8390**	2000	2850
4 Dr GL Htchbk (5 spd)	**8600**	2100	2950
2 Dr GL Diesel Htchbk (5 spd)	—	1500	2350
4 Dr GL Diesel Htchbk (5 spd)	—	1575	2425
2 Dr GT Htchbk (5 spd)	**9975**	2450	3325
4 Dr GT Htchbk (5 spd)	**10185**	2525	3400
GTI 4			
2 Dr Htchbk (5 spd)	**10325**	3100	4000
2 Dr 16-Valve Htchbk (5 spd)	**12240**	3825	4725
JETTA 4			
2 Dr Sdn (5 spd)	**9590**	2575	3450
4 Dr Sdn (5 spd)	**9810**	2725	3625
2 Dr Wolfsburg Sdn (5 spd)	**11340**	2975	3875
4 Dr GL Sdn (5 spd)	**10340**	2900	3800
4 Dr GLI Sdn (5 spd)	**12100**	3450	4350
QUANTUM 5			
4 Dr Wgn (5 spd)	**13920**	2900	3800
4 Dr Syncro Wgn (5 spd)	**17230**	3400	4300
4 Dr GL Sdn (5 spd)	**15510**	3250	4150
4 Dr GL Wgn (5 spd)	**15910**	3100	4000
4 Dr GL Syncro Wgn (5 spd)	**18870**	3675	4575
SCIROCCO 4			
2 Dr Cpe (5 spd)	**11110**	3550	4450
2 Dr 16-Valve Cpe			

Year-Model-Body Type	Original List	Current Whlse	Average Retail
(5 spd)	**13500**	4275	5200
VANAGON 4			
Conversion Bus (4 spd)	**12020**	2625	3525
GL 7-Seater (4 spd)	**15320**	3975	4875
GL Wolfsburg 7-Seater (4 spd)	**17315**	4525	5450
Camper (4 spd)	**17325**	5225	6200
Camper GL (4 spd)	**20100**	6200	7225
ADD FOR:			
Bestseller Pkg (Cabriolet)	**630**	185	225
Weekender Pkg (Vanagon GL)	**280**	100	125

NOTE: Power brakes standard on all models. Air conditioning standard on Quantum. Power windows standard on Quantum GL. Power door locks standard on Vanagon GL Wolfsburg. Power steering standard on GTI 16-Valve, Jetta Wolfsburg, Jetta GL, Jetta GLI, Cabriolet Wolfsburg, Scirocco 16-Valve, Quantum and Camper GL.

1986

Year-Model-Body Type	Original List	Current Whlse	Average Retail
CABRIOLET 4			
2 Dr Convertible (5 spd)	**11995**	4325	5250
GOLF 4			
2 Dr Diesel Htchbk (5 spd)	**7665**	1225	1950
2 Dr Htchbk (5 spd)	**7865**	1525	2375
4 Dr Diesel Htchbk (5 spd)	**7875**	1275	2000
4 Dr Htchbk (5 spd)	**8075**	1625	2475
2 Dr Wolfsburg Htchbk (5 spd)	**8170**	1675	2525
4 Dr Wolfsburg Htchbk (5 spd)	**8380**	1725	2575
GTI 4			
2 Dr Htchbk (5 spd)	**9925**	2250	3100
JETTA 4			
2 Dr Diesel Cpe (5 spd)	**9035**	1525	2375
2 Dr Cpe (5 spd)	**9235**	1925	2775
4 Dr Diesel Sdn (5 spd)	**9255**	1475	2300
4 Dr Sdn (5 spd)	**9455**	1925	2775
4 Dr GL Sdn (5 spd)	**9800**	2200	3050
4 Dr GLI Sdn (5 spd)	**11415**	2775	3675
4 Dr GLI Wolfsburg (5 spd)	**11420**	2850	3750
4 Dr GLI Wolfsburg (auto)	**10075**	3075	3975
QUANTUM 5			
4 Dr (5 spd)	**13995**	2175	3025
4 Dr Wgn (5 spd)	**12570**	1850	2700
4 Dr Syncro (5 spd)	**15645**	2300	3175
SCIROCCO 4			
2 Dr Cpe	**10370**	2075	2925
VANAGON 4			
Conversion Bus (4 spd)	**11320**	1900	2750
L 7-Seater (4 spd)	**13490**	2275	3150
L 9-Seater (4 spd)	**13545**	2300	3175
GL 7-Seater (4 spd)	**14340**	3150	4050
Camper (4 spd)	**16150**	3925	4825
Camper GL (4 spd)	**18640**	4825	5750
Camper Syncro 4WD (4 spd)	**18325**	4825	5750
ADD FOR:			
Bestseller Pkg (Cabriolet)	**595**	125	155
Weekender Pkg (Vanagon GL & L)	**265**	55	70
Leather Trim (GTI)	**495**	105	130

NOTE: Power brakes standard on all models. Power windows standard on Quantum Sedan. Power locks standard on Quantum Sedan. Power steering standard on Jetta GLI, Scirocco, Camper GL, Quantum and Vanagon GL. Air conditioning standard on Quantum.

1985

Year-Model-Body Type	Original List	Current Whlse	Average Retail
CABRIOLET 4			
2 Dr Convertible (auto)	**11595**	3350	4250
GOLF 4			
2 Dr Diesel Htchbk (5 spd)	**7085**	650	1225
2 Dr Htchbk (5 spd)	**7285**	1050	1775
4 Dr Diesel Htchbk (5 spd)	**7295**	750	1475
4 Dr Htchbk (5 spd)	**7495**	1125	1850
GTI 4			
2 Dr Htchbk (5 spd)	**9285**	1650	2500
JETTA 4			
2 Dr Base Diesel Cpe (5 spd)	**8350**	1250	1975
2 Dr Base Cpe (5 spd)	**8550**	1625	2475
4 Dr Base Diesel Sdn (5 spd)	**8570**	1275	2000
4 Dr Base Sdn (5 spd)	**8770**	1700	2550
4 Dr GL Sdn (5 spd)	**9070**	1725	2575
4 Dr GLI Sdn (5 spd)	**10570**	2125	2975
QUANTUM 5			
4 Dr GL Sdn (5 spd)	**13295**	1550	2400
4 Dr Wgn (5 spd)	**11570**	1275	2000
SCIROCCO 4			
2 Dr Cpe (5 spd)	**9980**	1575	2425
VANAGON 4			
7-Seater L (4 spd)	**12865**	2200	3050
9-Seater L (4 spd)	**12920**	2225	3075

Refer To Optional Equipment Schedules

Year-Model-Body Type	Original List	Current Whlse	Average Retail
7-Seater GL (4 spd)	**13715**	2525	3400
Campmobile (4 spd)	**17190**	3600	4500
5-Seat Conversion Bus	**11790**	1975	2825
ADD FOR:			
Triple White Bestseller Pkg (Cabriolet)	**500**	75	100
Leather Trim (Scirocco)	**735**	95	120

NOTE: Power brakes standard on all models. Power steering standard on Jetta GLI, Quantum and Vanagon Camper. Air conditioning standard on Jetta GLI and Quantum. Power windows standard on Quantum.

1984

Year-Model-Body Type	Original List	Current Whlse	Average Retail
JETTA 4			
2 Dr Diesel Sdn (4 spd)	**7955**	575	1075
2 Dr Sdn (5 spd)	**7955**	900	1625
4 Dr Diesel Sdn (4 spd)	**8175**	625	1175
4 Dr Sdn (5 spd)	**8415**	1075	1800
4 Dr GL Sdn (5 spd)	**8775**	1200	1925
4 Dr Turbo Diesel Sdn (5 spd)	**9775**	875	1600
4 Dr GLI Sdn (5 spd)	**9255**	1450	2225
QUANTUM 4			
4 Dr GL Turbo Diesel Sdn (5 spd)	**13530**	850	1550
4 Dr GL Sdn (5 spd)	**12980**	1025	1750
4 Dr Wolfsburg Ltd Ed Sdn (5 spd)	**13480**	1125	1850
4 Dr GL Turbo Diesel Wgn (5 spd)	**14330**	800	1500
4 Dr GL Wgn (5 spd)	**13780**	900	1625
4 Dr Wolfsburg Ltd Ed Wgn (5 spd)	**14280**	1050	1775
RABBIT 4			
2 Dr Conv (5 spd)	**10980**	2525	3400
2 Dr Conv Wolfsburg Ltd Ed (5 spd)	**11380**	2600	3475
2 Dr L Htchbk (4 spd)	**6695**	700	1325
2 Dr L Diesel Htchbk (4 spd)	**6555**	225	475
2 Dr Wolfsburg Ltd Ed Htchbk (4 spd)	**7160**	725	1375
2 Dr GTI Htchbk (5 spd)	**8515**	1200	1925
4 Dr L Htchbk (4 spd)	**6905**	750	1475
4 Dr L Diesel Htchbk (4 spd)	**6765**	300	575
4 Dr Wolfsburg Ltd Ed Htchbk (4 spd)	**7370**	800	1500
4 Dr GL Htchbk (4 spd)	**7295**	900	1625
SCIROCCO 4			
2 Dr Cpe (5 spd)	**10870**	1250	1975
2 Dr Wolfsburg Ltd Ed (5 spd)	**9975**	1275	2000
VANAGON 4			
7-Seater (4 spd)	**12240**	1550	2400
9-Seater (4 spd)	**12295**	1550	2400
7-Seater GL (4 spd)	**12740**	1650	2500
7-Seater Wolfsburg Ltd Ed (4 spd)	**13140**	1675	2525
Campmobile (4 spd)	**16365**	2575	3450
Campmobile Wolfsburg Ltd Ed (4 spd)	**17365**	2675	3575

1983 — ALL BODY STYLES

Year-Model-Body Type	Original List	Current Whlse	Average Retail
JETTA 4	—	800	1500
QUANTUM	—	625	1175
RABBIT CONVERTIBLE	—	1800	2650
RABBIT HATCHBACKS	—	550	1025
RABBIT PICKUPS	—	110	300
SCIROCCO	—	825	1525
VANAGON	—	1100	1825
CAMPMOBILE	—	1900	2750

VOLVO

1992

Year-Model-Body Type	Original List	Current Whlse	Average Retail
240 4			
4 Dr Sdn (5 spd)	**20820**	—	—
5 Dr Wgn (5 spd)	**21320**	—	—
4 Dr GL Sdn (5 spd)	**21495**	—	—
ADD FOR:			
Anti-Lock Brakes	**995**	—	—
Leather Seat Trim	**595**	—	—
Alloy Wheels	**325**	—	—
740 4			
4 Dr Sdn (auto)	**24285**	—	—
5 Dr Wgn (auto)	**24965**	—	—
5 Dr GL Wgn (auto)	**25675**	—	—
5 Dr Turbo Wgn (auto)	**27795**	—	—
ADD FOR:			
Leather Seat Trim	**895**	—	—
Alloy Wheels (Turbo)	**225**	—	—
(Base, GL)	**325**	—	—
940 4			
4 Dr GL Sdn (auto)	**24995**	—	—
4 Dr Turbo Sdn (auto)	**30795**	—	—
5 Dr Turbo Wgn (auto)	**31475**	—	—
ADD FOR:			
Leather Seat Trim (GL)	**895**	—	—
Alloy Wheels (GL)	**325**	—	—

Year-Model-Body Type	Original List	Current Whlse	Average Retail
960 6			
4 Dr Sdn (auto)	**33975**	—	—
5 Dr Wgn (auto)	**34655**	—	—

NOTE: Cruise control standard on 940. Power windows and power door locks standard on all models. Power sunroof standard on 240 GL, 740 Turbo and 940.

1991

Year-Model-Body Type	Original List	Current Whlse	Average Retail
240 4			
4 Dr Sdn (5 spd)	**19620**	13200	15525
5 Dr Wgn (5 spd)	**20115**	13875	16250
5 Dr SE Wgn (5 spd)	**22855**	—	—
740 4			
4 Dr Sdn (auto)	**23175**	15475	18125
5 Dr Wgn (auto)	**23855**	16150	18800
4 Dr Turbo Sdn (5 spd)	**25310**	16775	19425
5 Dr Turbo Wgn	**25990**	17275	19925
4 Dr SE Sdn (auto)	**28455**	—	—
5 Dr SE Wgn (auto)	**29135**	—	—
940 4			
4 Dr GLE Sdn (auto)	**27885**	20325	23375
4 Dr Turbo Sdn (auto)	**29985**	21550	24850
4 Dr SE Sdn (auto)	**33775**	—	—
5 Dr GLE Wgn (auto)	**28565**	21025	24325
5 Dr Turbo Wgn (auto)	**30665**	—	—
5 Dr SE Wgn (auto)	**34455**	—	—
COUPE 4			
2 Dr Turbo Cpe (auto)	**41945**	—	—
ADD FOR:			
Anti-Lock Brakes (240 Base, 740 Base)	**995**	500	600
Leather Upholstery (240 Base)	**595**	300	360
(740, 940 GLE)	**895**	450	550

NOTE: Power brakes, power door locks and power windows standard on all models. Power steering standard on 940 Turbo & SE and Coupe. Power sunroof standard on 740 Turbo & SE, 940 and Coupe.

1990

Year-Model-Body Type	Original List	Current Whlse	Average Retail
240 4			
4 Dr Sdn (5 spd)	**16725**	9100	10475
5 Dr Wgn (5 spd)	**17215**	9725	11200
240 DL 4			
4 Dr Sdn (5 spd)	**18820**	9975	11500
5 Dr Wgn (5 spd)	**19310**	10600	12225
740 BASE			
4 Dr Sdn (5 spd)	**21095**	10950	12625
5 Dr Wgn (5 spd)	**21775**	11575	13375
740 GL 4			
4 Dr Sgn (5 spd)	**22135**	11550	13350
5 Dr Wgn (5 spd)	**22815**	12150	14025
740 GLE 4			
4 Dr Sdn (5 spd)	**25950**	12975	15300
5 Dr Wgn (5 spd)	**26630**	13600	15975
740 TURBO 4			
4 Dr Sdn (4 spd)	**26285**	13425	15750
5 Dr Wgn (4 spd)	**26965**	14050	16500
760 GLE 6			
4 Dr Sdn (auto)	**33965**	16475	19125
760 TURBO 4			
4 Dr Sdn (auto)	**33965**	17025	19675
5 Dr Wgn (auto)	**34645**	17625	20275
780 GLE 6			
2 Dr Cpe (auto)	**38735**	19175	22225
780 TURBO 4			
2 Dr Cpe (auto)	**39950**	19725	22775
ADD FOR:			
Anti-Lock Braking System (740 Base & GL)	**1175**	450	525
Leather Upholstery (740)	**895**	375	450

NOTE: Power brakes and power door locks standard on all models. Anti-lock brakes standard on 740 GLE, 740 Turbo, 760 Series and 780 Series. Power seat standard on 760 Series and 780 Series. Power windows standard on 240 DL, 740 Series, 760 Series and 780 Series. Sunroof standard on 240 DL Sedan, 740 GL, 740 GLE, 740 Turbo, 760 Series and 780 Series.

1989

Year-Model-Body Type	Original List	Current Whlse	Average Retail
240 DL 4			
4 Dr Sdn (5 spd)	**17250**	8250	9525
5 Dr Wgn (5 spd)	**17740**	8825	10200
240 GL 4			
4 Dr Sdn (auto)	**20110**	9875	11375
5 Dr Wgn (auto)	**20850**	10450	12050
740 GL 4			
4 Dr Sdn (5 spd)	**20685**	9750	11225
5 Dr Wgn (5 spd)	**21365**	10300	11875
740 GLE 4			
4 Dr Sdn (5 spd)	**24565**	10925	12600
5 Dr Wgn (5 spd)	**26140**	11500	13275
740 TURBO 4			
4 Dr Sdn (5 spd)	**24925**	11325	13075
5 Dr Wgn (5 spd)	**25605**	11900	13750
760 GLE 6			
4 Dr Sdn (auto)	**32155**	13975	16350

VOLVO

Year-Model-Body Type	Original List	Current Whlse	Average Retail
760 TURBO 4			
4 Dr Sdn (auto)	**32940**	14500	17025
5 Dr Wgn (auto)	**32940**	15025	17675
780 GLE 6			
2 Dr Cpe (auto)	**37790**	16525	19175
780 TURBO 4			
2 Dr Cpe (auto)	**38975**	17025	19675

NOTE: Power brakes and power door locks standard on all models. Power windows standard on 240 GL, 740 Series, 760 Series and 780 Series. Power sunroof standard on 240 GL, 740 Series (manual on 740 GL), 760 Series and 780 Series.

1988

Year-Model-Body Type	Original List	Current Whlse	Average Retail
240 DL 4			
4 Dr Sdn (5 spd)	**17250**	6625	7700
5 Dr Wgn (5 spd)	**17740**	7125	8275
240 GL 4			
4 Dr Sdn (auto)	**20035**	7950	9225
5 Dr Wgn (auto)	**20775**	8475	9800
740 GLE 4			
4 Dr Sdn (4 spd)	**21850**	8075	9325
5 Dr Wgn (5 spd)	**23425**	8600	9925
4 Dr Turbo Sdn (5 spd)	**24925**	8850	10225
5 Dr Turbo Wgn (4 spd)	**25605**	9375	10800
760 GLE 6			
4 Dr Sdn (auto)	**32155**	11175	12900
4 Dr Turbo Sdn (auto)	**32940**	11650	13450
5 Dr Turbo Wgn (auto)	**32940**	12150	14025
780 GLE 6			
2 Dr Cpe (auto)	**39880**	13650	16025
ADD FOR:			
Anti-Lock Braking System (740 GLE)	**1175**	325	375
Leather Upholstery (240 GL Sdn)	**785**	250	300
(740 GLE Sdn, 740 GLE Sdn, 740 GLE Turbo Sdn & Wgn)	**895**	275	325
Metallic Paint (240 DL)	**380**	75	100
Pearlescent Paint (780 GLE)	**320**	75	100
Restraint System (740 GLE Sdn & Wgn)	**850**	200	250

NOTE: Power steering, power brakes, power door locks and air conditioning standard on all models. Power windows standard on 240 GL, 740 GLE, 760 GLE and 780 GLE. Sunroof standard on 240 GL, 740 GLE and 760 GLE. Power seat standard on 760 GLE and 780 GLE. Moonroof standard on 780 GLE.

1987

Year-Model-Body Type	Original List	Current Whlse	Average Retail
240 DL 4			
4 Dr Sdn (5 spd)	**15690**	4775	5700
5 Dr Wgn (5 spd)	**16180**	5250	6175
240 GL 4			
4 Dr Sdn (auto & sunroof)	**18385**	5975	6900
5 Dr Wgn (auto & sunroof)	**19070**	6475	7525
740 GLE 4			
4 Dr Sdn (4 spd & sunroof)	**20695**	5850	6775
5 Dr Wgn (4 spd & sunroof)	**22150**	6350	7400
4 Dr Turbo Sdn (4 spd & sunroof)	**22710**	6325	7350
5 Dr Turbo Wgn (4 spd & sunroof)	**23310**	6825	7950
760 GLE 4			
4 Dr Turbo Sdn (auto & sunroof)	**28340**	7675	8900
5 Dr Turbo Wgn (auto & sunroof)	**27765**	8175	9450
4 Dr Sdn (6 cyl) (auto & sunroof)	**28290**	7275	8450
780 GLE 6			
2 Dr Cpe (auto & moonroof)	**34785**	10050	11600
ADD FOR:			
Leather Upholstery (240 GL Sdn)	**730**	200	250
(740 GLE Sdn ex. Turbo)	**855**	225	275
Metallic Paint (240 DL)	**380**	75	100
Restraint System (740 GLE, 760 Turbos)	**850**	200	250

NOTE: Air conditioning, power steering, power brakes and power door locks standard on all models. Power windows and sunroof standard on 240 GL, 740 GLE, 760 GLE and 780 GLE.

1986

Year-Model-Body Type	Original List	Current Whlse	Average Retail
DL 4			
4 Dr Sdn (4 spd)	**14615**	3650	4550
5 Dr Wgn (4 spd)	**15105**	3975	4875
GL 4			
4 Dr Sdn (4 spd & sunroof)	**16695**	4250	5175
5 Dr Wgn (4 spd)	**17280**	4675	5600
740 GLE 4			
4 Dr Sdn (4 spd & sunroof)	**18525**	4700	5625

Year-Model-Body Type	Original List	Current Whlse	Average Retail
4 Dr Turbo Sdn (4 spd & sunroof)	**20505**	5275	6150
5 Dr Wgn (4 spd & sunroof)	**19750**	5125	6050
5 Dr Turbo Wgn (4 spd & sunroof)	**20995**	5525	6450
4 Dr Turbo Diesel Sdn (6 cyl) (auto)	**20095**	4500	5425
4 Dr Turbo Diesel Wgn (auto & sunroof)	**21320**	4850	5775
760 GLE 4			
4 Dr Turbo Sdn (4 spd & sunroof)	**24480**	5575	6450
4 Dr Turbo Wgn (auto & sunroof)	**25425**	6325	7350
4 Dr Sdn (6 cyl) (auto & sunroof)	**23625**	5525	6450
ADD FOR:			
Leather Upholstery			
(GL Sdn)	**630**	135	165
(740 GLE Sdn except Turbo)	**735**	155	190
Metallic Paint (DL)	**380**	50	75

NOTE: Power brakes, power locks and power steering standard on all models. Power windows and sunroof standard on GL, 740 GLE and 760 GLE. Power seat and air conditioning standard on 760 GLE. Automatic transmission standard on 740 GLE Turbo Diesel and 760 GLE (gas & turbo).

1985

Year-Model-Body Type	Original List	Current Whlse	Average Retail
DL 4			
4 Dr Sdn (4 spd)	**13920**	2525	3400
5 Dr Wgn (4 spd)	**14395**	2875	3775
GL 4			
4 Dr Sdn (4 spd & sunroof)	**16225**	3000	3900
5 Dr Wgn (4 spd)	**16755**	3325	4225
5 Dr Wgn (auto)	**17190**	3575	4475
GLT 4			
4 Dr Turbo Sdn (4 spd & sunroof)	**18420**	3425	4325
5 Dr Turbo Wgn (4 spd)	**18950**	3750	4650
5 Dr Turbo Wgn (auto)	**19385**	4000	4900
740 GLE 4			
4 Dr Sdn (4 spd & sunroof)	**18150**	3525	4425
4 Dr Turbo Sdn (4 spd & sunroof)	**20130**	4050	4950
4 Dr Turbo Diesel Sdn (4 spd w/overdrive)	**19015**	2825	3725
5 Dr Wgn (4 spd w/overdrive & sunroof)	**19360**	3850	4750
5 Dr Turbo Diesel Wgn (4 spd w/overdrive & sunroof)	**20760**	3050	3950
5 Dr Turbo Wgn (4 spd w/overdrive & sunroof)	**21340**	4350	5275
760 GLE 4			
4 Dr Sdn (auto & sunroof)	**21985**	4025	4925
4 Dr Turbo Sdn (4 spd & sunroof)	**22965**	4225	5150
4 Dr Diesel Turbo Sdn (auto & sunroof)	**23185**	3450	4350
5 Dr Turbo Wgn (4 spd w/overdrive & sunroof)	**23440**	4575	5500
ADD FOR:			
Metallic Paint (DL)	**380**	50	60
Audio Pkg (740 GLE)	**800**	100	125
Leather Upholstery			
(740 GLE)	**735**	95	120
(GL Turbo Sdn)	**590**	75	95

NOTE: Power steering, power brakes and air conditioning standard on all models. Sunroof and power windows standard on GL, GLT and 740 GLE and 760 GLE. Power door locks standard on GLT, 740 GLE and 760 GLE.

1984

Year-Model-Body Type	Original List	Current Whlse	Average Retail
760 6			
4 Dr (auto & sunroof)	**21657**	2525	3400
4 Dr Turbo (4 spd)	**22353**	2675	3550
4 Dr Turbo Diesel (4 spd)	**22655**	2175	3025
DL 4			
2 Dr (4 spd)	**11953**	2125	2975
4 Dr (4 spd)	**12583**	2225	3075
5 Dr Wgn (4 spd)	**13008**	2450	3325
GL 4			
4 Dr (4 spd & sunroof)	**15673**	2300	3175
4 Dr Diesel (4 spd & sunroof)	**15705**	1875	2725
5 Dr Wgn (4 spd)	**16228**	2575	3450
5 Dr Diesel Wgn (4 spd)	**16260**	2125	2975
GLT 4			
2 Dr Turbo (4 spd & sunroof)	**17142**	2375	3250
4 Dr Turbo (4 spd & sunroof)	**17452**	2475	3350
5 Dr Turbo Wgn (4 spd)	**18007**	2750	3650

Refer To Optional Equipment Schedules

Year-Model-Body Type	Original List	Current Whlse	Average Retail
1983 — ALL BODY STYLES			
760 GLE	—	2475	3400
DL 4	—	1900	2750
GL 4	—	2100	2950
GLT 4	—	2100	2950

YUGO

Year-Model-Body Type	Original List	Current Whlse	Average Retail
1991			
YUGO 4			
3 Dr GV Plus Htchbk (NA w/power steering)	**5824**	—	—
2 Dr Cabrio Conv (NA w/power steering)	**10168**	—	—
NOTE: Power brakes standard on all models.			
1990			
YUGO 4			
3 Dr GV Plus Htchbk (NA w/power steering)	**4435**	875	1600
2 Dr Cabrio Conv (NA w/power steering)	**10168**	—	—
NOTE: Power brakes standard on all models.			
1989			
YUGO 4			
3 Dr GV Htchbk (NA w/power steering)	**5607**	575	1075
3 Dr GVL Htchbk (NA w/power steering)	**5837**	725	1375
NOTE: Power brakes standard on all models.			
1988			
YUGO 4			
3 Dr GV Htchbk (4 spd)	**4349**	400	725
3 Dr GVL Htchbk (4 spd)	**4599**	500	925
3 Dr GVX Htchbk (5 spd)	**5699**	600	1225
NOTE: Power brakes standard on all models.			
1987			
YUGO 4			
3 Dr GV Htchbk (4 spd)	**3990**	350	625
3 Dr GVX Htchbk (5 spd)	**—**	525	1075
NOTE: Power brakes standard on all models.			
1986			
YUGO 4			
3 Dr Htchbk	**3990**	175	375
NOTE: Power brakes standard.			

LIGHT TRUCK PRICES

Add 5% to all models for points west of the Mississippi

CHEVROLET

Year-Model-Body Type	Original List	Current Whlse	Average Retail
1992			
S-10 BLAZER 2WD 6			
2 Dr Sport Utility	**15603**	—	—
4 Dr Sport Utility	**16563**	—	—
ADD FOR:			
CAA2 Tahoe/Sport Equip Pkg	**1024**	—	—
CAA3 Tahoe/Sport Equip Pkg	**2870**	—	—
DAA2 Tahoe/Sport Equip Pkg (2WD 4 Dr)	**554**	—	—
DAA3 Tahoe/Sport Equip Pkg (2WD 4 Dr)	**2575**	—	—
DAA3 Tahoe/Sport Equip Pkg (4WD 4 Dr)	**2202**	—	—
Tahoe LT Group	**3601**	—	—
Enhanced Powertrain Pkg	**1160**	—	—
K-1500 BLAZER 4WD 111.5" WB 8			
Wgn	**20125**	—	—
ADD FOR:			
K5A2 Silverado Pkg	**2276**	—	—
K5A3 Silverado Pkg	**2933**	—	—
Sport Silverado Pkg	**2926**	—	—

Year-Model-Body Type	Original List	Current Whlse	Average Retail
C-1500 PICKUPS 117.5" WB 6*			
Fleetside	13900	—	—
Sportside	14300	—	—
* For 8 cylinder models add $— wholesale and $— retail.			
C-1500 PICKUPS 117.5" WB 8			
454 SS Fleetside	20585	—	—
C-1500 PICKUPS 131.5" WB 6*			
Fleetside	14200	—	—
Work Truck Fleetside	11405	—	—
* For 8 cylinder models add $— wholesale and $— retail.			
C-1500 EXTENDED PICKUPS 141.5" WB 6*			
Fleetside	14850	—	—
Sportside	15250	—	—
* For 8 cylinder models add $— wholesale and $— retail.			
C-1500 EXTENDED PICKUPS 155.5" WB 6*			
Fleetside	15140	—	—
* For 8 cylinder models add $— wholesale and $— retail.			
ADD FOR:			
5.7 Liter 8 Cyl Eng	845	—	—
6.2 Liter 8 Cyl Diesel Eng	2400	—	—
Work Truck Group 2	790	—	—
Scottsdale Pkg	738	—	—
P1A3 Silverado Pkg	1948	—	—
P1A4 Silverado Pkg	2820	—	—
Sport Scottsdale Pkg	1378	—	—
Sport Silverado Pkg (2WD)	2881	—	—
(4WD)	3129	—	—
C-2500 PICKUP 131.5" WB 6*			
Fleetside	14840	—	—
* For 8 cylinder models add $— wholesale and $— retail.			
C-2500 HD PICKUP 131.5" WB 6*			
Fleetside	15673	—	—
* For 8 cylinder models add $— wholesale and $— retail.			
C-2500 EXTENDED PICKUP 141.5" WB 6*			
Fleetside	15960	—	—
* For 8 cylinder models add $— wholesale and $— retail.			
C-2500 EXTENDED PICKUP 155.5" WB 6*			
Fleetside	16240	—	—
* For 8 cylinder models add $— wholesale and $— retail.			
C-2500 HD EXTENDED PICKUP 155" WB 6*			
Fleetside	16733	—	—
* For 8 cylinder models add $— wholesale and $— retail.			
ADD FOR:			
5.7 Liter 8 Cyl Eng	845	—	—
7.4 Liter 8 Cyl Eng	1315	—	—
6.2 Liter 8 Cyl Diesel Eng	2400	—	—
6.5 Liter 8 Cyl Turbo Diesel Eng	3100	—	—
Scottsdale Pkg	853	—	—
Silverado Pkg	2453	—	—
S-10 PICKUPS 4*			
Fleetside EL (108" WB)	9883	—	—
Fleetside (108" WB)	10888	—	—
Fleetside (118" WB)	11188	—	—
Fleetside Maxi Cab (123" WB)	12113	—	—
* For 6 cylinder models add $— wholesale and $— retail.			
ADD FOR:			
4.3 Liter 6 Cyl Eng	620	—	—
C-1500 SUBURBAN 129.5" WB 8			
Panel Doors	19000	—	—
ADD FOR:			
NA2 Silverado Pkg	3507	—	—
NA3 Silverado Pkg	4796	—	—
C-2500 SUBURBAN 129.5" WB 8			
Panel Doors	20204	—	—
ADD FOR:			
7.4 Liter 8 Cyl Eng	470	—	—
Silverado Pkg	4528	—	—
ASTRO 111" WB 2WD 6			
Cargo Van	14840	—	—
Extended Cargo Van	15510	—	—
Pass Van	16030	—	—
Extended Pass Van	16720	—	—
ADD FOR:			
4.3 Liter 6 Cyl Eng (2WD models)	500	—	—
CL Decor Pkg	633	—	—
LT Decor Pkg	2848	—	—
LUMINA APV 6			
Cargo Van	15205	—	—
Wgn	16400	—	—
CL Wgn	17355	—	—
ADD FOR:			
3.8 Liter 6 Cyl Eng	619	—	—
G-10 VANS 110" WB 6*			
Chevyvan	15290	—	—
Sportvan	17030	—	—
* For 8 cylinder models add $— wholesale and $— retail.			
G-10 VANS 125" WB 6*			
Chevyvan	15570	—	—
Sportvan	17970	—	—
* For 8 cylinder models add $— wholesale and $— retail.			

Refer To Optional Equipment Schedules

Year-Model-Body Type	Original List	Current Whlse	Average Retail
ADD FOR:			
Beauville Group (Sportvan)	**3652**	—	—
Beauville Trim Pkg (Sportvan)	**818**	—	—
G-20 VANS 125" WB 6*			
Chevyvan	**15810**	—	—
Sportvan	**18160**	—	—
* For 8 cylinder models add $— wholesale and $— retail.			
ADD FOR:			
5.7 Liter 8 Cyl Eng	**845**	—	—
6.2 Liter LD 8 Cyl Eng	**2400**	—	—
1991			
S-10 BLAZER 2WD 6			
2 Dr Sport Utility	**14625**	11175	12775
4 Dr Sport Utility	**15865**	11875	13575
V-1500 BLAZER 4WD 106.5" WB 8			
Wgn	**18435**	13275	15475
Wgn, HD Diesel	**21363**	13750	16000
C-1500 GAS PICKUPS 117.5" WB 6*			
Fleetside	**12920**	8875	10125
Sportside	**13260**	9000	10250
454 SS Fleetside (8 cyl)	**19610**	12900	15100
Fleetside (131" WB)	**13220**	9225	10500
Fleetside Extended Cab (141" WB)	**13870**	9775	11125
Sportside Extended Cab (141" WB)	**14210**	9850	11200
Fleetside Extended Cab (155" WB)	**14160**	9875	11250
* For 8 cylinder models add $425 wholesale and $425 retail.			
C-1500 DIESEL PICKUPS 131.5" WB 8			
Fleetside	**16250**	10175	11600
Fleetside Extended Cab (141" WB)	**16690**	10650	12150
Sportside Extended Cab (141" WB)	**17030**	10725	12250
Fleetside Extended Cab (155" WB)	**16980**	10750	12275
C-2500 GAS PICKUPS 131.5" WB 6*			
Fleetside	**13860**	9650	10975
Heavy Duty Fleetside	**14514**	9900	11275
Fleetside Extended Cab (141" WB)	**14980**	10450	11925
Fleetside Extended Cab (155" WB)	**15260**	10575	12075
Heavy Duty Fleetside Extended Cab (155" WB)	**15564**	10875	12425
* For 8 cylinder models add $425 wholesale and $425 retail.			
C-2500 DIESEL PICKUPS 131.5" WB 8			
Fleetside	**16320**	10475	11950
Heavy Duty Fleetside	**16793**	10775	12300
Fleetside Extended Cab (141" WB)	**17430**	11325	12950
Fleetside Extended Cab (155" WB)	**17720**	11450	13100
Heavy Duty Fleetside Extended Cab (155" WB)	**17904**	11750	13425
S-10 REG CAB PICKUPS 4*			
Fleetside EL (108" WB) (NA w/power steering)	**9350**	5750	6550
Fleetside (108" WB)	**10645**	6325	7225
Fleetside (118" WB)	**10945**	6425	7350
Fleetside Extended Cab (123" WB)	**12226**	6925	7925
* For 6 cylinder models add $450 wholesale and $450 retail.			
R-1500 SUBURBAN 129.5" WB 8			
Panel Doors	**17405**	13575	15825
Tailgate	**17565**	13675	15925
Panel Doors, Diesel	**19843**	14050	16300
Tailgate, Diesel	**19998**	14150	16475
R-2500 SUBURBAN 129.5" WB 8			
Panel Doors	**18963**	14100	16425
Tailgate	**19113**	14200	16525
Panel Doors, Diesel	**20701**	14525	16925
Tailgate, Diesel	**20861**	14600	17000
ASTRO 111" WB 6			
Cargo Van	**14305**	9325	10600
CS Pass Van	**15425**	11250	12850
CL Pass Van	**16505**	11950	13675
LT Pass Van	**18055**	12500	14525
ASTRO EXTENDED 111" WB 6			
Cargo Van	**14975**	10075	11475
CS Pass Van	**16115**	12075	13800
CL Pass Van	**17195**	12750	14950
LT Pass Van	**18745**	13325	15525
LUMINA APV 6			
Cargo Van	**14422**	—	—
Wgn	**15560**	10900	12450
CL Wgn	**16450**	11600	13250
G-10 VANS 110" WB 6*			
Chevyvan	**14585**	9225	10500
Sportvan	**16315**	10700	12200
Beauville (125" WB)	**18155**	11950	13675
w/125" WB add (Chevyvan)	**280**	120	150
(Sportvan)	**950**	510	620
* For 8 cylinder models add $425 wholesale and $425 retail.			

Year-Model-Body Type	Original List	Current Whlse	Average Retail
G-20 VANS 110" WB 6*			
Chevyvan	**14765**	9400	10700
Chevyvan Diesel (8 cyl)	**17438**	10200	11625
Chevyvan Diesel (125" WB) (8 cyl)	**17728**	10400	11875
Sportvan (125" WB)	**17415**	11025	12575
Beauville Sportvan (125" WB)	**18295**	12100	13850
Sportvan Diesel (125" WB) (8 cyl)	**20085**	11875	13575
Beauville Sportvan Diesel (125" WB) (8 cyl)	**20838**	12950	15150
w/125" WB add (Chevyvan)	**290**	120	150
* For 8 cylinder models add $425 wholesale and $425 retail.			
ADD FOR:			
Baja Equip (S-10 4WD Pickups)	**1260**	690	850
Scottsdale Pkg (C-K Pickups)	**573**	290	350
Silverado Pkg (V-1500 Blazer)	**1298**	710	870
(C-K Pickups)	**1012**	1310	1590
(Suburban)	**1600**	1630	1970
Tahoe Equip Pkg (S-10 Blazer)	**841**	450	550
(S-10 Pickup)	**587**	290	360

1990

Year-Model-Body Type	Original List	Current Whlse	Average Retail
S-10 BLAZER 2WD 100.5" WB 6			
Sport Utility	**13695**	7550	8625
V-10 BLAZER 4WD 106.5" WB 8			
Wgn	**17305**	10000	11375
Wgn, Diesel	**19998**	10450	11925
C-1500 GAS PICKUPS 117.5" WB 6*			
Fleetside	**12080**	6900	7900
Sportside	**12405**	7000	8000
454 SS Fleetside (8 cyl)	**18295**	10250	11700
Fleetside (131" WB)	**12380**	7150	8175
Fleetside Extended Cab (141" WB)	**12990**	7725	8825
Fleetside Extended Cab (155" WB)	**13270**	7850	8975
Fleetside Work Truck (131" WB)	**11347**	6700	7650
* For 8 cylinder models add $400 wholesale and $400 retail.			
C-1500 DIESEL PICKUPS 131.5" WB 8			
Fleetside	**15170**	7825	8950
Fleetside Extended Cab (141" WB)	**15600**	8575	9775
Fleetside Extended Cab (155" WB)	**15875**	8725	9950
C-2500 GAS PICKUPS 131.5" WB 6*			
Fleetside	**12985**	7625	8725
Heavy Duty Fleetside	**13609**	7875	9000
Fleetside Extended Cab (141" WB)	**14055**	8375	9525
Fleetside Extended Cab (155" WB)	**14335**	8500	9675
Heavy Duty Fleetside Extended Cab (155" WB)	**14624**	8675	9875
* For 8 cylinder models add $400 wholesale and $400 retail.			
C-2500 DIESEL PICKUPS 131.5" WB 8			
Fleetside	**15235**	8475	9650
Heavy Duty Fleetside	**15694**	8725	9950
Fleetside Extended Cab (141" WB)	**16305**	9225	10500
Fleetside Extended Cab (155" WB)	**16585**	10450	12050
Heavy Duty Fleetside Extended Cab (155" WB)	**16759**	10525	12000
S-10 REG CAB PICKUPS 4*			
Fleetside EL (108" WB) (NA w/power steering)	**8951**	5075	5875
Fleetside (108" WB)	**10265**	5225	6025
Fleetside (118" WB)	**10430**	5350	6150
Fleetside Extended Cab (123" WB)	**11215**	6775	7750
* For 6 cylinder models add $425 wholesale and $425 retail.			
R-1500 SUBURBAN 129.5" WB 8			
Panel Doors	**16435**	11150	12750
Tailgate	**16586**	11250	12850
Panel Doors, Diesel	**18703**	11600	13250
Tailgate, Diesel	**18848**	11700	13375
R-2500 SUBURBAN 129.5" WB 8			
Panel Doors	**17058**	11550	13200
Tailgate	**17203**	11650	13325
Panel Doors, HD Diesel	**19286**	12000	13750
Tailgate, HD Diesel	**19436**	12100	13850
ASTRO 111" WB 6			
Cargo Van (4 cyl)	**12915**	6625	7575
CS Pass Van	**14610**	8875	10125
CL Pass Van	**15650**	9475	10775
LT Pass Van	**17145**	10000	11375
ASTRO EXTENDED 111" WB 6			
Cargo Van (4 cyl)	**14217**	7300	8350
CS Pass Van	**15312**	9550	10875
CL Pass Van	**16352**	10100	11525
LT Pass Van	**17847**	10700	12200

Refer To Optional Equipment Schedules

Year-Model-Body Type	Original List	Current Whlse	Average Retail
LUMINA APV 6			
Cargo Van	**13700**	—	—
Wgn	**14800**	10925	12475
CL Wgn	**15745**	11625	13300
G-10 VANS 110" WB 6*			
Chevyvan	**13600**	7100	8100
Sportvan	**15515**	8575	9775
Beauville (125" WB)	**17270**	9675	11000
w/125" WB add (Chevyvan)	**270**	140	170
(Sportvan)	**905**	410	510
* For 8 cylinder models add $400 wholesale and $400 retail.			
G-20 VANS 110" WB 6*			
Chevyvan	**13770**	7225	8250
Chevyvan Diesel (8 cyl)	**16408**	8075	9250
Chevyvan Diesel (125" WB) (8 cyl)	**16678**	8225	9375
Sportvan (125" WB)	**16565**	8975	10225
Beauville Sportvan (125" WB)	**17410**	9825	11175
Sportvan Diesel (125" WB) (8 cyl)	**18888**	9775	11125
Beauville Sportvan Diesel (125" WB) (8 cyl)	**19678**	10600	12100
w/125" WB add (Chevyvan)	**280**	140	170
* For 8 cylinder models add $400 wholesale and $400 retail.			
ADD FOR:			
Baja Equip (S-10 4WD Pickups)	**1260**	600	730
Scottsdale Pkg (C-K Pickups)	**557**	230	290
Silverado Pkg (V-10 Blazer)	**1281**	610	740
(Suburban)	**1583**	760	930
(C-K Pickups)	**1025**	470	580
Sport Pkg (S-10 Blazer)	**1038**	480	590
Tahoe Pkg (S-10 Blazer)	**841**	380	470
(S Pickups)	**574**	250	310

1989

Year-Model-Body Type	Original List	Current Whlse	Average Retail
S-10 BLAZER 2WD 100.5" WB 6			
Sport Utility	**11680**	6375	7275
V-10 BLAZER 4WD 106.5" WB 8			
Wgn	**15355**	8650	9850
Wgn, Diesel	**18085**	9050	10325
C-10 GAS PICKUPS 117.5" WB 6*			
Fleetside	**10335**	5750	6550
Sportside	**10553**	5825	6625
Fleetside Extended Cab (141" WB)	**11267**	6600	7550
Fleetside Extended Cab (155" WB)	**11467**	6775	7750
w/131" WB add	**200**	125	150
* For 8 cylinder models add $375 wholesale and $375 retail.			
C-10 DIESEL PICKUPS 131.5" WB 8			
Fleetside	**13318**	6550	7475
Fleetside Extended Cab (141" WB)	**13853**	7375	8425
Fleetside Extended Cab (155" WB)	**14053**	7575	8650
C-20 GAS PICKUPS 131.5" WB 6*			
Fleetside	**11143**	6450	7375
Heavy Duty Fleetside	**12378**	6700	7650
Fleetside Extended Cab (141" WB)	**12298**	7000	8000
Fleetside Extended Cab (155" WB)	**12498**	7200	8225
Heavy Duty Fleetside Extended Cab (155" WB) (8 cyl)	**13413**	7775	8900
* For 8 cylinder models add $375 wholesale and $375 retail.			
C-20 DIESEL PICKUPS 131.5" WB 8			
Fleetside	**13383**	7225	8250
Heavy Duty Fleetside	**13828**	7475	8550
Fleetside Extended Cab (141" WB)	**14538**	7775	8900
Fleetside Extended Cab (155" WB)	**14738**	7975	9125
Heavy Duty Fleetside Extended Cab (155" WB)	**14911**	8175	9300
R-20 GAS PICKUPS 164.5" WB 8			
Fleetside Bonus Cab	**14164**	7725	8825
Fleetside Crew Cab	**14664**	7925	9075
R-20 HD DIESEL PICKUPS 164.5" WB 8			
Fleetside Bonus Cab	**15164**	8125	9250
Fleetside Crew Cab	**15664**	8325	9475
S-10 REG CAB PICKUPS 4			
Fleetside EL (108" WB)	**7474**	4350	5150
Fleetside (108" WB)	**8585**	4525	5425
Fleetside (118" WB)	**8750**	4625	5425
Fleetside Extended Cab (123" WB)	**9435**	4975	5775
* For 6 cylinder models add $400 wholesale and $400 retail.			
R-10 SUBURBAN 129.5" WB 8			
Panel Doors	**14545**	9275	10550
Tailgate	**14585**	9375	10675

Year-Model-Body Type	Original List	Current Whlse	Average Retail
Panel Doors, Diesel	**16895**	9650	10975
Tailgate, Diesel	**16935**	9725	11075
R-20 SUBURBAN 129.5" WB 8			
Panel Doors	**15184**	9575	10900
Tailgate	**15224**	9650	10975
Panel Doors, HD Diesel	**17464**	9925	11300
Tailgate, HD Diesel	**17504**	10025	11400
ASTRO 111" WB 6*			
Cargo Van (4 cyl)	**10400**	4900	5700
CS Pass Van	**11900**	7100	8100
CL Pass Van	**12633**	7625	8725
LT Pass Van	**14144**	8175	9300
* For 6 cylinder models add $325 wholesale and $325 retail.			
G-10 VANS 110" WB 6*			
Chevyvan	**11145**	5125	5925
Sportvan	**12638**	6625	7575
Beauville (125" WB)	**14221**	7675	8775
w/125" WB add			
(Chevyvan)	**260**	110	140
(Sportvan)	**280**	120	150
* For 8 cylinder models add $375 wholesale and $375 retail.			
G-20 VANS 110" WB 6*			
Chevyvan	**11455**	5225	6025
Chevyvan Diesel (8 cyl)	**13853**	6050	6850
Chevyvan (125" WB)	**11725**	5350	6150
Chevyvan Diesel (125" WB) (8 cyl)	**14114**	6200	7075
Sportvan (125" WB)	**13121**	6850	7825
Beauville Sportvan	**14440**	7775	8900
Sportvan Diesel (125" WB) (8 cyl)	**15498**	7625	8725
Beauville Sportvan Diesel (125" WB) (8 cyl)	**16759**	8575	9775
* For 8 cylinder models add $375 wholesale and $375 retail.			
ADD FOR:			
High Country Pkg (T Blazer)	**1063**	410	510
Sport Pkg			
(S/T Blazer)	**1089**	420	520
(Astro)	**1070**	420	510
Tahoe Pkg			
(S/T Blazer)	**715**	260	320
(S/T Pickups)	**563**	200	250
Silverado Pkg			
(Blazer)	**1340**	530	650
(Suburban)	**1570**	640	780
(C-K10,20 Pickups)	**708**	260	320

Year-Model-Body Type	Original List	Current Whlse	Average Retail
1988			
S-10 BLAZER 100.5" WB 4*			
Sport Utility	**10505**	4300	5100
* For 6 cylinder models add $300 wholesale and $300 retail.			
V-10 BLAZER 106" WB 8			
Wgn	**14691**	6925	7925
Wgn, Diesel	**17422**	7250	8275
C-10 GAS PICKUPS 117.5" WB 6*			
Fleetside	**9894**	4000	4775
Sportside	**10102**	4100	4875
Fleetside Extended Cab (155" WB)	**10983**	4875	5675
w/131" WB add	**190**	80	90
* For 8 cylinder models add $325 wholesale and $325 retail.			
C-10 DIESEL PICKUPS 131.5" WB 8			
Fleetside	**12868**	4675	5475
Fleetside Extended Cab (155" WB)	**13569**	5550	6350
C-20 GAS PICKUPS 131.5" WB 6*			
Fleetside	**10671**	4550	5475
Fleetside Extended Cab (155" WB)	**11976**	5350	6150
* For 8 cylinder models add $325 wholesale and $325 retail.			
C-20 DIESEL PICKUPS 131.5" WB 8			
Fleetside	**12911**	5025	5825
Fleetside Extended Cab (155" WB)	**14216**	5750	6550
R-20 GAS PICKUPS 164.5" WB 8			
Fleetside Bonus Cab	**12922**	5850	6650
Fleetside Crew Cab	**13358**	6050	6850
R-20 HD DIESEL PICKUPS 164.5" WB 8			
Fleetside Bonus Cab	**14578**	6200	7075
Fleetside Crew Cab	**15015**	6400	7300
S-10 REG CAB PICKUPS 4*			
Fleetside EL (108" WB)	**6795**	2600	3425
Fleetside (108" WB)	**7890**	2750	3600
* For 6 cylinder models add $300 wholesale and $300 retail.			
S-10 EXTENDED CAB 4*			
Fleetside	**8815**	4175	4975
* For 6 cylinder models add $300 wholesale and $300 retail.			
R-10 SUBURBAN 129.5" WB 8			
Panel Doors	**13945**	7250	8275
Tailgate	**13968**	7350	8400
Panel Doors, Diesel	**16260**	7600	8675
Tailgate, Diesel	**16304**	7700	8800
R-20 SUBURBAN 129.5" WB 8			
Panel Doors	**14559**	7550	8625
Tailgate	**14602**	7650	8750
Panel Doors, Diesel	**16839**	7900	9025

Refer To Optional Equipment Schedules

Year-Model-Body Type	Original List	Current Whlse	Average Retail
Tailgate, Diesel	**16883**	8000	9150
ASTRO 111" WB 6*			
Cargo Van (4 cyl)	**9190**	3100	3950
CS Pass Van	**10696**	5225	6025
CL Pass Van	**11489**	5725	6525
LT Pass Van	**12828**	6250	7150
G-10 VANS 110" WB 6			
Chevyvan	**10240**	3225	4075
Sportvan	**11922**	4725	5525
Bonaventure (125" WB)	**13081**	5550	6350
Beauville (125" WB)	**13489**	5725	6525
w/125" WB add			
(Chevyvan)	**248**	90	100
(Sportvan)	**251**	90	110
* For 8 cylinder models add $325 wholesale and $325 retail.			
G-20 VANS 110" WB 6*			
Chevyvan	**10865**	3350	4200
Chevyvan Diesel (8 cyl)	**13262**	4050	4825
Sportvan (125" WB)	**12423**	4900	5700
Bonaventure Sportvan (125" WB)	**13330**	5600	6400
Beauville Sportvan (125" WB)	**13736**	5800	6600
Sportvan Diesel (125" WB) (8 cyl)	**14800**	5600	6400
Bonaventure Sportvan Diesel (125" WB) (8 cyl)	**15735**	6275	7175
Beauville Sportvan Diesel (125" WB) (8 cyl)	**16055**	6450	7375
* For 8 cylinder models add $250 wholesale and $250 retail.			
ADD FOR:			
High Country Pkg (T Blazer)	**1025**	320	400
Scottsdale Pkg			
(R-20 Pickups)	**243**	90	100
(C-K10,20 Pickups)	**326**	120	140
Silverado Pkg			
(Blazer)	**1249**	400	490
(Suburban)	**1300**	420	520
Sport Pkg			
(S/T Blazer)	**1068**	330	410
(S/T Pickups)	**925**	280	350
Tahoe Pkg			
(S/T Blazer)	**683**	200	250
(S/T Pickups)	**650**	180	230

1987

Year-Model-Body Type	Original List	Current Whlse	Average Retail
S-10 BLAZER 100.5" WB 4*			
Sport Utility	—	3500	4400
* For 6 cylinder models add $250 wholesale and $250 retail.			
V-10 BLAZER 106" WB 8			
Wgn	**13066**	5850	6650
Wgn, Diesel	**16027**	6150	6925
EL CAMINO 117" WB 6*			
El Camino	**10453**	4050	4825
El Camino Super Sport	**10784**	4425	5225
* For 8 cylinder models add $275 wholesale and $275 retail.			
R-10 PICKUPS 117.5" WB 6*			
Stepside	**8651**	3125	3975
Fleetside	**8503**	3125	3975
Stepside, Diesel (8 cyl)	**11842**	4300	5100
Fleetside, Diesel (8 cyl)	**11695**	4300	5100
w/131.5" WB add	**184**	50	60
* For 8 cylinder models add $275 wholesale and $275 retail.			
R-20 PICKUPS 131.5" WB 6*			
Stepside	**10077**	3725	4500
Fleetside	**9929**	3725	4500
* For 8 cylinder models add $275 wholesale and $275 retail.			
R-20 DIESEL PICKUPS 131.5" WB 8			
Stepside	**12722**	4300	5100
Fleetside	**12574**	4300	5100
R-20 HEAVY DUTY PICKUPS 131.5" WB 8			
Stepside	**11498**	4200	5000
Fleetside	**11351**	4200	5000
R-20 PICKUPS 164.5" WB 8			
Fleetside Bonus Cab	**12475**	4775	5575
Fleetside Crew Cab	**12842**	4950	5750
R-20 DIESEL PICKUPS 164.5" WB 8			
Fleetside Bonus Cab	**13693**	5050	5850
Fleetside Crew Cab	**14060**	5250	6050
S-10 EXTENDED CAB 4*			
Fleetside (122.9" WB)	**8167**	2725	3575
* For 6 cylinder models add $250 wholesale and $250 retail.			
S-10 REG CAB PICKUPS 4*			
Fleetside EL (108" WB)	**6295**	2175	2975
Fleetside (108" WB)	**7435**	2225	3025
Fleetside (118" WB)	**7702**	2275	3100
* For 6 cylinder models add $250 wholesale and $250 retail.			
R-10 SUBURBAN 129.5" WB 8			
Panel Doors	**12435**	5400	6200
Tailgate	**12477**	5525	6325
Panel Doors, Diesel	**15193**	5750	6550
Tailgate, Diesel	**15235**	5825	6625
R-20 SUBURBAN 129.5" WB 8			
Panel Doors	**13036**	5625	6425
Tailgate	**13077**	5750	6550
Panel Doors, HD Diesel	**15669**	5925	6725
Tailgate, HD Diesel	**15712**	5925	6725

Year-Model-Body Type	Original List	Current Whlse	Average Retail
ASTRO M10 111" WB 6*			
Cargo Van (4 cyl)	**8797**	2375	3200
Pass Van	**9833**	4075	4850
CS Pass Van	**10314**	4275	5075
CL Pass Van	**11079**	4475	5275
LT Pass Van	**12370**	4950	5750
G-10 VANS 110" WB 6*			
Chevyvan	**9464**	2375	3200
Sportvan	**11162**	3750	4525
Bonaventure (125" WB)	**12279**	4350	5150
Beauville (125" WB)	**12631**	4525	5325
w/125" WB add			
(Chevyvan)	**242**	70	80
(Sportvan)	**242**	70	80
* For 8 cylinder models add $275 wholesale and $275 retail.			
G-20 VANS 110" WB 6*			
Chevyvan	**10131**	2425	3250
Chevyvan Diesel (8 cyl)	**12753**	2925	3775
Sportvan (125" WB)	**11609**	3900	4675
Bonaventure Sportvan (125" WB)	**12483**	4425	5225
Beauville Sportvan (125" WB)	**12833**	4575	5375
Sportvan Diesel (125" WB) (8 cyl)	**14211**	4450	5250
Bonaventure Sportvan Diesel (125" WB) (8 cyl)	**15113**	4900	5700
Beauville Sportvan Diesel (125" WB) (8 cyl)	**15379**	5100	5900
Chevyvan Diesel (125" WB) (8 cyl)	**12995**	3100	3950
* For 8 cylinder models add $275 wholesale and $275 retail.			
ADD FOR:			
Durango Pkg (S/T Pickup)	**313**	90	110
High Country Pkg (S/T Blazer)	**1025**	250	310
Scottsdale Pkg			
(Suburban Diesel)	**329**	90	110
(Suburban Gasoline)	**485**	140	160
(C-K Pickups)	**353**	100	120
(R-V Pickups)	**274**	80	100
Silverado Pkg			
(Blazer)	**1073**	260	320
(Suburban)	**1330**	330	410
(C-K Pickups)	**681**	150	190
Sport Pkg (S/T Blazer)	**1042**	250	310
(S/T Pickups)	**965**	230	280
Tahoe Pkg (S/T Blazer)	**657**	130	170
(S/T Pickups)	**637**	130	170
1986			
K-10 BLAZER 8			
Utility w/HT	**12383**	4775	5575
Utility Diesel w/HT	**15330**	5025	5825
S-10 BLAZER 100.5" WB 4*			
Tailgate	**9582**	2475	3300
* For 6 cylinder models add $225 wholesale and $225 retail.			
EL CAMINO 117" WB 6*			
El Camino	**9850**	3150	4000
El Camino Super Sport	**10172**	4525	5325
* For 8 cylinder models add $250 wholesale and $250 retail.			
C-10 PICKUPS 117.5" WB 6*			
Stepside	**8133**	2625	3475
Fleetside	**7989**	2625	3475
Stepside, Diesel (8 cyl)	**11223**	3100	3950
Fleetside, Diesel (8 cyl)	**11080**	3100	3950
w/131.5" WB add	**179**	40	50
* For 8 cylinder models add $250 wholesale and $250 retail.			
C-20 PICKUPS 131.5" WB 6*			
Stepside	**9521**	3075	3925
Fleetside	**9377**	3075	3925
* For 8 cylinder models add $250 wholesale and $250 retail.			
C-20 DIESEL PICKUPS 131.5" WB 8			
Stepside	**12161**	3650	4425
Fleetside	**12017**	3650	4425
C-20 HEAVY DUTY PICKUPS 131.5" WB 6*			
Stepside	**10542**	3250	4100
Fleetside	**10399**	3250	4100
* For 8 cylinder models add $250 wholesale and $250 retail.			
C-20 PICKUPS 164.5" WB 6*			
Fleetside Bonus Cab	**11425**	3875	4650
Fleetside Crew Cab	**11783**	4100	4875
* For 8 cylinder models add $250 wholesale and $250 retail.			
S-10 EXTENDED CAB 4*			
Fleetside (122.9" WB)	**7909**	1775	2575
* For 6 cylinder models add $225 wholesale and $225 retail.			
S-10 REG CAB PICKUPS 4*			
Fleetside EL (108" WB)	**6161**	1550	2300
Fleetside (108" WB)	**7202**	1550	2350
Fleetside (118" WB)	**7444**	1625	2425
* For 6 cylinder models add $225 wholesale and $225 retail.			
C-10 SUBURBAN 129.5" WB 8			
Panel Doors	**11769**	4425	5225
Tailgate	**11809**	4500	5300
Panel Doors, Diesel	**14518**	4650	5450
Tailgate, Diesel	**14559**	4725	5525

Refer To Optional Equipment Schedules

CHEVROLET

Year-Model-Body Type	Original List	Current Whlse	Average Retail
C-20 SUBURBAN 129.5" WB 8			
Panel Doors	**12613**	4625	5425
Tailgate	**12653**	4725	5525
Panel Doors, HD Diesel	**15241**	4950	5750
Tailgate, HD Diesel	**15282**	5050	5850
ASTRO M10 111" WB 6*			
Cargo Van (4 cyl)	**8290**	1575	2375
Pass Van	**9299**	2950	3800
CS Pass Van	**9767**	3075	3925
CL Pass Van	**10512**	3375	4225
G-10 VANS 110" WB 6*			
Chevyvan	**8876**	1700	2500
Sportvan	**10529**	2825	3675
Bonaventure (125" WB)	**11617**	3300	4150
Beauville (125" WB)	**11959**	3550	4325
w/125" WB add			
(Chevyvan)	**232**	50	60
(Sportvan)	**236**	50	60
G-20 VANS 110" WB 6*			
Chevyvan	**9525**	1775	2575
Chevyvan Diesel (8 cyl)	**12143**	2275	3100
Sportvan (125" WB)	**10964**	2950	3800
Bonaventure Sportvan (125" WB)	**11815**	4425	5225
Beauville Sportvan (125" WB)	**12156**	4575	5375
Sportvan Diesel (125" WB) (8 cyl)	**13562**	3500	4275
Bonaventure Sportvan Diesel (125" WB) (8 cyl)	**14440**	3975	4750
Beauville Sportvan Diesel (125" WB) (8 cyl)	**14699**	4150	4950
w/125" WB add			
(Chevyvan)	**235**	55	65
(Chevyvan Diesel 8 cyl)	**236**	65	80
* For 8 cylinder models add $250 wholesale and $250 retail.			
ADD FOR:			
Conquista (El Camino)	**232**	50	60
Durango Pkg (S/T Pickup)	**305**	60	80
Scottsdale Pkg (Suburban)	—	100	120
Silverado Pkg			
(Blazer)	**1045**	170	210
(Suburban)	**1145**	190	240
(C-K Pickups)	—	100	130
Sport Pkg (S/T Blazer)	**1015**	170	210
(S/T Pickups)	**940**	150	190
Tahoe Pkg (S/T Blazer)	**640**	140	160
(S/T Pickups)	**620**	130	160

Year-Model-Body Type	Original List	Current Whlse	Average Retail
1985			
K-10 BLAZER 8			
Utility w/HT	**11380**	4025	4800
Utility Diesel w/HT	**14411**	4300	5100
S-10 BLAZER 100.5" WB 4*			
Tailgate	**8881**	2000	2800
* For 6 cylinder models add $200 wholesale and $200 retail.			
EL CAMINO 117" WB 6*			
El Camino	**9058**	2425	3250
El Camino Super Sport	**9327**	2600	3425
* For 8 cylinder models add $225 wholesale and $225 retail.			
C-10 PICKUPS 117.5" WB 6*			
Stepside	**7532**	2050	2850
Fleetside	**7397**	2050	2850
Stepside, Diesel	**10445**	2450	3275
Fleetside, Diesel	**10310**	2450	3275
w/131.5" WB add	**169**	30	40
* For 8 cylinder models add $225 wholesale and $225 retail.			
C-20 PICKUPS 131.5" WB 6*			
Stepside	**8798**	2400	3225
Fleetside	**8663**	2400	3225
* For 8 cylinder models add $225 wholesale and $225 retail.			
C-20 DIESEL PICKUPS 131.5" WB 8			
Stepside	**11274**	2825	3675
Fleetside	**11139**	2825	3675
C-20 HEAVY DUTY PICKUPS 131.5" WB 6*			
Stepside	**9756**	2575	3400
Fleetside	**9622**	2575	3400
* For 8 cylinder models add $225 wholesale and $225 retail.			
C-20 HD DIESEL PICKUPS 131.5" WB 8			
Stepside	**11575**	3000	3850
Fleetside	**11441**	3000	3850
C-20 PICKUPS 164.5" WB 6*			
Fleetside Bonus Cab	**10584**	2975	3825
Fleetside Crew Cab	**10920**	3150	4000
* For 8 cylinder models add $225 wholesale and $225 retail.			
C-20 DIESEL PICKUPS 164.5" WB 8			
Fleetside Bonus Cab	**12403**	3500	4275
Fleetside Crew Cab	**12379**	3700	4475
S-10 EXTENDED CAB 4*			
Fleetside (122.9" WB)	**7167**	1425	2125
Fleetside, Diesel (122.9" WB)	**7875**	1125	1800
* For 6 cylinder models add $200 wholesale and $200 retail.			
S-10 REG CAB PICKUPS 4*			
Fleetside (108" WB)	**5990**	1200	1875
Fleetside (118" WB)	**6702**	1275	1950

Year-Model-Body Type	Original List	Current Whlse	Average Retail
Fleetside, Diesel (108" WB)	**7349**	900	1600
Fleetside, Diesel (118" WB)	**7502**	1025	1700
* For 6 cylinder models add $200 wholesale and $200 retail.			
C-10 SUBURBAN 129.5" WB 8			
Panel Doors	**10812**	3600	4375
Tailgate	**10850**	3700	4475
Panel Doors, Diesel	**13369**	3875	4650
Tailgate, Diesel	**13407**	3975	4750
C-20 SUBURBAN 129.5" WB 8			
Panel Doors	**11598**	3800	4575
Tailgate	**11635**	3900	4675
Panel Doors, Diesel	**14042**	4075	4850
Tailgate, Diesel	**14079**	4175	4975
ASTRO 111" WB 4			
Cargo Van	**7821**	1125	1800
Pass Van	**8195**	2175	2975
CS Pass Van	**8623**	2250	3050
CL Pass Van	**9359**	2700	3550
G-10 VANS 110" WB 6*			
Chevyvan	**8099**	1225	1900
Sportvan	**9650**	2275	3100
Bonaventure (125" WB)	**10661**	2575	3400
Beauville (125" WB)	**10979**	2575	3400
w/125" WB add			
(Chevyvan)	**215**	30	40
(Sportvan)0	**220**	30	40
G-20 VANS 110" WB 6*			
Chevyvan	**8701**	1275	1950
Chevyvan Diesel	**11128**	1700	2500
Sportvan (125" WB)	**10054**	2325	3150
Bonaventure (125" WB)	**10845**	2350	3150
Beauville (125" WB)	**11161**	2600	3425
Sportvan Diesel (125" WB)	**12468**	2750	3600
Bonaventure Diesel 125" WB)	**13284**	3050	3900
Beauville Diesel (125" WB) (8 cyl)	**13525**	3175	4025
Chevyvan (125" WB)	**8921**	1325	2000
Chevyvan Diesel (125" WB) (8 cyl)	**11346**	1725	2525
* For 8 cylinder models add $225 wholesale and $225 retail.			
ADD FOR:			
Conquista (El Camino)	**195**	30	30
Durango Pkg (S/T Pickups)	**289**	40	50
Scottsdale Pkg			
(Suburban Diesel)	**311**	40	50
(Suburban Gasoline)	**459**	60	70
Silverado Pkg (Blazer)	**1015**	140	170

Year-Model-Body Type	Original List	Current Whlse	Average Retail
(Suburban)	—	120	150
(C-K Pickups)	**695**	100	110
Sport Pkg (S/T Blazer)	**972**	130	160
(S/T Pickups)	—	120	140
Tahoe Pkg (S/T Blazer)	**585**	80	100
(S/T Pickups)	—	80	100
1984			
K-10 BLAZER 8			
Utility w/HT	**10931**	3025	3875
Utility Diesel w/HT	**13664**	3225	4075
S-10 BLAZER 100.5" WB 4*			
Tailgate	**8580**	1700	2500
* For 6 cylinder models add $175 wholesale and $175 retail.			
EL CAMINO 117" WB 6*			
El Camino	**8622**	1850	2650
El Camino Super Sport	**8881**	2050	2850
* For 8 cylinder models add $200 wholesale and $200 retail.			
C-10 PICKUPS 117.5" WB 6*			
Stepside	**7213**	1700	2500
Fleetside	**7082**	1700	2500
Stepside, Diesel	**10257**	2050	2850
Fleetside, Diesel	**10126**	2050	2850
w/131.5" WB add	**157**	20	20
* For 8 cylinder models add $200 wholesale and $200 retail.			
C-20 PICKUPS 131.5" WB 6*			
Stepside	**8431**	2050	2850
Fleetside	**8300**	2050	2850
* For 8 cylinder models add $200 wholesale and $200 retail.			
C-20 HEAVY DUTY PICKUPS 131.5" WB 6*			
Stepside	**8945**	2200	3000
Fleetside	**8814**	2200	3000
* For 8 cylinder models add $200 wholesale and $200 retail.			
C-20 DIESEL PICKUPS 131.5" WB 8			
Stepside	**11038**	2375	3200
Fleetside	**10907**	2375	3200
C-20 HD DIESEL PICKUPS 131.5" WB 8			
Stepside	**11552**	2500	3325
Fleetside	**11421**	2500	3325
C-20 PICKUPS 164.5" WB 6*			
Fleetside Bonus Cab	**9757**	2600	3425
Fleetside Crew Cab	**10087**	2700	3550
* For 8 cylinder models add $200 wholesale and $200 retail.			
C-20 DIESEL PICKUPS 164.5" WB 8			
Fleetside Bonus Cab	**12364**	2950	3800
Fleetside Crew Cab	**12694**	1325	2000
S-10 EXTENDED CAB 4*			
Fleetside (122.9" WB)	**7036**	1325	2000

Refer To Optional Equipment Schedules

Year-Model-Body Type	Original List	Current Whlse	Average Retail
Fleetside, Diesel (122.9" WB)	**7939**	1075	1750
S-10 REG CAB PICKUPS 4*			
Fleetside (108" WB)	**6102**	1125	1800
Fleetside (118" WB)	**6663**	1200	1875
Fleetside, Diesel (108" WB)	**7413**	850	1550
Fleetside, Diesel (118" WB)	**7566**	950	1625
* For 6 cylinder models add $175 wholesale and $175 retail.			
C-10 SUBURBAN 129.5" WB 8			
Panel Doors	**10444**	2750	3600
Tailgate	**10480**	2825	3675
Panel Doors, Diesel	**13004**	2925	3775
Tailgate, Diesel	**13040**	3000	3850
C-20 SUBURBAN 129.5" WB 8			
Panel Doors	**10691**	2925	3775
Tailgate	**10727**	3000	3850
Panel Doors, Diesel	**13820**	3075	3925
Tailgate, Diesel	**13856**	3175	4025
G-10 VANS 110" WB 6*			
Chevyvan	**7653**	800	1475
Sportvan	**9201**	1700	2500
Bonaventure (125" WB)	**10174**	1950	2750
Beauville (125" WB)	**10439**	2075	2875
w/125" WB add			
(Chevyvan)	**212**	50	60
(Sportvan)	**212**	50	60
G-20 VANS 110" WB 6*			
Chevyvan	**8288**	850	1550
Chevyvan Diesel	**10846**	1175	1850
Sportvan (125" WB)	**9589**	1750	2550
Bonaventure (125" WB)	**10350**	2000	2800
Beauville (125" WB)	**10615**	2125	2925
Sportvan Diesel (125" WB)	**12134**	2125	2925
Bonaventure Diesel (125" WB)	**12920**	2325	3150
Beauville Diesel (125" WB)	**13110**	2400	3225
Chevyvan (125" WB)	**8500**	900	1600
Chevyvan Diesel (125" WB)	**11056**	1275	1950
* For 8 cylinder models add $200 wholesale and $200 retail.			

DODGE

1992

Year-Model-Body Type	Original List	Current Whlse	Average Retail
AD-150S 2WD 106" WB 8			
Ramcharger S	**17575**	—	—
AD-150 2WD 106" WB 8			
Ramcharger	**19600**	—	—
ADD FOR:			
5.9 Liter 8 Cyl Eng	**399**	—	—
LE Pkg	**1460**	—	—
Canyon Sport Pkg	**2365**	—	—
CARAVAN 4*			
Caravan, Base	**14358**	—	—
Caravan, SE	**16481**	—	—
Caravan, LE	**20340**	—	—
* For 3.0 liter 6 cylinder models add $— wholesale and $— retail.			
CARAVAN 6			
Caravan, SE AWD	**19539**	—	—
Caravan, LE AWD	**22442**	—	—
Caravan, ES	**20883**	—	—
GRAND CARAVAN 6			
Caravan, Base	**18233**	—	—
Caravan SE	**18463**	—	—
Caravan LE	**21060**	—	—
Caravan ES	**21571**	—	—
CARAVAN CARGO VAN 112" WB 4*			
Van	**13772**	—	—
* For 3.0 liter 6 cylinder models add $— wholesale and $— retail.			
CARAVAN CARGO VAN 119" WB 6			
Van	**16161**	—	—
ADD FOR:			
3.3 Liter 6 Cyl Eng	**796**	—	—
ES Decor Group	**543**	—	—
DAKOTA 2WD 4*			
S Sweptline (112" WB)	**10117**	—	—
Sweptline (112" WB)	**11773**	—	—
Sweptline (124" WB)	**12056**	—	—
Club Cab (131" WB)	**13040**	—	—
Sport Sweptline (112" WB)	**10542**	—	—
* For 6 cylinder models add $— wholesale and $— retail.			
DAKOTA 4WD 6			
Sweptline (112" WB)	**15081**	—	—
Sweptline (124" WB)	**15295**	—	—
Club Cab (131" WB)	**16235**	—	—
Sport Sweptline (112" WB)	**14269**	—	—
ADD FOR:			
5.2 Liter 8 Cyl Eng			
(2WD)	**1118**	—	—
(4WD)	**587**	—	—
RAM 50 2WD 4			
Standard Cab (105" WB)	**9571**	—	—
Standard Cab (116" WB)	**10126**	—	—
SE Standard Cab			

Year-Model-Body Type	Original List	Current Whlse	Average Retail
(105" WB)	10431	—	—
POWER RAM 50 4WD 4			
Standard Cab			
(105" WB)	12301	—	—
D150 PICKUPS 115" WB 6*			
Sweptline	13980	—	—
* For 8 cylinder models add $— wholesale and $— retail.			
D150 PICKUPS 131" WB 6*			
Sweptline	14197	—	—
* For 8 cylinder models add $— wholesale and $— retail.			
D150 PICKUPS 133" WB 8			
Club Cab	16062	—	—
D150 PICKUPS 149" WB 8			
Club Cab	16281	—	—
D250 PICKUP 131" WB 6*			
Sweptline	15138	—	—
* For 8 cylinder models add $— wholesale and $— retail.			
D250 PICKUPS 149" WB 8			
Club Cab	17022	—	—
ADD FOR:			
5.9 Liter 8 Cyl Eng			
(D250 Sweptline)	857	—	—
(D250 Club Cab, 4WD models)	270	—	—
5.9 Liter 6 Cyl Cummins Turbo Diesel Eng			
(D250 Sweptline)	4728	—	—
(D250 Club Cab)	4022	—	—
(4WD Sweptline)	3821	—	—
(4WD Club Cab)	3702	—	—
B150 VANS 6*			
109" WB Van	14749	—	—
127" WB Van	15578	—	—
* For 8 cylinder models add $— wholesale and $— retail.			
B250 VANS 6*			
109" WB Van	15297	—	—
127" WB Van	15991	—	—
127" WB Maxivan	16978	—	—
* For 8 cylinder models add $— wholesale and $— retail.			
ADD FOR:			
5.9 Liter 8 Cyl Eng	857	—	—
B150 WAGONS 6*			
109" WB Wgn	16137	—	—
127" WB Wgn	16995	—	—
* For 8 cylinder models add $— wholesale and $— retail.			
B250 WAGONS 6*			
127" WB Wgn	17639	—	—
* For 8 cylinder models add $— wholesale and $— retail.			
B250 WAGONS 8			
127" WB Maxiwagon	18925	—	—
ADD FOR:			
5.9 Liter 8 Cyl Eng			
(B250 ex. Maxiwagon)	857	—	—
(B250 Maxiwagon)	270	—	—
LE Pkg (B150 Wgn)	2996	—	—
(B250 ex. Maxiwagon)	3140	—	—

1991

Year-Model-Body Type	Original List	Current Whlse	Average Retail
AD-150S 106" WB 8*			
Ramcharger S	16494	10050	11450
AD-150 106" WB 8*			
Ramcharger	18656	11075	12650
* For 360 CID 8 cylinder engine add $300 wholesale and $300 retail.			
CARAVAN 4*			
Caravan, Base	14305	10150	11575
Caravan, SE	15551	11000	12550
Caravan, LE	17994	11750	13425
* For 6 cylinder models add $400 wholesale and $400 retail.			
CARAVAN 6			
Caravan ES	19489	12075	13800
GRAND CARAVAN 6			
Caravan SE	17301	12300	14125
Caravan LE	19604	13025	15225
CARAVAN CARGO VAN 112" WB 4*			
Van	13671	8375	9525
* For 6 cylinder models add $400 wholesale and $400 retail.			
CARAVAN CARGO VAN 119" WB 6			
Van	15411	9650	10975
DAKOTA 2WD 4			
S Sweptline (112" WB)	9926	6250	7150
Sweptline (112" WB)	11377	6925	7925
Sweptline (124" WB)	11528	7050	8075
Club Cab (131" WB)	12657	7525	8600
Sport Sweptline (112" WB)	13798	8150	9275
Sport Club Cab (131" WB)	15128	8750	9975
* For 6 cylinder models add $500 wholesale and $500 retail.			
RAM 50 2WD 4			
Standard Cab (105" WB)	9213	6400	7300
Standard Cab (116" WB)	9746	6500	7425
SE Sports Cab (116" WB)	10471	7725	8825
SE Standard Cab (105" WB)	10175	6775	7750
LE Sports Cab (116" WB)	11900	8150	9275

Year-Model-Body Type	Original List	Current Whlse	Average Retail
D150 PICKUPS 115" WB 6*			
S Sweptline	**11679**	7650	8750
Sweptline	**13144**	8150	9275
Club Cab (133" WB) (8 cyl)	**15185**	9475	10775
Club Cab (149" WB) (8 cyl)	**15394**	9650	10975
w/131" WB add	**209**	140	160
* For 8 cylinder models add $425 wholesale and $425 retail.			
D250 PICKUPS 131" WB 6*			
Sweptline	**14216**	8950	10200
Club Cab (149" WB) (8 cyl)	**16833**	10200	11625
* For 8 cylinder models add $425 wholesale and $425 retail.			
B150 VANS 6*			
109" WB Van	**14456**	9725	11075
127" WB Van	**15165**	9900	11275
* For 8 cylinder models add $425 wholesale and $425 retail.			
B250 VANS 6*			
109" WB Van	**14697**	9500	10800
127" WB Van	**15373**	10075	11475
127" WB Maxivan	**16334**	10250	11700
* For 8 cylinder models add $425 wholesale and $425 retail.			
B150 WAGONS 06*			
109" WB Wgn	**15719**	10825	12350
127" WB Wgn	**16555**	11400	13025
* For 8 cylinder models add $425 wholesale and $425 retail.			
B250 WAGONS 6*			
127" WB Wgn	**17183**	11175	12775
127" WB Maxiwagon (8 cyl)	**18436**	12075	13800
* For 8 cylinder models add $425 wholesale and $425 retail.			
ADD FOR:			
LE Decor Pkg (Dakota)	**1110**	600	740
(Ram Wagons)	**1152**	630	770
(Pickups)	**1160**	630	770
Premium Van Decor Pkg (Caravan Cargo Van)	**1451**	800	980
SE Decor Pkg (Dakota)	**682**	350	430
(Pickups)	**700**	360	450

1990

Year-Model-Body Type	Original List	Current Whlse	Average Retail
AD-150S 106" WB 8*			
Ramcharger S	**15334**	6625	7575
AD-150 106" WB 8*			
Ramcharger	**17195**	7500	8575
* For 360 CID V8 engine add $250 wholesale and $250 retail.			
CARAVAN 4*			
Caravan, Base	**12835**	7875	9000
Caravan, SE	**13515**	8625	9825
Caravan, LE	**16125**	9300	10575
Caravan, ES	**17350**	9475	10775
* For 6 cylinder models add $375 wholesale and $375 retail.			
GRAND CARAVAN 6			
Caravan, SE	**16235**	9725	11075
Caravan, LE	**18325**	10375	11825
CARAVAN CARGO VAN 112" WB 4*			
Van	**11965**	6050	6850
* For 6 cylinder models add $375 wholesale and $375 retail.			
CARAVAN CARGO VAN 119" WB 6			
Van	**14290**	7200	8225
DAKOTA 2WD 4*			
S Sweptline (112" WB)	**9290**	4775	5575
Sweptline (112" WB)	**10481**	5325	6125
Convertible (112" WB)	**14126**	6550	7475
Sweptline (124" WB)	**10626**	5450	6250
Club Cab (131" WB)	**11781**	5900	6700
Sport Sweptline (112" WB)	**13006**	6500	7425
Sport Convertible (112" WB)	**16281**	7700	8800
Sport Club Cab (131" WB)	**14081**	7075	8100
* For 6 cylinder models add $375 wholesale and $375 retail.			
RAM 50 2WD 4			
Standard Cab (105" WB)	**8780**	4825	5625
Standard Cab (116" WB)	**9313**	4900	5700
Sport Cab (116" WB)	**9819**	5325	6125
SE Standard Cab (105" WB)	**9853**	5200	6000
LE Sport Cab (116" WB)	**12030**	5975	6775
D150 PICKUPS 115" WB 6*			
S Sweptline	**11470**	5975	6775
Sweptline	**12206**	6375	7275
Club Cab (133" WB) (8 cyl)	**14156**	7600	8675
Club Cab (149" WB) (8 cyl)	**14356**	7750	8850
w/131" WB add	**200**	100	120
* For 8 cylinder models add $400 wholesale and $400 retail.			
D250 PICKUPS 131" WB 6*			
Sweptline	**13181**	7125	8125
Club Cab (149" WB) (8 cyl)	**15681**	8350	9500

Year-Model-Body Type	Original List	Current Whlse	Average Retail
* For 8 cylinder models add $400 wholesale and $400 retail.			
B150 VANS 6*			
109" WB Van	**13296**	7175	8200
127" WB Van	**13976**	7675	8775
* For 8 cylinder models add $400 wholesale and $400 retail.			
B250 VANS 6*			
109" WB Van	**13526**	7350	8400
127" WB Van	**14176**	7850	8975
127" WB Maxivan	**15096**	8075	9250
* For 8 cylinder models add $400 wholesale and $400 retail.			
B150 WAGONS 6*			
109" WB Wgn	**15096**	8650	9850
127" WB Wgn	**15896**	9150	10400
* For 8 cylinder models add $400 wholesale and $400 retail.			
B250 WAGONS 6*			
127" WB Wgn	**16496**	8950	10200
127" WB Maxiwagon (8 cyl)	**17696**	9475	10775
* For 8 cylinder models add $400 wholesale and $400 retail.			
ADD FOR:			
LE Decor Pkg			
(Ram Wagons)	**1130**	530	650
(Dakota Convertible)	**—**	300	370
(Dakota)	**1102**	520	640
(D & W Series Pickups)	**—**	400	500
Royal Decor Pkg			
(Caravan Cargo Van)	**1125**	520	640
SE Decor Pkg			
(Dakota Pickups)	**—**	220	270
(D150 Reg Cab Pickups)	**686**	300	370
(D250 Reg Cab Pickups)	**459**	180	230

1989

Year-Model-Body Type	Original List	Current Whlse	Average Retail
AD-100 106" WB 8			
Ramcharger	**12785**	5275	6075
AD-150 106" WB 8			
Ramcharger	**14927**	6150	6925
CARAVAN 4*			
Caravan, Base	**11312**	6625	7575
Caravan, Special Ed	**12039**	7300	8350
Caravan, Limited Ed	**13987**	7900	9025
* For 6 cylinder models add $325 wholesale and $325 retail.			
GRAND CARAVAN 6			
Caravan, Special Ed	**14526**	8375	9525
Caravan, Limited Ed	**16462**	9025	10275
DAKOTA 2WD 4*			
S Sweptline (112" WB)	**7497**	3850	4525
Sweptline (112" WB)	**9172**	4350	5150
Sweptline (124" WB)	**9228**	4425	5225
Sport Sweptline (112" WB) (6 cyl)	**11293**	5275	6075
Sport Convertible (112" WB) (6 cyl)	**14425**	6300	7200
* For 6 cylinder models add $325 wholesale and $325 retail.			
RAIDER 4*			
Sport Utility	**12550**	5750	6550
* For 6 cylinder models add $325 wholesale and $325 retail.			
RAM 50 2WD 4			
Pickup (105" WB)	**7664**	3825	4600
Sport Pickup (105" WB)	**9496**	4425	5225
Pickup (116" WB)	**8320**	3950	4725
Extended Cab Pickup (116" WB)	**8680**	4275	5075
Custom Pickup (116" WB)	**8769**	4375	5175
Sport Extended Cab Pickup (116" WB)	**10407**	4800	5600
D100 PICKUPS 115" WB 6*			
Sweptline	**9865**	5025	5925
w/131" WB add	**187**	90	110
* For 8 cylinder models add $375 wholesale and $375 retail.			
D150 PICKUPS 115" WB 6*			
Sweptline	**10693**	5400	6200
w/131" WB add	**200**	100	120
* For 8 cylinder models add $375 wholesale and $375 retail.			
D250 PICKUPS 131" WB 6*			
Sweptline	**11722**	6150	6925
* For 8 cylinder models add $375 wholesale and $375 retail.			
B150 VANS 6*			
109" WB Van	**11430**	5650	6450
109" WB Long Range Ram Van	**10729**	5725	6525
127" WB Van	**12000**	6100	6900
127" WB Long Range Ram Van	**11973**	6175	6950
* For 8 cylinder models add $375 wholesale and $375 retail.			
B250 VANS 6*			
109" WB Van	**11741**	5775	6575
127" WB Van	**12379**	6225	7100
127" WB Maxivan	**13250**	6700	7650
* For 8 cylinder models add $375 wholesale and $375 retail.			
B150 WAGONS 6*			
109" WB Ram Value Wgn	**13273**	7150	8175
109" WB Ram Wgn	**13339**	7225	8250
127" WB Ram Wgn	**13862**	7725	8825

Refer To Optional Equipment Schedules

DODGE

Year-Model-Body Type	Original List	Current Whlse	Average Retail
* For 8 cylinder models add $375 wholesale and $375 retail.			
B250 WAGONS 6*			
127" WB Ram Wgn	**14431**	7350	8400
127" WB Maxiwagon	**15573**	7850	8975
* For 8 cylinder Non-Maxi Wagons add $375 wholesale and $375 retail. For 8 cylinder Maxi-wagons add $375 wholesale and $375 retail.			
ADD FOR:			
LE Decor Pkg			
(Ramcharger)	**718**	260	320
(Ram Wagons)	**1179**	460	570
Snow Commander Pkg			
(Ramcharger)	**1573**	640	780
Prospector Pkg 1			
(Ramcharger)	—	150	190
(Ram Wagons)	**1179**	460	570
(Vans)	**320**	140	170
(Dakota)	**287**	120	150
(D & W 100 Pickups)	**655**	150	200
(D & W 250 Pickups)	**382**	120	150
Prospector Pkg 2			
(Ramcharger)	**2171**	900	1100
(Ram Wagons)	**521**	180	220
(Vans)	**571**	200	250
(Dakota 2WD)	**691**	250	310
(Dakota 4WD)	**1186**	470	570
(D & W 150 Pickups)	**536**	180	230
(D & W 250 Pickups)	**595**	210	260
Prospector Pkg 3			
(Ram Wagons)	**915**	350	430
(Vans)	**939**	360	440
(Dakota)	**1801**	740	900
(D & W 150 Pickups)	**621**	220	280
(D & W 250 Pickups)	**690**	250	310
Prospector Pkg 4			
(Ram Wagons)	**2888**	1210	1470
(Vans)	**1811**	740	910
SE Decor Pkg (Dakota)	**374**	110	150

1988

Year-Model-Body Type	Original List	Current Whlse	Average Retail
AD-100 106" WB 8			
Ramcharger	**11776**	3725	4500
AD-150 106" WB 8			
Ramcharger	**13640**	4450	5250
CARAVAN 4*			
Caravan, Base	**10887**	4900	5700
Caravan, Special Ed	**11587**	5525	6325
Caravan, Limited Ed	**13462**	6050	6850
GRAND CARAVAN 4*			
Caravan; Special Ed	**12502**	6225	7100
Caravan, Limited Ed			
(6 cyl)	**15509**	6700	7650
MINI RAM VAN 4*			
Mini Ram Van, Base	**9717**	3225	4075
Mini Ram Van, Extended	**10399**	3700	4475
* For 6 cylinder models add $300 wholesale and $300 retail.			
DAKOTA 2WD 4*			
S Sweptline (112" WB)	**6875**	2750	3600
Sweptline (112" WB)	**8244**	2850	3700
Sweptline (124" WB)	**8407**	2950	3800
Sport Sweptline (112" WB) (6 cyl)	**9995**	3725	4500
* For 6 cylinder models add $300 wholesale and $300 retail.			
RAIDER 4			
Sport Utility	**12053**	4225	5025
RAM 50 2WD 4			
Pickup (105" WB)	**7404**	2375	3200
Sport Pickup (105" WB)	**8976**	2825	3675
Pickup (116" WB)	**8060**	2450	3275
Extended Cab (116" WB)	**8416**	2700	3550
Custom Pickup (116" WB)	**8463**	2700	3550
Sport Extended Cab (116" WB)	**9886**	3150	4000
D100 PICKUPS 115" WB 6*			
Sweptline	**8853**	3050	3900
w/131.5" WB add	**177**	90	100
D150 PICKUPS 115" WB 6*			
Sweptline	**9988**	3300	4150
w/131" WB add	**191**	80	100
* For 8 cylinder models add $325 wholesale and $325 retail.			
D250 PICKUPS 131" WB 6*			
Sweptline	**11031**	3975	4750
* For 8 cylinder models add $325 wholesale and $325 retail.			
B150 WAGONS 6*			
109" WB Ram Value Wgn	**12705**	5250	6050
109" WB Ram Wgn	**12781**	5175	5975
B250 WAGONS 6*			
127" WB Ram Wgn	**13714**	5375	6175
127" WB Ram Maxiwagon (8 cyl)	**14812**	6100	6900
* For 8 cylinder models add $325 wholesale and $325 retail.			
ADD FOR:			
LE Decor Pkg			
(AD & AW 150 Ramcharger)	**625**	130	160
(Ram Wagons)	**1095**	260	330
(Caravan)	**603**	120	160

Year-Model-Body Type	Original List	Current Whlse	Average Retail
(Dakota)	**1073**	260	320
(D & W Pickups)	**469**	130	160
Prospector Pkg I			
(Ramcharger)	**—**	290	360
(Ram Value Wagon)	**725**	160	200
(Dakota)	**439**	120	150
Prospector Pkg II			
(Ramcharger)	**2006**	520	640
(Ram Wagons)	**465**	130	160
(Vans)	**450**	130	160
(Dakota)	**671**	140	180
Prospector Pkg III			
(Ram Wagons)	**803**	240	300
(Vans)	**800**	240	300
(Dakota 2WD)	**1031**	320	400
(D & W Pickups)	**1685**	560	680
Prospector Pkg IV			
(Ram Wagons)	**2869**	990	1200
(Vans)	**1875**	630	770
Royal Decor Pkg			
(Mini Ram Van)	**1043**	330	410
SE Decor Pkg (Dakota)	**499**	130	160

1987

Year-Model-Body Type	Original List	Current Whlse	Average Retail
AD-150 106" WB 8			
Ramcharger	**12820**	3600	4375
CARAVAN 4*			
Caravan, Base	**10411**	3550	4325
Caravan, Special Ed	**10875**	4100	4875
Caravan, Limited Ed	**11741**	4525	5325
GRAND CARAVAN 4*			
Caravan, Special Ed	**11751**	4575	5375
Caravan, Limited Ed	**12561**	4950	5750
* For 6 cylinder models add $250 wholesale and $250 retail.			
MINI RAM VAN 4*			
Mini Ram Van, Base	**9222**	2325	3150
Mini Ram Van, Royal	**10052**	2600	3425
* For 6 cylinder models add $250 wholesale and $250 retail.			
DAKOTA 4 2WD*			
S Sweptline (112" WB)	**6590**	2400	3225
Sweptline (112" WB)	**7529**	2475	3300
Sweptline (124" WB)	**7764**	2550	3375
* For 6 cylinder S Sweptline add $250 wholesale and $250 retail.			
RAIDER 4			
Sport Utility	**10501**	3800	4575
RAM 50 4 2WD			
Pickup (105" WB)	**6527**	1700	2500
Pickup (116" WB)	**6887**	1775	2575
Custom Pickup (116" WB)	**7289**	1950	2750
Sport Pickup (105" WB)	**7945**	2050	2850
D100 PICKUPS 115" WB 6*			
Sweptline	**7653**	2450	3275
w/131" WB add	**172**	90	100
D150 PICKUPS 115" WB 6*			
Sweptline	**8823**	2650	3500
w/131" WB add	**184**	90	110
* For 8 cylinder models add $275 wholesale and $275 retail.			
D250 PICKUPS 131" WB 6*			
Sweptline	**10493**	3125	3975
B150 VANS 6*			
109" WB Van	**9939**	2725	3575
109" WB Long Range Ram Van	**9295**	2775	3625
127" WB Van	**10178**	3025	3875
127" WB Long Range Ram Van	**10238**	3075	3925
* For 8 cylinder models add $275 wholesale and $275 retail.			
B250 VANS 6*			
109" WB Van	**10401**	2775	3625
127" WB Van	**10645**	3075	3925
127" WB Maxivan	**11333**	3150	4000
* For 8 cylinder models add $275 wholesale and $275 retail.			
B150 WAGONS 6*			
109" WB Ram Value Wgn	**11933**	4225	5025
109" WB Ram Wgn	**11980**	4175	4975
127" WB Ram Wgn	**12220**	4500	5300
* For 8 cylinder models add $275 wholesale and $275 retail.			
B250 WAGONS 6*			
127" WB Ram Wgn	**12559**	4600	5400
127" WB Ram Maxiwagon (8 cyl)	**14174**	4850	5650
* For 8 cylinder models add $275 wholesale and $275 retail.			
ADD FOR:			
LE Decor Pkg			
(Ramcharger)	**696**	150	190
(Ram Wgns)	**1203**	290	360
(D & W Pickups)	**630**	130	170
Prospector I Pkg (Dakota)	**607**	120	160
Prospector II Pkg (Dakota)	**1208**	290	360
Prospector III Pkg (Dakota)	**2599**	690	850
Prospector Van Conv Pkg (B150 & B250 Vans)	**2514**	670	820

Refer To Optional Equipment Schedules

DODGE

Year-Model-Body Type	Original List	Current Whlse	Average Retail
1986			
AD-150 106" WB 8			
Ramcharger	**11534**	2825	3675
CARAVAN 4			
Caravan, Base	**9659**	2750	3600
Caravan, Special Ed	**9938**	3075	3925
Caravan, Limited Ed	**10681**	3500	4275
MINI RAM VAN 4			
Mini Ram Van, Base	**8308**	1575	2375
Mini Ram Van, Royal	**9128**	1800	2600
D100 PICKUPS 115" WB 6*			
Sweptline	**7291**	1775	2575
w/131" WB add	**224**	110	140
D150 PICKUPS 115" WB 6*			
Sweptline	**8010**	1925	2725
w/131" WB add	**174**	90	100
* For 8 cylinder models add $250 wholesale and $250 retail.			
D250 PICKUPS 131" WB 6*			
Sweptline	**9333**	2350	3175
B150 VANS 6*			
109" WB Van	**9040**	1975	2775
109" WB Long Range Ram Van	**9109**	2050	2850
127" WB Van	**9266**	2275	3100
127" WB Long Range Ram Van	**9328**	2300	3125
* For 8 cylinder models add $250 wholesale and $250 retail.			
B250 VANS 6*			
109" WB Van	**9489**	2050	2850
127" WB Van	**9718**	2275	3100
127" WB Maxivan	**10349**	2375	3200
* For 8 cylinder models add $250 wholesale and $250 retail.			
B150 WAGONS 6*			
109" WB Ram Value Wgn	**10947**	3125	3975
109" WB Ram Wgn	**10987**	3075	3925
127" WB Ram Wgn	**11215**	3275	4125
* For 8 cylinder models add $250 wholesale and $250 retail.			
B250 WAGONS 6*			
127" WB Ram Wgn	**11535**	3300	4150
127" WB Ram Maxiwagon (8 cyl)	**13024**	3625	4400
* For 8 cylinder models add $250 wholesale and $250 retail.			
ADD FOR:			
LE Pkg (Dakota)	**1074**	180	220
Popular Equip Pkg			
(Caravan SE)	**1155**	190	240
(Caravan LE)	**851**	130	170
Royal SE Pkg			
(Ramcharger)	**680**	140	170
(Ram Wgns)	**1087**	180	220
(D & W Pickups)	**591**	120	150
SE Pkg (Dakota)	**501**	100	130

Year-Model-Body Type	Original List	Current Whlse	Average Retail
1985			
AD-150 106" WB 8			
Ramcharger	**10471**	1975	2775
CARAVAN 4			
Caravan, Base	**9238**	2125	2925
Caravan, Special Ed	**9487**	2350	3175
Caravan, Limited Ed	**10105**	2600	3425
MINI RAM VAN 4			
Mini Ram Van, Base	**8052**	1075	1750
Mini Ram Van, Royal	**8848**	1275	1950
D100 PICKUPS 115" WB 6*			
Sweptline	**6871**	1275	1950
w/131" WB add	**271**	120	140
D150 PICKUPS 115" WB 6*			
Utiline	**7693**	1325	2000
Sweptline	**7558**	1350	2050
w/131" WB add	**168**	70	90
* For 8 cylinder models add $225 wholesale and $225 retail.			
D250 PICKUPS 131" WB 6*			
Utiline	**8645**	1700	2500
Sweptline	**8510**	1750	2550
* For 8 cylinder models add $225 wholesale and $225 retail.			
B150 VANS 6*			
109" WB Van	**8574**	1125	1800
109" WB Long Range Ram Van	**8660**	1175	1850
127" WB Van	**8789**	1275	1950
127" WB Long Range Ram Van	**8868**	1325	2000
* For 8 cylinder models add $225 wholesale and $225 retail.			
B250 VANS 6*			
109" WB Van	**8994**	1175	1850
127" WB Van	**9213**	1300	1975
127" WB Maxivan	**9807**	1475	2250
* For 8 cylinder models add $225 wholesale and $225 retail.			
B150 WAGONS 6*			
109" WB Ram Value Wgn	**10386**	2200	3000
109" WB Ram Wgn	**10343**	2175	2975
127" WB Ram Wgn	**10560**	2300	3125
* For 8 cylinder models add $225 wholesale and $225 retail.			
B250 WAGONS 6*			
127" WB Ram Wgn	**10872**	2250	3050

Year-Model-Body Type	Original List	Current Whlse	Average Retail
127" WB Ram			
Maxiwagon (8 cyl)	**12283**	2600	3425
* For 8 cylinder models add $225 wholesale and $225 retail.			
ADD FOR:			
Prospector Pkg I			
(Pickups)	**1087**	100	130
Prospector Pkg II			
(Pickups)	**1510**	150	200
Prospector Pkg III			
(Pickups)	**2427**	280	350
Royal SE Pkg			
(Ramcharger)	**1161**	110	140
(Ram Wgns)	**1123**	100	130
(Pickups)	**452**	60	70
Travel Equip Pkg			
(Caravan SE & LE)	**1003**	140	160

1984

Year-Model-Body Type	Original List	Current Whlse	Average Retail
AD-150 106" WB 8			
Ramcharger	**9829**	1625	2425
AW-150 106" WB 8			
Ramcharger	**10945**	2250	3050
CARAVAN 4			
Caravan, Base	**8669**	1800	2600
Caravan Special Ed	**8906**	2025	2825
Caravan Limited Ed	**9494**	2250	3050
MINI RAM VAN 4			
Mini Ram Van, Base	**7698**	825	1500
Mini Ram Van, Royal	**8457**	1000	1675
D100 PICKUPS 115" WB 6*			
Sweptline	**6535**	975	1650
w/131" WB add	**208**	90	100
D150 PICKUPS 115" WB 6*			
Utiline	**7368**	1025	1700
Sweptline	**7236**	1100	1775
w/131" WB add	**157**	60	80
* For 8 cylinder models add $200 wholesale and $200 retail.			
D250 PICKUPS 131" WB 6*			
Utiline	**8274**	1325	2000
Sweptline	**8143**	1400	2100
* For 8 cylinder models add $200 wholesale and $200 retail.			
RAMPAGE 104" WB 4			
Rampage	**6899**	625	1175
Rampage 2.2	**7315**	750	1450
B150 VANS 6*			
109" WB Van	**7854**	800	1475
109" WB Long Range			
Ram Van	**7954**	825	1500
127" WB Van	**8064**	875	1575
127" WB Long Range			
Ram Van	**8157**	950	1575
* For 8 cylinder models add $200 wholesale and $200 retail.			
B250 VANS 6*			
109" WB Van	**8493**	825	1500
127" WB Van	**8703**	875	1575
127" WB Maxivan	**9322**	1050	1725
* For 8 cylinder models add $200 wholesale and $200 retail.			
B150 WAGONS 6*			
109" WB Ram Value			
Wgn	**9659**	1725	2525
109" WB Ram Wgn	**9559**	1700	2500
127" WB Ram Wgn	**9768**	1775	2575
* For 8 cylinder models add $200 wholesale and $200 retail.			
B250 WAGONS 6*			
127" WB Ram Wgn	**9987**	1750	2550
127" WB Ram			
Maxiwagon (8 cyl)	**11309**	1900	2700
* For 8 cylinder models add $200 wholesale and $200 retail.			

FORD

1992

Year-Model-Body Type	Original List	Current Whlse	Average Retail
EXPLORER 2WD 6			
2 Dr XL	**15854**	—	—
2 Dr Sport	**17780**	—	—
2 Dr Eddie Bauer	**21208**	—	—
4 Dr XL	**16692**	—	—
4 Dr XLT	**19427**	—	—
4 Dr Eddie Bauer	**22578**	—	—
ADD FOR:			
Leather Seats (Sport)	**1434**	—	—
(XLT)	**1368**	—	—
Cloth Sport Bucket			
Seats (Sport)	**1022**	—	—
(XLT)	**956**	—	—
BRONCO 4WD 6			
Custom Wgn	**19697**	—	—
XLT Wgn	**21841**	—	—
XLT Nite Wgn	**23202**	—	—
Eddie Bauer Wgn	**23201**	—	—
ADD FOR:			
5.0 Liter 8 Cyl Eng			
(Custom, XLT)	**637**	—	—
5.8 Liter 8 Cyl Eng			
(Custom, XLT)	**857**	—	—
(XLT Nite, Eddie Bauer)	**221**	—	—
ECONOLINE CLUB WAGON 138" WB 6			
Custom Wgn	**17713**	—	—

Refer To Optional Equipment Schedules

FORD

Year-Model-Body Type	Original List	Current Whlse	Average Retail
Custom HD Wgn	**18701**	—	—
Custom Super Wgn	**20751**	—	—
XLT Wgn	**20457**	—	—
XLT HD Wgn	**21667**	—	—
XLT Super Wgn	**22326**	—	—
Chateau Wgn	**23963**	—	—
Chateau HD Wgn	**24720**	—	—
ADD FOR:			
5.0 Liter 8 Cyl Eng	**716**	—	—
5.8 Liter 8 Cyl Eng	**937**	—	—
7.5 Liter 8 Cyl Eng	**1421**	—	—
7.3 Liter 8 Cyl Diesel Eng	**3733**	—	—
E-150 ECONOLINE VAN 138" WB 6*			
Cargo	**15933**	—	—
* For 8 cylinder models add $— wholesale and $— retail.			
E-250 ECONOLINE VANS 138" WB 6*			
Cargo	**16347**	—	—
Cargo, Heavy Duty	**16666**	—	—
Cargo, Super	**16997**	—	—
Cargo, Super HD	**17406**	—	—
* For 8 cylinder models add $— wholesale and $— retail.			
ADD FOR:			
5.8 Liter 8 Cyl Eng (E-150)	**937**	—	—
AEROSTAR VANS 119" WB 2WD 6			
Cargo	**14590**	—	—
Cargo, Extended	**15387**	—	—
Window	**14967**	—	—
Window, Extended	**15714**	—	—
ADD FOR:			
4.0 Liter 6 Cyl Eng (2WD models)	**316**	—	—
AEROSTAR WAGONS 119" WB 2WD 6			
Wgn, XL	**14596**	—	—
Wgn, XL Extended	**16388**	—	—
Wgn, XL Plus	**16092**	—	—
Wgn, XL Plus Extended	**17277**	—	—
Wgn, XLT	**17944**	—	—
Wgn, XLT Extended	**18621**	—	—
Wgn, Eddie Bauer	**21636**	—	—
Wgn, Eddie Bauer Extended	**22604**	—	—
ADD FOR:			
4.0 Liter 6 Cyl Eng (2WD models)	**300**	—	—
F-150 PICKUPS 117" WB 6*			
S Styleside	**11264**	—	—
Styleside	**13613**	—	—
Flareside	**14926**	—	—
* For 8 cylinder models add $— wholesale and $— retail.			

Year-Model-Body Type	Original List	Current Whlse	Average Retail
F-150 PICKUPS 133" WB 6*			
S Styleside	**11500**	—	—
Styleside	**13957**	—	—
* For 8 cylinder models add $— wholesale and $— retail.			
F-150 SUPER CAB PICKUPS 139" WB 6			
S Styleside	**13667**	—	—
Styleside	**14979**	—	—
Flareside	**15990**	—	—
* For 8 cylinder models add $— wholesale and $— retail.			
F-150 SUPER CAB PICKUP 155" WB 6			
S Styleside	**13771**	—	—
* For 8 cylinder models add $— wholesale and $— retail.			
ADD FOR:			
XL Pkg (2WD Styleside)	**621**	—	—
(4WD Styleside)	**465**	—	—
(Super Cab)	**416**	—	—
XLT Lariat Pkg			
(2WD Styleside)	**1263**	—	—
(4WD Styleside)	**1107**	—	—
(Flareside)	**1056**	—	—
(Super Cab)	**1257**	—	—
XLT Lariat Nite Pkg			
(2WD Styleside)	**2439**	—	—
(4WD Styleside)	**2283**	—	—
(Flareside)	**999**	—	—
(Styleside Super Cab)	**3227**	—	—
(Flareside Super Cab)	**999**	—	—
5.8 Liter 8 Cyl Eng	**857**	—	—
F-250 PICKUPS 133" WB 6			
Styleside (under 8500 lb. GVW)	**14697**	—	—
Styleside (over 8500 lb. GVW)	**15413**	—	—
F-250 SUPER CAB PICKUP 155" WB 8			
Styleside (over 8500 lb. GVW)	**17808**	—	—
ADD FOR:			
XLT Lariat Pkg			
(Styleside)	**2029**	—	—
(Super Cab)	**2179**	—	—
5.0 Liter 8 Cyl Eng (Styleside under 8500 lb. GVW)	**637**	—	—
5.8 Liter 8 Cyl Eng (2WD Styleside)	**857**	—	—
7.3 Liter 8 Cyl Diesel Eng			
(2WD Styleside over 8500 lb. GVW)	**3072**	—	—
(4WD Styleside, Super Cab)	**2215**	—	—
7.5 Liter 8 Cyl Eng			

Year-Model-Body Type	Original List	Current Whlse	Average Retail
(2WD Styleside over 8500 lb. GVW)	**1341**	—	—
(4WD Styleside, Super Cab)	**484**	—	—
RANGER S 2WD 4			
108" WB	**9820**	—	—
RANGER 2WD 4*			
Sport 108" WB	**9759**	—	—
Sport 114" WB	**9916**	—	—
Custom 108" WB	**10905**	—	—
Custom 114" WB	**11225**	—	—
* For 6 cylinder models add $— wholesale and $— retail.			
RANGER SUPER CAB 2WD 4			
125" WB	**12216**	—	—
ADD FOR:			
2.9 Liter 6 Cyl Eng (4WD Sport & Custom)	**556**	—	—
4.0 Liter 6 Cyl Eng (2WD Sport & Custom)	**620**	—	—
(4WD Sport & Custom)	**735**	—	—
(4WD Super Cab)	**179**	—	—

1991

Year-Model-Body Type	Original List	Current Whlse	Average Retail
EXPLORER 2WD 6			
2 Dr XL	**14586**	12225	13975
2 Dr Sport	**15961**	12925	15125
2 Dr Eddie Bauer	**18882**	14000	16250
4 Dr XL	**15541**	13225	15425
4 Dr XLT	**17642**	14200	16525
4 Dr Eddie Bauer	**20164**	14925	17400
BRONCO 105" WB 6*			
Wgn	**18463**	13550	15800
Silver Anniversary Wgn	**25690**	—	—
* For 8 cylinder models add $425 wholesale and $425 retail.			
E-150 CLUB WAGON 138" WB 6*			
8 Pass Wgn	**17530**	11550	13200
* For 8 cylinder models add $425 wholesale and $425 retail.			
E-250 CLUB WAGON 138" WB 6*			
12 Pass Wgn	**18614**	11925	13625
* For 8 cylinder models add $425 wholesale and $425 retail.			
E-150 ECONOLINE VANS 138" WB 6*			
Cargo	**14766**	9300	10575
Cargo, Super	**15712**	10000	11375
* For 8 cylinder models add $425 wholesale and $425 retail.			
E-250 ECONOLINE VANS 138" WB 6*			
Cargo	**15116**	9425	10725
Cargo, Heavy Duty	**15519**	9600	10925
Cargo, Super	**15851**	10300	11750
* For 8 cylinder models add $425 wholesale and $425 retail.			
AEROSTAR VANS 119" WB 2WD 6*			
Cargo	**13519**	8475	9650
Cargo, Extended	**14266**	9275	10550
Window	**13903**	8575	9775
Window, Extended	**14650**	9375	10675
* For 4.0 liter 6 cylinder models add $200 wholesale and $200 retail.			
AEROSTAR WAGONS 119" WB 2WD 6*			
Wgn, XL	**13986**	10400	11875
Wgn, XL Extended	**15121**	11325	12850
Wgn, XLT	**15909**	11400	13025
Wgn, XLT Extended	**16807**	12200	13950
Wgn, Eddie Bauer	**19025**	12275	14050
Wgn, Eddie Bauer Extended	**19922**	12975	15175
F-150 PICKUPS 117" WB 6*			
S Styleside	**11026**	8450	9625
Custom Styleside	**12745**	8800	10025
w/133" WB add			
(S)	**225**	140	160
(Custom)	**244**	140	160
* For 8 cylinder models add $425 wholesale and $425 retail.			
F-150 SUPER CAB PICKUPS 139" WB 6*			
S Styleside	**12318**	9450	10750
Custom Styleside	**14129**	9800	11150
* For 8 cylinder models add $425 wholesale and $425 retail.			
F-150 SUPER CAB PICKUPS 155" WB 6*			
S Styleside	**12544**	9600	10925
Custom Styleside	**14363**	9925	11300
* For 8 cylinder models add $425 wholesale and $425 retail.			
F-250 PICKUPS 133" WB 6*			
Styleside (under 8500 lb. GVW)	**13854**	9575	10900
* For 8 cylinder models add $425 wholesale and $425 retail.			
F-250 HD PICKUPS 133" WB 6*			
Styleside (over 8500 lb. GVW)	**14271**	9875	11250
F-250 HD SUPER CAB PICKUP 155" WB 8			
Styleside (over 8500 lb. GVW)	**16680**	10875	12425
RANGER S 2WD 4*			
108" WB	**9134**	5575	6375
* For 6 cylinder models add $400 wholesale and $400 retail.			
RANGER 2WD 4*			
Sport 108" WB	**9347**	6600	7550
Sport 114" WB	**9503**	6700	7650
Custom 108" WB	**10508**	6775	7750
Custom 114" WB	**10833**	6900	7900

Refer To Optional Equipment Schedules

Year-Model-Body Type	Original List	Current Whlse	Average Retail
* For 6 cylinder models add $400 wholesale and $400 retail.			
RANGER SUPER CAB 2WD 4*			
125" WB	**12020**	7175	8200
* For 6 cylinder models add $400 wholesale and $400 retail.			
ADD FOR:			
XL Pkg			
(Econoline)	—	260	330
(F-150 Reg Cab)	**445**	210	260
(F-250 Reg Cab)	**340**	150	190
(F-250 Super Cab)	**244**	140	170
XLT Pkg			
(Bronco)	**2378**	1350	1630
(Econoline E-150 Club Wgn)	**2278**	1290	1560
(Econoline E-250 Club Wgn)	**4672**	2700	3270
XLT Nite Pkg (Bronco)	**3589**	2060	2490
XLT Lariat Trim			
(F-150)	—	620	760
(F-250)	—	1190	1450
XLT Lariat Nite Trim			
(F-150)	—	1310	1580
Eddie Bauer Pkg			
(Bronco)	**4044**	2330	2820
1990			
BRONCO 105" WB 6*			
Wgn	**17619**	9925	11300
* For 8 cylinder models add $400 wholesale and $400 retail.			
BRONCO II 94" WB 6			
Bronco II 2WD	**13769**	7125	8125
E-150 CLUB WAGON 138" WB 6*			
8 Pass Wgn	**17569**	9650	10975
* For 8 cylinder models add $400 wholesale and $400 retail.			
E-250 CLUB WAGON 138" WB 6*			
12 Pass Wgn	**18094**	10025	11400
* For 8 cylinder models add $400 wholesale and $400 retail.			
E-150 ECONOLINE VANS 124" WB 6*			
Cargo	**13713**	7075	8100
* For 8 cylinder models add $400 wholesale and $400 retail.			
E-150 ECONOLINE VANS 138" WB 6*			
Cargo	**13983**	7200	8225
Cargo, Super	**14893**	7900	9025
* For 8 cylinder models add $400 wholesale and $400 retail.			
E-250 ECONOLINE VANS 138" WB 6*			
Cargo	**14272**	7350	8400
Cargo, Super	**15031**	8050	9200
* For 8 cylinder models add $400 wholesale and $400 retail.			
AEROSTAR VANS 119" WB 2WD 6*			
Cargo	**12726**	6225	7100
Cargo, Extended	**13473**	6925	7925
Window	**13110**	6325	7225
Window, Extended	**13857**	7075	8100
Wagon	**13152**	8100	9225
Wagon, Extended	**14050**	8850	10075
* For 4.0 liter 6 cylinder models add $200 wholesale and $200 retail.			
F-150 PICKUPS 117" WB 6*			
S Styleside	**11151**	6225	7100
Styleside	**12017**	6900	7900
w/133" WB add			
(2WD)	**216**	110	130
(4WD)	**335**	170	200
* For 8 cylinder models add $400 wholesale and $400 retail.			
F-150 SUPER CAB PICKUP 139" WB 6*			
Styleside	**13367**	7750	8850
* For 8 cylinder models add $400 wholesale and $400 retail.			
F-150 SUPER CAB PICKUP 155" WB 6*			
Styleside	**13591**	7875	9000
* For 8 cylinder models add $400 wholesale and $400 retail.			
F-250 PICKUPS 133" WB 6*			
Styleside (under 8500 lb. GVW)	**12962**	7625	8725
Styleside (over 8500 lb. GVW)	**13411**	7925	9075
* For 8 cylinder models (under 8500 lb. GVW) add $400 wholesale and $400 retail. For 8 cylinder models (over 8500 lb. GVW) add $400 wholesale and $400 retail.			
F-250 SUPER CAB 2WD 155" WB 6			
Styleside (over 8500 lb. GVW)	**15765**	8500	9675
F-250 SUPER CAB 4WD 155" WB 8			
Styleside (over 8500 lb. GVW)	**18070**	10125	11550
RANGER 2WD 4*			
108" WB	**10188**	5175	5975
114" WB	**10351**	5275	6075
* For 6 cylinder models add $400 wholesale and $400 retail.			
RANGER "S" 2WD 4			
108" WB	**8607**	4075	4850
114" WB	**8763**	4175	4975
RANGER SUPER CAB 2WD 4*			
125" WB	**11461**	5750	6550
* For 6 cylinder models add $375 wholesale and $375 retail.			

Year-Model-Body Type	Original List	Current Whlse	Average Retail
ADD FOR:			
Sport Appearance Pkg			
(Bronco II)	**695**	310	380
Sport Trim Pkg			
(Bronco II)	**824**	370	460
Eddie Bauer Pkg			
(Bronco)	**3578**	1790	2170
(Aerostar)	**6668**	3370	4080
XL Pkg			
(Econoline Van)	**794**	350	440
(F-150 Pickups)	—	350	440
(F-250 Pickups)	**767**	340	420
XL Plus Pkg			
(Aerostar)	**2072**	1010	1230
XL Sport Pkg			
(Bronco II)	**799**	350	440
XLT Pkg			
(Bronco II)	**640**	280	350
(Bronco)	**1197**	570	690
(Econoline Club Wgn)	**2416**	1190	1450
(Aerostar)	**3037**	1510	1830
(Ranger)	—	150	200
XLT Plus Pkg			
(Aerostar)	**4360**	2190	2650
XLT Lariat Pkg			
(F-Pickups)	—	800	970
Plus Pkg			
(Ranger S)	—	350	440

1989

Year-Model-Body Type	Original List	Current Whlse	Average Retail
BRONCO 105" WB 6*			
Wgn	**15983**	8625	9825
* For 8 cylinder models add $375 wholesale and $375 retail.			
BRONCO II 94" WB 6			
Bronco II 2WD	**12520**	6075	6875
E-150 CLUB WAGON 138" WB 6*			
5 Pass Wgn	**15289**	7625	8725
E-250 CLUB WAGON 138" WB 6*			
5 Pass Wgn	**16060**	7900	9025
* For 8 cylinder models add $375 wholesale and $375 retail.			
E-150 ECONOLINE VANS 124" WB 6*			
Cargo	**11443**	5450	6250
* For 8 cylinder models add $375 wholesale and $375 retail.			
E-150 ECONOLINE VANS 138" WB 6*			
Cargo	**11702**	5625	6425
Cargo, Super	**13291**	6325	7225
* For 8 cylinder models add $375 wholesale and $375 retail.			
E-250 ECONOLINE VANS 138" WB 6*			
Cargo	**12684**	5750	6550
Cargo, Super	**13400**	6450	7375
* For 8 cylinder models add $375 wholesale and $375 retail.			
AEROSTAR VANS 119" WB 6			
Cargo	**11126**	4925	5725
Cargo, Extended	**11666**	5625	6425
Window	**11509**	5025	5825
Window, Extended	**12049**	5750	6550
Wagon	**11645**	6850	7825
Wagon, Extended	**12292**	7525	8600
F-150 PICKUPS 117" WB 6*			
S Styleside	**10067**	5625	6425
Styleside	**10516**	6250	7150
w/133" WB add	**200**	90	100
* For 8 cylinder models add $375 wholesale and $375 retail.			
F-150 SUPER CAB PICKUP 138" WB 6*			
Styleside	**12027**	6650	7600
* For 8 cylinder models add $375 wholesale and $375 retail.			
F-150 SUPER CAB PICKUP 155" WB 6*			
Styleside	**12227**	6775	7750
* For 8 cylinder models add $375 wholesale and $375 retail.			
F-250 PICKUPS 133" WB 6*			
Styleside			
(under 8500 lb. GVW)	**11419**	6575	7525
Styleside			
(over 8500 lb. GVW)	**11843**	6900	7900
* For 8 cylinder models (under 8500 lb. GVW) add $375 wholesale and $375 retail. For 8 cylinder models (over 8500 lb. GVW) add $375 wholesale and $375 retail.			
F-250 SUPER CAB 2WD 155" WB 6			
Styleside			
(over 8500 lb. GVW)	**14250**	7300	8350
F-250 SUPER CAB 4WD 155" WB 8			
Styleside			
(over 8500 lb. GVW)	**16395**	7625	8725
RANGER 2WD 4*			
108" WB	**9045**	4650	5450
114" WB	**9208**	4725	5525
RANGER 'S' 2WD 4			
108" WB	**7693**	4075	4850
RANGER SUPER CAB 2WD 4*			
125" WB	**10458**	5100	5900
* For 6 cylinder 2WD models add $325 wholesale and $325 retail. For 6 cylinder 4WD models add $325 wholesale and $325 retail.			
RANGER SUPER CAB 4WD 6			
125" WB	**13451**	6450	7375
ADD FOR:			
XL Sport Pkg			
(Bronco II)	**1693**	690	840
XL Pkg			

Refer To Optional Equipment Schedules

FORD

Year-Model-Body Type	Original List	Current Whlse	Average Retail
(Econoline)	**590**	210	260
(F-Pickups)	**470**	160	200
XLT Pkg			
(Bronco II)	**1455**	580	710
(Bronco)	**1599**	650	790
(Aerostar)	**3770**	1600	1940
(Ranger)	**1400**	560	690
XLT Lariat Pkg			
(F-Pickups)	**2380**	990	1210
Eddie Bauer Pkg			
(Bronco II)	**3537**	1490	1810
(Bronco)	**5000**	2140	2590
(Aerostar)	**7350**	270	340
STX Pkg (Ranger)	**2500**	110	130
GT Pkg (Ranger)	**4655**	1990	2400
1988			
BRONCO 105" WB 6*			
Wgn	**15279**	7250	8275
* For 8 cylinder models add $325 wholesale and $325 retail.			
BRONCO II 94" WB 6			
Bronco II 2WD	**11707**	4775	5575
E-150 CLUB WAGON 138" WB 6*			
5 Pass Wgn	**14621**	6225	7100
E-250 CLUB WAGON 138" WB 6*			
5 Pass Wgn	**15462**	6350	7250
E-150 ECONOLINE VANS 124" WB 6*			
Cargo	**10949**	3975	4750
* For 8 cylinder models add $325 wholesale and $325 retail.			
E-150 ECONOLINE VANS 138" WB 6*			
Cargo	**11196**	4100	4875
Cargo, Super	**12724**	4725	5525
* For 8 cylinder models add $325 wholesale and $325 retail.			
E-250 ECONOLINE VANS 138" WB 6*			
Cargo	**12102**	4150	4950
Cargo, Super	**12818**	4775	5575
* For 8 cylinder models add $325 wholesale and $325 retail.			
AEROSTAR VANS 119" WB 6			
Cargo (4 cyl)	**10540**	3625	4400
Window	**10924**	4800	5600
Wagon	**11165**	5525	6325
F-150 PICKUPS 117" WB 6*			
S Styleside	**9676**	3725	4500
Styleside	**10038**	3850	4625
w/133" WB add	**189**	80	100
* For 8 cylinder models add $325 wholesale and $325 retail.			
F-150 SUPERCAB PICKUP 138" WB 6*			
Styleside	**11550**	5275	6075

Year-Model-Body Type	Original List	Current Whlse	Average Retail
* For 8 cylinder models add $325 wholesale and $325 retail.			
F-150 SUPER CAB PICKUP 155" WB 6*			
Styleside	**11739**	5400	6200
* For 8 cylinder models add $325 wholesale and $325 retail.			
F-250 PICKUPS 133" WB 6*			
Styleside (under 8500 lb. GVW)	**10849**	5125	5925
Styleside (over 8500 lb. GVW)	**11288**	5500	6300
* For 8 cylinder models add $325 wholesale and $325 retail.			
F-250 SUPER CAB 155" WB 6			
Styleside (over 8500 lb. GVW)	**12898**	6225	7100
F-250 SUPER CAB 4WD 155" WB 8			
Styleside (over 8500 lb. GVW)	**15734**	7775	8900
RANGER 4*			
108" WB	**8396**	3525	4300
114" WB	**8558**	3625	4400
RANGER 'S' 4			
108" WB	**7093**	2675	3525
* For 6 cylinder models add $300 wholesale and $300 retail.			
RANGER SUPER CAB 2WD 4			
125" WB	**9691**	3975	4750
RANGER SUPER CAB 4WD 6			
125" WB	**11956**	5275	6075
ADD FOR:			
XL Sport Pkg			
(Bronco II)	**1215**	390	480
XL Pkg (F-Pickups)	**430**	110	140
XLT Pkg			
(Bronco II)	**890**	270	340
(Bronco)	**1400**	460	560
XLT Lariat Pkg			
(F-Series)	**1440**	470	580
GT Pkg (Ranger)	**3460**	1200	1460
STX Pkg (Ranger)	**1460**	480	590
Eddie Bauer Pkg			
(Bronco II)	**3450**	1200	1460
(Bronco)	**3970**	1390	1680
1987			
BRONCO 105" WB 6*			
Wgn	**14166**	5500	6300
* For 8 cylinder models add $275 wholesale and $275 retail.			
BRONCO II 94" WB 6			
Bronco II 2WD	**11398**	3075	3925

Year-Model-Body Type	Original List	Current Whlse	Average Retail
E-150 CLUB WAGON 138" WB 6*			
5 Pass Wgn	**13171**	4800	5600
E-250 CLUB WAGON 138" WB 6*			
5 Pass Wgn	**14881**	4900	5700
E-150 ECONOLINE VANS 124" WB 6*			
Cargo	**10449**	2450	3275
Window	**10740**	2575	3400
* For 8 cylinder models add $275 wholesale and $275 retail.			
E-150 ECONOLINE VANS 138" WB 6*			
Cargo	**10688**	2550	3375
Window	**10979**	2625	3475
Cargo, Super	**11599**	2900	3750
Window, Super	**11890**	2975	3825
* For 8 cylinder models add $275 wholesale and $275 retail.			
E-250 ECONOLINE VANS 138" WB 6*			
Cargo	**11589**	2575	3400
Window	**11880**	2675	3525
Cargo, Super	**12302**	2850	3700
* For 8 cylinder models add $275 wholesale and $275 retail.			
AEROSTAR VANS 119" WB 6			
Cargo (4 cyl)	**10045**	1975	2775
Window	**10428**	2275	3100
Wagon	**10682**	3600	4375
F-150 PICKUPS 117" WB 6*			
Styleside	**9509**	3100	3950
Flareside	**9772**	3150	4000
w/133" WB add	**184**	90	110
* For 8 cylinder models add $275 wholesale and $275 retail.			
F-150 SUPER CAB PICKUP 155" WB 6*			
Styleside (139" WB)	**11405**	3725	4500
* For 8 cylinder models add $275 wholesale and $275 retail.			
F-250 PICKUPS 133" WB 6*			
Styleside (under 8500 lb. GVW)	**10566**	3725	4500
Styleside (over 8500 lb. GVW)	**10874**	3925	4700
* For 8 cylinder models add $275 wholesale and $275 retail.			
F-250 SUPER CAB 155" WB 6			
Styleside (over 8500 lb. GVW)	**12686**	4575	5375
F-250 SUPER CAB 4WD 155" WB 8			
Styleside (over 8500 lb. GVW)	**15834**	5500	6300
RANGER 4*			
108" WB	**7684**	2025	2825
114" WB	**7845**	2125	2925
* For 6 cylinder models add $250 wholesale and $250 retail.			
RANGER 'S' 4			
108" WB	**6393**	1950	2750
RANGER SUPER CAB 2WD 4			
125" WB	**8846**	2350	3175
ADD FOR:			
XL Pkg (F-Pickups)	**395**	110	140
XLT Pkg			
(Bronco II)	**830**	190	240
(Bronco)	**980**	230	290
(Ranger)	**780**	170	220
XLT Lariat Pkg			
(F-Pickups)	—	220	280
STX Pkg			
(Ranger)	—	250	310
Eddie Bauer Pkg			
(Bronco II)	**2260**	600	730

1986

Year-Model-Body Type	Original List	Current Whlse	Average Retail
BRONCO 104" WB 6*			
Wgn	**12782**	4450	5250
* For 8 cylinder models add $250 wholesale and $250 retail.			
BRONCO II 94" WB 6*			
Bronco II 2WD	**10420**	2475	3300
E-150 CLUB WAGON 138" WB 6*			
5 Pass Wgn	**12274**	3500	4275
E-250 CLUB WAGON 138" WB 6*			
5 Pass Wgn	**13839**	3600	4375
E-150 ECONOLINE VANS 124" WB 6*			
Cargo	**9439**	1700	2500
Window	**9710**	1775	2575
* For 8 cylinder models add $250 wholesale and $250 retail.			
E-150 ECONOLINE VANS 138" WB 6*			
Cargo	**9663**	1800	2600
Window	**9934**	1925	2725
Cargo, Super	**10593**	2400	3225
Window, Super	**10863**	2500	3325
* For 8 cylinder models add $250 wholesale and $250 retail.			
E-250 ECONOLINE VANS 138" WB 6*			
Cargo	**10561**	1850	2650
Window	**10831**	2000	2800
Cargo, Super	**11221**	2450	3275
* For 8 cylinder models add $250 wholesale and $250 retail.			
AEROSTAR VANS 119" WB 4			
Cargo	**8774**	1300	1975
Window	**9822**	1375	2075
Wagon	**9553**	2475	3300
F-150 PICKUPS 117" WB 6*			
Styleside	**8373**	2450	3300
Flareside	**8626**	2550	3375

Refer To Optional Equipment Schedules

Year-Model-Body Type	Original List	Current Whlse	Average Retail
w/133" WB add	**174**	90	100
* For 8 cylinder models add $250 wholesale and $250 retail.			
F-150 SUPER CAB PICKUP 138" WB 6*			
Styleside	**10272**	3000	3850
* For 8 cylinder models add $250 wholesale and $250 retail.			
F-150 SUPER CAB PICKUP 155" WB 6*			
Styleside	**10446**	3100	3950
* For 8 cylinder models add $250 wholesale and $250 retail.			
F-250 PICKUPS 133" WB 6*			
Styleside (under 8500 lb. GVW)	**9646**	3000	3850
Styleside (over 8500 lb. GVW)	**9978**	3350	4200
* For 8 cylinder models under 8500 lb. GVW add $250 wholesale and $250 retail. For 8 cylinder models over 8500 lb. GVW add $250 wholesale and $250 retail.			
F-250 SUPER CAB 155" WB 6			
Styleside (over 8500 lb. GVW)	**11645**	3550	4325
F-250 SUPER CAB 4WD 155" WB 8			
Styleside (over 8500 lb. GVW)	**14015**	4425	5225
RANGER 4*			
108" WB Pickup	**7065**	1450	2175
114" WB Pickup	**7221**	1550	2350
* For 6 cylinder models add $225 wholesale and $225 retail.			
RANGER 'S' 4			
108" WB Pickup	**5993**	1175	1850
RANGER SUPER CAB 2WD 4			
125" WB	**8053**	1675	2475
* For 6 cylinder models add $225 wholesale and $225 retail.			
ADD FOR:			
XL Pkg (F-Pickups)	**395**	80	100
XLT Pkg			
(Bronco II)	**830**	120	160
(Bronco)	**980**	160	200
(Ranger)	**780**	120	150
XLT Lariat Pkg			
(F-Pickups)	**625**	130	160
STX Pkg (Ranger)	—	140	180

1985

Year-Model-Body Type	Original List	Current Whlse	Average Retail
BRONCO 104" WB 6* E			
Wgn	**12050**	3500	4275
Eddie Bauer Wgn	**16029**	4050	4825
* For 8 cylinder models add $225 wholesale and $225 retail.			
BRONCO II 94" WB 6*			
Bronco II	**11102**	2650	3500
Bronco II Eddie Bauer	**13365**	3075	3925
E-150 CLUB WAGON 124" WB 6*			
5 Pass Wgn	**11641**	2375	3200
E-150 CLUB WAGON 138" WB 6*			
5 Pass Wgn	**13140**	2475	3300
E-150 ECONOLINE VANS 124" WB 6*			
Cargo	**8676**	1125	1800
Display	**8802**	1200	1875
Window	**8870**	1225	1900
* For 8 cylinder models add $225 wholesale and $225 retail.			
E-150 ECONOLINE VANS 138" WB 6*			
Cargo	**8888**	1200	1875
Display	**9015**	1275	1950
Window	**9082**	1300	1975
Cargo, Super	**9765**	1425	2125
Window, Super	**9959**	1550	2350
* For 8 cylinder models add $225 wholesale and $225 retail.			
E-250 ECONOLINE VANS 138" WB 6*			
Cargo	**9940**	1275	1950
Display	**10067**	1325	2000
Window	**10134**	1375	2075
Cargo, Super	**10570**	1550	2350
Window, Super	**10764**	1625	2425
* For 8 cylinder models add $225 wholesale and $225 retail.			
F-150 PICKUPS 117" WB 6*			
Styleside	**7902**	1950	2750
Flareside	**8066**	1925	2725
w/133" WB add	**166**	70	90
* For 8 cylinder models add $225 wholesale and $225 retail.			
F-150 SUPERCAB PICKUP 139" WB 6*			
Styleside	**9238**	2275	3100
* For 8 cylinder models add $225 wholesale and $225 retail.			
F-150 SUPER CAB PICKUP 155" WB 6*			
Styleside	**9404**	2375	3200
* For 8 cylinder models add $225 wholesale and $225 retail.			
F-250 PICKUPS 133" WB 6*			
Styleside (over 8500 lb. GVW)	**9563**	2400	3225
* For 8 cylinder models under 8500 lb. GVW add $225 wholesale and $225 retail. For 8 cylinder models over 8500 lb. GVW add $225 wholesale and $225 retail.			
F-250 SUPER CAB 4WD 155" WB 8			
Styleside (over 8500 lb. GVW)	**13177**	4075	4850
RANGER 4			
108" WB Pickup	**6675**	1100	1775

Year-Model-Body Type	Original List	Current Whlse	Average Retail
114" WB Pickup	**6829**	1175	1850
RANGER 'S' 4			
108" WB Pickup	**5995**	1250	1925
ADD FOR:			
California Pkg (E250 Club Wgn)	**492**	70	80
Camper Pkg (Econoline Vans)	**641**	90	100
Explorer Pkg A (F Series Pickups)	**525**	70	90
Explorer Pkg B (F Series Pickups)	**800**	110	130
Explorer Pkg C (F Series Pickups)	**1328**	130	170
Explorer Pkg D (F Series Pickups)	**1763**	190	240
XL Trim			
(Ranger)	**355**	50	60
(F Series Pickups)	—	50	60
XLT Trim			
(Ranger)	**737**	100	120
(F Series Pickups)	**655**	90	100

1984

Year-Model-Body Type	Original List	Current Whlse	Average Retail
BRONCO 104" WB 6*			
Wgn	**11468**	2925	3775
* For 8 cylinder models add $200 wholesale and $200 retail.			
BRONCO II 94" WB 6*			
Bronco II	**10446**	2175	2975
Bronco II Eddie Bauer	**12638**	2400	3225
E-150 CLUB WAGON 124" WB 6*			
5 Pass Wgn	**9621**	1825	2625
E-150 CLUB WAGON 138" WB 6*			
5 Pass Wgn	**9830**	1925	2725
E-250 CLUB WAGONS 138" WB 6*			
11 Pass Wgn	**11474**	2025	2825
5 Pass HD Extended Super Wgn	**11911**	2575	3400
5 Pass Extended Super Wgn	**11584**	2500	3325
E-150 ECONOLINE VANS 124" WB 6*			
Cargo	**7835**	1225	1900
Display	**7957**	1275	1950
Window	**8023**	1325	2000
* For 8 cylinder models add $200 wholesale and $200 retail.			
E-150 ECONOLINE VANS 138" WB 6*			
Cargo	**8045**	1300	1975
Display	**8167**	1350	2050
Window	**8233**	1400	2100
Cargo, Super	**8984**	1550	2350
Display, Super	**9106**	1625	2425
Window, Super	**9172**	1650	2450
* For 8 cylinder models add $200 wholesale and $200 retail.			
E-250 ECONOLINE VANS 138" WB 6*			
Cargo	**8889**	1050	1725
Display	**9011**	1125	1800
Window	**9077**	1200	1875
Cargo, Super	**9496**	1225	1900
Display, Super	**9618**	1275	1950
Window, Super	**9684**	1350	2050
* For 8 cylinder models add $200 wholesale and $200 retail.			
F-150 PICKUPS 117" WB 6*			
Styleside	**7209**	1550	2350
Flareside	**7371**	1550	2350
w/133" WB add	**157**	50	60
* For 8 cylinder models add $200 wholesale and $200 retail.			
F-150 SUPER CAB PICKUP 139" WB 6*			
Styleside	**8674**	1875	2675
* For 8 cylinder models add $200 wholesale and $200 retail.			
F-150 SUPER CAB PICKUP 155" WB 6*			
Styleside	**8832**	1975	2775
* For 8 cylinder models add $200 wholesale and $200 retail.			
F-250 PICKUPS 133" WB 6*			
Styleside (under 8500 lb. GVW)	**8130**	1925	2725
Styleside (over 8500 lb. GVW)	**9034**	2200	3000
* For 8 cylinder models under 8500 lb. GVW add $200 wholesale and $200 retail. For 8 cylinder models over 8500 lb. GVW add $200 wholesale and $200 retail.			
F-250 SUPER CAB 155" WB 6*			
Styleside (over 8500 lb. GVW)	**9811**	2475	3300
* For 8 cylinder models add $200 wholesale and $200 retail.			
RANGER 4			
108" WB Pickup	**6453**	950	1625
114" WB Pickup	**6612**	1050	1725

GMC

1992

Year-Model-Body Type	Original List	Current Whlse	Average Retail
YUKON 4WD 112" WB			
2 Dr Wgn	**20493**	—	—
ADD FOR:			
SLE Pkg (models w/o sport pkg)	**1135**	—	—
(models w/sport pkg)	**705**	—	—

Refer To Optional Equipment Schedules

GMC

Year-Model-Body Type	Original List	Current Whlse	Average Retail
Sport Pkg	**1197**	—	—
JIMMY 2WD 100.5" WB 6			
2 Dr Sport Utility	**15802**	—	—
JIMMY 2WD 107" WB 6			
4 Dr Sport Utility	**16762**	—	—
ADD FOR:			
SLE Pkg	**815**	—	—
SLS Pkg (2WD models)	**991**	—	—
(4WD models)	**744**	—	—
TYPHOON 4WD 100.5" WB 6			
2 Dr Sport Utility	**28995**	—	—
SONOMA REG CAB PICKUPS 2WD 4*			
Special Wideside (108" WB)	**10021**	—	—
Wideside (108" WB)	**11087**	—	—
Wideside (118" WB)	**11387**	—	—
* For 2.8 liter 6 cylinder engine add $— wholesale and $— retail.			
SONOMA GT 2WD 6			
Wideside	**16300**	—	—
SONOMA CLUB COUPE 2WD 4			
Wideside	**12312**	—	—
SONOMA SYCLONE TURBO 4WD 6			
Wideside	**26995**	—	—
ADD FOR:			
SLE Pkg	**522**	—	—
4.3 Liter EFI 6 Cyl Eng (2WD models)	**620**	—	—
4.3 Liter PFI 6 Cyl Eng (2WD models)	**1120**	—	—
(4WD models)	**500**	—	—
C-1500 PICKUPS 117.5" WB 6*			
Wideside	**14138**	—	—
Sportside	**14538**	—	—
* For 8 cylinder models add $— wholesale and $— retail.			
C-1500 PICKUPS 131.5" WB 6*			
Wideside	**14438**	—	—
Special Wideside	**11569**	—	—
* For 8 cylinder models add $— wholesale and $— retail.			
C-1500 CLUB COUPE PICKUPS 141.5" WB 6*			
Wideside	**15088**	—	—
Sportside	**15488**	—	—
* For 8 cylinder models add $— wholesale and $— retail.			
C-1500 CLUB COUPE PICKUP 155.5" WB 6*			
Wideside	**15378**	—	—
* For 8 cylinder models add $— wholesale and $— retail.			
ADD FOR:			
5.7 Liter 8 Cyl Eng	**845**	—	—
6.2 Liter 8 Cyl Diesel Eng	**2400**	—	—
SLE Pkg	**810**	—	—
SLX Pkg	**589**	—	—
Sport Pkg (2WD models)	**723**	—	—
(4WD models)	**1030**	—	—
Sport Handling Pkg	**805**	—	—
C-2500 PICKUPS 131.5" WB 6*			
Wideside	**15078**	—	—
Heavy Duty Wideside	**15911**	—	—
* For 8 cylinder models add $— wholesale and $— retail.			
C-2500 CLUB COUPE PICKUP 141.5" WB 6*			
Wideside	**16198**	—	—
* For 8 cylinder models add $— wholesale and $— retail.			
C-2500 CLUB COUPE PICKUPS 155.5" WB 6*			
Wideside	**16478**	—	—
Heavy Duty Wideside	**16971**	—	—
* For 8 cylinder models add $— wholesale and $— retail.			
ADD FOR:			
SLE Pkg	**794**	—	—
SLX Pkg	**589**	—	—
5.7 Liter 8 Cyl Eng	**845**	—	—
7.4 Liter 8 Cyl Eng	**1315**	—	—
6.2 Liter 8 Cyl Diesel Eng	**2400**	—	—
6.5 Liter 8 Cyl Turbo Diesel Eng	**3100**	—	—
C-1500 SUBURBAN 2WD 131.5" WB 8			
Panel Doors	**19238**	—	—
ADD FOR:			
SLE Pkg	**2109**	—	—
C-2500 SUBURBAN 2WD 131.5" WB 8			
Panel Doors	**20442**	—	—
ADD FOR:			
SLE Pkg	**2109**	—	—
7.4 Liter 8 Cyl Eng	**470**	—	—
SAFARI 2WD 111" WB 6			
Cargo Van	**14908**	—	—
Extended Cargo Van	**15578**	—	—
Pass Van	**16249**	—	—
Extended Pass Van	**16939**	—	—
ADD FOR:			
SLE Pkg	**1092**	—	—
SLT Pkg	**2952**	—	—
GT Sport Pkg (models w/SLE pkg)	**737**	—	—
(models w/o SLE pkg)	**1196**	—	—
4.3 Liter CPI 6 Cyl Eng (2WD models)	**500**	—	—
G-1500 VANS 110" WB 6*			
½ Ton Vandura	**15358**	—	—

Year-Model-Body Type	Original List	Current Whlse	Average Retail
Rally Wgn	**17174**	—	—

* For 8 cylinder models add $— wholesale and $— retail.

G-1500 VANS 125" WB 6*

Year-Model-Body Type	Original List	Current Whlse	Average Retail
½ Ton Vandura	**15638**	—	—
Rally Wgn	**18124**	—	—

* For 8 cylinder models add $— wholesale and $— retail.

ADD FOR:

Year-Model-Body Type	Original List	Current Whlse	Average Retail
STX Pkg (Rally Wgn)	**838**	—	—
5.7 Liter 8 Cyl Eng	**845**	—	—

G-2500 VANS 110" WB 6

Year-Model-Body Type	Original List	Current Whlse	Average Retail
¾ Ton Vandura	**15578**	—	—

G-2500 VANS 125" WB 6

Year-Model-Body Type	Original List	Current Whlse	Average Retail
¾ Ton Vandura	**15878**	—	—
Rally Wgn	**18314**	—	—

ADD FOR:

Year-Model-Body Type	Original List	Current Whlse	Average Retail
STX Pkg (Rally Wgn)	**838**	—	—
5.7 Liter 8 Cyl Eng	**845**	—	—
6.2 Liter 8 Cyl Diesel Eng	**2400**	—	—

1991

S-15 JIMMY 2WD 100.5" WB 6

Year-Model-Body Type	Original List	Current Whlse	Average Retail
2 Dr Sport Utility	**14840**	11250	12850

S-15 JIMMY 2WD 107" WB 6

Year-Model-Body Type	Original List	Current Whlse	Average Retail
4 Dr Sport Utility	**16080**	12225	13975

V-1500 JIMMY 106" WB 8

Year-Model-Body Type	Original List	Current Whlse	Average Retail
Wgn	**18519**	13400	15600
Wgn, Diesel	**21447**	13875	16125

SONOMA REG CAB PICKUPS 4*

Year-Model-Body Type	Original List	Current Whlse	Average Retail
Special Wideside (108" WB)	**9709**	5350	6150
Wideside (108" WB)	**10659**	6450	7375
Wideside (118" WB)	**10959**	6600	7550

* For 6 cylinder models add $400 wholesale and $400 retail.

SONOMA CLUB COUPE 2WD 4

Year-Model-Body Type	Original List	Current Whlse	Average Retail
Wideside	**12240**	7000	8000

* For 6 cylinder models add $400 wholesale and $400 retail.

SONOMA SYCLONE TURBO 4WD 6

Year-Model-Body Type	Original List	Current Whlse	Average Retail
Wideside	**25500**	—	—

C-1500 GAS PICKUPS 117.5" WB 6*

Year-Model-Body Type	Original List	Current Whlse	Average Retail
Wideside	**13214**	8975	10225
Sportside	**13554**	9075	10350
Special Wideside (131" WB)	**11572**	8300	9450
w/131" WB add	**300**	130	160

* For 8 cylinder models add $425 wholesale and $425 retail.

C-1500 GAS CLUB CPE PICKUPS 141.5" WB 6*

Year-Model-Body Type	Original List	Current Whlse	Average Retail
Wideside	**14164**	9825	11175
Sportside	**14504**	—	—
w/155" WB add	**290**	120	150

* For 8 cylinder models add $425 wholesale and $425 retail.

C-1500 DIESEL PICKUPS 131.5" WB 8

Year-Model-Body Type	Original List	Current Whlse	Average Retail
Wideside	**16544**	9900	11275

C-1500 DIESEL CLUB CPE PICKUPS 141.5" WB 8

Year-Model-Body Type	Original List	Current Whlse	Average Retail
Wideside	**16984**	10300	11750
Sportside	**17324**	—	—
w/155" WB add	**290**	120	150

C-2500 GAS PICKUPS 131.5" WB 6*

Year-Model-Body Type	Original List	Current Whlse	Average Retail
Wideside	**14154**	9725	11075
Heavy Duty Wideside	**14807**	10050	11450

* For 8 cylinder models add $425 wholesale and $425 retail.

C-2500 GAS CLUB CPE PICKUPS 141.5" WB 6*

Year-Model-Body Type	Original List	Current Whlse	Average Retail
Wideside	**15274**	10950	12500
Heavy Duty Wideside (155" WB)	**15858**	11400	13025
w/155" WB add	**280**	120	150

* For 8 cylinder models add $425 wholesale and $425 retail.

C-2500 DIESEL PICKUPS 131.5" WB 8

Year-Model-Body Type	Original List	Current Whlse	Average Retail
Wideside	**16614**	10600	12100
Heavy Duty Wideside	**17088**	10950	12500

C-2500 DIESEL CLUB CPE PICKUPS 141.5" WB 8

Year-Model-Body Type	Original List	Current Whlse	Average Retail
Wideside	**17724**	11450	13100
Heavy Duty Wideside (155" WB)	**18198**	11775	13475
w/155" WB add	**290**	120	150

R-1500 SUBURBAN 129.5" WB 8

Year-Model-Body Type	Original List	Current Whlse	Average Retail
Panel Doors	**17620**	13650	15900
Tailgate	**17780**	13750	16000
Panel Doors, Diesel	**20098**	14125	16450
Tailgate, Diesel	**20253**	14200	16525

R-2500 SUBURBAN 129.5" WB 8

Year-Model-Body Type	Original List	Current Whlse	Average Retail
Panel Doors	**19178**	14200	16525
Tailgate	**19328**	14275	16625
Panel Doors, HD Diesel	**20956**	14600	17000
Tailgate, HD Diesel	**21116**	14700	17125

SAFARI 111" WB 6*

Year-Model-Body Type	Original List	Current Whlse	Average Retail
Cargo Van	**14389**	9425	10725
Extended Cargo Van	**15059**	10175	11600
SLX Pass Van	**15660**	11350	12975
SLX Extended Pass Van	**16350**	11500	13150
SLE Pass Van	**16740**	12050	13775
SLE Extended Pass Van	**17430**	12175	13925
SLT Pass Van	**18290**	12600	14725
SLT Extended Pass Van	**18980**	12750	14950

* For 2WD models w/6 cylinder high output engine add $200 wholesale and $200 retail.

G-1500 VANS 110" WB 6*

Year-Model-Body Type	Original List	Current Whlse	Average Retail
½ Ton Vandura	**14669**	9250	10525
Rally Wgn	**16485**	10725	12250
Rally STX Wgn			

Refer To Optional Equipment Schedules

Year-Model-Body Type	Original List	Current Whlse	Average Retail
(125" WB)	**18345**	11975	13700
w/125" WB add			
(Vandura)	**280**	120	150
(Rally)	**950**	120	150
* For 8 cylinder models add $425 wholesale and $425 retail.			
G-2500 VANS 110" WB 6*			
¾ Ton Vandura	**14849**	9425	10725
¾ Ton Vandura Diesel (8 cyl)	**17522**	10250	11700
Rally Wgn (125" WB)	**17585**	11075	12650
Rally STX (125" WB)	**18485**	12125	13875
Rally Wgn Diesel (125" WB)	**20188**	11950	13675
Rally STX Diesel (125" WB)	**21028**	13100	15300
* For 8 cylinder models add $425 wholesale and $425 retail.			
ADD FOR:			
SLE Comfort Pkg			
(Sonoma Reg Cab Pickup)	**548**	270	330
(Sonoma Club Cab Pickup)	**683**	350	430
SLE Decor Pkg			
(V-1500 Jimmy)	**1286**	710	860
(R Pickups)	**947**	510	620
(V Pickups)	**905**	480	590
(C-K Pickups)	**771**	400	500
(Suburban)	**1600**	890	1090
SLX Decor Pkg			
(C-K Reg Pickups)	**573**	290	350
(C-K Club Cab Pickups)	**458**	210	270

1990

Year-Model-Body Type	Original List	Current Whlse	Average Retail
S-15 JIMMY 100.5" WB 6			
Sport Utility	**13888**	7650	8750
V-1500 JIMMY 106" WB 8			
Wgn	**17367**	9950	11325
Wgn, Diesel	**20060**	10400	11875
C-1500 GAS PICKUPS 117.5" WB 6*			
Wideside	**12352**	6950	7950
Sportside	**12677**	7075	8100
Wideside Extended Cab (141" WB)	**13262**	7775	8900
w/131" WB add	**280**	140	170
* For 8 cylinder models add $400 wholesale and $400 retail.			
C-1500 DIESEL PICKUPS 131.5" WB 8			
Wideside	**15442**	7875	9000
Wideside Extended Cab (141" WB)	**15872**	8625	9825
Wideside Extended Cab (155" WB)	**16147**	8775	10000
C-2500 GAS PICKUPS 131.5" WB 6*			
Wideside	**13257**	7675	8775
Heavy Duty Wideside	**13881**	8000	9150
Wideside Extended Cab (141" WB)	**14327**	8425	9600
Wideside Extended Cab (155" WB)	**14607**	8575	9775
Heavy Duty Wideside Extended Cab (155" WB)	**14896**	8875	10125
* For 8 cylinder models add $400 wholesale and $400 retail.			
C-2500 DIESEL PICKUPS 131.5" WB 8			
Wideside	**15507**	8525	9700
Heavy Duty Wideside	**15966**	8825	10050
Wideside Extended Cab (141" WB)	**16577**	9375	10675
Wideside Extended Cab (155" WB)	**16857**	9475	10775
Heavy Duty Wideside Extended Cab (155" WB)	**17031**	9750	11100
S-15 REG CAB PICKUPS 4			
Wideside EL (108" WB) (NA w/power steering)	**8812**	4600	5400
Wideside (108" WB)	**10458**	5275	6075
Wideside (118" WB)	**10623**	5400	6200
Wideside Extended Cab (123" WB)	**11408**	5850	6650
R-1500 SUBURBAN 129.5" WB 8			
Panel Doors	**16628**	11175	12775
Tailgate	**16778**	11275	12875
Panel Doors, Diesel	**18896**	11625	13300
Tailgate, Diesel	**19041**	11725	13400
R-2500 SUBURBAN 129.5" WB 8			
Panel Doors	**17251**	11575	13225
Tailgate	**17396**	11675	13350
Panel Doors, HD Diesel	**19479**	11975	13700
Tailgate, HD Diesel	**19629**	12075	13800
SAFARI 111" WB 6			
Cargo Van (4 cyl)	**12977**	6675	7625
SLX Pass Van	**14823**	8925	10175
SLE Pass Van	**15863**	9500	10800
SLT Pass Van	**17358**	10050	11450
* For 6 cylinder models add $375 wholesale and $375 retail.			
G-1500 VANS 110" WB 6*			
½ Ton Vandura	**13662**	7125	8125
Rally Wgn	**15663**	8875	10125
Rally STX (125" WB)	**17438**	9700	11050
w/125" WB add			
(Vandura)	**270**	140	170
(Rally)	**905**	140	170

* For 8 cylinder models add $400 wholesale and $400 retail.

G-2500 VANS 110" WB 6*

Year-Model-Body Type	Original List	Current Whlse	Average Retail
¾ Ton Vandura	**13832**	7250	8275
¾ Ton Vandura Diesel (8 cyl)	**16470**	8100	9225
Rally Wgn (125" WB)	**16713**	9000	10250
Rally STX (125" WB)	**17578**	9825	11175
Rally Wgn Diesel (125" WB) (8 cyl)	**19036**	9825	11175
Rally STX Diesel (125" WB) (8 cyl)	**19846**	10650	12150
¾ Ton Vandura (125" WB) (6 cyl)	**14112**	7500	8575
¾ Ton Vandura Diesel (125" WB) (8 cyl)	**16740**	8350	9500

* For 8 cylinder models add $400 wholesale and $400 retail.

ADD FOR:

Year-Model-Body Type	Original List	Current Whlse	Average Retail
Baja Equip (S15 4WD Pickups)	**1260**	600	730
Gypsy Pkg (S15 Jimmy)	**1239**	580	710
Safari GT Pkg (Safari 2WD SLE)	**905**	410	510
(Safari 2WD SLX)	**1309**	620	750
Sierra Classic Pkg (S-15 2WD Jimmy)	**841**	380	470
(S-15 4WD Jimmy)	**809**	360	450
(V1500 Jimmy)	**1281**	610	740
(Suburban)	**1583**	760	930
Sierra SLE Pkg (C & K Pickups)	**1040**	480	590
Sierra SLX Pkg (C & K Reg Cab Pickups)	**632**	270	340
(C & K Ext Cab Pickups)	**517**	210	260

1989

S-15 JIMMY 100.5" WB 6

Year-Model-Body Type	Original List	Current Whlse	Average Retail
Sport Utility	**11680**	6400	7300

V-1500 JIMMY 106" WB 8

Year-Model-Body Type	Original List	Current Whlse	Average Retail
Wgn	**15355**	8700	9900
Wgn, Diesel	**18085**	9100	10350

C-1500 GAS PICKUPS 117.5" WB 6*

Year-Model-Body Type	Original List	Current Whlse	Average Retail
Wideside	**10335**	5825	6625
Sportside	**10553**	5900	6700
Fleetside Extended Cab (141" WB)	**11267**	6450	7375
Wideside Extended Cab (155" WB)	**11467**	6675	7625
w/131" WB add	**200**	90	100

* For 8 cylinder models add $375 wholesale and $375 retail.

C-1500 DIESEL PICKUPS 131.5" WB 8

Year-Model-Body Type	Original List	Current Whlse	Average Retail
Fleetside	**13318**	6700	7650
Fleetside Extended Cab (141" WB)	**13853**	7200	8225
Fleetside Extended Cab (155" WB)	**14053**	7425	8475

C-2500 GAS PICKUPS 131.5" WB 6*

Year-Model-Body Type	Original List	Current Whlse	Average Retail
Wideside	**11143**	6500	7425
HD Fleetside	**12378**	6800	7775
Fleetside Extended Cab (141" WB)	**12298**	7125	8125
Wideside Extended Cab (155" WB)	**12498**	7275	8300
HD Fleetside Extended Cab (155" WB) (8 cyl)	**13413**	7875	9000

* For 8 cylinder models add $375 wholesale and $375 retail.

C-2500 DIESEL PICKUPS 131.5" WB 8

Year-Model-Body Type	Original List	Current Whlse	Average Retail
Wideside	**13383**	7275	8300
HD Fleetside	**13828**	7575	8650
Fleetside Extended Cab (141" WB)	**14538**	7875	9000
Wideside Extended Cab (155" WB)	**14738**	8050	9200
HD Fleetside Extended Cab (155" WB)	**14911**	8650	9850

R-2500 GAS PICKUPS 164.5" WB 8

Year-Model-Body Type	Original List	Current Whlse	Average Retail
Wideside Bonus Cab	**14164**	7775	8900
Wideside Crew Cab	**14664**	8000	9150

R-2500 DIESEL PICKUPS 164.5" WB 8

Year-Model-Body Type	Original List	Current Whlse	Average Retail
HD Wideside Bonus Cab	**15164**	8425	9600
HD Wideside Crew Cab	**15664**	8675	9875

S-15 REG CAB PICKUPS 4*

Year-Model-Body Type	Original List	Current Whlse	Average Retail
Wideside EL (108" WB)	**7474**	3575	4350
Wideside (108" WB)	**8585**	4525	5325
Wideside (118" WB)	**8750**	4600	5400
Wideside Extended Cab (123" WB)	**9435**	4950	5750

* For 6 cylinder models add $375 wholesale and $375 retail.

R-1500 SUBURBAN 129.5" WB 8

Year-Model-Body Type	Original List	Current Whlse	Average Retail
Panel Doors	**14545**	9325	10600
Tailgate	**14585**	9425	10725
Panel Doors, Diesel	**16895**	9675	11000
Tailgate, Diesel	**16935**	9775	11125

R-2500 SUBURBAN 129.5" WB 8

Year-Model-Body Type	Original List	Current Whlse	Average Retail
Panel Doors	**15184**	9675	11000
Tailgate	**15224**	9775	11125
Panel Doors, HD Diesel	**17464**	10250	11700
Tailgate, HD Diesel	**17504**	10350	11800

Refer To Optional Equipment Schedules

Year-Model-Body Type	Original List	Current Whlse	Average Retail
SAFARI 111" WB 6*			
Cargo Van (4 cyl)	**10400**	4925	5725
SLX Pass Van	**11900**	7175	8200
SLE Pass Van	**12633**	7700	8800
SLT Pass Van	**14144**	8275	9425
* For 6 cylinder models add $325 wholesale and $325 retail.			
G-1500 VANS 110" WB 6*			
½ Ton Vandura	**11145**	5175	5975
Rally Wgn	**12638**	6700	7650
Rally STX (125" WB)	**14221**	9650	11050
w/125" WB add			
(Vandura)	**260**	110	140
(Rally)	**260**	110	140
* For 8 cylinder models add $375 wholesale and $375 retail.			
G-2500 VANS 110" WB 6*			
¾ Ton Vandura	**11455**	5300	6100
¾ Ton Vandura Diesel (8 cyl)	**13853**	6100	6900
Rally Wgn (125" WB)	**13121**	6925	7925
Rally STX (125" WB)	**14440**	7850	8975
Rally Wgn Diesel (125" WB) (8 cyl)	**15498**	7675	8775
Rally STX Diesel (125" WB) (8 cyl)	**16759**	8625	9825
¾ Ton Vandura (125" WB) (6 cyl)	**11725**	5425	6225
¾ Ton Vandura Diesel (125" WB) (8 cyl)	**14114**	6500	7425
* For 8 cylinder models add $375 wholesale and $375 retail.			
ADD FOR:			
Timberline Pkg (S/T Jimmy)	**1063**	410	510
Gypsy Pkg (S/T Jimmy)	**1089**	420	520
Sierra SLE Pkg			
(Suburban)	**1560**	630	770
(C-K Pickups)	**601**	210	270
Sierra Classic Pkg			
(S/T Jimmy)	**715**	260	320
(Jimmy)	**1340**	530	650
(S/T Pickups)	**535**	180	230
(R-V Pickups)	**956**	370	450
Safari GT Pkg (Safari)	**1070**	420	510

1988

Year-Model-Body Type	Original List	Current Whlse	Average Retail
S-15 JIMMY 100.5" WB 4*			
Sport Utility	**10505**	4375	5175
* For 6 cylinder models add $300 wholesale and $300 retail.			
V-1500 JIMMY 106" WB 8			
Wgn	**14691**	7000	8000
Wgn, Diesel	**17422**	7325	8375
C-1500 GAS PICKUPS 117.5" WB 6*			
Wideside	**9894**	4200	5000
Sportside	**10102**	4300	5100
Wideside Extended Cab (155" WB)	**10983**	4900	5700
w/131" WB add	**190**	70	80
* For 8 cylinder models add $325 wholesale and $325 retail.			
C-1500 DIESEL PICKUPS 131.5" WB 8			
Fleetside	**12868**	4900	5700
Fleetside Extended Cab (155" WB)	**13569**	5625	6425
C-2500 GAS PICKUPS 131.5" WB 6*			
Wideside	**10671**	4725	5525
Wideside Extended Cab (155" WB)	**11976**	5400	6200
C-2500 DIESEL PICKUPS 131.5" WB 8			
Wideside	**12911**	5375	6175
Wideside Extended Cab (155" WB)	**14216**	6100	6900
R-2500 GAS PICKUPS 164.5" WB 6			
Wideside Bonus Cab	**12922**	5575	6375
Wideside Crew Cab	**13358**	5800	6600
R-2500 DIESEL PICKUPS 164.5" WB 8			
Wideside Bonus Cab	**14578**	6250	7150
Wideside Crew Cab	**15015**	6475	7400
S-15 REG CAB PICKUPS 4*			
Wideside EL (108" WB)	**6795**	2525	3350
Wideside (108" WB)	**7890**	2750	3600
* For 6 cylinder models add $300 wholesale and $300 retail.			
S-15 EXTENDED CAB 4			
Wideside	**8815**	3125	3975
R-1500 SUBURBAN 129.5" WB 8			
Panel Doors	**13945**	7300	8350
Tailgate	**13988**	7400	8450
Panel Doors, Diesel	**16260**	7650	8750
Tailgate, Diesel	**16304**	7750	8850
R-2500 SUBURBAN 129.5" WB 8			
Panel Doors	**14559**	7625	8725
Tailgate	**14602**	7725	8825
Panel Doors, HD Diesel	**16839**	8075	9250
Tailgate, HD Diesel	**16883**	8175	9300
SAFARI 111" WB 6*			
Cargo Van (4 cyl)	**9190**	3175	4025
SLX Pass Van	**10696**	5300	6100
SLE Pass Van	**11489**	5825	6625
SLT Pass Van	**12828**	6375	7275
G-1500 VANS 110" WB 6*			
½ Ton Vandura	**10240**	3250	4100
Rally Wgn	**11922**	4675	5475
Rally Cust Wgn			

Year-Model-Body Type	Original List	Current Whlse	Average Retail
(125" WB)	**13081**	5450	6250
Rally STX (125" WB)	**13489**	5725	6525
w/125" WB add			
(Vandura)	**248**	100	130
(Rally)	**251**	110	130
* For 8 cylinder models add $325 wholesale and $325 retail.			
G-2500 VANS 110" WB 6*			
¾ Ton Vandura	**10865**	3350	4200
¾ Ton Vandura Diesel (8 cyl)	**13262**	4100	4875
Rally Wgn (125" WB)	**12423**	4900	5700
Rally Cust Wgn (125" WB)	**13330**	5575	6375
Rally STX (125" WB)	**13736**	5850	6650
Rally Wgn Diesel (125" WB) (8 cyl)	**14800**	5625	6425
Rally Cust Wgn Diesel (125" WB) (8 cyl)	**15735**	6275	7175
Rally STX Diesel (125" WB) (8 cyl)	**16055**	6475	7400
¾ Ton Vandura (125" WB) (6 cyl)	**11117**	3550	4325
¾ Ton Vandura Diesel (125" WB) (8 cyl)	**13513**	4225	5025
ADD FOR:			
Gypsy Pkg			
(S/T Jimmy)	**1068**	330	410
(S/T Pickups)	**925**	280	350
Sierra Classic Pkg			
(S/T Jimmy)	**683**	200	250
(Jimmy)	**1249**	400	490
(S/T Reg Cab Pickups)	**637**	180	220
(S/T Extended Cab Pickups)	**729**	210	260
(R1500 Suburban)	**1369**	450	550
(R2500 Suburban)	**1248**	400	500
1987			
S-15 JIMMY 100.5" WB 4*			
Sport Utility	**10124**	3225	4075
* For 6 cylinder models add $250 wholesale and $250 retail.			
V-1500 JIMMY 106" WB 8			
Wgn	**13066**	5925	6725
Wgn, Diesel	**16027**	6225	7100
CABALLERO 117" WB 6*			
Caballero	**10453**	4000	4775
Caballero SS Diablo	**10784**	4375	5175
* For 8 cylinder models add $275 wholesale and $275 retail.			
R-1500 PICKUPS 117.5" WB 6*			
Fenderside	**8651**	3150	4000

Year-Model-Body Type	Original List	Current Whlse	Average Retail
Wideside	**8503**	3225	4075
Fenderside, Diesel (8 cyl)	**11842**	3725	4500
Wideside, Diesel (8 cyl)	**11695**	3825	4600
w/131.5" WB add	**183**	60	80
* For 8 cylinder models add $275 wholesale and $275 retail.			
R-2500 PICKUPS 131.5" WB 6*			
Fenderside	**10077**	3750	4525
Wideside	**9929**	3800	4575
* For 8 cylinder models add $275 wholesale and $275 retail.			
R-2500 DIESEL PICKUPS 131.5" WB 8			
Fenderside	**12722**	4325	5125
Wideside	**12574**	4375	5175
R-2500 HEAVY DUTY PICKUPS 131.5" WB 8			
Fenderside	**10077**	4050	4950
Wideside	**9929**	4100	4875
R-2500 HD DIESEL PICKUPS 131.5" WB 8			
Fenderside	**11498**	4350	5150
Wideside	**11351**	4400	5200
R-2500 PICKUPS 164.5" WB 8			
Wideside Bonus Cab	**12475**	4800	5600
Wideside Crew Cab	**12842**	5000	5800
R-2500 DIESEL PICKUPS 164.5" WB 8			
Wideside Bonus Cab	**13693**	5075	5875
Wideside Crew Cab	**14060**	5300	6100
S-15 EXTENDED CAB 4*			
Wideside (122.9" WB)	**8167**	2475	3300
S-15 REG CAB PICKUPS 4*			
Wideside EL (108" WB)	**6595**	2050	2850
Wideside (108" WB)	**7435**	2200	3000
Wideside (118" WB)	**7702**	2275	3100
* For 6 cylinder models add $250 wholesale and $250 retail.			
R-1500 SUBURBAN 129.5" WB 8			
Panel Doors	**12435**	5450	6250
Tailgate	**12477**	5575	6375
Panel Doors, Diesel	**15193**	5775	6575
Tailgate, Diesel	**15235**	5875	6675
R-2500 SUBURBAN 129.5" WB 8			
Panel Doors	**13036**	5750	6550
Tailgate	**13077**	5825	6625
Panel Doors, HD Diesel	**15669**	6025	6825
Tailgate, HD Diesel	**15712**	6150	6925
SAFARI M15 111" WB 6*			
Cargo Van (4 cyl)	**8797**	2375	3200
SL Pass Van	**9833**	4100	4875
SLX Pass Van	**10314**	4300	5100
SLE Pass Van	**11079**	4575	5375
SLT Pass Van	**12370**	5000	5800
G-1500 VANS 110" WB 6*			
½ Ton Vandura	**9464**	2375	3200
Rally Wgn	**11404**	3750	4525
Rally Cust Wgn			

Refer To Optional Equipment Schedules

Year-Model-Body Type	Original List	Current Whlse	Average Retail
(125" WB)	**12279**	4350	5150
Rally STX (125" WB)	**12631**	4525	5325
w/125" WB add			
(Vandura)	**242**	70	80
(Rally)	**242**	70	80

* For 8 cylinder models add $275 wholesale and $275 retail.

G-2500 VANS 110" WB 6*

Year-Model-Body Type	Original List	Current Whlse	Average Retail
¾ Ton Vandura	**10131**	2425	3250
¾ Ton Vandura Diesel (8 cyl)	**12753**	2925	3775
Rally Wgn (125" WB)	**11609**	3900	4675
Rally Cust Wgn (125" WB)	**12483**	4425	5225
Rally STX (125" WB)	**12833**	4575	5375
Rally Wgn Diesel (125" WB) (8 cyl)	**14211**	4425	5225
Rally Cust Wgn Diesel (125" WB) (8 cyl)	**15113**	4900	5700
Rally STX Diesel (125" WB) (8 cyl)	**15379**	5100	5900
¾ Ton Vandura (125" WB) (8 cyl)	**10374**	2775	3625
¾ Ton Vandura Diesel (125" WB) (8 cyl)	**12995**	3025	3875

* For 8 cylinder models add $275 wholesale and $275 retail.

ADD FOR:

Year-Model-Body Type	Original List	Current Whlse	Average Retail
Gypsy Pkg			
(S/T Jimmy)	**1042**	250	310
(S/T Pickups)	**965**	230	280
High Sierra Pkg			
(Suburban Diesel)	**329**	90	110
(Suburban Gasoline)	**485**	140	160
(R-V Pickups)	**274**	80	100
Sierra Classic Pkg			
(S/T Jimmy)	**657**	130	170
(Jimmy)	**1073**	260	320
(Suburban)	**1330**	330	410
(S/T Pickups)	**637**	130	170
(R-V Pickups)	**—**	140	180
Sierra SLE Pkg			
(C-K Pickups)	**681**	150	190
Timberline Pkg			
(S/T Jimmy)	**1025**	250	310

1986

K-1500 JIMMY 8

Year-Model-Body Type	Original List	Current Whlse	Average Retail
Utility w/HT	**12383**	4825	5625
Utility Diesel w/HT	**15330**	5075	5875

S-15 JIMMY 100.5" WB 4*

Year-Model-Body Type	Original List	Current Whlse	Average Retail
Tailgate	**9582**	2475	3300

CABALLERO 117" WB 6*

Year-Model-Body Type	Original List	Current Whlse	Average Retail
Caballero	**9850**	3175	4025
Caballero Diablo	**10172**	3500	4275

* For 8 cylinder models add $250 wholesale and $250 retail.

C-1500 PICKUPS 117.5" WB 6*

Year-Model-Body Type	Original List	Current Whlse	Average Retail
Fenderside	**8133**	2675	3525
Wideside	**7989**	2675	3525
Fenderside, Diesel (8 cyl)	**11223**	3100	3950
Wideside, Diesel (8 cyl)	**11080**	3100	3950
w/131.5" WB add	**179**	50	60

* For 8 cylinder models add $250 wholesale and $250 retail.

C-2500 PICKUPS 131.5" WB 6*

Year-Model-Body Type	Original List	Current Whlse	Average Retail
Fenderside	**9521**	3100	3950
Wideside	**9377**	3100	3950

* For 8 cylinder models add $250 wholesale and $250 retail.

C-2500 DIESEL PICKUPS 131.5" WB 8

Year-Model-Body Type	Original List	Current Whlse	Average Retail
Fenderside	**12161**	3350	4200
Wideside	**12017**	3350	4200

C-2500 HEAVY DUTY PICKUPS 131.5" WB 6*

Year-Model-Body Type	Original List	Current Whlse	Average Retail
Fenderside	**10542**	3375	4225
Wideside	**10399**	3375	4225

* For 8 cylinder models add $250 wholesale and $250 retail.

C-2500 PICKUPS 164.5" WB 6*

Year-Model-Body Type	Original List	Current Whlse	Average Retail
Wideside Bonus Cab	**11425**	4750	5550
Wideside Crew Cab	**11783**	4950	5750

* For 8 cylinder models add $250 wholesale and $250 retail.

C-2500 HD DIESEL PICKUPS 131.5" WB 8

Year-Model-Body Type	Original List	Current Whlse	Average Retail
Fenderside	**12482**	3725	4500
Wideside	**12339**	3725	4500

C-2500 HD DIESEL PICKUPS 164.5" WB 8

Year-Model-Body Type	Original List	Current Whlse	Average Retail
Wideside Bonus Cab	**13365**	5000	5800
Wideside Crew Cab	**13723**	5225	6025

S-15 EXTENDED CAB 4*

Year-Model-Body Type	Original List	Current Whlse	Average Retail
Wideside (122.9" WB)	**7909**	1850	2650

S-15 REG CAB PICKUPS 4*

Year-Model-Body Type	Original List	Current Whlse	Average Retail
Wideside EL (108" WB)	**6161**	1525	2325
Wideside (108" WB)	**7202**	1550	2350
Wideside (118" WB)	**7444**	1625	2425

* For 6 cylinder models add $225 wholesale and $225 retail.

C-1500 SUBURBAN 129.5" WB 8

Year-Model-Body Type	Original List	Current Whlse	Average Retail
Panel Doors	**11769**	4425	5225
Tailgate	**11809**	4525	5325
Panel Doors, Diesel	**14518**	4675	5475
Tailgate, Diesel	**14559**	4750	5550

C-2500 SUBURBAN 129.5" WB 8

Year-Model-Body Type	Original List	Current Whlse	Average Retail
Panel Doors	**12613**	4625	5425
Tailgate	**12653**	4725	5525

Year-Model-Body Type	Original List	Current Whlse	Average Retail
Panel Doors, HD Diesel	**15241**	4875	5675
Tailgate, HD Diesel	**15282**	4950	5750
SAFARI M15 111" WB 6			
Cargo Van (4 cyl)	**8290**	1600	2400
SL Pass Van	**9299**	2975	3825
SLX Pass Van	**9767**	3100	3950
SLE Pass Van	**10512**	3500	4275
G-1500 VANS 110" WB 6*			
½ Ton Vandura	**8876**	1725	2525
Rally Wgn	**10529**	2825	3675
Rally Cust Wgn (125" WB)	**11617**	3275	4125
Rally Wgn STX (125" WB)	**11959**	3525	4300
w/125" WB add (Vandura)	**232**	50	60
(Rally)	**236**	50	60
G-2500 VANS 110" WB 6*			
¾ Ton Vandura	**9525**	1775	2575
¾ Ton Vandura Diesel (8 cyl)	**12142**	2250	3050
Rally Wgn (125" WB)	**10964**	2950	3800
Rally Cust Wgn (125" WB)	**11815**	3350	4200
Rally STX (125" WB)	**12156**	3600	4375
Rally Wgn Diesel (125" WB) (8 cyl)	**13562**	3475	4250
Rally Cust Wgn Diesel (125" WB) (8 cyl)	**14440**	3950	4725
Rally STX Diesel (125" WB) (8 cyl)	**14699**	4150	4950
w/125" WB add (Vandura)	**237**	50	60
* For 8 cylinder models add $250 wholesale and $250 retail.			
ADD FOR:			
Amarillo Pkg (Caballero)	**232**	50	60
Gypsy Pkg (S/T Jimmy)	**1015**	170	210
(S/T Pickups)	**940**	150	190
High Sierra Pkg (Suburban Diesel)	**320**	70	80
(Suburban Gasoline)	**472**	100	120
(S/T Pickup)	**305**	60	80
Sierra Classic Pkg (Jimmy)	**1045**	170	210
(S/T Jimmy)	**640**	140	160
(Suburban Diesel)	**1145**	190	240
(Suburban Gasoline)	**1295**	230	280
(S/T Pickups)	**620**	130	160
(C-K Reg Pickups)	**720**	100	130
(C-K Bonus Pickups)	**800**	120	150
(C-K Crew Cab Pickups)	**885**	130	170

Year-Model-Body Type	Original List	Current Whlse	Average Retail
1985			
CABALLERO 117" WB 6*			
Caballero	**9109**	2450	3275
Caballero Diablo	**9378**	2625	3475
* For 8 cylinder models add $225 wholesale and $225 retail.			
K-1500 JIMMY 8			
Utility w/HT	**11431**	4075	4850
Utility Diesel HT	**14165**	4350	5150
S-15 JIMMY 100.5" WB 4*			
Tailgate	**8928**	2025	2825
C-1500 PICKUPS 117.5" WB 6*			
Fenderside	**7532**	2050	2850
Wideside	**7397**	2050	2850
Fenderside, Diesel	**10445**	2275	3100
Wideside, Diesel	**10310**	2275	3100
w/131.5" WB add	**169**	50	60
* For 8 cylinder models add $225 wholesale and $225 retail.			
C-2500 PICKUPS 131.5" WB 6*			
Fenderside	**8798**	2400	3225
Wideside	**8663**	2400	3225
* For 8 cylinder models add $225 wholesale and $225 retail.			
C-2500 HD PICKUPS 131.5" WB 6*			
Fenderside	**9756**	2625	3475
Wideside	**9622**	2625	3475
* For 8 cylinder models add $225 wholesale and $225 retail.			
C-2500 DIESEL PICKUPS 131.5" WB 8			
Fenderside	**11274**	2825	3675
Wideside	**11139**	2825	3675
C-2500 HD DIESEL PICKUPS 131.5" WB 8			
Fenderside	**11575**	3075	3925
Wideside	**11441**	3075	3925
C-2500 PICKUPS 164.5" WB 6*			
Wideside Bonus Cab	**10584**	2975	3825
Wideside Crew Cab	**10920**	3150	4000
* For 8 cylinder models add $225 wholesale and $225 retail.			
C-2500 DIESEL PICKUPS 164.5" WB 8			
Fenderside	**12403**	3500	4275
Wideside	**12379**	3500	4275
S-15 REG CAB PICKUPS 4*			
Wideside (108" WB)	**5990**	1225	1900
Wideside (118" WB)	**6702**	1300	1975
Wideside Diesel (108" WB)	**7349**	900	1600
Wideside Diesel (118" WB)	**7502**	1025	1700
S-15 EXTENDED CAB 4*			
Wideside (122.9" WB)	**7167**	1475	2250
Wideside, Diesel (122.9" WB)	**7875**	1275	1950

Refer To Optional Equipment Schedules

Year-Model-Body Type	Original List	Current Whlse	Average Retail
* For 6 cylinder models add $200 wholesale and $200 retail.			
C-1500 SUBURBAN 129.5" WB 8			
Panel Doors	**10812**	3600	4375
Tailgate	**10850**	3700	4475
Panel Doors, Diesel	**13369**	3875	4650
Tailgate, Diesel	**13407**	3975	4750
C-2500 SUBURBAN 129.5" WB 8			
Panel Doors	**11598**	3800	4575
Tailgate	**11635**	3900	4675
Panel Doors, Diesel	**14042**	4075	4850
Tailgate, Diesel	**14079**	4175	4975
G-1500 VANS 110" WB 6*			
½ Ton Vandura	**8150**	1200	1875
Rally Wgn	**9701**	2250	3050
Rally Cust Wgn (125" WB)	**17012**	2550	3375
Rally Wgn STX (125" WB)	**11030**	2675	3525
w/125" WB add			
(Vandura)	**215**	50	60
(Rally Wgn)	**220**	50	60
* For 8 cylinder models add $225 wholesale and $225 retail.			
G-2500 VANS 110" WB 6*			
¾ Ton Vandura	**8752**	1225	1900
¾ Ton Vandura Diesel	**11183**	1625	2425
Rally Wgn (125" WB)	**10105**	2300	3125
Rally Cust Wgn (125" WB)	**10896**	2600	3425
Rally STX (125" WB)	**11212**	2775	3625
Rally Wgn Diesel (125" WB)	**12523**	2725	3575
Rally Cust Wgn Diesel (125" WB) (8 cyl)	**13339**	3025	3875
Rally STX Diesel (125" WB) (8 cyl)	**13580**	3175	4025
Vandura (125" WB)	**8972**	1275	1950
* For 8 cylinder models add $225 wholesale and $225 retail.			
ADD FOR:			
Amarillo Pkg (Caballero)	**195**	30	30
Gypsy Pkg			
(S/T Jimmy)	**972**	130	160
(S/T Pickups)	**868**	120	140
High Sierra Pkg			
(Suburban Diesel)	**311**	40	50
(Suburban Gasoline)	**459**	60	70
(S/T Pickups)	**295**	40	50
Sierra Classic Pkg			
(S/T Jimmy)	**595**	80	100
(Jimmy)	**1015**	140	170
(Suburban)	**—**	120	150
(S/T Reg Cab Pickups)	**605**	80	100
(S/T Extended Cab Pickups)	**995**	140	160
(C-K Pickups)	**—**	90	110
Woody Dress Up Pkg			
(S/T Jimmy)	**1520**	160	200

1984

Year-Model-Body Type	Original List	Current Whlse	Average Retail
CABALLERO 117" WB 6*			
Caballero	**8622**	1850	2650
Caballero SS Sport	**8881**	2075	2875
* For 8 cylinder models add $200 wholesale and $200 retail.			
K-1500 JIMMY 8			
Utility w/HT	**10931**	3025	3875
Utility Diesel w/HT	**13664**	3200	4050
S-15 JIMMY 100.5" WB 4*			
Tailgate	**8580**	1700	2500
C-1500 PICKUPS 117.5" WB 6*			
Fenderside	**7213**	1700	2500
Wideside	**7082**	1700	2500
Fenderside, Diesel	**10257**	2075	2875
Wideside, Diesel	**10126**	2300	3075
w/131.5" WB add	**157**	40	50
* For 8 cylinder models add $200 wholesale and $200 retail.			
C-2500 PICKUPS 131.5" WB 6*			
Fenderside	**8431**	2050	2850
Wideside	**8300**	2050	2850
* For 8 cylinder models add $200 wholesale and $200 retail.			
C-2500 HEAVY DUTY PICKUPS 131.5" WB 6*			
Fenderside	**8945**	2225	3025
Wideside	**8814**	2225	3025
* For 8 cylinder models add $200 wholesale and $200 retail.			
C-2500 DIESEL PICKUPS 131.5" WB 8			
Fenderside	**11038**	2375	3200
Wideside	**10907**	2375	3200
C-2500 HD DIESEL PICKUPS 131.5" WB 8			
Fenderside	**11552**	2525	3350
Wideside	**11421**	2525	3350
C-2500 PICKUPS 164.5" WB 6*			
Wideside Bonus Cab	**9757**	2525	3350
Wideside Crew Cab	**10087**	2725	3575
* For 8 cylinder models add $200 wholesale and $200 retail.			
C-2500 DIESEL PICKUPS 164.5" WB 8			
Fenderside Bonus Cab	**12364**	2875	3725
Wideside Crew Cab	**12694**	3075	3925
S-15 EXTENDED CAB 4*			
Wideside (122.9" WB)	**7036**	1325	2000
Wideside, Diesel (122.9" WB)	**7939**	1100	1775

Year-Model-Body Type	Original List	Current Whlse	Average Retail
* For 6 cylinder models add $175 wholesale and $175 retail.			
S-15 REG CAB PICKUPS 4*			
Wideside (108" WB)	**6102**	1150	1825
Wideside (118" WB)	**6663**	1200	1875
Wideside, Diesel (108" WB)	**7413**	850	1550
Wideside, Diesel (118" WB)	**7566**	950	1625
* For 6 cylinder models add $175 wholesale and $175 retail.			
C-1500 SUBURBAN 129.5" WB 8			
Panel Doors	**10444**	2750	3600
Tailgate	**10480**	2825	3675
Panel Doors, Diesel	**13004**	2925	3775
Tailgate, Diesel	**13040**	3000	3850
C-2500 SUBURBAN 129.5" WB 8			
Panel Doors	**10691**	2925	3775
Tailgate	**10727**	3000	3850
Panel Doors, Diesel	**13820**	3075	3925
Tailgate, Diesel	**13856**	3175	4025
G-1500 VANS 110" WB 6*			
½ Ton Vandura	**7653**	800	1475
Rally Wgn	**9201**	1700	2500
Rally Cust Wgn (125" WB)	**10174**	1950	2750
Rally Wgn STX (125" WB)	**10439**	2050	2850
w/125" WB add			
(Vandura)	**212**	60	70
(Rally Wgn)	**212**	60	70
* For 8 cylinder models add $200 wholesale and $200 retail.			
G-2500 VANS 110" WB 6*			
¾ Ton Vandura	**8288**	825	1500
¾ Ton Vandura Diesel	**10846**	1175	1850
Rally Wgn (125" WB)	**9589**	1775	2575
Rally Cust Wgn (125" WB)	**10350**	2000	2800
Rally STX (125" WB)	**10615**	2125	2925
Rally Wgn Diesel (125" WB)	**12134**	2150	2950
Rally Cust Wgn Diesel (125" WB)	**13110**	2325	3150
Rally STX Diesel (125" WB)	**11056**	2425	3250
Vandura (125" WB)	**8500**	875	1575
* For 8 cylinder models add $200 wholesale and $200 retail.			

JEEP

Year-Model-Body Type	Original List	Current Whlse	Average Retail
1992			
CHEROKEE 2WD 101" WB 4*			
2 Dr Cherokee	**14346**	—	—
4 Dr Cherokee	**15357**	—	—
* For 6 cylinder models add $— wholesale and $— retail.			
CHEROKEE BRIARWOOD 4WD 101" WB 6			
4 Dr Cherokee	**24949**	—	—
CHEROKEE LIMITED 4WD 101" WB 6			
4 Dr Cherokee	**25484**	—	—
COMANCHE 2WD 4*			
Short Bed Pickup	**10673**	—	—
Long Bed Pickup	**11370**	—	—
* For 6 cylinder models add $— wholesale and $— retail.			
ADD FOR:			
Eliminator Pkg	**2217**	—	—
Pioneer Pkg	**1649**	—	—
Sport Pkg	**412**	—	—
WRANGLER 4WD 4*			
2 Dr "S"	**11993**	—	—
2 Dr Soft Top	**14067**	—	—
* For 6 cylinder models add $— wholesale and $— retail.			
ADD FOR:			
Islander Pkg	**1350**	—	—
Sahara Pkg	**2499**	—	—
Renegade Pkg	**4864**	—	—
1991			
CHEROKEE 101" WB 4* 2WD			
2 Dr Cherokee	**14229**	9950	11325
4 Dr Cherokee	**15212**	10650	12150
CHEROKEE BRIARWOOD 101" WB 6 4WD			
4 Dr Cherokee	**24562**	18200	20825
CHEROKEE LIMITED 101" WB 6 4WD			
4 Dr Cherokee	**25082**	18500	21425
COMANCHE 4* 2WD			
Short Bed Pickup	**10331**	6350	7250
Long Bed Pickup	**10716**	6650	7600
* For 6 cylinder models add $400 wholesale and $400 retail.			
GRAND WAGONEER 109" WB 8			
4 Dr Wgn	**29421**	—	—
WRANGLER 4* 4WD			
2 Dr "S"	**10480**	8275	9425
2 Dr Soft Top	**13534**	9325	10600
* For 6 cylinder models add $400 wholesale and $400 retail.			

Refer To Optional Equipment Schedules

Year-Model-Body Type	Original List	Current Whlse	Average Retail
ADD FOR:			
Hardtop Roof (Wrangler)	**755**	370	450
Eliminator Pkg (Comanche)	**3452**	150	200
Islander Pkg (Wrangler Base)	**738**	380	470
Pioneer Pkg (Comanche Short Bed)	**1635**	910	1110
(Comanche 2WD Long Bed)	**1434**	790	970
(Comanche 4WD Long Bed)	**1138**	610	750
Renegade Pkg (Wrangler Base)	**4266**	2460	2950
Sahara Pkg (Wrangler Base)	**1886**	1070	1300

1990

Year-Model-Body Type	Original List	Current Whlse	Average Retail
CHEROKEE 101" WB 4* 2WD			
2 Dr Cherokee	**14115**	8125	9250
4 Dr Cherokee	**14965**	8475	9650
* For 6 cylinder models add $375 wholesale and $375 retail.			
CHEROKEE LIMITED 101" WB 6 4WD			
2 Dr Cherokee	**24650**	15400	17925
4 Dr Cherokee	**25775**	15950	18475
COMANCHE 4* 2WD			
Short Bed Pickup	**9511**	4900	5700
Long Bed Pickup	**11797**	5175	5975
* For 6 cylinder models add $375 wholesale and $375 retail.			
GRAND WAGONEER 109" WB 8			
4 Dr Wgn	**27795**	13250	15450
WAGONEER 101" WB 6			
4 Dr Limited	**24795**	13150	15350
WRANGLER 4* 4WD			
2 Dr "S"	**9952**	6250	7150
2 Dr Soft Top	**12754**	7250	8275
* For 6 cylinder models add $375 wholesale and $375 retail.			
ADD FOR:			
Eliminator Pkg (Comanche)	**3384**	1690	2040
Islander Pkg (Wrangler)	**724**	320	400
Laredo Pkg (Wrangler)	**4023**	2020	2440
(Cherokee)	**3390**	1690	2050
Pioneer Pkg (Cherokee)	**1689**	810	990
(Comanche Short Bed)	**1603**	770	940
(Comanche 2WD Long Bed)	**1406**	670	810
(Comanche 4WD Long Bed)	**1116**	520	640
Sahara Pkg (Wrangler)	**1823**	890	1080
Sport Pkg (Cherokee)	**945**	440	540

1989

Year-Model-Body Type	Original List	Current Whlse	Average Retail
CHEROKEE 101" WB 4* 2WD			
2 Dr Cherokee	**12374**	6625	7575
4 Dr Cherokee	**13186**	7100	8100
* For 6 cylinder models add $325 wholesale and $325 retail.			
CHEROKEE LIMITED 101" WB 6 4WD			
2 Dr Cherokee	**23282**	12900	15100
4 Dr Cherokee	**24386**	13425	15625
COMANCHE 4* 2WD			
Short Bed Pickup	**7757**	4000	4775
Long Bed Pickup	**8585**	4200	5000
* For 6 cylinder models add $325 wholesale and $325 retail.			
GRAND WAGONEER 109" WB			
4 Dr Wgn	**26639**	12050	13775
WAGONEER 101" WB 6			
4 Dr Limited	**23455**	11350	12975
WRANGLER 4* 4WD			
2 Dr "S"	**8995**	5325	6125
2 Dr	**11022**	6200	7075
2 Dr Islander	**11721**	6500	7425
2 Dr Sahara	**12853**	6900	7900
2 Dr Laredo (6 cyl)	**14867**	7675	8775
* For 6 cylinder models add $325 wholesale and $325 retail.			
ADD FOR:			
Laredo Pkg (Cherokee)	**2937**	1230	1490
Pioneer Pkg (Cherokee)	**1217**	490	600
(Comanche Short Bed)	**1291**	520	640
(Comanche 2WD Long Bed)	**1100**	430	530
(Comanche 4WD Long Bed)	**810**	310	380
Eliminator Pkg (Comanche)	**2961**	1250	1510
Sport Pkg (Cherokee)	**945**	360	450
Off Road Pkg (Comanche)	**951**	370	450
Big Ton Pkg (Comanche)	**739**	270	340
Sport Pkg Opt Grp (Cherokee)	**1450**	580	710
Eliminator Pkg Grp 1 (Comanche)	**2783**	1170	1410
Eliminator Pkg Grp 2 (Comanche)	**3268**	1380	1670
Pioneer Pkg Opt Grp 1 (Cherokee)	**2420**	1010	1230

Year-Model-Body Type	Original List	Current Whlse	Average Retail
Pioneer Pkg Opt Grp 2			
(Cherokee)	**3067**	1290	1570
Laredo Pkg Opt Grp			
(Cherokee)	**3612**	1530	1860

1988

Year-Model-Body Type	Original List	Current Whlse	Average Retail
CHEROKEE 101" WB 4* 2WD			
2 Dr Cherokee	**11186**	4525	5325
4 Dr Cherokee	**11798**	4900	5700
* For 6 cylinder models add $300 wholesale and $300 retail.			
CHEROKEE LIMITED 101" WB 6 4WD			
2 Dr Cherokee	**22260**	10200	11625
4 Dr Cherokee	**23153**	10675	12175
COMANCHE 4* 2WD — *Schedule E*			
Short Bed Pickup	**7114**	3100	3950
Long Bed Pickup	**7906**	3175	4025
* For 6 cylinder models add $300 wholesale and $300 retail.			
GRAND WAGONEER 109" WB 8			
4 Dr Wgn	**24623**	9600	10925
JEEP TRUCK 8 4WD			
J-10 Pickup	**13128**	5825	6625
J-20 Pickup	**13525**	6325	7225
WAGONEER 101" WB 6			
4 Dr Limited	**21926**	9600	10925
WRANGLER 4* 4WD			
2 Dr "S"	**8995**	3725	4500
2 Dr	**10595**	4825	5625
2 Dr Sahara	**11995**	5525	6325
2 Dr Laredo	**13395**	6200	7075
ADD FOR:			
Chief Pkg (Cherokee)	**1881**	630	770
(Comanche)	**1322**	430	530
Eliminator Pkg			
(Comanche)	**2929**	1010	1220
Laredo Pkg (Cherokee)	**3204**	1110	1350
(Comanche)	**1428**	460	570
Pioneer Pkg			
(Base Cherokee)	**1158**	370	450
(Comanche)	**648**	180	230
(Jeep Trucks)	**304**	110	130
Olympic Pkg			
(Wrangler)	**1491**	490	600
(Cherokee)	**3037**	1050	1270
(Comanche)	—	600	740

1987

Year-Model-Body Type	Original List	Current Whlse	Average Retail
CHEROKEE 101" WB 4* 2WD			
2 Dr Cherokee	**10741**	3750	4525
4 Dr Cherokee	**11335**	4200	5000
* For 6 cylinder models add $250 wholesale and $250 retail.			
CHEROKEE LIMITED 101" WB 6 4WD			
4 Dr Cherokee	**22104**	8500	9675
COMANCHE 4* 2WD			
Short Bed Pickup	**6495**	2275	3100
Long Bed Pickup	**7860**	2375	3200
* For 6 cylinder models add $250 wholesale and $250 retail.			
GRAND WAGONEER 109" WB 8			
4 Dr Wgn	**23906**	8250	9400
JEEP TRUCK 6* 4WD			
J-10 Pickup	**11714**	4500	5300
* For 8 cylinder models add $250 wholesale and $250 retail.			
JEEP TRUCK 8 4WD			
J-20 Pickup	**13131**	4900	5700
WAGONEER 101" WB 4*			
4 Dr Wgn	**15531**	6625	7575
4 Dr Limited	**20400**	7650	8750
* For 6 cylinder models add $250 wholesale and $250 retail.			
WRANGLER 4* 4WD			
2 Dr "S"	**8795**	3725	4500
2 Dr	**10295**	4325	5125
WRANGLER LAREDO 4* 4WD			
2 Dr	**12693**	5075	5875
* For 6 cylinder models add $250 wholesale and $250 retail.			
ADD FOR:			
Chief Pkg			
(Cherokee)	**1788**	460	560
(Comanche)	**1399**	350	430
Laredo Pkg			
(Cherokee)	**3249**	880	1070
(Comanche)	**1299**	320	400
Pioneer Pkg			
(Cherokee)	**1080**	260	320
(Comanche)	**699**	150	190
(Jeep Trucks)	**586**	120	150
Sport Decor Grp			
(Wrangler)	**750**	170	210

1986

Year-Model-Body Type	Original List	Current Whlse	Average Retail
CHEROKEE 101" WB 4* 2WD			
2 Dr Cherokee	**9945**	2900	3750
4 Dr Cherokee	**10464**	3100	3950
* For 6 cylinder models add $225 wholesale and $225 retail.			
GRAND WAGONEER 109" WB 6*			
4 Dr Wgn	**21599**	5725	6525
* For 8 cylinder models add $250 wholesale and $250 retail.			

Refer To Optional Equipment Schedules

Year-Model-Body Type	Original List	Current Whlse	Average Retail
JEEP CJ 4* 4WD			
CJ-7 Open Body	**7725**	3175	4025
* For 6 cylinder models add $225 wholesale and $225 retail.			
COMANCHE 4* 2WD			
Custom Pickup	**7199**	1950	2750
* For 6 cylinder models add $225 wholesale and $225 retail.			
JEEP TRUCK 6* 4WD			
J-10 Townside	**10999**	3575	4350
* For 8 cylinder models add $250 wholesale and $250 retail.			
JEEP TRUCK 8 4WD			
J-20 Townside	**12329**	4125	4900
WAGONEER 101" WB 4*			
4 Dr Wgn	**14024**	4825	5625
4 Dr Limited	**18994**	5650	6450
* For 6 cylinder models add $225 wholesale and $225 retail.			
WRANGLER 4* 4WD			
2 Dr Open Body	**9899**	—	—
WRANGLER LAREDO 4* 4WD			
2 Dr Open Body	**12205**	—	—
* For 6 cylinder models add $225 wholesale and $225 retail.			
ADD FOR:			
Chief Pkg (Cherokee)	**1548**	270	340
Laredo Pkg			
(Cherokee)	**2969**	580	710
(CJ-7 Soft Top)	**2787**	540	660
(CJ-7 Hardtop)	**3304**	2390	2890
Pioneer Pkg			
(Cherokee)	**1039**	170	210
(Jeep Trucks)	**570**	120	150
Renegade Pkg (CJ-7)	**1253**	210	
270			
Sport Decor Pkg			
(Wrangler)	**721**	100	130
X Pkg (Comanche)	**605**	130	160
XLS Pkg (Comanche)	**931**	150	190

1985

Year-Model-Body Type	Original List	Current Whlse	Average Retail
CHEROKEE 101" WB 4 2WD			
2 Dr Cherokee	**9195**	2050	2850
4 Dr Cherokee	**9766**	2275	3100
* For 6 cylinder models add $200 wholesale and $200 retail.			
GRAND WAGONEER 109" WB 6*			
4 Dr Wgn	**20830**	4600	5400
* For 8 cylinder models add $225 wholesale and $225 retail.			
JEEP CJ 4* 4WD			
CJ-7 Open Body	**7282**	2700	3550
* For 6 cylinder models add $200 wholesale and $200 retail.			
JEEP TRUCK 6* 4WD			
J-10 Townside (131" WB)	**10497**	2825	3675
* For 8 cylinder models add $225 wholesale and $225 retail.			
JEEP TRUCK 8 4WD			
J-20 Townside (131" WB)	**11578**	3075	3925
SCRAMBLER 4* 4WD			
Scrambler	**7282**	2075	2875
* For 6 cylinder models add $200 wholesale and $200 retail.			
WAGONEER 101" WB 4*			
4 Dr Wgn	**13427**	4500	5300
4 Dr Limited	**18186**	5400	6200
* For 6 cylinder models add $200 wholesale and $200 retail.			
ADD FOR:			
Chief Pkg (Cherokee)	**1650**	300	370
Laredo Pkg			
(CJ-7 Soft Top)	**2678**	520	630
(CJ-7 Hardtop)	**3180**	630	760
(Scrambler Soft Top)	**2494**	480	590
(Scrambler Hardtop)	**2939**	570	700
(Cherokee)	**2907**	560	690
Pioneer Pkg (Cherokee)	**1171**	200	250
Renegade Pkg (CJ-7)	**1188**	200	250
(Scrambler)	**970**	150	200

1984

Year-Model-Body Type	Original List	Current Whlse	Average Retail
CHEROKEE 101" WB 4* 4WD			
2 Dr Cherokee	**10097**	2450	3275
4 Dr Cherokee	**10547**	2575	3400
2 Dr Cherokee Celebration Ed	**11810**	—	—
4 Dr Cherokee Celebration Ed	**12260**	—	—
* For 6 cylinder models add $175 wholesale and $175 retail.			
GRAND WAGONEER 109" WB 6*			
4 Dr Wgn	**19556**	4325	5125
* For 8 cylinder models add $200 wholesale and $200 retail.			
JEEP CJ 4* 4WD			
CJ-7 Basic	**7109**	2325	3150
* For 6 cylinder models add $175 wholesale and $175 retail.			
JEEP TRUCK 6* 4WD			
J-10 Townside (119" WB)	**9813**	2175	2975
J-10 Townside			

Year-Model-Body Type	Original List	Current Whlse	Average Retail
(131" WB)	**9963**	2275	3100
* For 8 cylinder models add $200 wholesale and $150 retail.			
JEEP TRUCK 8 4WD			
J-20 Townside (131" WB)	**10889**	2475	3300
SCRAMBLER 4* 4WD			
Scrambler	**7109**	2175	2975
* For 6 cylinder models add $175 wholesale and $175 retail.			
WAGONEER 101" WB 4*			
4 Dr Wgn	**12594**	3825	4600
4 Dr Limited	**17226**	4425	5225
* For 6 cylinder models add $175 wholesale and $175 retail.			

OLDSMOBILE

1992

Year-Model-Body Type	Original List	Current Whlse	Average Retail
BRAVADA 6			
Sport Utility	**24855**	—	—
ADD FOR:			
Leather Seats	**650**	—	—
SILHOUETTE 6			
Wagon	**19095**	—	—
ADD FOR:			
3.8 Liter 6 Cyl Eng	**800**	—	—
Leather Seats	**650**	—	—

1991

Year-Model-Body Type	Original List	Current Whlse	Average Retail
BRAVADA 6			
Sport Utility	**23795**	16975	19500
SILHOUETTE 6			
Wagon	**18195**	—	—
ADD FOR:			
Leather Pkg	**650**	330	410

PLYMOUTH

1992

Year-Model-Body Type	Original List	Current Whlse	Average Retail
VOYAGER 4*			
Voyager, Base	**14358**	—	—
Voyager, SE	**16481**	—	—
* For 6 cylinder models add $— wholesale and $— retail.			
VOYAGER 6			
Voyager, SE AWD	**19539**	—	—
Voyager, LE	**20202**	—	—
Voyager, LX	**20883**	—	—
GRAND VOYAGER 6			
Voyager, Base	**18233**	—	—
Voyager, SE	**18463**	—	—
Voyager, LE	**21011**	—	—
ADD FOR:			
3.3 Liter 6 Cyl Eng	**796**	—	—
LX Decor Pkg	**776**	—	—

1991

Year-Model-Body Type	Original List	Current Whlse	Average Retail
VOYAGER 4*			
Voyager, Base	**14305**	10175	11750
Voyager, Special Ed	**15551**	11025	12575
Voyager, Limited Ed	**17994**	11775	13475
* For 6 cylinder models add $400 wholesale and $400 retail.			
VOYAGER 6			
Voyager, LX	**19489**	12100	13850
GRAND VOYAGER 6			
Voyager, Special Ed	**17301**	12275	14050
Voyager, Limited Ed	**19604**	13050	15250
ADD FOR:			
Luxury Equip Pkg			
(Voyager SE, Grand Voyager SE)	**2376**	1350	1630
(Voyager LE, LX & Grand Voyager LE)	**1892**	1060	1290

1990

Year-Model-Body Type	Original List	Current Whlse	Average Retail
VOYAGER 4*			
Voyager, Base	**12835**	7825	8950
Voyager, Special Ed	**13515**	8575	9775
Voyager, Limited Ed	**16125**	9250	10525
Voyager, LX	**17240**	8100	9225
* For 6 cylinder models add $375 wholesale and $375 retail.			
GRAND VOYAGER 6			
Voyager, Special Ed	**16235**	9675	11000
Voyager, Limited Ed	**18325**	10325	11775
ADD FOR:			
Luxury Equip Pkg			
(Voyager SE)	**2070**	1010	1230
(Voyager Grand SE)	**1903**	920	1120

1989

Year-Model-Body Type	Original List	Current Whlse	Average Retail
VOYAGER 4*			
Voyager, Base	**11312**	6600	7550
Voyager, Special Ed	**12039**	7275	8300
Voyager, Limited Ed	**13987**	7900	9025

Refer To Optional Equipment Schedules

Year-Model-Body Type	Original List	Current Whlse	Average Retail
* For 6 cylinder models add $325 wholesale and $325 retail.			
GRAND VOYAGER 6			
Voyager, Special Ed	**14526**	8325	9475
Voyager, Limited Ed	**16462**	8975	10225
ADD FOR:			
LX Decor Pkg (Voyager LE)	**1469**	590	720
Lux Equip Pkg (Voyager)	**1828**	750	910

1988

Year-Model-Body Type	Original List	Current Whlse	Average Retail
VOYAGER 4*			
Voyager, Base	**10887**	4900	5700
Voyager, Special Ed	**11587**	5525	6325
Voyager, Limited Ed	**13462**	6025	6825
GRAND VOYAGER 4*			
Voyager, Special Ed	**12505**	6225	7100
Voyager, Limited Ed	**15509**	6750	7725
* For 6 cylinder models add $300 wholesale and $300 retail.			
ADD FOR:			
LE Decor Pkg (Voyager LE)	**603**	170	210
Lux Equip Pkg (Voyager)	**1281**	410	510

1987

Year-Model-Body Type	Original List	Current Whlse	Average Retail
VOYAGER 4*			
Voyager, Base	**10411**	3600	4375
Voyager, Special Ed	**10875**	4150	4950
Voyager, Limited Ed	**11741**	4600	5400
GRAND VOYAGER 4*			
Voyager, Special Ed	**11751**	4575	5375
Voyager, Limited Ed	**12561**	5000	5800
* For 6 cylinder models add $275 wholesale and $275 retail.			
ADD FOR:			
Lux Equip Pkg (Voyager)	**1722**	450	550
Travel Equip Pkg			
(Voyager SE & LE)	**1927**	500	610
(Voyager Grand Models)	**1538**	390	480

1986

Year-Model-Body Type	Original List	Current Whlse	Average Retail
VOYAGER 4			
Voyager, Base	**9659**	2725	3575
Voyager, Special Ed	**9938**	3075	3925
Voyager, Limited Ed	**10681**	3525	4300
ADD FOR:			
Luxury Equip Pkg (Voyager)	**1443**	260	320
Travel Equip Pkg (Voyager SE & LE)	**1633**	290	360

1985

Year-Model-Body Type	Original List	Current Whlse	Average Retail
VOYAGER 4			
Voyager, Base	**9238**	2125	2925
Voyager, Special Ed	**9487**	2350	3175
Voyager, Limited Ed	**10105**	2600	3425
ADD FOR:			
Luxury Equip Pkg (Voyager LE)	**1270**	120	160
Travel Equip Pkg (Voyager SE & LE)	**1003**	140	160

1984

Year-Model-Body Type	Original List	Current Whlse	Average Retail
VOYAGER 4			
Voyager, Base	**8669**	1800	2600
Voyager, Special Ed	**8906**	2000	2800
Voyager, Limited Ed	**9494**	2250	3050

PONTIAC

1992

Year-Model-Body Type	Original List	Current Whlse	Average Retail
TRANS SPORT SE 6			
Wagon	**17055**	—	—
TRANS SPORT GT 6			
Wagon	**20935**	—	—
ADD FOR:			
3.8 Liter 6 Cyl Eng	**819**	—	—

1991

Year-Model-Body Type	Original List	Current Whlse	Average Retail
TRANS SPORT 6			
Wagon	**16449**	11875	13575
TRANS SPORT SE 6			
Wagon	**18889**	12600	14725
ADD FOR:			
6 Pass Seating (Trans Sport)	**525**	260	320
7 Pass Seating (Trans Sport)	**675**	350	430

Used Car Buying Work Sheet

ITEM	Car "A"	Car "B"	Car "C"	Car "D"
BODY:	$	$	$	$
RUST				
DENT				
CHROME				
PAINT				
GLASS				
MOTOR:				
VALVES				
PISTONS				
RINGS				
TRANSMISSION:				
ADJUST				
OVERHAUL				
TIRES:				
RETREAD				
WORN				
BRAKES:				
ADJUST				
REPLACE				
ELECTRICAL:				
BATTERY				
WIRING				
GENERATOR				
REGULATOR				
PLUGS & POINTS				
TUNE UP:				
MISCELLANEOUS				
COOLING SYSTEM:				
HOSE				
RADIATOR				
WATER PUMP				
EXHAUST:				
MUFFLER				
FRONT EXHAUST				
TAIL PIPE				
LIGHTS:				
HEAD				
TAIL				
DIRECTIONAL				
WIPER:				
BLADES				
MOTOR				
TOTAL REPAIR COST	$	$	$	$
ASKING PRICE OF CAR				
+ or – = NET PRICE				

√ **Side-by-side comparison** of any __two__ 1992 and currently released 1993 vehicles.

√ **Customized:** based on your personal driving profile, annual mileage, and state taxes and fees, etc..

√ **Immediate delivery:** shipped first class mail within 24 hours or FAXED directly to you.

√ **Convenient:** comparison shopping in the comfort of your home or office.

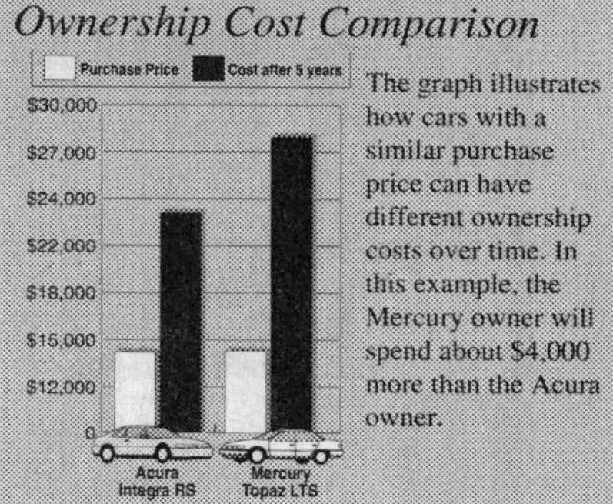

Ownership Cost Comparison
Purchase Price
Cost after 5 years
$30,000
$27,000
$24,000
$22,000
$18,000
$15,000
$12,000
0
Acura Integra RS
Mercury Topaz LTS
The graph illustrates how cars with a similar purchase price can have different ownership costs over time. In this example, the Mercury owner will spend about $4,000 more than the Acura owner.

__For complete pricing, equipment__, and ownership costs order **The ArmChair Compare®** **Report, *compares side-by-side two vehicles*** *for only $17.95 plus $2.00 shipping*

The AutoInvestigator™ any __two__ vehicles for only $12.95 plus $2.00 shipping

Call 1-800-227-2665 *ext.* 5 *or* Fax to: (408) 253-4822

Complete this form

Name ____________________
Address ____________________
City __________ ***State*** _____ ***Zip*** _______
Day Phone ( ) ____ – _____
Your Annual Mileage __ __, __ __ __
Desired Down Pmt: ☐ ____ % ***OR*** ☐ $________
☐ **Mastercard** ☐ **VISA** ***Exp. date*** __________
Credit card Account # ________________
Signature X ____________________

*Include order form with Personal check/charge information for **$14.95** and mail to:*

IntelliChoice, Inc.
1135 S.Saratoga-
Sunnyvale Rd.
San Jose, CA 95129

__Vehicle One__ Describe the vehicle below:
Year _____ Make ____________________
Model __________________________
Number of Doors ☐ 2–dr ☐ 4–dr
Drive ☐ 2 WD ☐ 4 WD
Style ☐ Sedan ☐ Hatch ☐ Convert. ☐ Wagon ☐ Coupe ☐ Van ☐ Pickup ☐ Other_________

__Vehicle Two__ Describe the vehicle below:
Year _____Make ____________________
Model __________________________
Number of Doors ☐ 2–dr ☐ 4–dr
Drive ☐ 2 WD ☐ 4 WD
Style ☐ Sedan ☐ Hatch ☐ Convert. ☐ Wagon ☐ Coupe ☐ Van ☐ Pickup ☐ Other_________

__Trade-In__ 1981-1991 vehicles only
Describe the vehicle below:
Year ______Make ____________________
Model __________________________
Number of Doors ☐ 2–dr ☐ 4–dr
Condition ☐ Excellent ☐ Average ☐ Poor
Style ☐ Sedan ☐ Hatch ☐ Convert. ☐ Wagon ☐ Coupe ☐ Van ☐ Pickup ☐ Other_______

Brought to you by IntelliChoice, Inc., publisher of the award-winning *The Complete Car Cost Guide* and *The Complete Small Truck Cost Guide* featured in *Road & Track*, *USA Today*, and *Changing Times*.

This is not an offer to sell, broker, or finance a vehicle. IntelliChoice, Inc. has no business relationship with any car dealer. The sole purpose of the AutoInvestigator™ report is to help you make the wisest automobile choice and to best prepare you for the purchase.

All products names are trademarks or registered trademarks of IntelliChoice, Inc.. This ad is presented to you in association with Edmund Publications Corp.

REBATES AND DEALER INCENTIVES

- Car/Puter's full disclosure **up to the minute Rebate and Confidential Dealer Incentive** information helps makes sure you don't get beaten by the dealer.
- Many **cars purchased below Dealers Factory Invoice** with Car/Puter's service.
- **Money Magazine** calls Car/Puter's Service "...one of the 100 best deals in America".

PERSONAL COUNSELOR

- Once you have selected the options you want, your Personal Counselor, tells you what rebates and discounts currently apply.
- They can often help you **find a better equipped car for less** then the car you were considering.

FLEET SIZED DISCOUNTS

- The dealers that Car/Puter uses for it's own purchases provide Fleet-Sized discounts. **Massive Volume Means — Lowest Prices.**
- Forget dealer preparation costs! Two window stickers... No More. Rust Proofing -Fabric Protection, never overpay again!

FINANCING AND LEASING ASSISTANCE

- **Don't give up your rebate for so called low cost financing** again. Let us help you find the best financing for you.
- Leases provided by national lease companies with simple-interest 1% over prime. —Low payments and best of all **no prepayment penalties** after first year.

Car Salesmen Give The Impression Of Not Telling Me Everything. Why Would NATIONWIDE Be Any Different?

We have no reason to keep things from you. Our 20 plus year approach has been to be straightforward in working with our clients. The printout you receive clearly reveals our "hand".

I Don't Live In Michigan, How Will I Get My New Vechicle?

You have three options -

1) You may designate a local dealership as your pick up point. (Please provide us with a choice of three.)
2) We will deliver your vehicle to your home via a licensed ICC driveaway service.
3) Your vehicle may be picked up at our headquarters in Southfield, MI.

When I Buy From NATIONWIDE, Is The Vehicle Under Warranty?

All cars and trucks sold by NATIOWIDE Auto Brokers, Inc are fully factory warranteed and all authorized dealerships throughout the United States and Canada will honor the warranty.

MASTERCARD/VISA CUSTOMERS ONLY! **1-800-521-7257**

Monday - Friday — 9 am to 8 pm: Saturday — 9 am to 1 pm Eastern Time

Please have your credit card number and expiration date ready for our operators

FAX PRICE: $9.95 for first two quotes of $11.95 each. $2.50 each additional fax.

Nationwide Auto Brokers, Inc.

17517 West Ten Mile Road • Southfield, Michigan 48075

Name ____________________

Address ____________________

City ____________ State ________ Zip ________

❑ MC/Visa/Discover ❑ Check ❑ Money Order

MC/Visa/Discover Card No. ____________________

Exp. Date ____________ Signature ____________________

MAKE	MODEL/ DESCRIP.	BODY TYPE (Check all that apply)	PRICE EACH
		▫ 2 door ▫ 4 door ▫ station wagon ▫ diesel ▫ turbo ▫ automatic ▫ manual ▫ hatchback ▫ notchback ▫ front wheel drive ▫ all wheel drive	$11.95
		▫ 2 door ▫ 4 door ▫ station wagon ▫ diesel ▫ turbo ▫ automatic ▫ manual ▫ hatchback ▫ notchback ▫ front wheel drive ▫ all wheel drive	$11.95
		▫ 2 wheel drive ▫ 4 wheel drive ▫ diesel ▫ turbo ▫ ½ ton ▫ ¾ ton ▫ 1 ton	$11.95

FAX PRICE: $9.95 for first two quotes of $11.95 each. $2.50 each additional fax.

NOTE: Attach sheet with additional body type specs only if necessary (do NOT list options).

Each Quote $11.95 TOTAL ________

PLEASE NOTE: Some specialty imports and limited production models and vehicles may not be available for delivery to your area or through our pricing service. A message on your printout will advise you of this eventuality. You will still be able to use the printout in negotiating the best deal with the dealer of your choice. New car pricing and purchasing services void where prohibited by law. Some limited vehicles are slightly higher.

From *Edmund's*, "The Original Consumer Price Authority"

AMERICA'S MOST-WANTED:

American Dream Cars

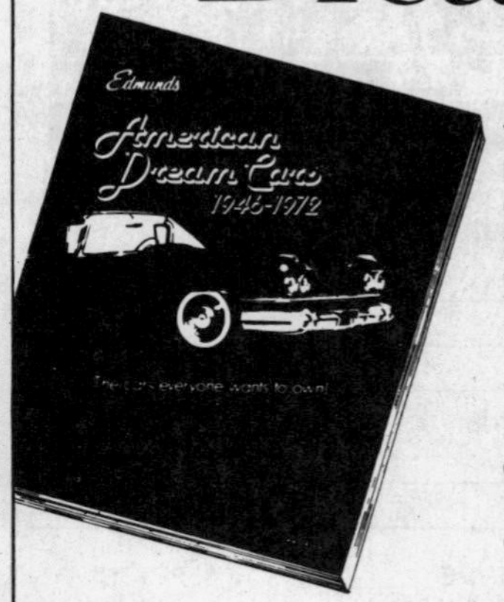

Get this year's hottest book on yesterday's hottest cars. For car collectors and enthusiasts, *American Dream Cars* provides detailed price and investment information on the most popular American-made cars from 1946 to 1972.

For only **$10.95** (includes shipping) you can have this collector's item. Included in the over 200 pages is detailed pricing, based on current market value, and color photographs of prized collectible cars.

☐ Enclosed is my check for ________ for ________

☐ I prefer to use my ☐ MasterCard ☐ Visa

Acct.# ____-____-____-____ Exp. ____/____

Name ________________________

Address ________________________

____

City/State/Zip ________________________

Edmund's

Edmund's Publication Corporation
200 Baker Avenue, Concord, MA 01742

Subscription Options for 1992

Get a complete picture of the 1992 automotive market

A

USED CAR PRICES — This 1 year subscription includes five updated versions of USED CAR PRICES.
Domestic: (includes bulk rate shipping & handling) **$25.95**
Other Countries: (includes air mail shipping & handling) **$32.95**

B

NEW VEHICLE PRICES — This 1 year subscription covers the complete automotive market of new vehicles for a total of 10 books: three NEW CAR (Domestic); three IMPORT CAR; three VAN, PICKUP, SPORT UTILITY; and one ECONOMY CAR.
Domestic: (includes bulk rate shipping & handling) **$49.95**
Other Countries: (includes air mail shipping & handling) **$74.95**

C

NEW and **USED CAR PRICES** — This 1 year subscription includes: three NEW (Domestic); five USED CAR; and three IMPORT CAR - for a total of 11 books.
Domestic: (includes bulk rate shipping & handling) **$54.95**
Other Countries: (includes air mail shipping & handling) **$79.95**

D

PREMIUM SUBSCRIPTION — *Exciting New Offer for 1992.* This 1 year subscription offers our full-line of books PLUS a *Free* copy of our *New* ULTIMATE OWNER'S MANUAL (an $8.95 value). The total of 16 books includes: three NEW CAR (Domestic); five USED CAR; three IMPORT CAR; three VAN, PICKUP, SPORT UTILITY; one ECONOMY CAR; and the *Free* ULTIMATE OWNER'S MANUAL all at a substantial savings to you.
Domestic: (includes bulk rate shipping & handling) **$77.95**
Other Countries: (includes air mail shipping & handling) **$109.95**

E

PREMIUM PLUS — Includes all of our Premium Subscription *PLUS* two *New, exciting publications* — 20 Best 1992 Cars, Vans, & Trucks; and 20 Best Used Cars, Vans, and Trucks.
Domestic: (includes bulk rate shipping & handling) **$82.95**
Other Countries: (includes air mail shipping & handling) **$114.95**

SCHEDULED RELEASE DATES FOR 1992

(Prices accurate thru cover date)

VOL. 26 (1992)

		Release Date	Cover Date
U2601	USED CAR PRICES	Dec. '91	April '92
N2601	NEW CAR PRICES (Domestic)	Jan. '92	June '92
S2601	VAN, PICKUP, SPORT UTILITY BUYER'S GUIDE	Jan. '92	June '92
I2601	IMPORT CAR PRICES	Feb. '92	July '92
E2601	ECONOMY CAR BUYER'S GUIDE	Feb. '92	1992
U2602	USED CAR PRICES	Mar. '92	July '92
N2602	NEW CAR PRICES (Domestic)	May '92	Nov. '92
S2602	VAN, PICKUP, SPORT UTILITY BUYER'S GUIDE	May '92	Nov. '92
U2603	USED CAR PRICES	June '92	Oct. '92
I2602	IMPORT CAR PRICES	June '92	Dec. '92
U2604	USED CAR PRICES	Sept. '92	Jan. '93
N2603	NEW CAR PRICES (Domestic 1993)	Nov. '92	Feb. '93
S2603	VAN, PICKUP, SPORT UTILITY BUYER'S GUIDE	Nov. '92	Feb. '93

PLUS NEW 1992 PUBLICATIONS

O2601	ULTIMATE OWNER'S MANUAL	1992
A2601	AMERICAN DREAM CAR	1992
CG2601	IMPORT CAR COLLECTOR'S GUIDE	1992
BN2601	20 BEST NEW CARS	1992
BU2601	20 BEST USED CARS	1992